PRAISE FOR *BY WHAT METHOD?*

The challenge today is not to talk about change, but to lead it. This book offers practical, step-by-step advice for all those engaged in the hard work of quality and productivity improvement. Its blend of theory, case examples, and self-guided exercises provides helpful tools applicable to a variety of organizations and situations. Professionals inside and outside of companies will find this a useful resource.

> Rosabeth Moss Kanter, Harvard Business School
> Author of *The Challenge of Organizational Change,*
> *When Giants Learn to Dance,* and *The Change Masters*

By What Method? does a highly commendable job of bringing together literature and experience from a broad array of disciplines to aid the change master in developing improved knowledge and skills for improving quality and productivity. Bill Morris and Scott Sink, industrial and systems engineers, have helped us understand how to accomplish the transformation that Dr. Deming, Dr. Juran, and others have argued for.

> Tom Murrin, Dean, School of Business, Duquesne University

Utilizing methods described in this book has been consistent with my own models of leadership and positive change. Work with the Virginia Quality and Productivity Center to establish this approach has complemented and enhanced my efforts to improve quality and productivity in the federal government. Doing these things over the past eight years was never easy. I do believe that this approach is sound and if led properly will help leadership make this crucial transformation to a quality organization.

> Dr. Dominic J. Monetta
> past Technical Director, Naval Ordnance Station, Indian Head
> Program Director, New Production Reactors, Department of Energy
> Under-Secretary of Defense for Research, Development, Testing, and Evaluation

I have been exposed to the evolution of these ideas and methods for the past eleven years. They have continued to evolve in a fashion that caused us to consider adopting them in National Grocers. In the past two years we have been immersed in applying them in our distribution system and have seen impressive results both qualitative and quantitative. We are so convinced that this approach has merit and a solid method for making the transformation that we are expanding into our finance and information systems divisions as well as other areas of our firm. There are no quick fixes and there isn't one best way. It has not been easy to implement and deploy what is described in this book. It took a strong partnership between National Grocers and Virginia Tech to accomplish what we have to this point. We believe we are on the path to accomplish our visions with a solid method that is facilitated by doing things described herein.

> David F. Poirier
> Senior Vice President, National Grocers Company, Ltd.

BY WHAT METHOD?

BY WHAT METHOD?

ARE YOU:

• DEVELOPING THE KNOWLEDGE AND SKILLS TO LEAD LARGE-SCALE QUALITY
AND PRODUCTIVITY IMPROVEMENT EFFORTS?

• MASTERING IMPLEMENTATION AND DEPLOYMENT?

• PUTTING TOGETHER THE PIECES OF THE TRANSFORMATION PUZZLE?

• ACHIEVING RESULTS WHILE BUILDING ORGANIZATIONAL COMPETENCE AND CAPABILITY?

D. SCOTT SINK
WILLIAM T. MORRIS
WITH CINDY S. JOHNSTON

INDUSTRIAL ENGINEERING & MANAGEMENT PRESS

ALSO BY D. SCOTT SINK

*Productivity Management: Planning, Measurement and Evaluation,
Control and Improvement*

WITH THOMAS C. TUTTLE

Planning and Measurement in Your Organization of the Future

Printed in the United States of America.

99 98 97 96 95   5 4 3 2 1

Additional copies may be obtained by contacting:
Institute of Industrial Enginers
Member & Product Services
25 Technology Park/Atlanta
Norcross, Georgia 30092 USA
(404) 449-0460 phone
(404) 263-8532 fax

Quantity discounts available

Library of Congress Cataloging-in-Publication Data

Sink, D. Scott, 1951–
    By what method?: have you developed the skills and knowledge to lead large-scale quality and productivity improvement efforts/D. Scott Sink, William T. Morris.
              p.   cm.
    Intended to "rewrite, update, and enhance" William T. Morris's implementation strateges for industrial engineers.
    Includes bibliographical references and index.
    ISBN 0-89806-141-5 (softcover)
    1. Total quality management. 2. Industrial productivity. 3. Quality of products. 4. Organizational change. I. Morris, William Thomas, 1928– . II. Morris, William Thomas, 1928– Implementation strategies for industrial engineers. III. Title.
HD62. 15.S58 1994
658.5'62–dc20   94-38235
                                                                         CIP

DEDICATION

To the change masters of the past, the present, and the future who have relentlessly worked to improve quality and productivity in their organizations and in doing so have created a rich body of wisdom and experience.

To our clients and sponsors and their organizations for providing the opportunity to reduce to practice and to learn and grow in doing so.

To the faculty and staff in the Virginia Quality and Productivity Center for their commitment to our vision of being a "teaching hospital" in quality and productivity improvement.

In particular, to Ms. Cindy Johnston, Mr. Scott Cypher and Ms. Angie Smibert for their original contributions, their project management skills, and their invaluable support to us as we completed this update and revision to *Implementation Strategies for Industrial Engineers*. Cindy's contributions extended far beyond the role of project manager; she wrote original material, significantly enhanced much of my work and the original manuscript, and re-engineered the outline to ensure that flow was orderly.

And, finally, to Maura Reeves, Ellen Snodgrass, Eric Torrey and IIE for their support efforts to ensure that this book got published in a quality fashion.

Table of Contents

*If there is anything
that characterizes life,
it is change.*

—*M. Scott Peck*

For the better part of thirty years now, North America has been going about the business of quality and productivity improvement. From simple and somewhat naive beginnings in the sixties, continuous improvement has become something akin to a national obsession: we've thrown tremendous energy and resources at the task and have seen mixed, if not in some cases questionable, results. The road leading to the transformation has been littered with false starts, false learning curves, failed attempts, and "programs of the month and year."

Why do we struggle? It is, of course, incorrect to cite a single cause since there are many and they are interdependent. However, one cause does loom large—lack of effective implementation and deployment. This is where our organizations get stuck. And our organizations get stuck here because many of us in positions of leadership for positive change are ill-equipped for the challenges we face. We simply lack the knowledge and skills necessary to lead and manage the transformation.

This book was written for those tasked with helping one or multiple organizations improve quality and productivity. Your title may be TQM Coordinator, Quality Manager, Human Resources Director, Industrial Engineer, Consultant, Performance Improvement Engineer, Corporate Development Specialist, or Organizational Development Specialist. Rosabeth Moss Kanter and others have labeled those leading improvement efforts as change agents or change masters. We will use the term change master throughout the following chapters.

WHY THIS BOOK WAS WRITTEN

In 1979, William T. Morris, my co-author, spent his last summer in academia writing a book entitled *Implementation Strategies for Industrial Engineers*. It blended, in a practical fashion, literature, research, and experience from a variety of fields and professions and provided a structured way of thinking about the change management aspect of an industrial engineer's job. The book is a classic, but unfortunately it is out of print. Over the years, the book has guided me as I have struggled to help individuals, groups, and organizations improve.

As is the case with most classics, it has become more salient with age. Change management has grown in interest and importance. Change masters are increasingly critical to improvement efforts. Yet throughout these twenty years, I haven't found a book that synthesized the theory and practice of positive change as well as *Implementation Strategies*. So, several years ago I asked Bill Morris if he would be interested in working with me to rewrite, update, and enhance that book. The project has taken far longer than it should have; nevertheless, I feel this book will be an important contribution to the field of quality and productivity improvement, to management of change, and to implementation and deployment.

It's a fact of life that change masters today are frustrated and battle fatigued. Our contention is that most do not have a complete body of knowledge and skill necessary to succeed. Through this book, we aim to assist change masters as you work to develop the knowledge and skills necessary for success in your roles. This book is not "instant pudding," a panacea, or a quick fix. The focus, as the title suggests, is on methods; however, we understand that methods rotely followed do not offer much promise. Organizational behavior is far too dynamic and complex. Simple solutions won't solve complex, dynamic, system-wide problems. On the other hand, change masters are faced with perplexities, problems, programs, projects, and processes — the five pursuits as Harold Kurstedt calls them. While we must aim to improve performance from a systems perspective, we simultaneously must solve problems, capture opportunities, and improve processes within specific domains of responsibility.

The purists suggest our approaches to improvement are too "reductionist" and analytical, hence we optimize the subsystem at the expense of the larger system. The pragmatists strive for quick fixes and immediate results in the absence of any theoretical foundation. The key, of course, is balance. We will encourage that you think systems, think statistically, improve performance within your immediate domain of responsibility while understanding the relationships between your strategies, measures, and actions and the next larger system. The alternatives are to continue as we have, suboptimizing and becoming more immobilized by the inherent and inevitable problems we create, or becoming paralyzed because the system and associated problems are so large that there are no perceived controllables. We will encourage balance; that you become a **profound pragmatist**. You'll have to study and apply the methods presented herein order to achieve the goal of being a successful change master.

Dr. Kanter did an outstanding job of introducing us to the concept of change masters, the roles they play, and the challenges they face. We believe it is important to go beyond the foundation she established. It is becoming clear that change masters are critical to successful efforts to improve quality and productivity; it is also becoming clear that the knowledge and skills of these change masters are deficient in most organizations. **This is the focal problem we address in this book.**

Our hope is that you will use this book throughout your career as a self-development guide for mastering the art and science of leadership for positive change.

ABOUT THE TITLE

We hear a lot today about continuity of leadership and constancy of purpose. Clearly, these two factors are important to rate of improvement. However, we think another factor is equally important: consistency of method. "By what method?" was the oft-bellowed phrase at the famous W. Edwards Deming four-day seminar. Inconsistent methods won't achieve consistent results. As change masters, you must work to achieve consistency in the methods by which your organizations increase their rate of improvement. This is a reduction of variation issue and is central to progress.

The subtitles reveal major themes developed in the book. Learning is a subtheme. How do those entrusted with leading positive change continually improve their knowledge and skills for the task? How do we lead large-scale organizational change? How do we improve the quality of implementation and deployment? There are certain "requirements for success" that must be met (they are necessary but not sufficient conditions) in order for your organization to succeed at increasing rates of improvement. We focus on these requirements in the pages that follow.

WHO WILL LEAD THE TRANSFORMATION?

The study of the rise and fall of civilizations has shown that the emergence of leadership in periods of need is necessary for continued survival and progress. Recently, I was working with an organization that is faced with a life or death situation. I had been working on integrating TQM and strategic planning, and on deployment, with the top leaders of the organization for many years. Each year we struggled to follow through. We couldn't maintain momentum; there was always this sense that we hadn't achieved the desired results. Over the years, this feeling had grown stronger and people became more skeptical and cynical toward the method, toward me, and even toward themselves.

But this year was different. If no results were achieved this year, they would be out of business in two years. The level of discipline with respect to implementation and deployment throughout the organization, and with follow-through, was amazing. They really managed their plans like projects; they held themselves accountable; they set aggressive targets for themselves.

Later, I was meeting with the School Board in the community in which this organization is located. The School Board was in the first year of an integrated Total Quality and Strategic Planning effort. I shared the story of the organization in their community, our eight years of frustration and now this seeming ability to perform miracles. I suggested to the School Board that **organizational leadership is the ability to perform miracles in the absence of a crisis.** Good management can often perform miracles in the presence of a crisis, but it takes good leadership to perform them in the absence of one. **Change masters have to create good leadership in the absence of crises.**

They say there are bold pilots and old pilots but no old, bold pilots. Not so with change masters. Old, bold change masters are necessary. It takes a boldness to lead change whether from within or without, from a position of power or from a position of informal power. At times, change masters have to operate at the "envelope" (outer limits) of their knowledge and skills. You won't become a change master from just reading and studying; you have to be willing to experiment, to get into the ring and mix it up. As you will see, being a change master is at the same time immensely rewarding and tremendously frustrating and fatiguing. It is not a role for everyone, but it's a crucial role in the organization of the future.

Who will lead the transformation? The answer is a lot of people, but someone has to get the ball rolling. Once that happens, there are usually more leaders than necessary because enthusiasm is contagious. In start-up, however, inertia is often hard to overcome. Someone has to step up to the plate and accept the obligation to get things moving. If you are fortunate enough to be one of the 5–10% that have their very top leadership and management doing this, then you're ahead of the game. If you are not in this group, then you have an added start-up task that will take time, patient impatience, discipline, persistence, technical competence, intellectual honesty, unrelenting dedication, individual responsibility, political astuteness, civility, conflict management, and a few other things we probably have either forgotten or haven't learned yet. As Dr. Deming said, "You can begin whenever you want as long as you start now." If not you, then who? If not now, when?

NOTES FROM THE AUTHOR
• Throughout the text, all first person references are the voice of D. Scott Sink.
• The case studies in Chapters 2, 3, 5, 10 and 12 are based on actual organizations (or composite profiles); however, names, locations, and other details have been changed.

ACKNOWLEDGEMENTS

The science of quality and productivity improvement is lagging the art. This is often the case in emerging disciplines and professions. We have spent the past twenty years practicing the art in the absence of a fully developed and integrated science. Among our partners in this process have been:

- National Grocers Company, Ltd.
- City of Worthington, Ohio
- Burlington Industries
- Marshall Space Flight Center
- Goddard Space Flight Center
- NASA productivity coordinators
- Department of Navy
  — Naval Aviation Depot at North Island
  — Charleston, Puget and Norfolk Naval Shipyards
  — NAVSEA 05, 06 (SSD), 07
  — Naval Ordnance Station – Indian Head
  — Explosive Ordnance Disposal Technical Center
  — Aircraft Intermediate Maintenance Support Office
  — Navy Productivity Advocate
  — AEGIS Program
  — NAVSEACENLANT
  — NAVAIR 00
- Tennessee Valley Authority
- City of Portsmouth, Va., and Portsmouth Public Schools
- Virginia Fibre
- U.S. Senate Productivity and Quality Award Board for Virginia
- Virginia Tech, Industrial and Systems Engineering, College of Engineering, University Challenge Partnership
- Department of Defense Aerospace and Defense Contractor Quality and Productivity Management Guide
- Department of Energy (New Production Reactors Program, Strategic Planning, Measurement, and Program Evaluation)
- City of Columbus Data Center
- State of Ohio Data Center
- Environmental Protection Agency, Region III
- Institute of Industrial Engineers
- Oklahoma State Univ., Industrial Engineering and Mgmt., College of Engineering
- The Ohio State University, Industrial and Systems Engineering
- RHODIA, SA (Brazil) and Rhone Poulenc (France)
- Virginia Quality and Productivity Center
- Virginia Tech Research and Graduate Studies
- Botswana Telecommunications Corporation
- Botswana National Productivity Center.

These organizations represent the learning laboratories of the past and present. They have been the sponsors and customers for our research, development, and reduction-to-practice efforts. In general, all of our work with these organizations has been aimed at helping them improve quality and productivity. Their listing here does not imply endorsement of the ideas presented in this book, nor does it imply that all our efforts with them were successful. We would not be honest if we suggested that there have not been failures in the past two decades. We have been asked to engage in some change efforts that we knew at the outset had a very low probability of success. But there was a sponsor, there was a champion, and there was a need. Our intent is to always learn, so we cannot discount the value these experiences provide. With every opportunity and effort we engage in, we learn and grow, sharing what we find out about ourselves with those around us.

— *D. Scott Sink*

ACHIEVING RESULTS:
THE CHALLENGE OF IMPLEMENTATION AND DEPLOYMENT

The key barometer of success in the '90s and beyond will be rate of improvement. You will read this several times in the following chapters because it is important. Rate of improvement cannot be increased significantly unless visions, strategies, and actions are effectively deployed and implemented at all levels of your organization. Appreciation for a system, one of Dr. W. Edwards Deming's four elements of profound knowledge, is necessary to effectively implement and deploy improvements; understanding vertical and horizontal linkages and cause-and-effect relationships within your organizational systems is necessary, but not sufficient, for success. As discussed in *The Goal* (Goldratt 1986), and stressed by Dr. Deming, optimizing the subsystem at the expense of the larger system is common today. Managers don't intend to have this happen; it is simply a phenomenon that occurs in complex organizational behavior unless we lead and manage to avoid it. As a change master working for and with organizational leaders, you must translate "appreciation for a system" into language and behaviors that people at all levels in the organization understand and follow (Figure 1).

As a change master, you also must be able to manage the life cycle of your improvement efforts effectively: envision the desired results of change and the methods by which to accomplish those results; motivate champions, sponsors, and followers for the changes; sell those directly involved or affected by change to overcome resistance; maintain momentum; and evaluate results for the benefit of future improvement efforts. In today's environment, the change master must balance immediate results with laying the foundation for long-term results and benefits. This requires clear, tangible improvement **now** in addition to setting the stage for mid-term and longer-term successes.

Change masters are members of a helping profession. You work for and with the formal leaders and managers in the organization to increase rate of improvement. You are in the business of enabling individuals, groups, and organizations to improve performance. As we have learned from the helping professions (medicine, psychiatry, counseling, organizational development), achieving results requires different methods in different situations. Sometimes we teach, sometimes we challenge, sometimes we observe, sometimes we coach and counsel, and sometimes we just listen.

Change masters must be skilled at problem solving and at helping their change target(s) solve problems. But change masters also create problems. Every solution creates new problems. The more active an organization is in performance improvement, the more rapidly new problems and opportunities are created, and the more pressure there is to

Figure 1. Depending upon how we look at our subsystems, their relationship to the overall system will change.

become effective and efficient at problem solving. This means that change masters will face the juggler's problem of keeping at least three balls in the air at once (Figure 2):

1. **Solve the focal problem** (e.g., re-engineering a business process, training people in statistical process control, improving system performance by thirty percent in eighteen months, getting a measurement system up and running). Solving the focal problem is the "ball" that most of us are trained, in some way, to address. We use our tools to solve problems.
2. **Allocate (what are most often) scarce resources to the improvement project** (*i.e.*, determine how much effort to put into each step in the Plan-Do-Study-Act [PDSA] improvement cycle). This is the "ball" that is commonly thought of as project management. In an environment filled with uncertainty, risk, and demands to do more with less, it is a challenge to find and maintain the right resources for our improvement efforts.
3. **Implementation** focuses on the change master architecting and engineering what will be done, when it will be done, how it will be done, who will do it, how to orchestrate the change target through phases of change (change process management), and balancing the quality of the solution with acceptance of the solution. This "ball" focuses on change master skills and behaviors and on managing through the phases of change.

All three balls must be juggled to achieve implementation and deployment effectiveness. Many, if not most, organizations struggle with this problem. Our book assists change masters in developing the improved knowledge and skills of juggling.

The 3^n-ball problem occurs when the change master is leading, managing, or participating in a program or a system of large-scale changes across many "fronts." Many organizations and change masters simultaneously are engaged in more than one change project (Figure 3). With increasingly scarce resources, change masters are being asked to do more with less and in a shorter period of time.

The role of a change master is vital to successful implementation and deployment. In the following chapters, we will refer often to the three-ball problem and the 3^n-ball problem as related to change mastering. In this first section, we discuss where organizations get stuck, develop the concept of change masters in more detail, provide a short case example of a change master at work, and close with some early development work you may want to do before moving on to the next section.

OPERATIONAL DEFINITIONS
Dr. Deming (1986) defined an operational definition as "one you can do business with." At the beginning of each section we provide operational definitions for terms and concepts utilized. We use the following terms in this section and throughout the book in our discussions of the art and science of managing complex organizational change.

ABC(D) Model: Dr. Harold Kurstedt, director of Management Systems Laboratories at Virginia Tech, has developed a useful model of how managers and leaders spend their time. It is called the ABC model. Dr. James Tompkins, noted author and consultant, has added a fourth component to the model. I'll take some liberties with it and use it as a shorthand throughout the book, so it will be beneficial for you to become comfortable with the constructs behind "A," "B," "C," and "D" (Figure 4).

Figure 2. Being a change master requires the ability to juggle roles, responsibilities, and tasks in improvement projects.

Figure 3. Ultimately, the successful change master needs to learn how to handle the 3"-ball problem.

The key concept in TQM is that if we improve the quality of "A" (administering the system, methods, processes, business) then the amount of "C" (fire-fighting, catering to crises) will be reduced, and we will have more time to do "B" (building the business, performance improvement). Jim Tompkins suggests we do a lot of the "dumb"—things ("D") that aren't important or urgent—and that it takes discipline to stop doing these things. We see the change master's primary job as ensuring that the "B" wedge gets driven in and is not forced back out by the pressures of "A," "C" and "D." There is a theorem associated with this model: Poorly designed, developed, and executed "B" will always be driven out by "A," "C" and "D." The job of the change master is, therefore, to ensure that "B" is well "architected and engineered," implemented, and maintained. Think about your role in the context of the ABC(D) model.

Change Master: "Those people and organizations adept at leading and managing positive

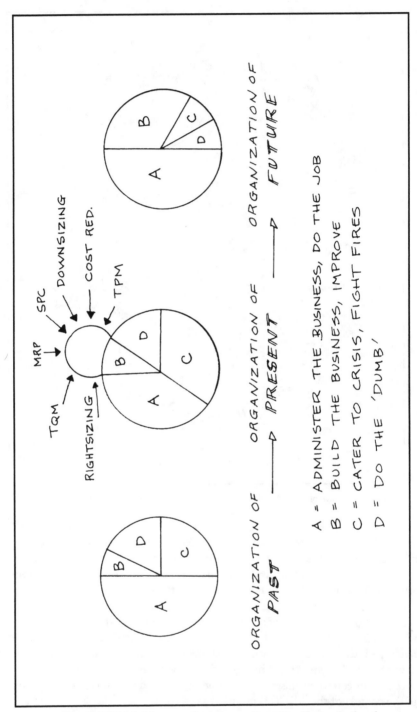

Figure 4. The ABC(D) Model portrays how we spend out time. To be a leader of improvement efforts, the way we allocate our time must shift.

change" (Kanter 1983). Also called change agents, these individuals or groups have been given the task of leading improvement efforts. We will refer to change masters as the "architects and engineers" of positive change or quality and productivity improvement efforts, particularly large-scale improvement efforts (Figure 5).

Change Sponsor: Individuals in pivotal positions of power who: can ensure that the cross-functional "battles" that must be fought are fought and won; can ensure resource application requirements are met; and can help maintain a system of communication, a willingness to cooperate, and ensure continuing integrity of purpose ("functions of the executive," as documented by Barnard 1939).

Change Target: The individuals, groups and organizations that are the focus of improvement efforts; the **unit of analysis** for improvement. Those who must participate in, cooperate with, or play a role in improvement efforts. Also referred to as **client** throughout this text.

Deployment: The word "total" in Total Quality Management can have many meanings. One interpretation is "system wide." Another is "life cycle," which includes a temporal dimension. Yet another is that it means "everybody." In recent years we have heard more and more about policy deployment and quality function deployment. The emphasis on these methods is a result of our increasing recognition that we have been attacking the parts but not the whole and in doing so have optimized the parts at the expense of the whole. Our operational definition of deployment is **successful implementation vertically and horizontally in the organizational system.** In other words, implementation is effected throughout the system. In a sense, deployment adds other dimensions to the concept of implementation, those of time and space. We manage improvement over time, and we manage improvement, in an integrated fashion, throughout the organizational system.

Fronts: We've borrowed this term from military history. As change masters, many if not most of you feel as though you are waging a battle. In all great battles, there are fronts, or subsystems that must be managed to win the war or battle. If one front gets too far ahead of other fronts or if one front lags too far behind, bad things happen (e.g., the front is "cut off," we lose momentum, progress in one front is stymied by lack of progress in another).

There are subsystems within your organization that are like fronts. We have identified nine: (1) Education/Training/Development; (2) Planning; (3) Measurement; (4) Culture/Community; (5) Motivation; (6) Infrastructure; (7) Communication; (8) Politics; (9) Technology. So, fronts are major organizational subsystems that must be managed in a wholistic sense.

Implementation: Although the term deployment is relatively new, the term implementation is not. Implementation is a complex concept. In layperson terms, implementation means the successful completion of a decision, solution, or project. It means that a new plan, method, or system becomes a routine part of the life. Implementation is related to effectiveness. We say we will do something, and we do it.

Successful implementation, to us, implies the presence of evaluation. In others words, it is not enough to just implement; we must follow through, ensuring accomplishment of

Figure 5. The change master is an architect and engineer for quality and productivity improvement.

the desired outcomes associated with what we were implementing. This is central to our operational definition of implementation and a key cause of failure of improvement efforts. So, implementation includes both the "Do" and the "Study" in PDSA. The degree to which implementation occurs is the degree to which the intended changes in behavior, policies, and methods become a way of doing business.

Improvement: Implementation and improvement, at least in this book, are interwoven. We are implementing change to cause improvement. There are at least two kinds of improvement discussed in the literature:

1. Step-function, breakthrough, re-engineering, recreating;
2. Continuous, incremental, "baby step," tuning, reorienting.

Recently, much attention has been given to business process re-engineering. A business process is really a system, a large process that begins with the customer and ends with the customer.

We can develop a process breakdown structure, similar to a work breakdown structure, and identify various levels of processes. In that context, a business process represents a Level 1 process. For example, Texas Instruments only identified seven business processes in the whole corporation.

Figure 6 depicts the two categories of improvement (tuning and overhaul) as it relates to operational and business processes.

Westinghouse utilizes an even more refined model of improvement, as shown in Figure 7.

Organizational System: Organizational system is a term we use to mean a firm, corporation, school, university, department, branch, section, work cell, team, city, community, division, function, plant, warehouse, cross-functional system, etc. Barnard (1938) defines an organization as two or more people who have come together to accomplish some common purpose. Rather than use the word organization, which can conjure up stereotypes (a university president will infer we aren't addressing universities, or a cross-functional team will infer we don't mean them), we choose to use the term organizational system and let you know that we mean "organization" in the sense that Barnard did.

Performance: As used in this book, performance means an integrated relationship among seven dimensions: effectiveness, efficiency, quality, productivity, quality of work life, innovation, and profitability/budgetability. (Figure 8).

Professional Modes of Functioning: Roles, behaviors, or styles that change masters utilize as they help individuals, groups, or organizations improve.

Transformation: Transformation probably means something different to each of us; it may be situationally defined. To M. Scott Peck (1993), it might mean the creation and maintenance of "community." "Community requires its members to honestly and openly speak their minds, to risk intimacy, to confess what is appropriate, to make the hidden known when doing so is helpful...The bedrock of community is commitment, a willing-

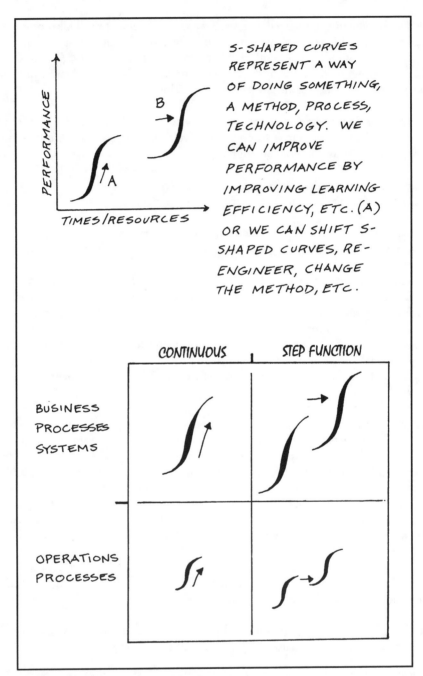

PERFORMANCE

TIMES/RESOURCES

B

A

S-SHAPED CURVES
REPRESENT A WAY
OF DOING SOMETHING,
A METHOD, PROCESS,
TECHNOLOGY. WE
CAN IMPROVE
PERFORMANCE BY
IMPROVING LEARNING
EFFICIENCY, ETC. (A)
OR WE CAN SHIFT S-
SHAPED CURVES, RE-
ENGINEER, CHANGE
THE METHOD, ETC.

CONTINUOUS   STEP FUNCTION

BUSINESS
PROCESSES
SYSTEMS

OPERATIONS
PROCESSES

Figure 6. Simplistically, there are four basic types of improvement.

ness for people to 'hang in there' together when the going gets rough." To Marvin Weisbord and others involved in "search conferences" it might mean discovering common ground (Weisbord 1992). To Dr. W. Edwards Deming (1986) it might have meant operationalizing the fourteen points. To Dr. Edward Lawler (1986) it might mean achieving high involvement. To many organizations today it might mean winning the Malcolm Baldrige Award. At the end of the chapter, we invite you to operationally define "the transformation" in the context of your organization and your understanding of the concept. In our view, the transformation means developing the competence and capacity to learn and to improve at rates that allow for the organization to survive and thrive.

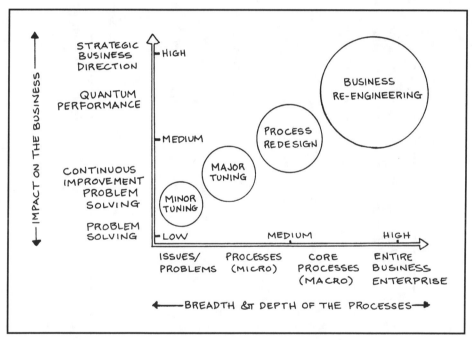

Figure 7. Improvement efforts vary from tune-ups to completely new designs (adapted from Westinghouse).

Performance	=	f (effectiveness, efficiency, quality, productivity, quality of work life, innovation, profitability/budgetability)
Effectiveness	=	f (rightness, timeliness, accomplishment, output, outcomes, quality)
Efficiency	=	f (inputs/resource consumption, budgets, time, quality, actual resource consumption)
Quality	=	f (perception, requirements, process capability, discipline, caring, engineering and design)
Productivity	=	f (output compared to input for a period of time, quality, effectiveness, efficiency)
Innovation	=	f (creativity, reduction to practice, teamwork, driving out fear, ideas put into action)
Quality of Work Life	=	f (affects, turnover, absenteeism, job characteristics, conditions, pay, benefits, leadership)
Profitability	=	f (revenue and costs)
Budgetability	=	f (what was promised versus what was delivered, budget versus actual costs)

Figure 8. Performance of organizations is a function of many dimensions. Those dimensions are, in turn, a function of certain characteristics of an organization.

CHAPTER 1

COMMON IMPLEMENTATION AND DEPLOYMENT PROBLEMS

Organizations get stuck with implementation and deployment, and while there seems to be no comprehensive data on the degree to which improvement efforts are implemented, there is enough anecdotal evidence for most professionals to take the problem very seriously indeed. For example, TQM has come under heavy fire recently for not achieving results. Among the growing list of criticisms for TQM and other improvement-oriented "technologies" are the following:

1. There is a long-running discussion in the literature concerning "sophisticated" designs and methods which are not implemented and are believed by some to be impossible to implement.
2. Failures to achieve implementation are a part of the professional history of many practicing performance improvement professions and functions.
3. There is useful evidence that some implementation strategies lead to intended behavior changes more reliably than others.
4. Managers, leaders, and change masters take implementation to be a significant and time consuming responsibility, often spending up to ninety percent of their time in client relations.
5. Although it is frequently observed that published reports of successful implementation are limited, this may be difficult data to interpret. Organizations often prefer not to make public their successful improvement efforts since these may be regarded as important aspects of their competitive advantage. Professionals who regularly achieve high degrees of implementation seldom find strong incentive to publish their results unless they seek to develop academic credentials.
6. There is a rich body of literature which analyzes specific failures to achieve implementation; however, it is often not prominent and is difficult to find because journals are reluctant to publish failures. We will utilize our substantial experience with failures in this book.
7. TQM and other current "fads" are likened to ceremonial rain dancing—a lot of hoopla and activity but most often without results.
8. The current environment requires quick results, short cycle times, and rapid improvements; anything complex, sophisticated, or strategic in nature is irrelevant.
9. There isn't time for theory today; we need practical, simple solutions. There are strong pressures against systems thinking. There are strong sentiments against theory. There are strong feelings in support of simplicity in spite of the increasing complexity of the problems.

It is important, however, not to grow pessimistic about the prospects for implementing large-scale or even small-scale improvement efforts. Our viewpoint is that implementation may be a problem, but it is a problem that can be approached consciously, methodically, and by drawing on the relevant research and experience base. By being ever attentive to the strategy of implementation and working diligently to acquire knowledge and skills, the change master will be rewarded by an increase in the probability that improvement will occur and by the greater degree to which it occurs.

Organizations are getting stuck with both implementation and deployment, but far and away the biggest problems are with deployment. Deployment forces leaders and managers of improvement efforts to think of the total system. This is difficult and requires an appropriate balance between theory and experience. Deployment forces change masters, leaders, and managers to address the *implementation*" problem (multiple interdependent improvement projects). Accomplishing the transformation, doing TQM, or whatever you have chosen to call efforts to improve your organization, clearly requires systems thinking or, as Dr. Deming called it, appreciation for systems.

WHY ORGANIZATIONS GET STUCK

The first reason most organizations get stuck is because they lack a critical mass of people who have a sufficient body of knowledge necessary to do the things required of the transformation. Implementing and deploying improvement initiatives within a complex organizational system requires a unique set of knowledge and skills, yet our universities have not devised plans of study for creating change masters. The informal education we get once we leave our formal educational settings is too haphazard, random, inconsistent, ineffective, unstructured, and unpurposeful to have a positive and predictable impact.

Poor selection of change masters is a second major reason organizations get stuck. We see organizations failing to make the transformation because they have selected change masters who are not capable. It is not uncommon for a person to be selected for an improvement leader or coordinator position in the following fashion. Top management decides they need a TQM program even though they really don't know what this means. Maybe a customer is putting pressure on them to do so. They put their heads together and try to come up with names of people inside the organization to do this. "Sam," someone suggests. Another replies, "No, Sam is too important for this job." " How about Mary?" another suggests. "No, Mary is on too many other important projects. She is an up and comer; this wouldn't be good for her resume." Finally, in desperation, someone suggests Joe. There is a moment of silent reflection, followed by the top, most senior manager saying, "Yes, Joe is perfect for the job. He is a year away from retirement. He's marginally competent. He can't do much damage. He will try hard. We will check the box with him for sure. He's perfect!" In my fifteen years in this field, I have encountered people selected for "change master" positions who were good people, well intended, but often technically incompetent, not socially or politically astute, sometimes not intellectually honest, often not individually responsible, and most did not possess unrelenting dedication for the task. It is necessary but not sufficient to select the right people to lead and manage the transformation in conjunction with sponsors and formal leadership within the organization.

The third reason most organizations get stuck is because managers and leaders fail to conceptualize the problem in the context of the "three balls" mentioned in the introduction. Many, if not most, do not have a grand strategy—a plan for improvement that is thought through strategically, reflects appreciation for a system, conveys appreciation of the past while planning for the future, integrates all initiatives for improvement, and is comprehensive. To illustrate this point, I compare and contrast what I saw during a Senate Productivity and Quality Award site visit at Canon of Virginia (Japanese improvement system with American managers and workers) versus what I saw during a similar site visit at an American manufacturing plant (American improvement system with American managers, leaders and workers). I'll use the step aerobic versus a staircase analogy. At Canon, I saw a well conceived staircase approach. They had clearly progressed up the staircase, building each year on what had been accomplished the years before, giving improvement methods and programs time to work. I saw no evidence of a program of the month or year or "quick fix" mentality. They knew where they were going over the next five years, both from an improvement process and method standpoint and from a product and service standpoint.

Compare this with the step aerobics approach I observed in the uniquely American plant. One month or year the organization had stepped up on one program. They didn't give it time to work, didn't see it as part of an evolutionary process. The next year (or month) the organization predictably stepped down from that program and then proceeded to step up again on yet another program for improvement. The outcome was chaos, frustration, apathy, cynicism, skepticism, and poor results over time.

The fourth reason organizations get stuck has to do with integration. General systems theory (von Bertalanffy 1968) tells us it is easier to differentiate than to integrate. Mechanisms for differentiation (e.g., organizational charts, restructuring, downsizing) are easier to employ than are mechanisms for integration (e.g., communication, planning, team building). With respect to quality and productivity improvement, we have differentiated the problem into pieces and assumed a group of people with all the pieces could integrate them into a meaningful whole. It hasn't worked. Solving the quality and productivity problems we are faced with requires integration and synthesis.

Maintaining communication and coordination while making large-scale system changes requires much effort and attention to detail. Ed Lawler talks about the importance of learning to share information, then share knowledge, then share power, then, finally, share rewards when moving toward high-involvement systems. Deployment of performance improvement initiatives requires managing the sharing of information and knowledge as a precursor to sharing power. It is often the case that power is shared through an infrastructure change before adequate information and knowledge are shared. When there isn't an adequate infrastructure for sharing information, knowledge, power, or vertical and horizontal deployment of strategies, policies, actions, measures, and methods, then it is almost impossible not to get stuck. Lack of integration causes predictable and undesirable results. "Management is prediction" (Deming 1993). Therefore, we can assume that we are simply failing to manage. Management and leadership are to blame. But, as Deming has said, "How could they know?"

The fifth and major reason organizations get stuck is because their leaders and managers do not possess profound knowledge and are not trying to acquire it. When leadership in an organization does not actively engage in learning about the transformation, or if there isn't a common body of knowledge among the leadership and management team, it is almost impossible not to get stuck. When leaders cannot participate as the "architects and engineers" for overall performance improvement efforts, then getting stuck is almost a certainty. If you are the change master and not in a formal position of power (traditional leadership role), then you must set as one of your major objectives the establishment of a common and sufficient body of knowledge among your organization's leadership team.

CONSISTENCY OF METHOD

Continuity of leadership and constancy of purpose are elements of Dr. Deming's fourteen points and widely espoused in the literature as being necessary for success. Perhaps implicit in these is the notion of consistency of method; yet we feel the issue is far too important to be left to inference. Consistency of method for doing "B" (building the business) is as important as continuity of leadership and constancy of purpose. In fact, they are inextricably interwoven. We can't begin to communicate the damage inflicted every time a new leader or top manager takes over and announces to his or her management team that they are going to change how they are doing strategic planning, team-building, measurement, etc. Most often it is not minor adjustments; it is full-scale tampering, often jumping on the bandwagon of the latest fad described in the most popular consultant book. The changes are not thought through in the context of understanding where the organizational system has been—what has and has not worked and the lessons learned.

It is an obligation of top leadership and management to define, document, understand, and be able to articulate with clarity and conviction how the organizational system plans, measures, rewards, improves, caters to crises, builds the business, shares information and knowledge, learns, grows, maintains community, and manages linkages. It's not an option; it is an obligation. Unfortunately, it is an obligation often not met. If there isn't a solid understanding of the method(s) by which top leadership and management is guiding and participating in the transformation, then there isn't much hope for success. The change master must solve this problem.

When you ask a top management team how it does strategic planning, who is involved, how plans are shared and deployed, challenge them if you get arm waving and lack of detail. They need to be honest and accept that the method by which they do these things is not understood or defined well enough, and, consequently, not a good way of doing business. When a new top leader or manager comes into an organization, why is it that they would almost never think to change the accounting system? Because it is well established, a way of doing business. Why, then, do they not give a second thought to changing how the organization plans or measures? Because these systems are not well established as ways of doing business. The Plan-Do-Study-Act process for improvement should be a way of doing business; however, it is not in most organizations.

Many American managers tend to rate Japanese-led American plants or companies low on the leadership dimension of the Baldrige guidelines. The top manager in one of these plants often is not charismatic, not verbally or physically that visible in the "system." We tend to view it differently, rating them higher on leadership when the leadership comes from the process, system, or method. This was the case at Canon of Virginia. Leadership, relative to consistency of method, comes from the "Canon Production System." The method for doing "A" and "B" is clearly articulated in that guidance document. They work to document the methods, train the methods, then they work to reduce variation in how the methods are applied. Leadership concentrates less on catering to crisis because the systems for "A" and "B" are stable and predictable. They deal with exceptions only, separating common cause of variation from special cause. They focus on strategic leadership of the organization as opposed to operational tampering. Once the Canon

Production System is established, the method for improvement is defined, documented, trained, communicated, and executed. Strategies, actions, and measures are deployed via the visible management system. This isn't a Japanese innovation (Boeing has been doing this for well over forty years.); this is good systems management for the '90s and beyond. You could completely switch the top management team in the Canon plant in Virginia and it wouldn't change how they plan, measure, deploy, and communicate. The system for improvement is established and is a way of doing business. Fixing the consistency-of-method problem will help to solve the continuity-of-leadership problem.

Again, compare and contrast this with most American plants. The method for doing "B" is often not well established. Most managers would be hard pressed to articulate the method for doing "B" in their organizations. "B" is subject to incessant tampering by leaders or managers who lack profound knowledge but know they want to leave their mark on the organization. "B" is driven out as easily as a tree with shallow roots is ripped from the soil by the slightest breeze. As change master, it is your job to correct this. This book is about accepting this challenge and succeeding.

Who will answer the question, "By what method?" in your organization? Who will lead the transformation? You will be tempted to say, "They will." "Who is they?" we will ask. You will say, "Top management." But who will get them to accept their obligation to lead? We believe you must accept this obligation. You have been given the task of leading, managing, coordinating, and participating in the transformation. You are a change master. You have informal power and in some cases formal power. You may be the top leader or manager in your organization; in this case, the answer is simpler than if you are working for or with top leadership and management. If you aren't the top leader or manager you must work with them and through them to make the transformation occur in your organization.

ORGANIZATIONAL SYSTEM LINKAGES: A KEY TO THE TRANSFORMATION

We have seen that developing appreciation for a system is important to the transformation. When we think about the system we are trying to improve, how do we draw the boundaries? What is the unit of analysis? TQM forces us to think about suppliers and customers as part of the system. What about subsystems? Do we see them as part of the system? Internal suppliers, internal customers, and support service functions are all part of the system and require integration. How do we manage the integration of these subsystems? How do we ensure that strategies, actions, and measures are aligned, congruent, and communicated among subsystems in the organization?

A study panel for the National Research Council recently examined "the productivity paradox" and the issue of organizational linkages. The productivity paradox is that U.S. corporations have invested huge sums of capital in information technology with the intent of improving productivity, yet evaluations tend to find limited results. Consider your own organization. Look at the investment in information technology and evaluate the impact on organizational productivity. Try evaluation using facts and data. What are the correlations? The implications the panel wrestled with were: (1) the investments in information technology are not paying off; (2) although the yields exist, we aren't measuring and evaluating properly; (3) there are major lag factors that obscure yields (related to 2); and (4) there are linkage issues that we aren't considering (related to 2 and 3). The linkage issues dominated the study and the overall book (NRC 1994).

In the highly popular book *The Goal*, Goldratt and Fox (1986) describe a situation where the goal of a plant was to maximize machine utilization of a very expensive piece of equipment. This was causing suboptimization of the larger system; in fact, the plant was going out of business. An invited outsider with profound knowledge shared with the plant manager the folly of optimizing a subsystem at the expense of the larger system. The plant manager adjusted the system (the plant), causing its performance to improve. Performance (as measured by machine utilization) of the subsystem (very expensive piece of equipment) went down; however, plant performance went up. Key performance indicators for the plant (throughput, efficiency, cycle time, quality, inventory costs) got better. Interestingly, the comptroller monitored subsystem measures and put pressure (we would call this tampering) on the plant manager to improve machine utilization. In other words, those "superior" to the plant manager were, in essence, pressuring him to optimize the performance of the subsystem at the expense of the performance of the system.

Why would they do this? Stupidity? Doubtful. Lack of appreciation for a system and insufficient understanding of linkages? Absolutely.

George Smith and I, partners on the NRC Study Panel on Linkages and the Productivity Paradox, concluded that an incomplete understanding of cause-and-effect relationships in an organizational system was a key culprit in the productivity paradox. As a change master, your understanding of the system in its environmental context, and how well you understand the business of your system, will determine the quality of your decisions and actions to improve performance. Profound knowledge isn't just about quality, statistics and psychology, it's about your business too. In the absence of knowing your business, none of the other issues related to performance improvement make any difference. You must understand the requirements of success of the organizational system you, as change master, are trying to improve. If you don't have valued products and services and can't maintain them, don't understand your markets and customers, don't understand your customers' business as well as they do, don't partner with your suppliers, and don't understand the economics of staying in business, then the other things we have been talking about are moot.

The comptroller in *The Goal* didn't have profound knowledge relative to the system. Strategies, actions, and measures from level to level in the organization were not thought through in a cause-and-effect sense. Figure 9 depicts the notion of system and levels in the context of appreciation for the system and being able to ensure you are truly improving performance of the right system.

Dixon, Nanni, and Volmann (1990) introduce the concept and importance of ensuring strategies, actions, and measures are integrated vertically and horizontally within an organizational system. Most planning and measurement systems are not designed, developed, or implemented in this fashion. As a result, we commonly experience the consequences described in *The Goal*.

It seems that a number of people are nibbling at the edges of the solution (e.g., Goldratt, Peck, Lawler, Kanter, Kilmann, Ishikawa, Crosby, Juran, Deming, Senge, Mintzberg, Conway, Covey, Scherkenbach, Weisbord). There are some powerful thinkers in this list, and this is not to imply that I know something they don't. I like the theories and concepts espoused by these highly regarded professionals. But after reading all their work, I still come away pondering practical applications. How do I do what they are saying? The theory and concepts ring true, but I'm left trying to help people figure out what to do next. This is what we have tried to accomplish in this book. Our ideas, theories, concepts, and, most importantly, methods may not be novel, but we think they reduce to practice and integrate

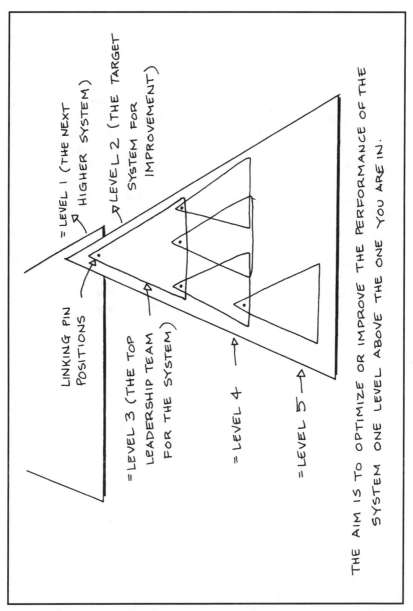

Figure 9. Appreciation for systems requires the ability to draw the system and subsystems and understand the linkages between them.

the works of a great many who are far more profound than us. We hope this integration and attempt at reduction to practice helps you become a better change master for your organization.

CONCLUSION

Ultimately, it seems to us that we are getting stuck on implementation and deployment because we don't know enough. There isn't enough learning going on in most organizations. Learning isn't measured, it isn't rewarded, it isn't practiced by most leaders, therefore it isn't pervasive. We suspect this may be why Peter Senge's recent book, *The Fifth Discipline*, is so popular; he has hit on a root cause, something that is consistently and commonly getting us stuck (1990).

The education, training, and development front must be managed better in your organization if you are to get unstuck. We believe there is a science to quality and productivity improvement, to implementation and deployment, to change management. We know that it is not being taught in a single curriculum or plan of study. We know that it is happenstance if someone or some organization acquires the body of knowledge necessary to succeed with the transformation.

You are stuck and your organizations are stuck because your level of knowledge and your bodies of knowledge are deficient. You will get unstuck when you commit to the development of profound knowledge.

CHAPTER 2

CHANGE MASTERS:
THE ARCHITECTS AND ENGINEERS OF THE TRANSFORMATION

The term change master seems awfully pretentious to me. What is a change master anyway? We learned from the '70s that productivity centers and directors weren't the answer; we know that quality has to be everybody's job. So why do we need this person called a change master? And, by the way, profound knowledge is pretty presumptuous. Who could even aspire to know everything that a change master might have to know? Leave running the organization to the formal organizational structure. They've done a pretty good job to this point. Sure times are tough, but it's tough all over. We don't need some "expert" in improvement, inside or outside the organization, messing with things. They couldn't possibly understand our problems and the complexities of running our business. All this change master stuff is much ado about nothing.

Sound familiar? Organizations need a lot of improvement today. We are in the middle of a revolution not any less significant than the industrial revolution around the turn of the last century. Tom Peters (1987) has suggested that the world has been turned upside down. Peter Drucker (1988) calls this the knowledge revolution. We have witnessed over twenty-five years of serious attention to productivity, quality, quality of work life, quality of life, competitiveness, employee involvement, and innovation. If anything, the attention given and resources allocated to improvement have intensified. Yet there is this nagging sense that there is no end in sight. Leaders, managers, and employees are stressed and strained, tired of change, tired of incessant exhortations to improve, tired of working harder and living poorer, tired of unfulfilled promises of rewards for working smarter. They are frustrated with lack of trust and fearful of their jobs, anxious about the global and national economies, and perhaps many are just "future shocked" (Toffler 1970). Popular psychology on stress management and self-help abounds. We are clearly in the midst of change with no apparent end in sight. One must be agile, quick, and innovative to keep up.

Maintaining an organization's ability to perform today is clearly a new challenge. Conventional organizational structures, systems, strategies, policies and procedures, staffing, measurement systems, and methods appear not to be working well in the face of new technologies and a global economy. Clearly, the concept of "equifinality" (one of the basic characteristics from general systems theory which states that there is no one best way, there are many paths to the same satisfactory solution) suggests that there will be variation in how organizations approach the challenge of maintaining competitive levels of performance. Yet it seems there is a fundamental fact that remains constant when we study human behavior in the context of complex socio-technical systems: individuals, groups, and organizations do get stuck. The science and art of getting individuals and groups healthy again is immature but developing rapidly, as did the medical profession in the late 19th century.

Who will lead the large-scale organizational change necessary for organizations to survive and thrive in the '90s and beyond? What discipline or profession will emerge as the leader in this field? How will all the change, all the improvement, all the innovation required be organized, led, managed, and coordinated? What does it take to be a change master? Does an organization need change masters? How do we use change masters effectively? How do we create change masters? These are the questions we hope to answer in this chapter and in following chapters.

WHAT DOES THE POSITION DESCRIPTION LOOK LIKE?

You may get the impression that we are expecting the change master to live up to the job advertisement in Figure 10 as you study this book. Of course, this is not the case. Our goal is to help leaders, managers, TQM coordinators, industrial engineers, psychologists, sociologists—those in positions with expectations of leading and managing improvement (particularly those with large-scale organizational change tasks)—better understand the requirements of this task and to begin to improve their associated knowledge and skills. We believe that more and more leaders and managers will be called upon, expected, even required to lead and manage positive change in the future. What are the expectations and requirements? By what method will you respond to these new expectations? How do you meet these and still do your job? How do you satisfy the requirements of the position? What are the requirements, anyway?

We believe that change masters, in general, will be expected to be proficient at leading and managing positive change on a continual basis. They will be expected to be proactive, anticipating necessary improvements in advance of competition. They will be required to be a professional that is part organizational development expert, part industrial engineer, part counselor, part statistician, part leader, part follower, part historian, part communications specialist, part visionary, part researcher, part pragmatic business owner, part humanitarian and ecologist, part scientist, part philosopher — part everything.

At a psychology convention some time ago, after Dr. Deming had completed his keynote address, someone from the audience challenged him with the following statement. "Dr. Deming, it would take a lifetime to learn to do all you have lectured to us about this morning." Dr. Deming's response was, "That's all the time you have." And so it is with the challenges of learning to become more effective change masters. It is a calling that may take a lifetime. Our goal is to help those who want to pursue this calling to develop a personal and professional plan of study that, if worked at diligently, will begin to create knowledge and skills necessary to be more effective.

We believe the requirements of becoming an effective change master can be met, and in some cases exceeded, in a program of study approximately ten to twenty years in length. We'll explain what we mean by program of study and defend the length of time a little later.

DO THESE JOBS EXIST?

Of course they do. First, in some respects all managers and leaders have a job requirement called change mastering. "B" is a part of all leaders' and managers' jobs, whether they understand that or not. The question being addressed in this book is how do we improve the performance of managers and leaders at the "B" tasks? One could argue that those

Figure 10. A position description for the change master of the '90s.

managers and leaders who have instinctively learned to lead "B" in the face of demanding "A" and "C" are, in fact, those who get ahead. There are, of course, special positions that are by nature change master positions. TQM coordinators, industrial engineers, organizational development specialists, quality and productivity coordinators, human resource positions, performance improvement engineers, management systems specialists, and operations research analysts, to name a few, have a strong, if not primary, change master component to them.

NATURE OR NURTURE?

We suspect you have known high-performing change masters—individuals who were knowledgeable and skilled at causing positive change with individuals, groups, or organizations. How did they acquire their knowledge and skills? How many of those skills are attributable to nature versus nurture? Clearly, as is the case with most professions, natural instincts and skills explain some of the abilities and proficiencies. Opportunity also explains some of the performance. Willingness or motivation to work hard, study, accept risks, create and capture opportunities, continue to develop, and stick with things even when times are tough also explains some of their performance.

Natural ability, opportunity, and motivation are three very important variables in explaining the performance of those who are skilled and successful at helping shape and create positive change in individuals, groups, and organizations. However, change mastering also can be learned. There is, we believe, a fairly specific albeit extensive "curriculum" or program of study which will lead to knowledge and skills that ultimately will enable one to perform as a change master. This program of study consists of a balanced mixture of formal study and informal self-directed study, experiential learning, on-the-job experimentation and learning, reading, thinking, writing, observing, listening, going to workshops, watching videos — the list goes on.

The cause-and-effect relationships associated with such a program of study and ultimate performance are not understood, even at the rudimentary level. At this point we have only reverse engineering, inference, hypotheses, hunches, replication (prototype development), maybe even, at worst, just speculation. In an engineering sense, however, we think we do have a fair understanding of the requirements for such a role or position. We have catalogued knowledge requirements and resources available for attaining that knowledge. So, we have a start at understanding the value-adding process necessary to "make" a change master.

We know the value-adding process is lengthy, that making a change master is like making a medical specialist: four years of pre-med, four years of medical school, another two to four years of specialty education, internships, and residencies, and then a lifetime of continued study and professional development. The development process for a change master is no less demanding. Life is at stake in both cases — quality of life and quality of work life, jobs, and organizational survival in the case of the change master.

Nature or nurture? Both are necessary. Not everyone has the ability to be a pilot, doctor, engineer, leader, manager, teacher, or change master. Our focus is on helping those with the ability, willingness, and opportunity to develop a program of study that will expedite improvement of their personal and professional performance.

WHAT'S IN IT FOR YOU? WHAT'S IN IT FOR YOUR ORGANIZATION?

We think the need to improve performance of individuals, groups, organizations, nations, and our world in general is clear. It also should be clear that effective leaders and managers for improvement are not as plentiful as is required. Leading and managing positive change today is more complex than ever. Special knowledge and skills are required to cope with the stresses and strains placed on individuals, groups and organizations. The opportunities in the area of quality and productivity improvement, for those technically competent, are increasing and significant. Those who develop special skills and knowledge to lead improvement efforts in organizations will experience rich, challenging, rewarding lives.

It is worth repeating that all this is not without attendant difficulties. As M. Scott Peck said so well in *The Road Less Traveled* (1978), "Life is difficult. Once we accept that life is difficult, it becomes less difficult." So it is with quality and productivity improvement. Every solution creates new problems. The success of a change master is not measured only in his or her solutions to existing problems but in the ability to become an even better problem solver for future problems. Leading and managing change will necessarily create crisis and conflict. So, the change master and the organization will experience pain and difficulty on the road to making the transformation. But the rewards are truly significant.

CASE EXAMPLE 1: A CHANGE MASTER AT WORK

Twelve top managers gather for a 9:00 a.m. meeting, the latecomers covertly eyeing the new "change master" (insert industrial engineer, industrial psychologist or sociologist, organizational development specialist, productivity or quality coordinator, TQM coordinator, etc.) who is getting acquainted with two of the production (insert academic, functional, accounting, engineering, design, etc. if more appropriate) department supervisors. The twelve include the manager, administrative support manager, heads of personnel, purchasing, management information systems, engineering, as well as supervisors from each of the six production departments. These people, along with the plant change master, constitute the entire management group for the plant. All are present, in response to a request from the plant manager, and all are aware that the topic for discussion is improving the quality and productivity of the plant—a topic to which they bring a broad range of experience, frustration, and anxiety.

The plant manager had curiously referred to the meeting as "a working session with our new change master" and mentioned the need for promptness. After a couple of minutes of the usual comfortable social interaction, the change master asks for attention. The following is a heavily edited transcript of what takes place.

"Dave [the plant manager] and I [Eileen] appreciate your attendance this morning to work on ways to improve our quality and productivity. As you know far better than I, this is a high-priority problem for the company, and we have been getting an increasing amount of heat from headquarters to bring our performance up to the level of the St. Louis plant [a plant that is similar in many ways].

"Having been here only a few weeks, it's obvious that I'm not going to tell you how to do this. With your experience, you know far more than I ever will about the opportunities we have for improving our quality and productivity. My job as the change master is to see if we can find efficient and effective ways to translate your knowledge and judgment into action. You are the folks who can improve performance, and my efforts are going to be aimed at helping you do this. I should say that when I speak of the performance of our plant I mean a complex interrelationship between effectiveness, efficiency, quality, productivity, quality of work life, innovation, and profitability. We are emphasizing quality and productivity right now because they are key performance criteria on which we are measured and evaluated. Our job this morning is to identify the quality and productivity improvement opportunities in our plant and see if you can reach some consensus as to which are the most important for us to tackle."

In the days immediately prior to this meeting, Eileen had interviewed each member of the management group individually, encouraging them to talk about their past frustrations with improvement efforts and their beliefs about where the most serious problems and opportunities were to be found. These interviews permitted the management group to relieve some of the stress caused by past attempts and then turn their thinking toward what might be done in the future. Each has thus come to the meeting with some prior thought as to what should be done.

Eileen has discussed with Dave the possibility of an efficient collaborative, consultative, or participative approach to performance improvement. She explained when participation was appropriate, the basic concepts of TQM and management of change, and made sure that he understood the costs, risks, benefits and advantages, and, most importantly, the amount of time involved. She assured him that this approach did not mean he was losing control or power, rather that he was gaining it in the long run. She explained the need to share information and knowledge before sharing power and eventually rewards. In passing, she mentioned that she wanted to work with him to improve the gainsharing system because she felt it was premature in this plant and not working effectively. She mapped out a very rough, overall "grand strategy" for the plant that addressed: planning, measurement (visible management systems), culture and community, education, training, and development, infrastructure for improvement, politics (particularly upline between the plant and the division), technology (methods, equipment, MIS, etc.), communication, and motivation. She explained how this current intervention fit into her overall grand strategy outline.

Dave was overwhelmed at first, but he had been a learner and an early adopter in the past; that's what had caused his rapid movement upward in the company. He admitted to Eileen that he was unclear about a lot of things, maybe even skeptical, but that he would keep an open mind. He was impressed by her ability to conceptualize her assignment in the bigger scheme of things, recognize system interdependencies, and think broadly and strategically. He had to admit he even felt a bit defensive and challenged, thinking to himself that he should be doing what she was doing for him. It seemed pretty logical and simple when she explained it, yet it sure did seem like "eating an elephant."

Dave agreed to try her first steps and to decide on the overall "grand strategy" later. Dave agreed to participate and to legitimize the effort by issuing invitations to the first meeting.

Eileen continues: "I'm inviting you to tackle this task using a well-proven method called the Nominal Group Technique (NGT). We'll use a slightly modified version of this technique I learned when at Virginia Tech. On the sheet in front of you is our task statement, 'Please list below the most important opportunities for performance (let's focus primarily on quality and productivity for now) improvement in our plant.' I'm going to ask you to take ten minutes or so to list as many important opportunities as you can on the sheet. During this period, let's not disturb each other and just work quietly at the generation of opportunities. Research has repeatedly shown that this 'silent generation' process works better than the old 'brainstorming' method. This is called the Nominal Group Technique because during this ten-minute period you will be working as individuals and will be a group in name only."

Next, we will go around the table, each of you taking turns to suggest one of the opportunities from your list. I will record these on the flip chart here so we can all see them. If, for any reason, you don't want to take your turn, just say 'pass.' We'll keep going around the table until you feel that all of the important opportunities are up on the board. Feel free to add to your list at any time during this process. Then we'll review the ideas or opportunities one by one to see if we understand what each means and to clarify them if necessary. You all read the 'learning organization' article by Peter Senge as pre-work to this session so you understand the difference between inquiry and advocacy. We are looking for inquiry only during the clarification session."

Finally, I'll invite you to select what you take to be the seven best opportunities and rank them using a voting card system to simplify the process. I'll collect the cards and, with help from a couple of you, put your rankings up on the board so we can see what kind of consensus there is among you. Afterwards, I'll explain to any of you who are interested the reasons why this method has been designed in this particular way. Any questions?"

The group went through this process, a little skeptically at first, but with increasing enthusiasm as ideas began to flow. At the end of an hour and a half, there were forty-one opportunities on the board, together with the ranks that have been assigned, expressed as seven points for the most important, and so on.

The five objectives in Figure 11, in a Pareto analysis sense, represented the major "consensus" ideas for improvement. The numbers under the ideas are the actual votes received. The numbers over on the right hand side are, in this order, the number of participants voting for the idea, sum of the votes, and the product of number of participants times sum of votes. So, all twelve voted for "implement TQM," the votes total 19, and the product of 12 and 19 is 228. Eileen ranked the ideas on the basis of the product.

There was substantial discussion on the meaning of the results. There were some disagreements and a lot of advocacy. Eileen sat back and listened carefully, taking notes on who said what, what the major issues were, and reflecting on what her next steps would be. She didn't intervene during this period; at times Dave looked over at her wondering why she didn't take charge. At the end of the meeting time, she called the group to attention again and explained what would happen next.

Eileen promised to supply everyone with a copy of the list after the meeting and to identify the "most important" opportunities on the basis of the product of the sum of scores assigned and number of participants voting for the idea. She also suggested that, having made this much progress, the group have a second meeting to consider who might become involved in working on these opportunities and what some of the first steps might be, keeping in mind that the actual commitment of time and money would be decided in the normal way by the plant manager himself.

One of the supervisors pointed out that the plant and the division had already tried quality circles and that they had failed miserably and that this seemed a lot like that. Eileen explained that she was developing a comprehensive understanding of what had been done over the past five years and was sensitive to past attempts to improve performance. She tried to explain the difference between what she was doing and quality circles but wasn't familiar enough with quality circles or the root causes of their failure in this plant to do this. She got stuck, and it was awkward. She did the only thing possible, she "punted, " and she said she would study the past failure with quality circles and get back to them. Eileen assured them that she had no intention of repeating the same mistakes.

She invited them to "press-on" with this effort and encouraged them to jump in and help her if they saw anything she was doing wrong. Most of the group seemed to buy this, or perhaps they were just being polite to the only female in the group; Eileen couldn't tell at this point. They did agree to a second meeting the following week, largely because they saw Dave giving positive body language to what had gone on that morning. In general, most had gotten caught up in the participation associated with the NGT and did feel they had a pretty good list of things to work on. They all, however, left skeptical that they would be successful in implementing even the simplest idea on the list. Things were unusually hectic in the company and division, and this all rolled down to the plant. Between doing their jobs (already 10-hour days) and fighting fires they would never have time to work on these

Figure 11. *Nominal Group Technique results in the top five performance improvement objectives.*

things. They were interested in seeing how well Eileen did in solving these problems.

In later casual discussions, the members of the management group mentioned several interesting things to each other. At no point in the meeting did Eileen make value judgments or inject substantive or "expert" contributions. Eileen's role was strictly limited to designing and executing the process which the group used to undertake its task. Everyone had an equal chance to participate; nobody dominated the session, and no single subject was dominant. Some participants didn't think much of the silent generation activity at first, but when they looked around and saw others working away, particularly the plant manager, they began to think and write as well. When somebody tried to be critical during the listing process, the plant manager quietly told him to wait, and reminded them to inquire, not advocate. During the clarification phase there was some expression of frustration, blame casting, and indications of anxiety, but Eileen kept the session moving and did not permit these moments to become shouting matches. By the time the meeting adjourned (almost exactly at the end of the two hours mentioned in the plant manager's invitation), enthusiasm had risen, there was general agreement that a very useful result had been achieved, and some were willing to say that it was the most productive meeting they could recall.

At the second meeting the following week, Eileen once again structured the process the group used with various combinations and modifications of silent generation, round-robin listing, clarification, and aggregating individual rankings into a crude measure of group consensus. Eileen provided structured processes for the group to accomplish two tasks:

1. Considering the top performance improvement opportunities resulting from the first meeting, classify them as:
   A. Easy for us to do   Hard for us
   B. Short run   Long run
   C. Resources available   Resources and approval
       at plant   required from headquarters

   Having shared these judgments in a structured way, the participants had a clearer understanding of what their consensus was about the magnitude of the effort in - volved in moving ahead with the top-priority opportunities.

2. For each of the top opportunities, who could make an important contribution to the effort or would be importantly involved in its implementation?

Eileen made it clear that this was not an invitation to nominate someone for a significant additional responsibility. Rather, it should be viewed as an important resource to help the plant manager form advisory groups that would work with Eileen on any of the opportunities the plant manager decided should be pursued. Eileen encouraged people to nominate themselves (on the basis of willingness, ability, and knowledge) where appropriate and a large number did so, noting that the plant manager nominated himself in several cases.

Again, after two hours, the group had produced a significant information base for their performance improvement effort. An ownership for the effort clearly was beginning to emerge. They began to feel more comfortable with Eileen, and they were surprised that a young, so-called "change master" would be so willing to allow this effort to reflect their extensive experience and judgment. Nothing about the effort seemed imposed by top management or created by outside experts. It was clear where they agreed and where they disagreed about these opportunities, but more importantly the participants felt pleased at their accomplishment and tended to identify with the result which came back to them in the form of a written summary from Eileen. They were extremely interested in what the plant manager would decide to do next.

Early in the following week, the plant manager devoted one of the regular operating meetings to a discussion of his concept of where the group should go next in the quest for performance improvement. He asked and received the group's approval for the establishment of three working groups, each consisting of three to five appropriate nominees, to attack three performance improvement opportunities that enjoyed a high level of support in terms of group consensus: (1) developing a new layout for the entire plant, (2) quality improvement, and (3) redesigning a particularly troublesome bottleneck operation in the production process. He explained how their ideas from the NGT fit into these rather broad initiatives. The plant manager made it clear that moderate time commitments were being sought from the working group participants, that Eileen would play a major role in each working group, and that appropriate budgetary support would be available or sought from headquarters as needs became clear. The group established for itself a series of future meeting dates at which progress would be reviewed, new working groups formed, and new opportunities undertaken.

Over the next several weeks, Eileen worked closely with the three working groups. The group members determined the general direction of their efforts, depended on Eileen for much of the hard work involved, contributed their judgment freely, and sought consensus among themselves on all major procedural decisions. Eileen's role during this period often resembled that found in more traditional industrial engineering groups. She devoted considerable time to collecting information, meeting the group needs for the special analytical methods that are the expertise of the industrial engineering profession, and proposing design alternatives for consideration by the participants.

However, there was another dimension to her work that was very nontraditional for industrial engineering and, in fact, more like industrial psychology or organizational development. She spent quite a bit of time making "just-in-time" educational interventions and process interventions. She had to ensure that the groups understood enough small-group behavior to manage both the content and process associated with solving their problem. She knew they weren't ready for self-management, but kept them thinking about how they would manage the project, not allowing them to rely too much on her for all the work. She kept trying to operationalize the "three-ball problem" and all the things she had learned in management systems engineering at Tech as she met with these groups. She wanted to successfully implement these three improvement projects, but she also wanted to build the capacity of the plant's management team to self-manage improvement. She spent as much time coaching, teaching, training, building confidence, and active listening as she did using her technical skills. When the group got stuck, she often had to challenge them to get unstuck; this was hard for her because it wasn't her "personality," but she learned to act and play the role she felt was most appropriate for the situation. When the groups met, they often asked Eileen to provide some structure for their group deliberations to achieve some of the efficiency and effectiveness of the two original meetings with which the program began.

In working with the groups, Eileen tried to follow three basic operating guidelines:

1. When bringing data to the group, let the participants interpret them.
2. When creating models, simulations, or system designs, put these before the participants at a very early stage in their development, encouraging and incorporating criticisms and suggestions.
3. All major decisions should be made by the participants, selecting from alternatives presented by the change master. Eileen attempted to supply as much technical insight into the workings of professional tools and methods as the participants appeared to want, explaining to their satisfaction computer simulation, plant layout algorithms, and so on.

In working with the group that developed the new plant layout, Eileen charted the present flow through the plant and provided much of the relevant data on quantities, frequencies, and space and utility requirements. A structured group session was used to generate and evaluate suggestions for major new layout concepts. Ultimately, Eileen used a computer-based algorithm to generate several layouts, which were evaluated and modified at another structured group session.

At the request of the working group, Eileen organized a series of sessions in which production people who would be involved in making the new layout work were given structured opportunities to evaluate the possibilities and to contribute their judgments and suggestions. When the working group had reached consensus on the two best layout alternatives, Eileen played a major role in presenting these to the plant manager, in helping to get funding and approval from headquarters, and in structuring the groups that planned the elaborate implementation process to bring the new layout into being.

Under the general guidance of the working group on quality improvement, Eileen conducted a series of structured group sessions that permitted people involved in all important plant functions to identify and evaluate quality problems. She used these opportunities to provide educational overviews on TQM basics, covering topics such as: appreciation for systems, customer focus, process improvement, statistical thinking, tools of quality, employee involvement, partnerships with vendors, the relationship between quality and productivity and gainsharing, root-cause analysis (why and how diagrams), and measurement. She devoted considerable time to collecting the background data on scrap rates, causes of defects, and other key variables for those problems rated as most important. Following a structured session where the working group interpreted this data, she suggested two basic approaches to quality improvement in the plant, both of which involved application of the techniques of statistical quality control.

After a somewhat long and difficult meeting during which Eileen attempted to put the working group at ease with the basic concepts of statistics and sampling, she helped the group reach consensus on a plan that was subsequently approved by the plant manager. She knew that their work had just begun on TQM with the establishment of statistical process control and was even herself a bit overwhelmed by the magnitude of this project.

She was surprised, after working with the top management team and the working groups, at how little actual improvement was going on in the company, division, and plant. She also was surprised at how little knowledge had been acquired over the past five years. The world around them was changing rapidly, yet this company seemed to be content with the status quo. Things were very reactive around here. Her grand strategy timeline and activities would have to be amended a bit, but having an overall strategy in her head helped her avoid the depression that set in when she got too realistic about the situation. Now she had to get her boss, Dave, and his boss, the division vice-president, to understand and buy into her strategy.

Eileen then organized a series of sessions in which production supervisors and key operators were shown how to set up and interpret the appropriate quality assurance tools. Her involvement continued with the working group which sought to redesign the particularly troublesome bottleneck operation. The production people themselves, having been given full assurances of job security and shares in the resulting savings through the gainsharing system, were involved in structured group sessions to obtain and evaluate their judgments and suggestions about the operation. During these sessions Eileen appropriately wove in educational interventions on the "theory of constraints" (Goldratt 1986) as best she could, attempting to develop at least a rudimentary understanding of linkages, bottlenecks, constraints, and optimization.

Three possible redesigns began to emerge, and Eileen collected the data necessary for their analysis and worked out the details of their execution. The working group asked the same production people to choose which approach should be recommended to the plant manager. Following approval by the plant manager and the inclusion of the necessary funds in the next year's budget, the production people showed considerable skill and enthusiasm in putting the new design into operation.

CASE EXAMPLE IN THE CONTEXT OF SOME THEORY

This scenario portrays a highly condensed report of the life of a change master. It is by no means comprehensive or complete, but it is representative of the range of activities in which change masters are engaged. It clearly demonstrates the multiple roles, or modes of professional functioning, that change masters are required to play in order to be successful at promoting quality and productivity improvement. Here we see the change master functioning as:

- **Facilitator of change:** helping the organization to change itself rather than imposing change on it;
- **Change process designer:** designing the overall process by which change takes place, rather than simply applying techniques or solving problems;
- **Grand strategy developer:** architecting and engineering the overall, strategic change effort, building on the past, taking the long view, shaping the strategy, selling it to leadership, and transferring ownership of the grand strategy to them once fully developed;
- **Structured group process coordinator:** accepting participation and collaboration as essential conditions for change but realizing that unplanned and unstructured participation is almost inevitably costly and frustrating;
- **Acceptant listener:** helping people put their anxieties, frustrations, and conflicts out in the open and eventually aside in favor of constructive approaches to change by being a concerned and effective listener;
- **Technical expert:** introducing the special tools, techniques, and methods of improvement by acting as a technical resource or a broker of technical resources to those who are participating in the change process;
- **Honest broker:** focusing on the use of facts and data, being intellectually honest, thinking systems, not being parochial;

• **Data collector:** bringing together the evidence needed by those who participate in the change process to make informed decisions;

• **Teacher:** using both personal example and traditional instruction to enhance the knowledge and skills of those involved in the change process, knowing when it is appropriate to weave in educational interventions; developing a common body of appropriate knowledge and skills in the organization so they can work together on performance improvement;

• **Change process supporter:** supporting, reinforcing, and encouraging the process of change in which those whose behavior will be influenced by the change remain the principal actors;

• **Challenger, conflict manager:** knowing when to challenge as a method for getting an individual or group unstuck, managing conflict by sharing issues, sponsoring openness, knowing when to confront versus when to smooth, managing process and task.

To the experienced change master, these multiple modes of professional functioning may be fully familiar. Others will see these modes as nontraditional and will be more concerned with behavioral aspects of improvement than with the technology of improvement. Our objective in the chapters that follow is to show that the skills needed to bring about effective change have a research background, can be learned, *and lead to an explicitly enhanced perception of the change master's professional modes of operation.* Our goal is to improve the performance of change masters by developing the art and science of that "helping profession."

Some of the other aspects of this scenario include:

• The philosophy that those whose behavior will be affected by change must participate in the planning of change; a philosophy that typifies most current management thought and requires skill and planning to execute effectively. Many managers who have tried participation without this prior planning are understandably disenchanted with this style of management.

• The need for top management to legitimize the effort and the importance of preserving the normal decision-making processes for the allocation of resources is explicitly recognized. Sharing of power, and the establishment of new decision rules in an organization, must follow, not precede, the sharing of information and knowledge. The evolution of power sharing and alteration in decision rules are necessarily slow and cautious.

• The viewpoint of the change master is that of stimulating and supporting the process by which an organizational system changes. Effective functioning from this viewpoint will require a working knowledge of some of the findings of the behavioral sciences. The change master must be engaged in the development of profound knowledge (theory of psychology, appreciation for systems, theory of knowledge, understanding of variation).

• Participative or collaborative approaches to change will require planning, facilitation, and support. They also may require the acceptance of some decline in the quality of the solutions developed in return for an increase in the acceptance of these solutions. The goal is effective implementation and an increase in the rate of improvement in our organizations. Over time, as the organization acquires more skill and knowledge, quality will improve.

DEVELOPMENT WORK

At the close of each SECTION we provide a set of developmental activities. The first is what we call **inquiry questions**. Senge (1990) presents the notion of inquiry versus advocacy. Inquiry, simply put, is active listening. You are trying to inquire as to intent and meaning. You are trying to uncover assumptions. You are trying to better understand what is being said. You are avoiding criticism, judgment, defensiveness, and evaluation. So, at the end of each chapter, we invite and encourage you to write down inquiry questions relative to the chapter. What didn't you understand? What would you like to know more about? What questions were prompted as you read the chapter? If you were going to "test" on this chapter, what questions would you ask? The intent here is for you to reflect on what you have read and to ask questions as a form of learning.

The **learning exercises** are short activities designed to help you move from theories and concepts to methods and skills. These are study-group types of activities that you may find helpful individually or as a group. They would be good exercises for your Design and Development (Architect and Engineering) Team, the group in your organization that is leading, guiding, crafting the overall quality and productivity improvement effort. Some of the exercises also would be useful for your top management team, others for various performance improvement teams you have set up.

The **feedback questions** are questions we have for you about the content of this chapter. Again, we invite and encourage you to answer them, to think about them, to discuss them in study groups. Some may prefer to do this formally, others informally. Do what works best for you, but at least read them.

And, finally, the **plan of study** is a list of references used in the chapter, suggested readings related to the chapter, but most importantly it is a resource for you to begin to develop your personal and professional plan of study (discussed in Section 6). We encourage you to scan the list of suggested further study at the very minimum. You might mark those that you have read, those you want to study, and those you want to get and read. We encourage you to mark up this book. Add value to it. Make it a study guide and a workbook. At the end of the book, we will have a formal exercise for your plan of development for the next six months and will invite you to integrate the section-by-section plans of study into an overall six-month to three-year effort.

INQUIRY QUESTIONS

These are questions you have for yourself or for others to help you better understand what was covered in this section. Feel free to send them to us, and we will develop a users' group and share questions and answers periodically.

Inquire First

What didn't you understand, what do you want to know about, what assumptions or beliefs do we posit that you want us to explain, what do you want clarification on?

Advocate Second

What did you disagree with, what do you want to argue about, what didn't you like, what do you want to challenge, in what areas do we appear to have different assumptions, databases, beliefs, or attitudes?

LEARNING EXERCISES

LE 1.1 We have used the term "the transformation," as used by Dr. Deming, many times to this point in the book and have provided you with our operational definition. What does the transformation mean to you and your organization? Operationally define the transformation. By what method has your organization attempted to make the transformation? What has worked? Why? What hasn't worked? Why?

LE 1.2 Interview top and senior leaders and managers in your organizational system and ask them to describe your organization's "B", or methods for making the transformation. If your organization has an executive steering group, a TQM council, or some other group that oversees and coordinates improvement efforts, interview them to see what their plans and strategies have been and are.

LE 1.3 Identify some "change masters" in your organization. Interview them. Try to discover what motivates them to stir things up, to work for positive change. Ask them what methods they employ in managing positive change. Find out what their backgrounds are. See if you can detect some common traits, behaviors, attitudes, and approaches among the group you interview. What are their mental models of quality and productivity improvement and of leading, orchestrating, and managing positive change?

LE 1.4 Listed below are some general characteristics sometimes attributed to managers and leaders. Assuming for the moment that these are useful characterizations of most managers, what do they suggest for the design of improvement efforts?

• Having strong need for achievement, needing money and power as symbols of success; apprehensive of failure but often risk prone;
• Having an aversion toward theory, oriented toward "reality," pragmatic, not given to introspection, favoring action over abstraction (e.g., ENTJs or ESTJs on the Meyers-Briggs type indicator, High Ds (dominance) on the DISC personality profile, comfortable with conflict—don't avoid, tend to compete, collaborate, challenge on the Thomas-Kilmann Conflict Mode instrument);
• Tolerant of ambiguity, able to decide on the basis of limited evidence;
• Self-confident, optimistic;
• Tolerant of pressure;
• Tolerant of perplexities and dilemmas, confusion;
• Intellectually honest, individually responsible, demonstrate unrelenting dedication, are technically competent (are generalists but have a core speciality);
• Used to making policies and rules rather than following them;
• Able to work toward goals without being bound by conventional methods;
• Able to adjust quickly to change, failure, and unforeseen circumstances;
• Tend to work best under deadlines, like to build a plan and work the plan but also are very intuitive about what has to get done when;
• Low tolerance for incompetence and for those without individual responsibility and intellectual honesty.

LE 1.5 Find an organization locally that has been struggling with implementation and deployment of TQM or other improvement efforts. The organization should be a typical American-style organization in terms of planning and improvement (PDSA). Collect data from the company such that you can sketch out a cause-and-effect diagram for their perceptions of why they have been struggling. Find out what has worked and what hasn't worked.

Identify a company locally or at least within your state that is practicing some form of Hoshin Kanri or policy deployment; doing Japanese-style planning and improvement (PDSA). Collect data from that organization and do a cause-and-effect diagram on why they have been struggling with implementation and deployment. What has worked and why? What hasn't worked and why?

Now compare and contrast the root causes for struggling between the traditional American PDSA organization and the Hoshin Kanri-style organizations. What do you find?

Do the same type of comparative analysis on employee involvement. Collect first-hand data on a typical American employee involvement method (suggestion system, quality circles, ad hoc teams) and on a "Japanese"-style employee involvement system (Kaizen, quality circles with a much more disciplined infrastructure and set of policies). Why have employee involvement techniques failed, largely, in this country? What do your methods analysis and cause-and-effect diagram tell you? What are the methods one should use to assess success and performance? What levels of performance against those measures are good benchmarks (e.g., 30-45 suggestions per employee per year, usually coming from teams not individuals, with $\geq 90\%$ acceptance and implementation rate, formal recognition and reward system is integrated, decision rules of empowerment are clearly defined, roles are understood, and people are trained to participate and contribute)?

LE 1.6 Compare and contrast the Malcolm Baldrige Award (get a copy of the latest version of the application package from the American Society for Quality Control) with the eight attributes of excellent American firms in *In Search of Excellence* (Peters and Waterman 1982), the National Aeronautics and Space Administration (NASA) Quality and Productivity Application criteria, the Federal Government/Office of Management and Budget (OMB) Quality and Productivity Application criteria, the Virginia (or other States) Senate Productivity and Quality Award criteria, with Dr. Deming's Seven Deadly Diseases, Fourteen Points, and other guidelines; Kilmann's five tracks; our nine fronts; and with other articles and books that have prescribed what criteria on which to make the transformation. What are the common threads? How do these coincide with your mental models of what an organization needs to focus on to make the transformation?

LE 1.7 The factors listed below are thought by some to be significant in determining the technical success and implementation of quality and productivity improvement efforts. Discuss the ways in which each of these may be considered and dealt with in the design-of-change process.

1. Previous experience of the organization with the quality and productivity improvement activity
2. Availabililty of time and resources
3. Support by top management

4. Involvement of the client (direct supervision or management) throughout the course of the improvement effort
5. Client relations in general
6. Project selection and planning
7. Planning and implementation throughout the improvement effort
8. Design and modus operandi of the task force
9. Methodology chosen to accomplish the improvement effort
10. Data collection methods and requirements
11. Continuous reporting and solicitation of inputs (both to users and top management)
12. Demonstrated system improvements
13. Detailed implementation plan (including time, people, resources)
14. Post-audit, evaluation, and follow-through by the improvement team.

LE 1.8 Below are some of the ways clients are thought to evaluate or judge the merits of quality and improvement efforts. Based on your experience and study, suggest examples of each of these. Discuss the impacts of these ways of evaluation on the design of the improvement or change process.

Scientific criteria:
• Consistency with assumptions stipulated by staff;
• Consistency with managerial beliefs and intuitive understanding;
• Consistency with the objective evidence.
Fundamental difficulties:
• Difficulty of demonstrating validity or prior economics;
• Designed to supplement and reformulate management conceptualizations;
• Usually implies changing human behavior;
• Concerns efficiency rather than feasibility.
Extra-scientific criteria:
• Acceptability to superiors;
• Consistent with what others, especially competitors, are doing;
• Resources used: money, technologies, computer time, Ph.D.s, consultants, models, theories;
• Ease of assimilation into management thinking;
• Appropriateness for the institution;
• Ad hominem, staff credentials, bases of power;
• Uniqueness of each problem;
• Disruption of normal operations;
• Degree of staff responsibility for implementation within power, interest, and motivation to act;
• Degree of uncertainty reduction;
• Agreement with expectations;
• Ease of scapegoating, ability to fence sit.

FEEDBACK QUESTIONS
FBQ 1.1 What is the infrastructure for "B" in your organization? Who are the A&E, construction management, and owner and operator/management groups in your organi-

zation relative to "B" (Figure 4)? Do these components work well together? Are they effective? Are they crafting strategy for leadership? Are they guiding efforts? Are they engineering improved management systems and processes? Are they navigating the organization through the transformation?

FBQ 1.2 Who are the change masters in your organization? Are they working as a coordinated team? Are their efforts aligned?

FBQ 1.3 How good is your organization at implementation and deployment? Where are the major difficulties you have faced with both implementation and deployment over the past several years? Let's treat these difficulties as symptoms or effects and prioritize them first. Now, taking the most important or significant difficulty, do a root-cause analysis and an error-cause removal on it. What did you learn?

FBQ 1.4 Depict and describe the method by which your organization:

- Plans
- Measures
- Rewards
- Implements
- Deploys
- Does PDSA.

FBQ 1.5 Operationally define the following quality and productivity improvement terms. Note they are clustered; also think through the relationship between the terms in the cluster.

What is your language of quality and productivity? What is your organization's? Do you have any elegant variation (overuse of synonyms that might cause confusion, a non-mutually exclusive list of terms you use)?

- Performance, effectiveness, efficiency, quality, productivity, quality of work life, innovation, profitability, budgetability;
- Measurement, evaluation, assessment, data, information, analysis, portrayal, knowledge, decisions, actions, strategies, control, improvement, standards, specification, requirements, expectations, process capability, metric, measure, criterion, attribute, indicator, key results area, key performance indicator, quota;
- Goals, objectives, strategies, vision, mission, guiding principles, values, implementation, deployment, bold goals, great performance, stretch goals, actions, tasks, activities, planned strategy, inferred strategy, policies;
- Total quality management, benchmarking, re-engineering, root-cause analysis and error-cause removal, Hoshin Kanri, Kanban, just-in-time, self-managing teams, ISO 9000, Malcolm Baldrige Award, quality function deployment, statistical process control, exploratory data analysis, strategic planning, quality circles, suggestion systems, gainsharing, cross-functional teams.

PLAN OF STUDY

What follows is a list of resources that support, in general, the material introduced in this section. Scan the list, indicate which you have read (R), studied (S), attempted to use (U), and which you would like to become acquainted with (TBD).

LITERATURE CITED

Barnard, C. I. 1938. *The Functions of the Executive.* Cambridge, Mass.: Harvard University Press.

Crosby, P. B. 1979. *Quality is Free.* New York: McGraw-Hill Book Co.

Crosby, P. B. 1984. *Quality Without Tears.* New York: McGraw-Hill.

Conway, W. E. 1992. Quality management in an economic downturn. *Quality Progress.* XXV(5): 27-29.

Covey, S. 1989. *Seven Habits of Highly Effective People.* New York: Simon and Schuster.

Covey, S. 1991. *Principle Centered Leadership.* New York: SummitBooks.

Covey, S. R., A. R. Merrill, and R. R. Merrill. 1994. *First Things First.* New York: Simon and Schuster.

Deming, W. E. 1986. *Out of the Crisis.* Cambridge, Mass.: MIT Center for Advanced Engineering Study.

Deming, W. E. 1993. *The New Economics.* Cambridge, Mass.: MIT Center for Advanced Engineering Study.

Dixon, J. R., A. J. Nanni, and T. E. Vollmann. 1990. *The New Performance Challenge: Measuring Operations for World-Class Competition.* Homewood, Ill.: Business One Irwin.

Drucker, P. F. 1988. The coming of the new organization. *Harvard Business Review.* January-February:45-53.

Drucker, P. F. 1993. *Post Capitalist Society.* New York: Harper Collins.

Goldratt, E. M., and J. Cox. 1986. *The Goal: A Process of Ongoing Improvement* (revised edition). Croton-on-Hudson, NY: North River Press.

Ishikawa, K. 1985. *What is Total Quality Control?—The Japanese Way.* Translated by D. J. Lu. Englewood Cliffs, N.J.: Prentice-Hall, Inc.

Ishikawa, K. 1990. *Guide to Quality Control.* Tokyo: Asian Productivity Organization.

Kanter, R. M. 1983. *The Change Masters.* New York: Simon & Schuster.

Kilmann, R. H. 1989. *Managing Beyond the Quick Fix: A Completely Integrated Program for Creating and Maintaining Organizational Success.* San Francisco: Jossey-Bass.

Kurstedt, H. A. 1993. *The Industrial Engineer's Systematic Approach to Management.* MSL Working Draft and articles and Responsive Systems Article. Blacksburg, Va.: Management Systems Laboratories.

Kurstedt, H. A. 1990. Catering to crises—how to escape. *Quality and Productivity Management.* 8(2).

Lawler, E. E. III. 1986. *High-Involvement Management: Participative Strategies for Improving Organizational Performance.* San Francisco: Jossey-Bass.

Mintzberg, H. 1989. *Mintzberg on Management: Inside Our Strange World of Organizations.* New York: Free Press.

Morris, W. T. 1979. *Implementation Strategies for Industrial Engineers.* Columbus, Ohio: Grid Publishing.

NRC. Harris, D. H. (ed.). 1994. *Organizational Linkages: Understanding the Productivity Paradox.* Committee on Human Factors, Commission on Behavioral and Social Sciences Education, National Research Council. Washington, D.C.: National Academy Press.

Peck, M. S. 1993. *A World Waiting to be Born: Civility Rediscovered.* New York: Bantam Books.

Peck, M. S. 1978. *The Road Less Traveled.* New York: Simon and Schuster.

Peters, T. 1987. *Thriving on Chaos.* New York: Harper Collins.

Scherkenbach, W. W. 1988. *The Deming Route to Quality and Productivity: Road Maps and Roadblocks.* Washington, D.C.: CEEPress.

Scherkenbach, W. W. 1991. *Deming's Road to Continual Improvement.* Knoxville, Tenn.: SPC Press.

Senge, P. M. 1990. *The Fifth Discipline.* New York: Doubleday/Currency.

Senge, P. M. 1990. The leaders's new work: building the learning organization. *Sloan Management Review.* Fall.

Sink, D. S. 1983. Using the nominal group technique effectively. *National Productivity Review.* Spring: 173-184.

Westinghouse Corporate Productivity and Quality. 1993. University Challenge Partnership with Virginia Tech. WesTIP® Workshop, Aug. 16-19, Blacksburg, Va.

Weisbord, M. R. (ed.). 1992. *Discovering Common Ground: How Future Search Conferences Bring People Together to Achieve Breakthrough Innovation, Empowerment, Shared Vision, and Collaborative Action.* San Francisco: Berrett-Koehler.

Weisbord, M. R. 1991. *Productive Workplaces: Organizing for Dignity, Meaning, and Community.* San Francisco: Jossey-Bass.

von Bertalanffy, L. 1968. *General Systems Theory: Foundations, Development, Applications* (revised edn.). New York: George Braziller, Inc.

BIBLIOGRAPHY

Adizes, I. 1988. *Corporate Lifecycles.* Englewood Cliffs, N.J.: Prentice-Hall.

Argyris, C., and D. Schon. 1978. *Organizational Learning: A Theory of Action Perspective.* Reading, Mass.: Addison-Wesley.

Barker, J. A. 1986. *The Power of Visions.* Minneapolis, Minn.: Filmedia.

Barker, J. A. 1988. *Discovering the Future: The Business of Paradigms.* St. Paul, Minn.: ILI Press.

Beer, M., R. Eisenstat, and B. Spector. 1990. Why change programs don't produce change. *Harvard Business Review.* 67:158-166.

Belasco, J. A. 1990. *Teaching the Elephant to Dance: Empowering Change in Your Organization.* New York: Crown Inc.

Bennis, W. 1989. *Why Leaders Can't Lead: The Unconscious Conspiracy Continues.* San Francisco: Jossey-Bass.

Berquist, W. 1993. *The Postmodern Organization: Mastering the Art of Irreversible Change.* San Francisco: Jossey-Bass.

Block, P. 1987. *The Empowered Manager.* San Francisco: Jossey-Bass.

Bolman, L. G., and T. E. Deal. 1991. *Reframing Organizations: Artistry, Choice and Leadership.* San Francisco: Jossey-Bass.

Canon of Virginia. 1992 and 1994. Senate Productivity and Quality Award Application Site Visit Materials. Blacksburg, Va.: Virginia Quality and Productivity Center.

Davenport, T. H., and J. E. Short. 1990. The new industrial engineering: information technology and business process redesign. *Sloan Management Review.* Summer.

Davis, S., and B. Davidson. 1991. *2020 Vision: Tranform Your Business Today to Succeed in Tomorrow's Economy.* New York: Simon & Schuster.

Davis, S. M. 1987. *Future Perfect.* Reading, Mass.: Addison-Wesley.

DeBono, E. 1970. *Lateral Thinking.* Harmondsworth, U.K.: Penguin.

Drucker, P. 1968. *The Age of Discontinuity.* New York: Harper Collins.

Drucker, P. 1989. *The New Realities.* New York: Harper Collins.

Drucker, P. F. 1980. *Managing in Turbulent Times.* New York: Harper and Row.

Foster, R. 1986. *Innovation.* New York: Summit.

Goldratt, E. M., and R. Fox. 1986. *The Race.* Croton-on-Hudson, NY: North River Press.

Goss, T., R. Pascale, and A. Athos. 1993. The reinvention roller coaster: risking the present for a powerful future. *Harvard Business Review.* November-December: 97-108.

Grayson, C. J., and C. O'Dell. 1988. *American Business: A Two-Minute Warning.* New York: The Free Press.

Hammer, M. 1990. Reengineering work: don't automate, obliterate. *Harvard Business Review.* July-August.

Hammer, M., and J. Champy. 1993. *Reengineering the Corporation: A Manifesto for Business Revolution.* New York: Harper Collins.

Handy, C. 1990. *The Age of Unreason.* Boston, Mass.: Harvard Business School Press.

Jaques, E. 1989. *Requisite Organization.: The CEO's Guide to Creative Structure and Leadership.* Arlington, VA.: Cason Hall.

Mintzberg, H. 1986. The manager's job: folklore and fact. *Management Classics.* Edited by M. T. Matteson and J. M. Ivancevich (3rd edn.). Plano, Tex.: Business Publications.

Monetta, D. J., and D. S. Sink. 1991. Continuous improvement: implementing a grand strategy system at the office of new production reactors. *Quality and Productivity Management.* 9(3).

Morris, W. T. 1975. *Work and Your Future: Living Poorer, Working Harder.* Reston, Va.: Reston Publishing.

Naisbitt, J. 1984. *Megatrends.* New York: Warner.

Naisbitt, J., and P. Aburdene. 1985. *Re-inventing the Corporation: Transforming Your Job and Your Company for the New Information Society.* New York: Warner Books.

Ouchi, W. 1981. *Theory Z: How American Business Can Meet the Japanese Challenge.* Reading, Mass.: Addison-Wesley.

Pascale, R., and A. Athos. 1981. *The Art of Japanese Management.* New York: Simon and Schuster.

Peters, T., and R. Waterman. 1982. *In Search of Excellence.* New York: Warner Books.

Quinn, R. E. 1991. *Beyond Rational Management: Mastering the Paradoxes and Competing Demands of High Performance.* San Francisco: Jossey-Bass.

Richover, H. G. 1991. Thoughts on man's purpose in life. *Quality and Productivity Management.* 9(3).

Schaffer, R. H., and H. A. Thomson. 1992. Successful change programs begin with results. *Harvard Business Review.* January-February.

Scott Morton, M. S. (ed.) 1991. *The Corporation of the 1990s: Information Technology and Organizational Transformation.* New York: Oxford University Press.

Sink, D. S. 1992. Can IE's become masters of change? *Industrial Engineering.* 24(12).

Sink, D. S., and G. L. Smith. 1994. The influence of organizational linkages and measurement practices on productivity and management. *Organizational Linkages: Understanding the Productivity Paradox.* Washington, DC: National Academy Press.

Taylor, F. W. 1911. *Principles of Scientific Management.* New York: Harper & Row.

Thompson, J. D. 1967. *Organizations in Action.* New York: McGraw-Hill.

Thurow, L. 1992. *Head to Head: The Coming Economic Battle Among Japan, Europe and America.* New York: William Morrow.

Thurow, L. C. 1985. *The Zero-Sum Solution: Building a World-Class American Economy.* New York: Simon and Schuster.

Toffler, A. 1970. *Future Shock.* New York: Bantam Books.

Toffler, A. 1980. *The Third Wave.* New York: Morrow.

Toffler, A. 1990. *Power Shift: Knowledge, Wealth, and Violence at the Edge of the 21st Century.* New York: Bantam Books.

Vail, P. B. 1991. *Managing as a Performing Art: New Ideas for a World of Chaotic Change.* San Francisco: Jossey-Bass.

Weick, K. E. 1979. *The Social Psychology of Organizing.* Reading, Mass.: Addison-Wesley.

HOW INDIVIDUALS, GROUPS, AND ORGANIZATIONS CHANGE TO IMPROVE QUALITY AND PRODUCTIVITY

How do you change? Can you think of examples where you changed for the better? What led up to that? What triggered it? What did you go through to improve? How did you maintain the change? Think of losing weight, getting in shape, New Year's Resolutions you kept (or didn't keep), getting a degree, finding a new job. Relate to positive change, first, on the personal level.

Now think about positive change at the group level. Think about an experience you've had in this situation. What triggered it? How did it transpire? Did the positive change "stick?" Why or why not? What differences can you think of between group and individual change and improvement?

Now think about positive change at the organizational level. What triggered it? Was it successful? Why or why not? How was the improvement initiated? How was the improvement effort managed and sustained? What was different about organizational improvement than individual or group improvement?

As you answered these questions, you may have been struck by a number of similarities in the process for positive change at the individual, group, and organizational level. We each know a lot more about positive (and not so positive) change than is apparent at first glance. Our personal experiences, combined with a little theory, a little research and experience, and some conceptual models, provide a rich foundation for understanding what the change master attempts to accomplish.

There is a wealth of information available today about managing change, and there are numerous common threads among the various approaches prescribed. We have attempted to extract those common threads and present them in this chapter:

1. Individuals, groups, and organizations move through distinct phases as they change to improve.
2. Resistance to change is common and predictable, comes in many forms, and has identifiable root causes which can be removed. In other words, resistance to change is manageable because it is predictable and understandable.
3. Although the most successful form of positive change, self-change (individual, group, organizational) has predictable difficulties that must be resolved.
4. Positive change looks easier on paper than it is in reality. The subtleties of change leadership and management are substantial.

Our case example in this section presents a more complex improvement effort than our first case study. It is set in a community and in an academic setting. We highlight, in the context of this chapter, the phases-of-change aspect of this case. In Section Three we highlight the professional-modes-of-functioning aspect of an improvement project.

OPERATIONAL DEFINITIONS

5-P Model: Harold Kurstedt (1993) discusses five types of endeavors: perplexities, programs, projects, problems, and processes. Each of these types of endeavors has different characteristics in terms of degree of complexity, amount of uncertainty, risk, level of ambiguity, etc. Different approaches, methods, and tools may be useful in addressing these endeavors. We introduce the 5-Ps in the context of improvement to trigger your thinking about different types of endeavors you will be confronted with as a change master and different tools you might use to address these endeavors.

Desired Outcomes/Desired Outputs: The distinction between an output and an outcome is one of time. If we plan a meeting, for example, we can identify some tangible product (e.g., a decision, report, action item) that we want to occur by the end of the meeting; this is an output. Anything we plan or expect to occur after the meeting is over, as a result of the meeting but not during the meeting, could be considered an outcome. In a service organization, for example, our service would be an output; the outcome is what the customer achieves as a result of the service. Customer satisfaction is an outcome, by definition. Repeat business is an outcome. Getting a good job is an outcome of the educational process.

Front Owner: We have introduced the term front or subsystem in the context of total-system or large-scale organizational change. In that context, we use the concept and term "front owner." In business process re-engineering, there is a step that requires the organization to identify the owner of the business process. This is an important step because many business processes don't have owners. Things that aren't owned aren't led and managed. Fronts, or subsystems (such as planning, measurement, motivation, communication, and infrastructure) also need owners for them to improve. So, when we speak of "front owner" we imply someone (or some group of people) who is responsible for and accountable for continued improvement of a given front.

I, G, O: As a shorthand notation, we will be referring to organization-level improvement as O-level, group-level improvement as G-level, and individual-level improvement as I-level.

Input/Output Analysis: Input/Output analysis is really just a system picture or model. It depicts the organizational system, inputs, outputs, upstream systems, upline systems, downstream systems, customers or users, desired outcomes, and measures of performance. Figure 12 is an example. It is useful in ensuring that domain, scope, and unit of analysis are clear and developmental when done in a group exercise. A learning exercise on this tool is provided at the end of this section (LE 2.10).

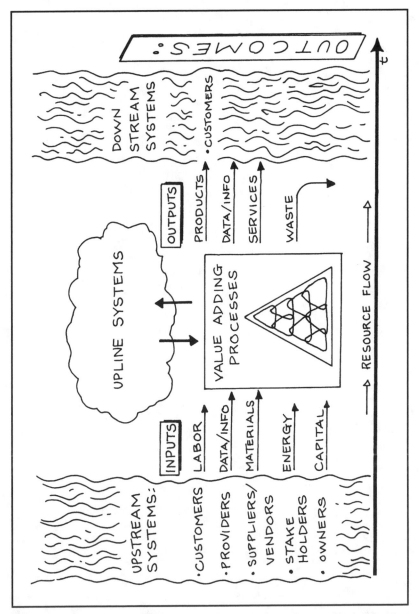

Figure 12. The input–output analysis is another way to depict the organizational system.

CHAPTER 3

FUNDAMENTALS OF CHANGE

A variety of change models have been developed through theory building, research, and through reduction-to-practice and consulting. Group change has been modeled in many ways, with the forming, storming, norming, and performing model being perhaps the most popular. Kurt Lewin's model of change (1951)—unfreezing, changing, refreezing—is simple but powerful. Organizational change is well theorized and researched; the subdiscipline of organizational-development contains numerous models for understanding organizational level change. The field of psychiatry, of course, is also replete with a variety of paradigms and models for changing human behavior.

However, organizations don't change; they don't do anything. Individuals and groups (but mostly individuals) improve things through their decisions, actions, and behaviors. Organizations improve because individuals and groups improve. This does not imply that there aren't organizational-level interventions that can be made to improve performance. It simply means that even O-level performance improvement decisions and actions are made by individuals and groups.

It seems there are a number of "burning questions" facing leaders of change:

• How do we get individuals and groups to optimize the performance of an organizational system in a systematic, coordinated fashion?
• How do we empower people to make positive change?
• How do we motivate people to make decisions and take actions when the consequences of those decisions and actions are not clear, there is risk and uncertainty involved, or there is a lag between actions and results or consequences? How do we motivate individual and group decisions and actions aimed at improvement when there may well be "winners and losers," at least in the near-term or smaller-system perspective?

We know these are questions you already have been wrestling with, and you want answers, not good questions. But it is important to make sure we identify the right questions and right problems before we march off to improve things. It is also clear that "examples in the absence of proper theory" are useless (Deming 1992). So, it is important we build a theoretical foundation sufficient to address our questions.

Our understanding of the theory, research, and practical experience associated with change for quality and productivity improvement leads us to believe that ultimately:

1. Change will occur when clients accept the need for it, make their own decisions in favor

of it, and determine for themselves the directions it will take.
2. The most effective way to encourage change is to make the client a collaborator or co-worker in the process. Change is most likely to occur when it is primarily a process of self-awareness and self-direction.

These conclusions are, of course, far from original. They are an old story to professions concerned with helping individuals and groups change. Behavioral scientists, management consultants, clinical psychologists, career counselors, physicians, and clergymen long have operated on the basis of similar conclusions.

In this chapter, we bring together what is at least a rough, underlying model from all of these change-oriented professions. The model can be used by the change master to provide an awareness of what is happening as the quality and productivity improvement effort goes forward. We believe the model is applicable at the I-level, G-level, and O-level. Obviously, as the size and complexity of the target system increase, the model becomes more difficult to implement and apply, and significant peripheral theory, research, knowledge, and experience must be brought to bear to succeed.

FRAMEWORKS FOR UNDERSTANDING CHANGE FOR IMPROVEMENT

Change masters not only must consider the various stages of their own personal and professional development, they must at all times be aware of the particular state of their change target. Let's consider for a moment the characteristics of the change target. Here, we present three models. The first is a readiness-for-change model developed by Beckhard (1986) (The formula was developed by David Gleicher of Arthur D. Little.) It suggests that determining readiness and capability for change can be modeled conceptually with the formula in Figure 13.

Most of the current management-of-change models build off this basic but fairly complete formula. A gap between current reality and the vision brings about creative tension, as discussed by Senge in his excellent book titled *The Fifth Discipline* (1990). Benchmarking can be used to create factual, data based understanding of gaps between current performance levels and "best of best" levels of performance. These factual gaps should bring about the creative tension that sparks decisions and actions aimed to close the gap. The "burning platform" metaphor commonly used in introducing change management supposes that individuals, groups, and organizations need to confront the pain of not changing within the context of the pain of changing. If the perceived cost, pain, or benefits of changing are not sufficient to motivate change, then resistance (sometimes rational and sometimes not) to change may be inevitable.

Creating awareness of the need to change by clarifying the vision and the goals of change is clearly important. But, as we found in the '70s, this is necessary but not sufficient to ensure that positive change to affect bottom-line performance is created. The late W. Edwards Deming shouted to his audiences of hundreds: "By what method?" By what method will we close the gap, make the transformation, improve quality? Practical first steps are needed. We can understand the goal, buy into the goal, understand the need to change, but if we don't know what to do, change will not occur.

This is the key domain of the change master: assisting in the design of paths to achieve goals. Design skills are crucial to a change master's ability to affect the "D" in this model. Again, we find that it must go beyond practical first steps. If the transformation that

Figure 13. Change models help consolidate theory so we can reduce it to practice (adapted from Beckhard 1986).

Deming and others are prescribing, in fact, will take multiple years to accomplish, then a complete project plan must be thought through.

Seven somewhat distinct phases of client change (Figure 14) serve as a foundation for discussion in Chapter 4. We will examine, through the use of a case example presented later in this section, how organizational systems pass through these phases, how they get stuck in phases, and will come to understand each of these phases more completely. You will learn how to plan for moving a change target through these phases in a systematic fashion.

In the interest of simplification, we have omitted from our discussion the important preliminary phase involving the entry of the change master into the client organization and the process by which the change master becomes legitimized. Others, such as Block (1981), discuss this in some detail. Clearly trust, chemistry, credibility, visibility, experience, and cultural issues all play a key role in determining opportunities that change masters will have to help improve organizational systems.

It should not be supposed that the following phases are necessarily well defined or distinct. Nor do all clients or client organizations move through all of the phases. The order in which they are presented here suggests a certain logic, but an actual change process may involve not only a different ordering but also a shifting back and forth among the phases. It may be helpful to think of the following seven phases as descriptive of individual change, group change, and organizational change, permitting the term client, again, to refer to all three.

1. **Situation Appraisal (Scouting, Targeting, Diagnosis).** The client's attention comes to focus on a limited, although perhaps vaguely understood, problem area. The client begins to refine feelings about "what is wrong" or where change is likely to have the best benefits-to-burdens ratio.
2. **Catharsis (Stress Relief).** The client reduces the inhibiting effects of past frustrations, anxieties, and conflicts. Blame casting, fault finding, injustices, and so on are expressed, set aside, and the client's attention is to some degree freed for concentration on the change process.
3. **Self-Awareness.** Data and fact gathering, modeling the present system (e.g., input/output analysis) and studies of "how we do it now" increase the client's self-perception and self-objectification.
4. **Self-Evaluation.** The client comes to make his or her own evaluation of current behavior. The client better understands goals, standards, and objectives and their relation to existing behavior. There is a growing appreciation of the need for change, the material and psychological costs of change, and the development of realistic expectations about the change process.
5. **Self-Designed Change Strategies.** The client plans or accepts plans for new behaviors, methods, and systems. The greater the degree to which the client participates in the planning of change, the greater is the probability that change will actually occur. This phase also includes the planning of tests, experiments, and trials of the new behavior.
6. **Trying Out the New Behaviors.** The client experiments with new methods and systems. Experiential learning leads to modifications and refinements.
7. **Reinforcing the New Behavior.** To be replicated, the new behavior must be rewarded and reinforced.

Figure 14. Individuals, groups, and organizations tend to pass through these phases as they change and improve.

This model of the client change process rests on several widely held assumptions for which there is a good deal of both casual and systematic evidence:

- Frustration, anxiety, conflict, and anger reduce the probability of behavior change, and the stress they create can be significantly relieved by expression and sharing.
- Collaboration, participation, and involvement of the client in the change process are essential. People and organizations cannot be changed by consultants; they change themselves.
- Change is most likely to occur if clients take responsibility for understanding their own behavior, clarifying their own standards and goals, and comparing these themselves.
- The greater the degree to which the client sees the new behavior or system as self-designed, the greater is the probability that change will occur.
- Lasting behavior change requires a support system that limits the fear of failure and rewards the new behavior, thus reinforcing it.

THE SELF-CHANGE PROBLEM

With all of this emphasis on individual, group, and organizational change as a self-designed process, it is reasonable to ask why a change master is required at all. Why don't individuals, groups, and organizations, recognizing their own dissatisfactions, simply change themselves? Many change masters clearly have a significant contribution to make as a system designer, creator of new methods, technical specialist, or expert, but why must their contribution go beyond this? Why must the change master take responsibility for the larger process of bringing about actual change? Why, indeed, is it necessary to redefine the traditional roles that various professions, disciplines, and positions play, embedding the technical contributions in the larger task of change process designer?

Given that a person or a group recognizes the need for change, it would seem that they would simply ask key people to work out new methods and new ways of making decisions. They would then implement the solutions deemed acceptable. While many leaders and managers encounter situations in which something like this happens, far more frequently they encounter clients who recognize the need for change but fail to achieve it. The basic facts of self-change which the leader and manager can usefully recognize include the following:

1. Deliberate self-change by individuals, groups, and organizations rarely happens without assistance from someone else in the form of planning, motivation, and support.
2. Clients, working by themselves, seldom are able to find and marshal the time, resources, knowledge, and sustained motivation to create and put into practice new ways of doing things.
3. Attempts at unassisted and unsupported self-change suffer from a variety of difficulties:
   - They are simply forgotten after awhile.
   - They get displaced on the client's agenda by more immediate concerns ("A," "C," and "D" squeeze "B" out).
   - Rewards and reinforcements are not present to motivate change efforts.
   - There is little social pressure or tension to drive the change process (if anything, there is social pressure to maintain the status quo, and in our present environment this just isn't acceptable).

- It is not easy to plan a program of change in which the anticipated effort seems to be justified by the probability and payoff of success.
- Efforts are easily stalled by minor frustrations, discouraging early results, and the failure to realize unrealistically high expectations. Often, those attempting change and improvement don't know what to expect, can't separate what is predictable and normal from what is not, and can't distinguish between special cause and common cause of variation because they have single data points. A change master will have multiple data points and will be less susceptible to this type of error.
- It is necessary to extinguish habits and customs that have a long history of use and reinforcement.

4. Planned change programs succeed when they supply:
    - A complete design for the process of creating and testing new methods and systems;
    - Support and reinforcement throughout this process;
    - Realistic expectations about the benefits and burdens of new ways of doing things;
    - Assistance to the client in clarifying goals and objectives;
    - Ways of freeing the client from "fire fighting."

5. Change seldom occurs as the result of:
    - Reading about new methods;
    - Telling about or showing new methods;
    - Hearing about new methods.

6. It is seldom helpful to say to a client, directly or by implication, "If you really wanted to change, you could," or "If change is not occurring, you're not really trying."

CASE EXAMPLE 2A: MANAGING PHASES OF CHANGE— THE BUCKSBURG 2000, COMMUNITY OF THE FUTURE INITIATIVE

The setting for this case study is the community of Bucksburg, Ohio, population 250,000. Like a number of other communities and localities, Bucksburg is faced with serious and pressing issues: education, infrastructure, economic, cultural, and political challenges prevail.

Bucksburg Tech, the state's largest university, is located within the community, and is home to the Ohio Quality and Productivity Center (OQPC), a quality and productivity center housed within Tech's Industrial and Systems Engineering Department.

CAST OF CHARACTERS
The Mayor and City Manager of Bucksburg: The sponsors of the Bucksburg 2000 initiative.

Elizabeth: Director of OQPC and assistant professor in the Industrial and Systems Engineering Department at Bucksburg Tech. Elizabeth has fifteen years of experience in the area of quality and productivity improvement and has been a center director for over ten years.

Kurt: A management systems engineer at OQPC who is serving as project manager on the Bucksburg 2000 initiative. Kurt has been with the center full-time for two years. As a masters student in the Management Systems Engineering Department at Bucksburg Tech, Kurt held a graduate research assistantship with the OQPC and gained hands-on experience by working to support the center's projects.

Ellen: The newly designated total quality coordinator for the City of Bucksburg. Ellen has been with the city for approximately eighteen months, the first sixteen of which she served as public information officer. She only recently transitioned into the role of Total Quality Coordinator.

Harry: President of Bucksburg Bank and Trust and prominent social, civic, and professional figure in the community of Bucksburg. Harry is politically astute, a networker, a progressive thinker, and has recently become enamored with the concept of total quality.

Garry, Ken, Marta, and Paul: Management systems engineers at OQPC and members of the Bucksburg improvement effort project team.

Harry, a bank president and self-appointed change master from Bucksburg, Ohio, took it upon himself to orchestrate a total quality movement in the city and in the entire community. He contacted the OQPC at Bucksburg Tech, having learned of the organization through a local company they had worked with successfully for over eight years. Harry arranged a meeting with the director of the OQPC, Elizabeth.

Elizabeth was impressed that the president of a local bank would initiate a community-based change effort. She was challenged by the opportunity, worried about how the effort would be funded, and initially skeptical that something this large could be managed. No one in OQPC, including herself, was experienced with a change effort this large. Furthermore, Bucksburg had a diverse population: an added dimension that her center had not dealt with extensively. But Elizabeth was aware of similar efforts in other states and knew she could benchmark for ideas.

The initial meeting with Harry in the boardroom at Bucksburg Bank and Trust was a fact finding session. Elizabeth was always optimistic with clients during these initial meetings. She struggled a bit to think through the right questions to ask: funding, key players, politics, desired outcomes, scope and duration, hidden agendas, and next steps are examples of the information she knew she needed.

Harry was a GO, GO, GO type person, charismatic and a visionary, and Elizabeth respected this, but she was concerned about his operational understanding and skills. Did he fully appreciate what was involved and what he was getting into? Was he starting an effort he would stick with, that the community would stick with, and that would be supported for the duration? She knew this was a crusade with a beginning and no end— did Harry?

The meeting ended well, and they decided to hold another meeting with additional change masters in the community and with the Mayor and City Manager. Elizabeth committed to organizing a statement of the "problem/project" using information she had obtained from this initial meeting. She also agreed to scope out the project, which would include mapping out a high-level project plan, complete with major milestones and a rough order of magnitude (ROM) budget. She had no idea how she would do this when she made her commitment but was confident that her colleagues in the OQPC would assist in putting something together; they had done this many times in the past.

Back at OQPC Elizabeth met with Kurt, Garry, Marta, Ken, and Paul and briefed them on the opportunity. Predictably, there was a wide range of reactions:

> "I've lived here all my life. This community is in trouble. They have too many problems. And besides, how can we expect to pull this off when we are struggling with much simpler projects?"
>
> "I'm not comfortable with Harry's motives. What's in it for him? Are there hidden agendas we don't know about?"
>
> "Great opportunity! When do we start? Who will be the principal investigator, project manager, and other team members?"
>
> "I need some time to think about this. I'm not comfortable making a commitment until I understand more about the situation."

At the conclusion of the discussion, Ken and Paul agreed to conduct some one-on-one and small-group interviews with key potential players in the Bucksburg effort to collect more data on the situation. Elizabeth, Garry, Kurt, and Marta set aside some time to work on the version 1.0 strategy.

A week later, Elizabeth reconvened her ad-hoc project team to discuss what Ken and Paul had learned in their interviews and to review the first-cut strategy and agenda design for the upcoming meeting with community leaders. Paul and Ken summarized their conclusions: The project was too complex and had too many problems, including no centralized leadership, no critical mass of effective change masters within the community, and strict budget constraints, which would mean that OQPC would have to do the project at a loss. Elizabeth tried her best at inquiry versus advocacy but wasn't sure she succeeded. She was committed, with support from Garry, Kurt, and Marta, to going a little further before deciding not to proceed.

Sensing this, Ken and Paul became "prisoners" for the rest of the meeting. (It is said there are three types of people in meetings: participants, prisoners, and tourists — Monetta 1991.) Elizabeth didn't have the physical or mental energy to try to change this. She knew she had a potential client that needed help, she knew it was unexplored territory for her center, and that this project was consistent with OQPC's mission. Besides, Elizabeth was intrigued by the challenge. She had a strong sense of vision about where the center should head and this guided her strategies and actions. Often in the past, she had made executive decisions that she didn't have strong consensus for on this basis. She knew Ken and Paul were experienced and knowledgeable, valued their judgment, and liked working with them, but sometimes Elizabeth questioned the extent to which they had bought into the center's vision. She informed the group that she wanted to press on a bit longer before making a go/no-go decision.

They reviewed the community meeting agenda, discussed and enhanced it as well as the first-cut strategy, and decided who would be involved in the next meeting with key players in the Bucksburg community. It was decided that Elizabeth, Paul, and a graduate student would make the next field site visit.

The following week they met with the Mayor, City Manager, Harry, and several other change masters from various businesses as well as from within the city government. Elizabeth reviewed her proposal and assessment of the situation. She provided several educational interventions on total quality, planning, and improvement and provided examples of efforts underway in communities such as Madison, Wisconsin; Philadelphia, Pennsylvania; and Portsmouth, Virginia.

Elizabeth found the Mayor and City Manager receptive and eager to get started but, as with Harry, questioned their intents and potential hidden agendas. It was becoming clear that politics were heavy and would be a key front in this effort. It also was clear that the education, training, and development front would be key. Elizabeth didn't get the impression that these meeting participants had even a superficial acquaintance with total quality.

Elizabeth presented the three-year ROM budget, and Harry said he was working with the business community and with several foundations to obtain grants to support the effort. The Mayor and City Manager said even though Bucksburg had budget problems they felt they would be able to free up some funds for the project. Elizabeth informed them that the center would do this project on a total-cost break-even basis, and the University would waive overhead charges, although her center couldn't. Funding, for the moment, seemed to be resolved.

Unknown to Elizabeth, Harry had set up several briefings on what was now being called the "Bucksburg 2000" initiative with key community leaders. There were receptions, meetings with the press, and strategy sessions all lined up for a day and a half. Elizabeth felt this effort was getting completely out of control. Paul said he told her this would happen and that he absolutely wouldn't work on the project. The graduate student was overwhelmed and had mentally shut down on overload an hour into the day. Feeling manipulated by Harry, Elizabeth went on automatic pilot, became part saleswoman for the project and part change master, trying to posture a wide variety of stakeholders and participants for what would come. She was clearly at the "envelope" of her skills, but she felt challenged and knew she would survive and grow from the experience.

It was 10:30 p.m. before she got home. She poured herself a glass of Chardonnay and sat back to unwind a bit before preparing for the next day. It was midnight before she retired. She knew 6:00 a.m. would roll around fast and that tomorrow would be another long day. At moments like this, Elizabeth sometimes questioned why she did this for a living, but she knew she would feel different in the morning.

The next morning, Elizabeth met from 6:30 to 8:00 with Paul and the graduate student to strategize about what to do next. What she needed most right now was a sounding board for the ideas that had formed throughout her night of fitful sleep.

Ninety minutes and two cups of black coffee later, Elizabeth was meeting with Harry and his growing assembly of community colleagues to map out a six-month strategy. Five minutes into the meeting, she realized a change of mode was in order, so she confronted Harry with the issue of roles and responsibilities. "Who's going to do what?" she asked. This shifted the power from Harry to her for the moment. Elizabeth seized the opportunity and took control by mapping out how she saw the effort taking shape, specifying accountabilities and major milestones, and even wove in subtle educational interventions as appropriate.

As a result of her facilitation, the group was able to map out potential interventions relative to the communication, infrastructure, planning, measurement, culture, motivation, education/training/development, political, and technology fronts for the six months, in some detail, and for months seven to twelve in less detail. Front owners were temporarily assigned to spread the work.

Elizabeth knew she had to "crash" the education, training, and development front with this core group of community change masters quickly. She called for an immediate five-day "boot camp" session designed to get them up to speed with concepts, language, theory, methods, and overall strategy. She hadn't thought of this in her version 1.0 strategy and therefore hadn't budgeted for it, but she realized this morning this would be a key requirement for success.

Once back at the OQPC, Elizabeth designated Kurt as project manager for the Bucksburg 2000 effort. Paul, whom she had originally envisioned playing this role, had made it very clear he was not going to be involved with this initiative. Ken, too, Elizabeth was certain, would refuse to take the role. Marta and Garry, although willing and capable, were consumed with other projects and had little remaining time or energy to expend. Kurt became the obvious choice: what he lacked in experience, he compensated for with hard work and a desire to learn.

The boot camp went well, a work hard, play hard environment. The OQPC team had spent considerable time up front on agenda design, and they executed it successfully. The participants left the session better informed, educated, highly motivated, charging in the same direction, and with clear individual roles and responsibilities. All this had happened in what seemed like an instant to the project team from OQPC.

A design team or "architect and engineering" group was assembled and, together with the core group of community change masters, represented a critical mass of people to work on this project. Collectively, they had knowledge, experience, political astuteness, strong ties to people in pivotal positions of power, willingness, and opportunity to accomplish the Bucksburg 2000 effort. Elizabeth reminded her project team, particularly Kurt, that the hard part was going to be to keep this group of twelve people coordinated, communicated with, motivated, productive, "in control," vectored in the same direction, and learning.

The next major milestone was a summit, scheduled for two months into the project. No evidence of entropy was visible until the week of that event. Kurt had let his guard down and not stayed closely in touch with what was going on within the community. As a result, for example, the size of the group participating in the summit soared from the planned thirty to over sixty-five. By the time Elizabeth and others found out about this it was too late to do anything but make necessary adjustments in logistics, agenda, and process.

The increase in size caused a corresponding increase in the complexity of leading and facilitating the session. It forced the OQPC project team to place more burden on Elizabeth, the most experienced with large-group planning sessions. For her, it would be a long two days. Another critical incident involved the unwillingness or inability of Kurt to maintain quality communication with the Mayor and City Manager. Clearly, they were the people in positions of power. Kurt, much younger and less experienced, had avoided these two key figures in the community, using excuses of "not necessary" or "couldn't get on their schedules." The result was that the night before the summit, Elizabeth felt ill-prepared and began to realize that some significant details, like a meeting with the Mayor and City Manager the day before the summit, had been overlooked.

All things considered, the next three days went pretty well. Elizabeth's experience and skill with large groups paid off. She found herself relying on tips gained from reading M. Scott Peck's method of community building and from Weisbord's work with search conferences, in addition to many years of running strategic planning sessions with groups ranging from six to 100. However, when she got mentally fatigued Elizabeth had a tendency to revert to preferred professional modes of functioning and had to watch out for that. She had to continually work with her support personnel to get them to anticipate and support the needs of the deliverer, to think ahead of her in the agenda (Figure 15), and to help her keep perspective.

The summit created a community vision, community guiding principles and values, assumptions, mission, current performance level information, input/output analysis, five-year goals, near-term objectives, and ad hoc teams organized to develop scoping proposals for the top priority improvement objectives for the community. Leaders from the Public School System, Police and Fire Departments, local business and industry, area churches, and city government all participated. Most of the participants were predictably skeptical, unhappy, and frustrated throughout the first day. However, on the second day and third day, they were amazed at how productive they had been, how much consensus they were able to achieve with the modified Nominal Group Technique and other structured group processes, and at the early feelings of community building.

One big disappointment was the lack of participation from the City Council members. They were constantly in and out of the meeting room and generally speaking were "tourists" rather than active participants. It seemed that the council was polarized over racial issues and other hidden agendas and that all past efforts to get the council to work better as a team and get on board had failed. This was another critical incident left unmanaged and unrecognized by Kurt. Elizabeth wished she had paid more attention to the inner workings of the political front; she felt she might have found a way to better manage the City Council's participation, but it was too late now.

Elizabeth spent three hours after the summit was adjourned briefing her colleagues on next steps, going over what went right and what could have gone better, and documenting critical incidents. Kurt scheduled a project team meeting for the next day to finalize next steps and ensure assignments were clear.

Output from the summit, including an updated "Bucksburg 2000" project plan, was distributed to all participants (or so the OQPC staff assumed) by Ellen, the internal (city employee) project manager and change master for this effort. Teams had been voluntarily (on the basis of willingness and ability) formed to create scoping proposals for top-priority objectives. A quarterly review session was scheduled for three months after the summit to present these proposals. It seemed the Bucksburg initiative was hitting stride and gaining momentum. All was well for the moment.

Kurt went on to other projects that heated up, assuming Ellen and the Bucksburg design team would self manage and keep the ball rolling. He was out of the office a lot, traveling frequently across the state to work with a manufacturing company on a business process re-engineering project, and then every two weeks to Washington, D.C., where he conducted TQM tools training for a large Navy client.

Two months had passed when Elizabeth, completely immersed in project work, research, publishing, teaching, and managing the center, suddenly realized she wasn't clear on where the Bucksburg 2000 project stood. She hadn't spoken with Kurt for any length of time since the summit; they had both been out of the office so much. Elizabeth called Kurt and asked him to set up a project team meeting to assess the status of the Bucksburg initiative. Kurt asked Elizabeth to remind him just who exactly was on the project team. Elizabeth blew her stack and told Kurt that a project manager had no business asking her

---

AGENDA I
July Mini Summit

DAY 1

When: 4:00 to 4:15
What: Introduction to the City of the Future Initiative
Who: Kurt

When: 4:15 to 4:45
What: Prework Review
Who: Kurt

When: 4:45 to 5:30
What: VideoTape - Business of Paradigms (Joel Barker)
Who: Kurt

When: 5:30
What: Happy Hour/Reception

DAY 2

When: 8:00 to 8:15
What: Opening Remarks
Who: Mayor and City Manager

When: 8:15 to 8:30
What: Day 1 Review
Who: Kurt

When: 8:30 to 10:00
What: Day 2 Overview/Introduction
Who: Elizabeth

When: 10:00
What: Break

When: 10:29 to 11:45
What: Group Exercise
Who: Elizabeth
What: OSA, Input/Output, Vision, Assumptions, Mission,
Roadblocks, Guiding Principles
Who: Kurt

When: 11:45 to 1:00
What: Lunch

When: 1:00 to 1:45
What: Exercise Debriefs by Team

When: 1:45 to 2:30
What: Assumption Expansion
Who: Kurt

When: 2:30 to 3:30
What: Working Brea

When: 3:30 to 5:00
What: Roadblock Expansion
Who: Elizabeth

When: 5:00
What: Adjourn

DAY 3

When: 8:00 to 8:30
What: Day 2 Review/Day 3 Overview
Who: Elizabeth

When: 8:30 to 10:00
What: Objective Generation
Who: Elizabeth

When: 10:00 to 10:30
What: Break

When: 10:30 to 11:30
What: Review Voting and second round
Who: Elizabeth

When: 11:30 to 1:00
What: Lunch

When: 1:00 to 2:00
What: Expanded Definitions & Strategy Statements (in small groups)
Who: Kurt/Elizabeth

When: 2:00 to 2:30
What: Exercise Debriefs by Team

When: 2:30
What: Next Steps
Who: Elizabeth/Ellen

Figure 15. The agenda for the summit was ambitious and designed to share information, build community, and reach consensus on how to improve.

this question.

The next day Kurt assembled a support service team member, a graduate student, himself and Elizabeth, in the Director's office. Kurt asked Elizabeth what the meeting was all about and, calmly, she said that having periodic project team meetings to communicate progress, performance, and plans was good practice for a change master in training.

"Where do we stand on the Bucksburg project? How are we doing budget wise? Where are we on the project plan and schedule? When is the quarterly review? How are the teams progressing? What's going on in the community? What was the aftermath from the summit, positive and negative? What's the level of customer satisfaction? What's going on with the change master group and the design team? What can I do to help?" Elizabeth questioned.

Kurt seemed for the most part caught off guard. He clearly wasn't prepared to answer many of the questions. Once again, Elizabeth silently wondered why she was in this business but then reminded herself that no one ever said running a "teaching hospital" dedicated to training change masters would be easy. Not thinking too much about the change process or professional modes of functioning or even situational leadership theory, she spelled out exactly what she wanted to see done, hoping that Kurt could take notes fast enough.

A week later, Elizabeth got a call from Kurt asking for dates on her calendar that she could be available to facilitate the quarterly review session. She asked him why he thought she had to be involved in the session, whether her labor for this was in the budget, and whether Kurt could manage to run that meeting without her. Kurt hadn't even considered the possibility of Eizabeth not being involved; he was concerned about how the client might react to her not being present for the session. Elizabeth told Kurt to think about it, talk with the design team, and let her know.

Kurt ended up handling that first quarterly review session. Most teams "crammed for the final," working up their scoping proposals the night before the session; therefore the quality was predictably less than desirable. Kurt came away with a strong sense of the level of effort this project was going to require and how much more attention to detail would be needed to keep the client focused on accomplishing objectives, let alone moving forward on the other fronts.

After the quarterly review session, Kurt called an emergency meeting of the Bucksburg change master group and design team to relate his concerns. Some team members shared his sense of urgency about the situation, but it was clear that some degree of entropy had set in, even with this group. Clearly, "A" and "C" and in some cases "D" had driven the "B" out of the planning teams' efforts and from the change masters and design team.

Kurt had a sinking feeling in his stomach as he began to realize there was more to starting up a large-scale organizational change effort than he had thought. It sounded so easy in the books and when he heard the professor speak about it in his ISE 5015 class. Self-doubt began to creep in, but Kurt acknowledged that perhaps this was better than being too confident and not knowing what he didn't know. Maybe he needed to work more closely with Elizabeth on the project over the next several months. It was hard to get a lot of quality time with her because of her demanding schedule, but this was important.

Kurt struggled to recall the theory and concepts of phases of change, the change process, and professional modes of functioning as he worked with the design team that afternoon, but he just didn't have it clear enough in his head. He would have to get the books out again and study it in the context of this project. He was clearly being called upon to put into practice what Dr. Morris had suggested in his book *Implementation Strategies for Industrial Engineers* (1979).

Surprisingly, he found that it wasn't difficult to get the change masters and design team back where they had been during boot camp. Focus and motivation were regained after about two hours of discussing issues and confronting root causes for the poor performance since the summit. They re-committed to ensuring the success of the Bucksburg initiative and identified specific group and individual tasks they would undertake to ensure that too much entropy didn't set in prior to the next session, the mid-year review. They knew that they needed an early success, so they focused on working with those teams that had significant but doable objectives.

The design team worked for some time on the communication front, ensuring that pivotal people in positions of power were kept informed and involved. They developed some tactics to try with the City Council. They confronted the issue of hidden agendas and decided to take time to surface underlying concerns and issues. It appeared to Kurt as if this group of twelve had suddenly moved out of storming and norming into performing. He wasn't quite sure how this happened but was relieved it had. He wondered silently if they could regress. He concluded that if the group composition stayed constant it was less likely than if members left or new members joined. He'd have to manage that if possible.

The mid-year review went well. Participants were prepared. The Mayor and City Manager took a more active role because they had been "managed" over the past several months. On a more disappointing note, the City Council problem had not been solved, and while some teams were making progress, others were struggling to survive. Kurt remembered something Dr. Deming said at his famous four-day seminar, "Variation is inherent."

Kurt was gaining credibility, knowledge, and skill as a result of having been forced to take responsibility for this project. He was doing better at working with Elizabeth and at keeping her informed. Whenever she had time available, he asked her to take an hour and meet with the City Manager and Mayor, which she gladly did.

One serious conflict arose about eight months into the project. Kurt allowed Ellen (the City's project manager for Bucksburg 2000) to get cross-wise with Elizabeth during a change master training course held at OQPC headquarters. Ellen was not making progress as a change master; she had some significant skill deficiencies, particularly in the area of meeting management, large-scale change conceptualization, strategizing, and communication skills. Elizabeth challenged the change masters in the course to be intellectually honest and technically competent. She made it clear that some people have the ability to perform in the capacity and some don't. Ellen became personally offended by Elizabeth's challenging and tried to "fire" the OQPC from the community effort. Elizabeth made an intervention with the City Manager and Mayor, emphasizing the importance of having an effective internal change master and project manager. The situation was resolved, but not without additional conflict and a number of problems that had to be addressed.

Kurt continued to have a difficult time maintaining communication and coordination with the design team. On a limited budget, he was constantly having to make trade-offs between what he knew he should do and what he could afford. He knew he had to delegate, to work with and through Ellen, the community change masters, and the design team, but maintaining momentum and continuity with them was a constant struggle. He was encouraged when he read M. Scott Peck's new book, *A World Waiting to be Born* (1993). The section on community building and maintenance clearly indicated that this is not easy.

CONCLUSION

The management of improvement-oriented change has become ever more crucial to the survival of organizations in the '90s and beyond. Management of change has taken over as one of the most demanded consulting specialties, is the focus of a growing body of literature, and has sparked countless seminars, conferences, and workshops on the subject. Many models and theories of change could be adopted; we have utilized our preferences hoping that they may be insightful for you. Certainly a model and theory to guide the planning and execution of change is useful. Our biases regarding the management of improvement-oriented change are already somewhat apparent and will become ever more so as you continue to read and study this book. The methodology presented in this book has served as a useful guide in our careers, and we think you may find them useful, too.

A fundamental premise in our approach to the management of improvement-oriented change is that ownership, involvement, participation, and acceptance are central to success. We advocate management of participation, not just participative management. As you will see, certain situations call for centralized decision-making and problem solving, others require participation, some consultation, yet others delegation. Empowerment is an important term but more important is the knowledge of when and how to empower.

In short, the role of change master in a large-scale, system-wide improvement effort such as establishing TQM in any large organization, as you have seen, is much more challenging than making smaller interventions with individuals or groups in some subsystem. It truly could be characterized as the 3^n-ball problem. The change master is managing multiple projects within a very large overall project across many fronts. The sheer number of dyadic and group relationships that must be established and maintained over time is a challenge. Is this doable? Yes. Is it required and important? You bet it is. Is it doable without discipline, a systematic strategy, a model, good methods, sufficient knowledge and skills, problem solving, and conflict management? No way. That's why we wrote this book.

CHAPTER 4

PHASES OF CLIENT CHANGE:
A CLOSER LOOK AND SOME PRACTICAL APPLICATIONS

We turn now to a more detailed examination of this general model of the phases through which individuals, groups, and organizations pass when change occurs. For each phase, we present the goals and objectives, cite typical change master strategies, discuss the phase in the context of the preceding case example, and, finally, mention some of the difficulties involved. In the next chapter, we consider the professional modes a change master employs in moving a client through these phases.

PHASE 1: SITUATION APPRAISAL (SCOUTING, TARGETING, DIAGNOSIS)

An important objective of the change master is to get the client to turn aside from the pressures of ongoing affairs ("A" and "C" and "D," sometimes both personally and professionally) and focus attention on the problem of performance improvement ("B"). During situation appraisal, the change master and the client attend to an opportunity, a symptom, a problem, or a situation about which they share a common belief that the benefits of change will have a positive impact on the performance of the organizational system, and they, at least intuitively, believe that the benefits outweigh the costs. Improvement efforts typically are undertaken on the basis of "beliefs in cause-and-effect relationships" rather than on the basis of "knowledge of cause-and-effect relationships" (Thompson 1967, Chapters 7 and 10).

Goals and Objectives of Situation Appraisal

The change master seeks to reach agreement with the client on problem areas and change process concepts that have the greatest promise of yielding net benefits. In addition, the change master seeks to:

1. Enlist the client's support and make maximum use of the client's knowledge through a process of joint diagnosis.
2. Have top management legitimize the presence and efforts of the change master. Get them involved in startup by ensuring their needs and expectations are articulated and understood. Ensure that they understand their roles during the life cycle of the project and that they are committed to support for the entire life cycle.

3. Focus client attention and begin to sort through symptoms, causes, problems, opportunities, hoped for or needed results, perplexities, programs, projects, problems, and processes. Make sense of a situation that is often ambiguous, uncertain, messy, confusing, and frustrating.
4. Obtain enough data such that appropriate next phases of change will progress on the basis of facts and data rather than just emotion, opinion, and affect.
5. Sort out the "voice of the customer(s)." Understand who the customer(s) are and their expectations, longer-term desired outcomes, shorter-term results expectations, needs, and requirements.
6. Attempt to collect data for the $C = a \cdot b \cdot d \geq R$ change model. What is the level of dissatisfaction with the status quo? What is the extent of the shared vision? Is there a common understanding of "great performance?" Is the aim of the system clear? Are practical next steps (by what method) clear and agreed upon?
7. Begin to develop an overall strategy in the mind of the change agent. The change master, as a result of data collected during this first phase, begins to envision what results will be achieved at the end of the project and how he or she will guide the client(s) through methods for achieving the results.
8. Build momentum, enthusiasm, excitement, hope, and trust gradually as this phase progresses.

All this and more must be accomplished during an appropriate period of time, given the overall length of the improvement project. It seems worthwhile to mention at this point that the client more often than not will be very impatient and not particularly aware of the importance of the early phases of change. They, particularly top management, will be pushing for results, quick fixes, trying out new behaviors (Phase 6), action before reflection, and will view Phases 1 and 2 as a waste of time.

The change master must conceptualize, during this first phase, the overall pace for the project. We suggest you build a high-level (Level 1) project plan with Phases 1-7 as the rows (y-axis) and time as the scale on the x-axis (Figure 16). How much time can you afford to devote to each phase and still complete the project on schedule? How much time does each phase deserve? How much time does each phase require based on your situation appraisal? Once this is done, the change master can begin to think about the "how" (method) for each phase of change. In short projects, it is often the case that Phase 1 must occur in one day or even one meeting. Also remember that phases-of-change activities often overlap: you will be in more than one phase at one time in many situations.

Typical Change Master Strategies

Often the benefits of change are obvious, and the symptoms of the problem are clearly perceived by the client. Identifying sponsors, champions, targets, and potential collaborating agents is an early task. Interviews with key players in the organization (individual and group) often are used to gather data from a variety of perspectives. In a large, complex organizational system such as a community, this task can be sizable. Attempting to identify the focal problem(s) is key: Are you dealing with a perplexity, a program, a project, a problem, or a process? The goal is to gain focus, reduce ambiguity and uncertainty, and bring structure to the initial situation.

Clients generally have a very high level of knowledge about where change is most likely

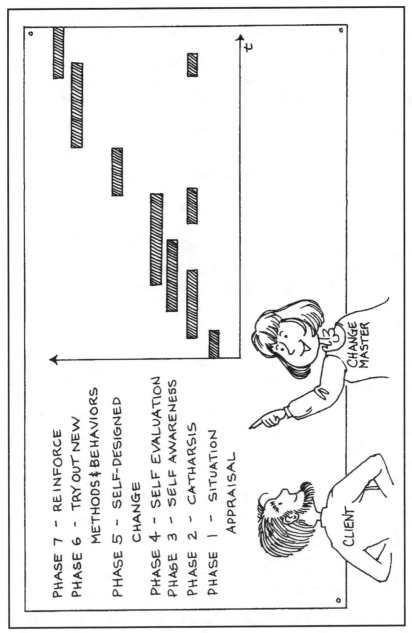

Figure 16. A high-level phase-of-change plan helps the change master move improvement projects forward.

to pay off. The change master gets client participation in the diagnosis through interviews and structured group processes aimed at getting them to be explicit about problems, road blocks, and difficulties that can be usefully changed.

Situation appraisal, particularly on the basis of the short exposure of a "walk-through" of an operation is a particularly difficult one. Where in an operation can the efforts of the change master staff be applied to achieve the best relationship between the costs of the staff effort and the resulting benefits?

A variety of common targeting strategies are used, including the following:

1. The change master staff should look at everything from a systems perspective.
2. Use the 80-20 principle (twenty percent of operations account for eighty percent of costs, benefits, problems, and opportunities).
3. Stamp out the horror stories. The best relationship between costs and benefits results if efforts are applied to the "worst" operations.
4. Work on those operations that have been neglected longest by the change master staff, or areas that have gone the longest without "B."
5. Work on the newest, most recently started operations.
6. Develop a portfolio of improvement projects consisting of a mix of:
   • Pet projects of management;
   • Short-term, modest-payoff projects;
   • Long-term, high-payoff projects.

The problem of what to look for on a walk-through, during an assessment audit, in benchmarking, or in a Malcolm Baldrige-type self-appraisal is one which change masters frequently face.

The most efficient strategy is to recognize that one's effectiveness as an observer can be increased greatly by generating a list of symptoms that must be considered uncertain indications and thus merit further investigation. A change master's basic list of symptoms grows with experience, but the following might serve as a start (We have blended government, industry, service, academia and education, nonprofit, etc. into one list, so think about the ones that are most appropriate in your organization.):

1. High in-process inventories;
2. High internal customer dissatisfaction;
3. High initial or final inventories;
4. Poor morale and attitudes, low commitment, feeling that nothing will change or get better, believing things are pretty good already;
5. Idle people, equipment, or space;
6. Presence of expediters, troubleshooters, problem solvers, separation of "A" and "C" and "B";
7. Change masters and managers sitting at their desk a disproportionate amount of time, leaders and managers who are complacent, leaders and managers who appear to be out of date;
8. Large amounts of scrap, waste, rejects, rework; errors that get to the customer;
9. Manual handling, poor processes and methods in general, processes that people say are in control and stable but you sense would fall apart if the person doing them left for

some reason, labor-intensive processes and methods that could be significantly simplified;

10. Large computer printouts, a sense that the organization is data rich and information poor; visible management systems are not evident.;

11. Extensive equipment repair and setup operations, poorly maintained equipment; downtime or slowness is common;

12. Old equipment, technology front is not well managed, hardware, equipment, software, methods, processes are not kept current, no system for doing so;

13. Unpunched cards at time clock, no indication of time management throughout the organization, no recognition of the importance of knowing where time is going from a measurement and performance assessment standpoint;

14. Obvious environmental and safety problems, human factors such as working conditions, office quality, and quality of work life in general are not of apparent importance, general housekeeping;

15. Rough relationship between numbers of production and nonproduction people, direct to indirect, billed to non-billed, value-adding to non-value adding. Is there awareness throughout of the importance of these ratios? Are they managed and controlled?;

16. Extent and condition of employee services: lockers, showers, eating facilities;

17. Presence of change orders, tracers, duplicate requisitions;

18. Difficulty making eye contact with working people, sense you get when talking to line employees, secretaries, sales people, teachers, students, customers (if possible), managers at all levels;

19. Extent to which plans, goals, strategies, actions, and measures are visible, understood, influencing day-to-day behaviors (deployment);

20. Extent to which measurement, evaluation, and improvement are self-managing;

21. What does the strategic plan look like? How is it created? Who is involved? How is it shared and deployed?;

22. Strong provider orientation, resistance to using the word customer, lack of understanding of internal customer importance;

23. Widely divergent opinions of what the focus of improvement should be, difficulty getting sponsors and champions to decide what the problem is or where to start, high variation in terms of people's perception of current performance levels;

24. Sense that there is a lot of "not invented here" syndrome, strong initial resistance to new ideas and approaches.

The change master is forced to be a good listener, a good observer, and a good senser during this phase. This phase often occurs under pressure to move forward either with a solution or with a clear strategy. The client often is testing the change master at this phase to see how quickly they can size up the situation. Change masters often must rely on their experience, instinct, and judgment. They must be able to focus quickly. They may have a chance later to reflect and alter their assessment and strategy, but often the client expects an initial diagnosis and prescription.

Establishing trust may require that the change master reveal early assessments. There are situations where the change master is best served with an "I don't know at the moment" or "I don't have enough data yet" approach. Again, however, most often the client expects a quick startup. The political astuteness of the change master often will come into play at this phase. Knowing who the people in pivotal positions of power are will be important to completing a situation appraisal. Knowing who to collect information from is as important as knowing what information to collect.

Case Example 2A in the Context of Situation Appraisal

In the Bucksburg 2000 case example, there are multiple clients, not uncommon for large-scale organizational change efforts. The initial client was Harry, the person with the vision and perhaps the hidden agendas. As the project evolved, the change model infrastructure (sponsor, champion, agent, target) got more complex. Clearly this wasn't just a three-ball problem. The director of OQPC quickly established a group of clients who, collectively, had the knowledge, information, experience, and influence within the community to ensure that this initial phase was completed.

The strategic performance improvement planning process (Sink and Tuttle 1989) utilized to move the planning front forward incorporates situation appraisal in early steps of the process, so the method accommodates this phase on the part of the planning team. In large-scale organizational change, it is just as important to worry about who isn't involved as who is involved. Planning for who will participate is a key to success. In the case example, assessment occurred on an ongoing basis. Elizabeth utilized a situation appraisal-type methodology (Kepner-Tregoe 1965) and a strategy-building and agenda-building methodology (see Chapter 6) to get started and to attempt to ensure that she understood the desired outcomes and outputs of key decision makers and other "internal" change agents early on. In doing this, she was attempting to collect adequate data to move forward, perhaps prepare her and them for the next phase of catharsis, and lay the foundation for later phases of self-awareness and evaluation and self-design.

Difficulties

This is the stage at which client expectations about the outcomes of the change process are formed. The change master needs to encourage the client to be open about these expectations and to make early and immediate efforts to assure that they are reasonable and realistic. This is the stage, also, at which misunderstandings occur. The change master should consider the use of a written:

- Statement of objectives of the effort, including the desired outputs and outcomes;
- Statement of both change master and client responsibilities and definition and description of the project infrastructure (roles and responsibilities);
- Change process plan, to include the boundaries, scope and life-cycle of the effort (should contract to go through evaluation);
- Agreement on deadlines, use of client personnel, use of additional change master staff, reporting methods;
- Agreement on responsibilities for implementation.

For an excellent discussion on "contracting" and the entry and scoping process (whether you are an internal or external change master) please see the book entitled *Flawless Consulting* (Block 1981), an excellent companion book for this one.

The client also should be alerted to the possibility that during the unfolding of the change process, the "real problem" may emerge as something quite different from present perceptions. The proposal and plan for this improvement effort should be viewed as a living plan.

Clearly, this is an important phase. It is the foundational phase, and the stronger the foundation, the stronger the overall project. Nothing will improve performance on Phase 1 like gaining more knowledge from books such as *Flawless Consulting*, practicing more discipline and structure with this phase in your improvement projects, devoting a little more time and attention to this phase, and experience.

PHASE 2: CATHARSIS (STRESS RELIEF, STORMING)

 Clients are subject to a variety of psychological stresses which must be dealt with before the change process can proceed effectively. These may include:

- Resentment toward the change master;
- Concern about job security;
- Anxiety about effects of possible changes;
- Resentment of criticism, both expressed and implied;
- Frustration over past failures;
- Discouragement: "We tried that before and it didn't work";
- Anger at being ignored, seeing others get credit for their ideas;
- Blame casting;
- Conflicts over responsibilities and authority;
- Not being fully informed;
- Chemistry problems between the change master and clients;
- Client has had change master thrust on him or her by his predecessor;
- False perceptions of downside risks and consequences that often go unstated;
- Lack of trust (intent, commitment, contribution, competence);
- Strong disagreement with the vision, aim, focus, path or method, or the overall project itself.

Stresses such as these compromise decision-making ability, inhibit clear self-perception, and build a resistant, closed attitude toward change processes. It is also well established that expressing these kinds of stresses tends to relieve them and makes it possible for the client to take a more constructive, open attitude toward change. The key is how to get these subsurface, often subconscious affects, attitudes, and emotions expressed. This is sometimes easier to do in a one-on-one setting; however, the change master most often is in a group setting.

Goals and Objectives for Catharsis

The goal of this phase is to get the client(s) to express these stresses, put them aside, and move on toward a more rational view of change and improvement. It sets the stage for the next phase of the process: self-awareness. These stresses will come out eventually as the change process unfolds, and it is far more effective to get them out early and have them put to rest. Most change process designers believe that stress relief as a specific activity undertaken very early will enhance the effectiveness of subsequent efforts to lead the client toward change.

The change master seeks to:

• Get the stresses out in the open;
• Have the client recognize and dispose of what is past;
• Focus on the future and on actions aimed at improvement;
• Establish the concept that the facts are almost always friendly;
• Get clients to accept responsibility for self-perception and ultimately for self-designed change;
• Bring out any subsurface fears, tensions, concerns, or subtleties that may linger in the minds of key individuals in the effort;
• Determine sources of mistrust;
• Surface hidden agendas.

Typical Change Master Strategies

The change master may achieve catharsis through:

• Additional individual interviews with client personnel;
• Structured group processes (although, again, group settings often do not allow for individual stress relief);
• Questionnaires;
• Unstructured group sessions;
• Having clients write anonymous letters;
• Confronting, exposing, and challenging key issues you suspect are unspoken but of concern, followed by active listening.

The change master primarily seeks to be a recipient of the expressions of stress, to receive them without being judgmental and with empathetic concern. Among the simplest and best change master methods are:

• Being open and available to clients, active listening;
• Cultivating informal contacts;
• Making sure everyone is fully informed about what is going on when a change process is underway;
• Making sure that either the change master or someone else is perceived as being very approachable during this early phase.

The process of catharsis is important to the change master in that it provides a wealth of data about the client and the problem area. The change master learns something about the history of the problem, the conflicting interests involved, the distribution of knowledge among clients, their openness to change, and so on. All of this information, as we will see in following chapters, is important in the design of change processes.

Case Example 2A in the Context of Catharsis

The complexity of a community change effort makes the first and second phases of change particularly challenging, as illustrated in the Bucksburg 2000 case example. Understanding the infrastructure (roles, responsibilities, accountabilities) for an improvement project such as this, and managing the political front are extremely difficult. Elizabeth found this out at several points. First, there was some disagreement within the OQPC at the outset. Some OQPC associates felt the effort was not well advised, while others wanted to proceed. This internal disagreement was never confronted—those who were willing to proceed pressed on, those who were not dropped out.

Role conflict between Harry and the external change agent (Elizabeth) was a running battle. Early in this project, Elizabeth actually took every opportunity possible, with different groups of people, to continue to process Phases 1 and 2. The first summit created more than ample opportunity to surface affects regarding this project. In fact, as mentioned, surfacing stress relief and achieving a catharsis with a group as heterogeneous and large as the one present at the first summit is almost impossible. Elizabeth quickly found herself in a situation of once again focusing on the key players and trying to expose their stresses and strains relative to the effort. In the midst of the summit, this didn't take much more than being an active listener.

Organizations, especially communities, are very dynamic. The stresses and strains, priorities, politics, and players can change very quickly. It is important to work hard to maintain focus, continuing to review the growing data from Phases 1 and 2 as the improvement project proceeds. As key players change and time passes, the change master should continue efforts to provide stress relief in the context of the project. Individual meetings with key players, where the change master plays the active listener role, are a mechanism for doing this. As the case example highlights, maintaining high-quality communication with the key players is critical to success. If key players do not see that this effort is leading to valued consequences for them, they will abandon the project.

The fact is that Elizabeth did not (perhaps did not have the luxury of or the experience to) process through this phase adequately. The complexity of trying to relieve stresses and develop openness with a group as large as was involved with this project overwhelmed Elizabeth. She became paralyzed as to who to focus on, lost sight of the sponsor, targets, champions — the infrastructure in general. There were not enough individual interviews early on in which affects could be openly expressed. It is not uncommon for the change master to rely primarily on group meetings (they are efficient), and as a result not collect certain data that would come out in one-on-one sessions. Hence, we are sacrificing effectiveness and quality of data for efficiency. This was true to some extent in this case.

There was a tight project budget. There was a preconceived notion, on the part of the OQPC, as to the method and path. Elizabeth and the OQPC jumped to prescription before adequate diagnosis and support were developed. In a sense, the change master skipped over Phases 1-5 and jumped immediately to Phase 6 (trying out new behaviors). This is a common problem when the change master has a preferred solution and hence becomes a trigger-happy doctor with the prescription pad. The client, in this case, was a willing accomplice (not uncommon). They were also a bit naive in terms of how to ensure lasting positive change. In particular, the Mayor and City Manager did not become active sponsors for the project. This was as much a political issue (fence sitting) as it was a failure on the part of the change master to create ownership of the aim and the path.

In short, both situation appraisal and catharsis were not done adequately in this case. The only solution is to take a bit more time up front to process through these phases. It's the "pay me now or pay me later" phenomenon.

Difficulties

The change master seeks to prevent stress-relieving activities from:

• Further entrenching previously held positions;
• Leading the client to assume that expressing stresses means something will be done about them;
• Leading the client to assume that the change master will take over and change things for the better;
• Leading the client to rush immediately toward solutions rather than trying to understand the problem;
• Creating a period of low morale and discouragement by focusing exclusively on anxieties, frustrations, and conflicts.

The change master wants to leave the client with the impression that the stresses expressed are understood and appreciated but that it is now time to move toward further self-awareness and self-designed change — dealing with their social needs but making it clear there are tasks that must be completed. This is similar to the storming and norming phases in group development prior to entering the performing stage. Timing, as might be imagined, is of the essence. Too little time in this phase and the client's performance might be affected. Too much time in this phase and the focal problem's solution may be jeopardized.

In improvement projects where multiple clients are involved, such as Bucksburg 2000, achieving healthy catharsis is often a real challenge. There are so many "clients" that it stretches the ability and time of the change master to manage this phase of change. It is important to focus time and energy in these situations: Who are the people associated with the improvement effort that you need to ensure move through this phase of change? As the project proceeds there will be a need, and more time, to process others through this phase. Often those needing this will seek out you or someone on your project team and provide ample indication of this need; then all you have to do is listen and capture the data, adding it to your growing database of Phase 1 and 2 information.

Maintaining this level of openness and catharsis is difficult. You will find that you get "in control" and then suddenly it is gone. Many personality types and cognitive styles will not appreciate the importance of this phase. Those who are highly analytical and pragmatic may see this phase as a waste of time and energy. If you try to process affects about the improvement project in a group setting, you must deal with variations in tolerance for this type of activity. In these cases, process those with a need for this individually.

It is important to remember that the product of this phase may not be tangible. It may well be that the greatest need is just to talk through fears, negative fantasies, concerns, hidden agendas, etc. There may be no resolution to some of the issues raised during this phase. They get surfaced, and you press on. Some change masters may have difficulty with this phase knowing that they may, in fact, do nothing with the data.

PHASE 3: SELF-AWARENESS

The ancient prescription, "know thyself," has always been an essential aspect of change for individuals and groups. As Peck (1993) emphasizes, "To become more civil, humans must become ever more conscious of themselves, of others, and of the organizations that relate them together. We only become civil through development and learning...We can choose to become more conscious and more civil, although it is seldom totally explainable why the choice is made or fails to be made." Consciousness, use of data and facts, and being intellectually honest go hand in hand.

To become self-aware is to come to an objective perception of present behavior, existing methods and systems, and "the way we do it now." It is a problem simply because clients are very often so busy doing what they do that there is little time or inclination to appreciate with any objectivity just what is happening or how it is being done.

Self-perception is an obvious and logical prelude to self-directed change. Getting the facts, finding out what we are really doing in a certain area, finding out how much we spend, how many people are involved, what our methods and systems actually are, and what assumptions underlie our behavior and strategies — these are aspects of the process of moving toward self understanding.

Goals and Objectives of Self-Awareness

Self-awareness includes achieving a shared, explicit, open understanding of present methods and systems. It also includes learning about attitudes, performance, problems, perceptions, values, styles, assumptions, and individual, group, and organizational objectives. In short, it provides the factual basis that forms both the starting point and the motivation for change. Important objectives in this phase include:

• Reaching a clear and accurate understanding of what is happening now;
• Sharing this understanding in an open, nonevaluative way;
• Facing up to all of the difficulties, shortcomings, and differences between how things are supposed to work and how they actually do work;
• Achieving a high level of client participation in both the collection and understanding of these data;
• Gaining a shared understanding of where the organizational system has been, how it has performed over time, what has worked, what is working, what should be stopped, what should be continued;
• Creating awareness on the part of key leaders regarding the need for improvement and a sense of urgency to improve; pursuading top management to be active in shaping consensus regarding the need for improvement and in a focus for what to improve;
• Attaining intellectual honesty on the part of top leadership about themselves and about the organizational system they are trying to improve.

Typical Change Master Strategies

The change master role in this phase is one of exposing data, with the intent of creating more shared awareness of the need for improvement and what and how to improve.

The whole array of traditional methods change masters have used to describe the "present system" is applicable here. The basic objective is simply that of making the client aware of what is going on. You want to work to help the client(s) think statistically, using longitudinal data about past and current performance levels. You want the client(s) to be objective (use facts and data) in their assessment of the current situation. The change master may collect this data, may design data collection programs for client personnel to execute, or may join with client personnel in collaborative efforts to understand existing methods and symptoms.

Process flow charts, material flow diagrams, methods descriptions, attitude measures, surveys, and cost studies are examples of the accepted and well understood techniques for enhancing self-perception on the part of the client. Interviews, structured group processes, analysis of organization records, and self-observation programs also are widely used methods of getting the appropriate information. The change master may offer tools, training, educational materials, software, templates, logs and forms, or benchmarking examples to facilitate the process. Many organizations today are utilizing benchmarking and self-assessment using Malcolm Baldrige-type guidelines to promote more self-awareness. In Virginia, we find many organizations utilizing the U. S. Senate Productivity and Quality Award Process as a way of doing this annually. Many quality and productivity centers provide "audits" as a service. These audits, coupled with internal activities, can heighten awareness of areas requiring improvement.

Case Example 2A in the Context of Self-Awareness

The fact is that the OQPC, Elizabeth in particular, was very ineffective at creating self-awareness. This was partly due to the fact that a community is a very large system. Nobody really "owns" a community. Who are we helping to improve self-awareness? What are we creating self-awareness about? How does this build from the first two phases? These are the questions that plagued Elizabeth as she tried to progress with the project.

She had a technology she wanted to apply to the situation. Her staff had done this many times before but never in a community setting. How could she move them (and who is "them?") through the phases of self-awareness and evaluation and eventually get them to a method for improving their community? She was continually ahead of the process, in Phase 6 (trying out new behaviors). She didn't know if this was bad or good. She was tempted to just give them the solution. Furthermore, the client reinforced this. They had a "just do it to us" mentality and at times acted as if they just wanted to get the project over with.

Elizabeth began to realize this would be fatal. She realized that she was being pulled into a trap of providing what was perceived as a quick fix. She knew, in theory, that her best strategy was to slow down and process through Phases 2, 3, and 4 more deliberately, but she didn't know how to pull this off. Harry and the other community change masters were constantly moving the process forward faster than she felt appropriate. Every time she met with the client, she would find that Harry and others had moved the project further and further into Phase 6. She was losing control of expectations and pace. She knew it was because she had inadequately processed through Phase 2 with all the key actors in the project, but she failed to stop and take action. Instead, she plundered ahead hoping that these Phase 2 problems would go away. We know from experience that these types of problems seldom evaporate.

When Phase 2 is incomplete, it is often difficult—if not impossible—to properly process through Phase 3. The leadership of this project for Bucksburg never fully achieved consensus. The planning session itself is designed to work toward consensus regarding self-awareness, but when the leadership of an improvement project doesn't have it going into the session, it becomes more difficult. There was not a high quality, explicit review of the past or of current performance levels at this point. Hence, the shared database for self-awareness was not created.

Difficulties

Bringing out data that can be interpreted as "showing people up" or implying criticism may, of course, harden attitudes, increase defensiveness, and simply build further resistance toward the change process. Protection of participants, maintenance of psychological safety, and appropriate assurances of confidentiality are a major concern in this phase. Evaluation, especially self-evaluation, comes later. Ideally, the change master hopes to cultivate the attitude among client personnel that the facts are almost always friendly, that change is exciting rather than threatening, and that ultimately there is no need to be apprehensive about an open appreciation of the way things are going.

As we move to the next phase it is important to re-emphasize that this phase is a measurement phase not an evaluation phase. The next phase involves converting information into decisions and, eventually, actions. It is often very difficult for clients, and even change masters, to separate measurement from evaluation, awareness from evaluation, understanding from judgment.

Separating opinions from facts also is difficult. The opinion-giving role often is used in group settings; opinion seeking is used less often. Opinions imply advocacy and evaluation. The intent of this phase is data sharing. We are trying to defer evaluation, conclusions and opinions until the next phase of change.

Getting clients to participate effectively in the self-awareness process often is difficult. Many clients are not particularly skilled at fact and data gathering about their organizational system. Measurement systems in most organizations are not adequate to support this phase of change. This means that special data gathering efforts must be made.

We have found that the technique of "echoing" what we hear clients say is valuable. They say something, we repeat it back in a way that forces some introspection. They imply, we infer, they confirm or modify. The change master may want to, at some point, synthesize a position and state it to the clients: "This is how I see things on the basis of what you have said to me at this point," or "Is this a fair self-assessment on the basis of the data we have to this point?"

PHASE 4: SELF-EVALUATION

 In this phase, the client comes to some conclusions about the effectiveness, efficiency, or benefit-cost relationship for the present methods and systems in use. They begin to be concerned about how to use the information and understanding created in the last phase for the purpose of improvement. How good is the way we are doing it now? Where do we need improvement? Where do we begin? The client also comes to formulate criteria by which future methods and systems may be judged. This may involve:

• Clarification of client goals;
• Measurement of system effectiveness;
• Exploration and adoption of standards for performance or effectiveness;
• Benchmarking;
• Predictions by the change master of levels of effectiveness that might be attained.

The degree of dissatisfaction with existing systems is closely related to the client's motivation to change. Recall the simple model presented in Chapter 3:

$C = a \cdot b \cdot d \geq R$ (where C = readiness for change, a = level of dissatisfaction with the status quo, b = clear or understood desired future state, d = clear practical first steps and ensuing steps, and R = perceived or real cost or risk of changing).

Goals and Objectives of Self-Evaluation

The change master seeks to bring the client to a clearer conceptualization of goals, standards, desired levels of performance, criteria, and measures of effectiveness. The aim is to have the client apply these to existing operations and systems in a dispassionate, guiltless way, leading to a clear conclusion about their shortcomings. A coincident goal is the development of more explicit criteria by which future changes may be evaluated. This phase requires exploring meaning in the data created as part of the self-awareness phase. We now move from inquiry (a mode used in awareness) to advocacy and evaluation.

The end product of self-evaluation is to come away with information and conclusions that posture us to move to decisions and actions — the self-designed change phase. We want to ensure that our information is adequate, valid, unbiased, and that it represents the voice of the process and the voice of the customers.

Typical Change Master Strategies

The change master seeks to assist the client's self-evaluation by:

* Designing measurement systems for performance assessment;
* Helping the client to become clearer and more explicit about goals through the use of multiple-criterion decision models, utility analysis, cost-effectiveness analysis, cost-benefit analysis, consensus-seeking methods;
* Suggesting standards that are reflective of industry performance, competitor performance, past client performance, and reasonably attainable rates of improvement;
* Designing evaluation systems involving structured group processes which help to depersonalize the necessary measurements and judgments;
* Exploring data for meaning, interpreting data, using statistics to understand variation, moving from measurement to evaluation in an unbiased fashion.

Change master knowledge and skills in data analysis, survey analysis, statistical analysis, logic, problem solving and decision-making frequently will be called upon in this phase. If Phase 2 was done adequately, then subjectiveness, opinions, affects, pet peeves, etc. should be well understood and accounted for.

Case Example 2A in the Context of Self-Evaluation

In the Bucksburg 2000 effort, self-evaluation took place; however, the evaluations were not effectively merged early on. There were wide variations in readiness for change in Bucksburg. Because the self-awareness step was incomplete and inadequate, it necessarily meant that self-evaluation would be flawed. There was too little use of data and facts in this phase of the project. The preparation for the community building and planning sessions and the sessions themselves involved self-evaluation, but it was not coordinated or systematic enough.

OQPC failed to accomplish the goals and objectives of this phase, as spelled out in the next section. Again, inadequate execution of the previous three phases created problems for this phase. The planning process overcame some of these deficiencies; however, the follow-up from the planning sessions suffered as a result of incomplete self-awareness and evaluation.

Difficulties

The basic difficulty is that client personnel will arrive at unrealistically high or low standards for evaluating new systems, thus leading to either frustration or to trivial change. Self-evaluation is often seriously inhibited by:

- The need to defend past positions and methods;
- The threat of exposure as ineffective or incompetent;
- The resentment of measurement systems, standards, or criteria imposed from "the outside";
- Fear of exposing good or bad performance, since often both are associated with the loss of power, resources, etc.;
- Inability or fear of accepting the fact that old paradigms, past practices, beliefs in cause-and-effect relationships are inappropriate or even wrong.

A part of being open to change is being open to evaluation of present performance. This openness is most frequently found among highly successful clients who are least in need of self-evaluation and self-change.

Facts and data converted to information in a rational fashion and portrayed in an effective and useful way appear to be the most predictable method for posturing a client for the next phase of improvement and change. This assumes a very rational and logical approach to change; however, if previous phases in the change model have been completed, these assumptions appear to be appropriate. It is when prior phases are ignored or prematurely interrupted that the rational and logical approach to improvement often fails.

The knowledge and skill for moving from data to information, for being rational in our evaluation of data is underdeveloped in most organizations. The change master will find that individual and group behavior often does not support smooth transitions from Phase 3 (awareness) to Phase 4 (evaluation). Statistical thinking and appreciation for a system will not be common in most situations. Structured and systematic decision-making, particularly group decision-making, will not be well developed or practiced. Measurement systems to support awareness and evaluation will be far from adequate. This means the change master will be confronted with many behaviors and situations that simply make it difficult to move through this phase successfully. A longer-term perspective may have to be adopted, assuming there will be multiple improvement cycles and that, over time, knowledge and skills to support these two phases will increase.

PHASE 5: SELF-DESIGNED CHANGE

 To maximize the probability of change actually occurring is to involve the client to the greatest degree reasonably possible in the planning and design of the new methods and systems. In some cases the design of change is almost entirely in the hands of client teams, with the change master seeking to stimulate and support their efforts. In other

situations, the special professional resources of the change master are essential to the planning and design process, but client inputs are continually sought and major decisions made by client personnel. Even when the change master plays a major technical role in the creation of new systems, the client should make a choice between two or more alternatives, thus making it fundamentally a client-determined change process. When the need for change and the readiness to accept it have been established, the change master assumes the role of facilitator in the design process. This very often means that the client lays out the broad shape of change and the change master supplies the professional knowledge that makes it feasible.

However, structuring the design and development of improvements is crucial to success. Much of the work in implementing total quality has focused on providing teams with structured approaches for analyzing problems, designing a solution, or selecting from alternative solutions. Meeting management often becomes either a key advantage or a source of frustration and failure in this phase as teams struggle to identify alternatives or design solutions in a consensus fashion.

Goals and Objectives of Self-Designed Change

The change master seeks to bring about the creation of new systems which:

• Fully reflect client knowledge and experience;
• Respond to the special, individual, local, and unique aspects of the client situation;
• Clients will accept and support because of their central role in the design process;
• Clients understand and believe will in fact capture the opportunity, solve the problem, or cause the required improvement.

The key is to bring together in a participative fashion the knowledge and experience of the client with the professional skills of the change master.

Typical Change Master Strategies

The change master facilitates self-designed change by working as a design guide, team member, or group process coordinator. The change master undertakes a role of stimulator, technical resource, honest broker, broker of technical assistance, support person, and creativity enhancer. The change master sees the client as the primary source of change, operates as an expert when professional skills are called for, but does little "selling" of expert-produced solutions to the client's problems. In doing so, the change master comes to focus more closely than ever on the special nature of the client and the problem. As mentioned earlier, the change masters and leaders in the organization may have to accept trade-offs or compromises between the quality of the solution and the acceptance of the solution. The ultimate criterion of success is effective implementation and deployment of the solution.

Case Example 2ᴀ in the Context of Self-Desisgned Change

Elizabeth, as mentioned earlier, relied, somewhat predictably, on the Strategic Performance Improvement Planning Process as a method for involving the client in self-designed change. Step 1 of that planning process is intended to move a planning team through the first four phases of change. Unfortunately, the pre-work for the planning session and the time allotted for Step 1 of the process were inadequate to successfully move the clients and participants through those crucial phases of the change process.

The product of the planning sessions was group consensus on a vision for the community, guiding principles, longer-range goals, specific improvement objectives, and teams to work on the improvement objectives. As a result of incomplete work in Phases 1-4 of the change process, Elizabeth and the OQPC found that the planning session did **not,** in fact, create enough consensus on the part of key participants to ensure effective implementation and deployment. This was not immediately apparent; however, over the next several months, it was clear that something was amiss.

The problem wasn't necessarily with the quality of the improvement plan, it was more with the acceptance of the plan from key people in pivotal positions of power. The sponsors (City Manager and Mayor), Elizabeth believed, did not see a close tie between the actions to be taken in the plan, results that would be achieved, and the kinds of consequences that would be positive for them politically. Like most high-level leaders and managers, they were interested in results that would benefit both the organization and them personally. Behavior is a function of its consequences. Elizabeth believed that the consequences of not supporting the plan and the process beyond the Bucksburg 2000 sessions were not clear enough to maintain sponsor support. As a result (as we will see in the next chapter), the effort died, although it did spawn some subsystem performance improvement efforts that were significantly more successful than the community-level effort.

Difficulties
Collaboration in the process of self-designed change often runs counter to client expectations. Many clients anticipate that:

- The change master will promptly produce the expert solution;
- They will not be called upon to involve themselves in the often difficult and time-consuming process of working with a team to design new systems;
- The possible sacrifice in quality of a collaborative design will not be warranted by its greater credibility, suitability, and acceptability;
- They will not be exposed to a somewhat extended participative undertaking.

PHASE 6: TRYING OUT THE NEW BEHAVIOR

The change master supports, encourages, and facilitates the client's testing of the newly designed systems and methods. The trials may be partial, sequential, and gradual, but the change master works to assure that the new ways are tested. The change master tries to move client personnel toward making definitive plans for experimentation. These plans, which ideally are largely client created, include not only the testing of new systems but also ways in which the results of the tests may be assessed. The change master cultivates an experimental attitude, emphasizing that the most important product of these trials may be information which can lead to still greater improvements.

Goals and Objectives of Trying Out the New Behavior
A primary aim of this phase is for clients to experience the proposed changes and modify them to reflect the realities of actual use. To achieve this, the change master tries to cultivate the concept that the trials are experiments to reduce uncertainty, that some failures are

possible, and that revisions and modifications are the expected and desired result. The change master wants to avoid the presumption that a new design is a commitment by the client and to support the view that the most important aspect of the test may be the information it produces which permits improvement of the design. The change master hopes to cultivate in the client:

• A willingness to learn from experience and to experiment with an openness to change that does not imply a personal threat or challenge;
• An inclination to consider the risks and payoffs from learning by doing;
• An awareness of the usefulness of planned measurement and evaluation of the test outcomes.

Typical Change Master Strategies

The change master works as a collaborator, supporting and encouraging the testing of the new behaviors, systems, and methods. Professional skills are supplied in the form of technical knowledge of measurement, experimental design, statistical analysis, decision analysis, and fact and data-based evaluation. The change master often seeks to relieve client personnel of the data collection tasks but sometimes offers them training in the methods of measurement and data interpretation.

Case Example 2A in the Context of Trying Out the New Behavior

Elizabeth struggled to get Kurt and Ellen to understand the importance of constancy of method and discipline during this phase. She kept stressing the importance of attention to detail, perfect practice, staying true to the method, making sure they knew and clearly communicated where they had been and where they were going.

She tried using the "piano teacher and parent" analogy to get them to understand the importance of discipline during this phase of change. The piano teacher understands the theory, has the skill, and knows how to transfer the knowledge and skill to the student but can't ensure that the student practices from lesson to lesson. Often, the parent is the one that enforces discipline in the student to practice between sessions (mine sure did). Unless the student practices sufficiently they will never develop their skill to the point where "intrinsic" motivation takes over. They will never get to the point where they start wanting to practice more because they are seeing results.

So Elizabeth tried to get the external and internal change masters (Kurt and Ellen) to be both the "piano teacher" and the "parent" for the community and the city. She also had each of them read M. Scott Peck's *The Road Less Traveled* (1978) to give them an appreciation for the importance of discipline. She required that Kurt do detailed planning and that his project plan be a "living plan."

Maintaining close contact, communication, and coordination with the client was crucial during this phase because it is all too easy not to stick with new methods and behaviors. Elizabeth kept struggling to help Kurt and Ellen keep momentum going in the face of inconsistent and declining attention from the City Manager and Mayor. The handwriting was on the wall in Elizabeth's mind; if they could not achieve a higher level of interest, commitment, and involvement from these two pivotal leaders, the effort would be lost. If the new methods and behaviors aren't tried out there can be no results; if there are no visible results, leadership will simply abandon the effort.

Difficulties

Some tests, experiments, and Study and Act activities are seen by clients as:

- Overly risky;
- Potentially damaging to the client's career or job security;
- Irreversible;
- Excessively costly;
- Unnecessary elements of the improvement cycle.

While these may or may not be reasonable judgments, the change master may experience difficulty in getting a commitment to undertake even a modest test or simulation of a new method. The other prominent difficulty in this phase is the tendency of initially disappointing results to cause premature cancellation of a program of experimentation. Knowing when and how long to encourage evaluation and Study and Act activities is, perhaps, one of the artful aspects of change mastering. It is important to know that the Study and Act stages of the improvement cycle are rarely done or rarely done properly. It is impossible for an individual, group, or organization to develop improved understanding of cause-and-effect relationships and to avoid the consequences of tampering or improper improvement interventions in the absence of more disciplined and systematic Study and Act.

Trying out new behaviors, methods, and systems takes time to establish. Predicted positive linkages may not appear immediately. It is common for lag factors to delay expected results. Further, it may well be that predicted positive results are masked or hidden by the presence of certain moderating variables. Sufficient evaluation and systematic study and act are required to fully appreciate or understand whether or not a given improvement intervention has or will create the desired outcomes. It is in this phase that the change master needs to encourage "staying the course." Wisdom, judgment, and experience are essential for the change master to guide client behaviors and decisions properly.

PHASE 7: REINFORCING THE NEW BEHAVIOR

In this phase, the test is evaluated, and the use of the new methods and systems is reinforced, supported, and demonstrated to others. This process is based on the fundamental principle for both people and organizations that behavior is most likely to be sustained if it is reinforced and rewarded in some appropriate way.

Goals and Objectives of Reinforcing the New Behavior

The goal is to assure that those who design the change and those whose behavior is influenced by it experience some sort of positive feedback or consequences, which they perceive as rewarding. Without this, change design and testing tend to die out.

Typical Change Master Strategies

The change master seeks to alert the client to the importance of this phase by inserting it specifically into the change process design to which the client agrees. Note that the motivation front is where appropriate interventions would be planned and made. The change master, recognizing that progress itself is frequently very rewarding, makes reports to participants, project advisory groups, and top management as the change process progresses. The change master supports the collection and analysis of data which show the results of the tests. When it is appropriate, the change master arranges meetings, training sessions, briefings for top management, and written reports which serve to bring the work of those who have planned and carried out the new systems to the attention of others.

Case Example 2A in the Context of Reinforcing the New Behavior

Elizabeth realized that something can't be reinforced if it isn't being tried. Improvement teams were established within the community, but the method they used to "solve the problems" they had identified was unspecified and inconsistent. Periodic review sessions of the community planning team kept slipping, thus making it more and more difficult to maintain momentum.

Elizabeth knew the quarterly review sessions were great opportunities to reinforce successes, regardless of how few they might be. She knew Kurt and Ellen had to keep the pressure on, using these meetings as a forcing function for improvement teams to make progress. Elizabeth was confident that if she could get the meetings scheduled regularly, peer pressure alone would build momentum over time. She relied on keeping things moving enough to get to the annual recycle where a major infusion of energy and method and enthusiasm would be relatively easy to negotiate. But Kurt and Ellen continued to allow the City Manager's and Mayor's attention and interest to wane. They were not following the method as it was intended to be executed. They did not have a clear strategy of next steps mapped out for 12-18 months. There was too much dead time between interventions. There simply weren't enough opportunities to reinforce anything. Lack of clear methodology, lack of discipline and attention to detail, inability to maintain interest and involvement of top leadership, absence of enough structure for the improvement teams, and inconsistent periodic reviews all were adding up to a failure with this attempt to improve the performance of Bucksburg.

The critics had argued that this effort was, in fact, not well advised. Elizabeth knew better; she knew that key variables or requirements for success were simply not being managed. Part of the problem was with the maturity of the two change masters. They were allowing themselves to be managed by change and were being overtaken by events. Political astuteness and unwillingness or reluctance to be bold and demanding of the City Manager and Mayor were major areas of deficiency. Ellen increasingly shied away from the community as the unit of analysis and began concentrating on the city itself, which was more managable and controllable. Kurt was caught up in the 3^n-ball problem; he wasn't staying ahead of the power curve with this client due to demands from other clients. He tended to spend more time on the projects that were less ambiguous and more well structured, thus fueling the entropy with Bucksburg. The whole infrastructure of champion, sponsor(s), change agent, and target was coming undone. In the meantime, Harry was off on another initiative, disappointed that this hadn't taken hold but, true to the style of an entrepreneur, very caught up in the next innovation. In short, there was not much to reinforce at this point — a common failure of quality and productivity improvement efforts.

Difficulties

This phase often requires a long-term commitment from the change master and tends to prolong his or her association with each project. It assumes a long-term and somewhat continuous association with the client. It is difficult to deal with disappointing results in a way which reinforces progress toward change. It is difficult, also, to hold the attention of clients over an extended period of time and to elicit reinforcing behaviors from managers whose style may be primarily authoritarian.

The motivation front is the most complex subsystem to plan for, alter, and manage. It requires working effectively with those specialties most likely to have the knowledge and skills in this area. Reward and recognition systems in many organizations are "a mess," needing significant redesign or re-engineering, and the challenges in doing so are significant. As mentioned previously, offsetting entropy requires continuous or at least periodic infusion of energy, in this case reinforcement. Attention to detail in this phase is crucial to success. Planning to ensure that this phase will receive appropriate resources and attention is critical to ensure that positive changes become a way of doing business.

USING THE CLIENT CHANGE MODEL – SUMMARY

The usefulness of the model for the change master concerned with the design and execution of change processes aimed at quality and productivity improvement efforts may be summarized in a small number of conjectures:

1. The change master should continually be aware of which phase is involved during all interactions with client personnel and what effect is being sought. Know why you are doing what you are doing. This takes study and practice.
2. Process consciousness requires a simple model that can be kept readily in mind and to which you may constantly refer. The model presented in this chapter may be enriched for completeness and greater understanding, but in this simple form it can be used by the change master in action. It provides a continual basis for self-orientation. What am I doing now? Why am I doing it? What do I want to be happening to the client? What do I want to happen next? What are my ultimate desired outcomes? Accepting equifinality, is this path likely to achieve the desired outcomes? Which fronts are in need of movement? Which are ahead? Which are behind? What are recent critical incidents? What have I learned to this point in this improvement effort? How does what we have done fit into our ultimate vision? What are potential problems or crises that I can anticipate? Are there any details I am overlooking?
3. As the change master gains experience, process consciousness becomes increasingly internalized and intuitive. This is both good and bad. It is good because it frees up mental, emotional, and physical capacity for other things. It is potentially bad because it is a source of errors and mistakes. The change master can get sloppy, forget details, develop paradigms, make too many assumptions, and become too rigid.
4. The client should be made aware of the model, not in the language used here but in "shop language" or the language of the "local culture." Making the client aware of the **grand strategy** of the change process increases its effectiveness, reduces anxiety about what is going to happen, creates openness and trust, assures psychological safety, and helps develop realistic expectations about results.

5. Planning a change process in which separate and distinct attention and concern are given to each of the phases of the client change model increases the probability of its success. This separation conjecture does not imply a necessary order for the phases or that the phases be dealt with only once but only that each of the phases be addressed one at a time.

DEVELOPMENT WORK

INQUIRY QUESTIONS
These are questions you have for yourself or for others to help you better understand what was covered in this section. Feel free to send them to us, and we will develop a users' group and share questions and answers periodically.

Inquire First
What didn't you understand, what do you want to know about, what assumptions or beliefs do we posit that you want us to explain, what do you want clarification on?

Advocate Second
What did you disagree with, what do you want to argue about, what didn't you like, what do you want to challenge, in what areas do we appear to have different assumptions, data bases, beliefs, of attitudes?

LEARNING EXERCISES
LE 2.1 What model(s) of change for individuals, groups, and organizations are you familiar with? How do they compare to the one presented in this section?

LE 2.2 Select an improvement project case study described in a professional publication and interpret the discription in terms of the client change model presented in this section. What phases appear to be missing from the explicit report of the project? Does the way in which the phases were carried out suggest any useful explanation of the ultimate outcome of this project?

LE 2.3 The Schaeffer and Thomson article in *Harvard Business Review* (1992) is very critical of TQM. There has been a significant backlash against TQM and related improvement programs. Explain this backlash in the context of the change model presented in this section.

LE 2.4 Prepare a briefing on this section. Give the briefing to your colleagues, your work team, your boss, your spouse, a close friend. Try to explain the model in this section to a variety of audiences. What did you learn about this section that you didn't know just from reading it? How did the various audiences react to it? Could they relate to it? Which phases of change seem more intuitive than others?

LE 2.5 Identify a low-risk opportunity to apply this model (senior chapter of your professional society, church group, social group, civic group, your immediate work group).

Try it out. What insights did you gain? What would you change in the model based on moving from knowledge to application?

LE 2.6 Consider a professional whose work is helping people change their behavior and with whom you have some experience. Interpret their style and method in terms of the client change model. Consider, for example, a guidance counselor, clergyperson, parent, teacher, parole officer, counseling psychologist, physician, management consultant, or organization development specialist. Talk about their model of change and their methods. Compare and contrast their models and methods with the one presented in this chapter.

LE 2.7 Recognizing that much would depend on the specifics of the client's situation, outline how you would plan each of the following improvement projects in terms of the change model presented in this section:

- Building or enhancing a performance measurement system;
- Dealing with an absenteeism or safety problem;
- Downsizing the organization;
- Installing an MRP-II system;
- Improving the productivity of an older plant;
- Improving the process of budgeting in the organization;
- Increasing the level of involvement of top management in your improvement effort;
- Implementing TQM in your organization;
- Team-building in your organization;
- Implementing your strategic plan when you have been unable to do so for the past five years;
- Implementing a system for budgeting and allocating capital funds;
- Installing a visible management system;
- Involving the union and all employees in improvement;
- Re-engineering the most important business process in your organization;
- Developing an office automation plan;
- Improving motivation of the workforce.

LE 2.8 Interpret the case application in this section in the context of the change model. What did you see in the application that we did not discuss?

LE 2.9 Consider a client situation in which you have worked or would like to work as a change master. Specify the aspects of the client situation you feel are relevant for the design of a change process having a high probability of success with the sort of quality and productivity improvement work you have done or would like to do.

In designing and evaluating your change or improvement process, consider the following criteria:

A. The design should be something you could keep in your desk drawer or in an electronic file and refer to as a useful guide when working with a client.
B. The design should take account of at least three major contingencies. A contingency is a specification of what you would do if event E happens and what you would do if event

E does not happen. Event E might be, for example, "the problem we are working on turns out to be very high on top management's agenda," or "the problem we are working on was a high priority but is now a low priority on top management's agenda."

C. Your change process design should include the following sorts of evidence, listed in decreasing order of worth:

1. Systematic evidence from the research literature;
2. Anecdotal case-study evidence involving one or a few instances;
3. Your own personal experience, common sense, or professional judgment.

LE 2.10 Identify an improvement project with which you have had personal involvement. Who were the sponsors, champions, targets, agents? Do an input/output analysis for the organizational system you were trying to improve. Analyze the success, failure, or level of performance of the improvement effort in the context of what has been presented to this point in the book.

FEEDBACK QUESTIONS

FBQ 2.1 The following are short descriptions of alternative models of the client change process. What sorts of modifications of the model outlined in this section do these suggest to you, if any?

- Plan-Do-Study-Act;
- Unfreeze the old behavior, change, refreeze;
- Contentment with status quo, denial, confusion, renewal;
- Become aware their is a problem or opportunity, determine what to do to solve or capture, do it, evaluate the results.

FBQ 2.2 Revisit the questions at the beginning of this section and think through the answers now that you have read and perhaps studied this section. Have your answers to these questions changed? How so? Have your insights to these questions been altered?

FBQ 2.3 How could one validate the change model presented in this section? How could one test its usefulness? How could you confirm that using this model, or one similar, would improve your performance as a change master?

FBQ 2.4 Operationally define the following terms:

- Change
- Improvement
- Implementation
- Deployment
- Behavior
- Attitudes
- Skills
- Knowledge
- Performance
- Quality

- Productivity
- Habit
- Way of doing business
- Program, process, project, problem, opportunity
- Reinforcement
- Learning
- Regression
- Continuity of leadership, constancy of purpose, consistency of method.

What is the relationship and importance of these terms in the context of leading and managing improvement?

FBQ 2.5 What are the difficulties associated with implementing change models such as the one presented in this section?

- At the individual and personal level
- At the group level
- At the organizational level.

How do you or would you address these difficulties?

FBQ 2.6 Do a force field analysis (forces for and forces against) for positive change and improvement. Force field theory tells us that we must address forces against (restraining forces) first to succeed in making progress. What are the forces against positive change in your organization? How can you reduce the impact of these forces?

FBQ 2.7 It seems the "reinforcing new behaviors" phase is one that is most frequently ignored, and, as a result, improvement methods do not become a way of doing business. Do a cause-and-effect diagram and analysis on why this is the case. Once you have identified root causes, identify specific actions you will take to eliminate these root causes. Is reinforcing new behaviors the final phase of the change model? If not, what is the next phase?

PLAN OF STUDY AND DEVELOPMENT
What follows is a list of resources that support, in general, the material introduced in this section. Scan the list, indicate which you have read (R), studied (S), attempted to use (U), and which you would like to become acquainted with (TBD).

LITERATURE CITED
Barker, J. A. 1988. *Discovering the Future: The Business of Paradigms.* St. Paul, Minn.: ILI Press.
Beckhard, R. 1986. *Organization Development: Strategies and Models.* Reading, Mass.: Addison-Wesley.
Block, P. 1981. *Flawless Consulting.* San Diego, Calif.: University Associates.
Camp, R. C. 1989. *Benchmarking: The Search for Industry Best Practices that Lead to Superior Performance.* Milwaukee, Wis.: Quality Press.

Deming, W. E. 1986. *Out of the Crisis*. Cambridge, Mass.: MIT Center for Advanced Engineering Study.

Deming, W. E. 1991. *Quality, Productivity, and Competitive Position* (famous four-day seminar held Sept. 10-13 in Atlanta, Ga.). Los Angeles: Quality Enhancement Seminars.

Deming, W. E. 1992. *Instituting Dr. Deming's Methods for Management of Productivity and Quality* (seminar held Jan. 21-22 in Washington, D.C.). Los Angeles: Quality Enhancement Seminars.

Deming, W. E. 1993. *The New Economics*. Cambridge, Mass.: MIT Center for Advanced Engineering Study.

Kepner, C. H., and B. B. Tregoe. 1965. *The Rational Manager*. New York: McGraw-Hill.

Kepner, C. H., and B. B. Tregoe. 1981. *The New Rational Manager*. Princeton, N.J.: Princeton Research Press.

Kurstedt, H. A. 1993. *The Industrial Engineer's Systematic Approach to Management*. MSL Working Draft and articles and Responsive Systems Article. Blacksburg, Va.: Management Systems Laboratories.

Malcolm Baldrige National Quality Award
  • 1993 Handbook for the Board of Examiners
  • 1993 Verifilm Case Study
  • 1993 Case Study Packet, Executive Summary
  • Application Scorebook
  • 1993 Varifilm Evaluation Notes
  • 1993 Site Evaluation Book
  • 1993 Varifilm Feedback Report
  • 1994 Award Criteria.
Available from American Society for Quality Control, Milwaukee, Wis.

Mizuno, S. (ed.) 1988. *Management for Quality Improvement: The 7 New QC Tools*. Cambridge, Mass.: Productivity Press.

Morris, W. T. 1979. *Implementation Strategies for Industrial Engineers*. Columbus, Ohio: Grid Publishing.

Ozeki, K., and T. Asaka. 1990. *Handbook of Quality Tools*. Cambridge, Mass.: Productivity Press.

Peck, M. S. 1993. *A World Waiting to be Born: Civility Rediscovered*. New York: Bantam Books.

Peck, M. S. 1978. *The Road Less Traveled*. New York: Simon and Schuster.

Schaffer, R. H., and H. A. Thomson. 1992. Successful change programs begin with results. *Harvard Business Review*. January/February.

Scholtes, P. R. 1988. *The Team Handbook*. Madison, Wis.: Joiner Assoc.

Senge, P. 1990. *The Fifth Discipline*. New York: Doubleday.

Sink, D. S., and T. C. Tuttle. 1989. *Planning and Measurement in Your Organization of the Future*. Norcross, Ga.: Industrial Engineering and Management Press.

Thompson, J. D. 1967. *Organizations in Action*. New York: McGraw-Hill.

Weisbord, M. R. 1991. *Productive Workplaces: Organizing for Dignity, Meaning, and Community*. San Francisco: Jossey-Bass.

Weisbord, M. R. (ed.). 1992. *Discovering Common Ground: How Future Search Conferences Bring People Together to Achieve Breakthrough Innovation, Empowerment, Shared Vision, and Collaborative Action*. San Francisco: Berrett-Koehler.

BIBLIOGRAPHY

Adizes, I. 1988. *Corporate Lifecycles.* Englewood Cliffs, N.J.: Prentice-Hall.

Argyris, C. 1982. *Reasoning, Learning, and Action: Individual and Organizational.* San Francisco: Jossey-Bass.

Argyris, C., and D. Schon. 1974. *Theory in Practice.* Reading, Mass.: Addison-Wesley.

Argyris, C., and D. Schon. 1978. *Organizational Learning: A Theory of Action Perspective.* Reading, Mass.: Addison-Wesley.

Barker, J. A. 1986. *Discovering the Future: The Business of Paradigms.* Minneapolis, Minn.: Filmedia.

Barker, J. A. 1986. *The Power of Visions.* Minneapolis, Minn.: Filmedia.

Beer, M. 1980. *Organizational Change and Development.* Santa Monica, CA: Goodyear.

Bennis, W. G. 1966. *Changing Organizations.* New York: McGraw-Hill.

Bennis, W. G., K. D. Benne, and R. Chin. 1985. *The Planning of Change,* (4th edn.). New York: Holt, Rinehart, Winston.

Berquist, W. 1993. *The Postmodern Organization: Mastering the Art of Irreversible Change.* San Francisco: Jossey-Bass.

Burke, W. 1987. *Organization Development: A Normative Approach.* Reading, Mass.: Addison-Wesley.

Fishbein, M., and I. Ajzen. 1975. *Belief, Attitude, Intention and Behavior: An Introduction to Theory and Research.* Philippines: Addison-Wesley.

French, W. L., and C. H. Bell. 1978. *Organization Development: Behavioral Science Interventions for Organizational Improvement.* Englewood Cliffs, N.J.: Prentice-Hall.

French, W. L., C. H. Bell, and R. A. Zawacki. 1978. *Organizational Development: Theory, Practice, and Research,* (3rd edn.). Homewood, Ill.: Richard D. Irwin, Inc.

Hackman, J. R. 1975. Group influences on individuals. In *Handbook of Industrial and Organizational Psychology.* Edited by M. Dunnette. Chicago: Wiley.

Hackman, J. R. 1990. *Groups that Work (and Those that Don't).* San Francisco: Jossey Bass.

Hirschman, A. O. 1970. *Exit, Voice and Loyalty: Responses to Decline in Firms, Organizations and States.* Cambridge, Mass.: Harvard University Press.

Huse, E. F. 1980. *Organizational Development and Change,* (5th edn.). St. Paul, Minn.: West.

Kanfer, F. H., and A. P. Goldstein, editors. 1975. *Helping People Change.* New York: Pergamon Press.

Katz, D., and R. L. Kahn. 1966. *The Social Psychology of Organizations.* New York: John Wiley and Sons.

Kerr, S. 1975. On the folly of rewarding A, while hoping for B. *Academy of Management Journal.* 18(3): 769-783.

Kilmann, R., T. J. Covin, and Associates. 1988. *Corporate Transformations,* San Francisco: Jossey Bass.

Kimberly, J. R., R. H. Miles, and Associates. 1980. *The Organizational Life Cycle: Issues in the Creation, Transformation and Decline of Organizations.* San Francisco: Jossey-Bass.

Kuhn, T. S. 1970. *The Structure of Scientific Revolutions.* Chicago: University of Chicago Press.

Lundstedt, S. B., and T. H. Moss (eds.). 1989. *Managing Innovation and Change.* Boston: Kluwer Academic.

March, J. G., and H. A. Simon. 1958. *Organizations.* New York: John Wiley.

Michael, D. 1973. *Planning to Learn and Learning to Plan.* San Francisco: Jossey-Bass.

Mills, D. Q. 1991. *Rebirth of the Corporation.* New York: John Wiley.

Mintzberg, H. 1985. Of strategies, deliberate and emergent. *Strategic Management Journal.* 6: 257-272.

Mintzberg, H. 1987. Crafting strategy. *Harvard Business Review.* 64: 66-75.

Naisbitt, J. and P. Aburdene. 1985. *Re-inventing the Corporation: Transforming your job and your company for the new information society.* New York: Warner Books.

Porter, L. W., E. E. Lawler III, and J. R. Hackman. 1975. *Behavior in Organizations.* New York: McGraw-Hill.

Shaw, M. E. 1976. *Group Dynamics: The Psychology of Small Group Behavior.* New York:

Steeples, M. M. 1992. *The Corporate Guide to the Malcolm Baldridge National Quality Award.* Milwaukee, Wis.: ASQC Quality Press.

Thoreson, C. E., and M. J. Mahoney. 1974. *Behavioral Self-Control.* New York: Holt, Rinehart and Winston.

Tichy, N. 1983. *Managing Strategic Change.* New York: John Wiley.

Walton, R. 1988. *Innovating to Compete.* San Francisco: Jossey-Bass.

Weick, K. E. 1979. *The Social Psychology of Organizing.* Reading, Mass.: Addison-Wesley.

Zand, D. E., and R. E. Sorensen. 1975. Theory of change and the effective use of management science. *Administrative Science Quarterly.* 20(12):000.

ON BECOMING A CHANGE MASTER: PROFESSIONAL MODES OF FUNCTIONING

Clients (individuals, groups, and organizations) pass through predictable phases of change as they attempt to improve. We reviewed those phases in Chapter 4. At the same time, it was impossible to present and discuss those phases of change independent of behaviors exhibited on the part of the change master.

In this section, we focus on what we call professional modes of functioning that the change master can adopt to manage phases of change. These professional modes of functioning represent not so much "what" the change master does, rather they represent "how." They are roles that the change master can play to move clients successfully through the phases of change.

Style is as much a part of professional modes of functioning as platform skills, verbal and written skills, adaptability, conflict management, and the ability to deal with ambiguity. Situational leadership theory has exposed many to the notion of a leader and manager altering their strategies, tactics, and behaviors with different people in different situations. Those who have studied this theory know it is intuitively appealing but difficult to put into practice.

Although the model of professional modes of functioning does characterize change master behaviors somewhat differently than the traditional leadership models, it is no less difficult to operationalize. Concentrate, for now, on understanding the types of behaviors that would be exhibited in each of the seven modes. In the next section, we will invite you to do a more thorough job of integrating modes with phases.

OPERATIONAL DEFINITIONS

Design and Development Team (DDT/A&E): This group, normally 9–12 in size, is the "architect and engineering" (A&E) team for the improvement effort. They design, develop, and solve problems. They help the organization maintain momentum, get unstuck, and maintain the plans and strategies for improvement. The DDT does not often implement improvement strategies. They are change agents/masters in the organization. They represent people with willingness and ability to learn how to help the organization accelerate improvement. They should be a multidisciplinary and experienced team. Coverage of the fronts on the team is of some importance. Their customers are the sponsors for the improvement efforts (e.g., top management and leadership team, executive steering group, steering council, quality and productivity improvement council). They are chartered by the "A" and "B" leadership group in the organization. They are not expected to "DO"; they are expected to "PLAN", design, develop, solve problems, maintain momentum, offset entropy, think statistically, understand systems, learn at a faster rate than the rest of the organization, lead, serve, manage and lead change, think ahead, pay attention to details, etc.

There will be a network of DDTs in a large system. Coordination between the DDTs is the responsibility of the highest system level DDT.

False Learning Curves(Scholtes 1988): The concept of a false learning curve was introduced to me at a Deming two-day seminar. Simply put, it represents the notion that we learn about something, get the jargon down, grasp the concepts, then try to apply it and find that our understanding is insufficient. We normally see a drop off in interest, motivation, energy, etc. at this point. Continued study, learning, and attempts to reduce to practice are required to get us past this "wall" and the false learning curve. (Shown later in the book, Figure 47.)

Levels of Knowledge:

Level 1: Theory, Concepts, Philosophy, Principles. Level 1 is the understanding of something at the conceptual level. To gain proper knowledge, the origins of the knowledge must be understood. The concepts and principles are the building blocks for gaining knowledge. We build upon each level, adding to and using the previous level in our ascent.

Level 2: Operational Definitions. An operational definition is having a definition you can do business with. It's when you accept the theories, and put them into terms you understand.

Level 3: Method. Now you know what to do. You understand the method or process, the step-by-step way to do some task. Knowledge of how to do doesn't necessarily mean you also have the skill to do, just that you understand how the job gets done.

Level 4: Skill. You know what to do, how to do it, and are down on the learning curve into actually doing it. You practice your Level 3 knowledge, testing, refining, adding to it as you actually perform.

Level 5: Profound Knowledge. Profound knowledge is when you can teach something and improve upon it. You understand the theory, have internalized or operationally defined it for yourself; you've found out how to do it and have been successful in doing it. In fact, you do it so well that you are beginning to gain insight about why you are successful. You have determined the critical pieces of the puzzle, can improve the puzzle, and can demonstrate "by what method" to others coming up the levels of knowledge.

Management Systems Model: A model developed by Dr. Harold Kurstedt at Virginia Tech portrays the management system as three basic components—what is being managed, what we manage with, and who manages—and three basic interfaces: measurement to data, information portrayal to information perception, and decisions to actions.

It is a powerful conceptual way of getting management teams to gain appreciation for a system and for developing improved understanding of the domain of responsibility and accountability for the team in context of continuous improvement (shown in adapted form later in the book, Figure 23).

Startup Phase: The startup phase of anything—be it a program, a project, a process—creates unique situations and characteristics. During startup, things are less stable, less predictable, and there are often surprises to manage. The leader/manager is forced to determine which subsystems to lay in place and get stable and in what order. Keeping things stable while other systems are being worked on is a challenge. There is an art to startup management and leadership. Leadership must reinforce those struggling in the system and fight off the critics, and they must be able to take a long view of things and maintain that perspective. I always try to think about what the startup phase of anything would look like if I could repeat the startup 100 times. If the leader of the improvement effort can do this, then he or she will be able to get the participants to stay the course.

Strategic Performance Improvement Planning Process: An effective mechanism for integrating strategic planning with Total Quality Management, providing the critical linkage between vision, strategy, actions, measures, and results.

Step 1   Organizational System Analysis
Step 2   Strategic Objectives
Step 3   Tactical Objectives
Step 4   Implementation Planning
Step 5   Implementation Management
Step 6   Performance Measurement
Step 7   Implementation Review, Evaluation and Recycle.

CHAPTER 5

MODES OF PROFESSIONAL FUNCTIONING: AN OVERVIEW

CASE EXAMPLE 2B: MANAGING PHASES OF CHANGE AND PROFESSIONAL MODES OF FUNCTIONING—BUCKSBURG 2000 AND BEYOND

This case example is an evolution of the previous case. The setting is Bucksburg, Ohio; however, the focus here is on improvement initiatives within Bucksburg Tech and the Bucksburg Public School System. These initiatives were spawned by the Bucksburg 2000 effort, which, ultimately, was not successful.

CAST OF CHARACTERS
Bucksburg 2000 and Bucksburg Public Schools
Kurt: OQPC project manager for the Bucksburg 2000 initiative and now for the Bucksburg Public School System initiative

Mayor and City Manager of Bucksburg: Sponsors for the Bucksburg 2000 initiative

Frank: The Superintendent of Bucksburg Public Schools

Tom: Chairperson of the School Board for the Bucksburg Public Schools initiative.

Bucksburg Tech
Elizabeth: OQPC director and startup project manager for the Bucksburg Tech initiative

Wayne and Rich: Deans of Engineering and Business at Bucksburg Tech

The President, Provost, and Chief Financial Officer of Bucksburg Tech

Bob, Ann, and Wayland: Internal change agents at Bucksburg Tech

Jay: A top manager at Westin, Inc. and a project manager for Bucksburg Tech's University Challenge TQM Partnership.

A year into the Bucksburg 2000 effort, Elizabeth had developed an uneasy feeling that Kurt was not managing one of the key requirements for success on the project: support and commitment from the sponsors. Elizabeth tried to push Kurt to keep pressure on the Mayor and City Manager, but he was uncomfortable challenging them and continued to target most of his communication efforts toward Ellen (and to a lesser extent the design team). Elizabeth kept reminding Kurt that Ellen had no power and that to some extent his time was wasted unless he could re-establish commitment from the two key sponsors.

Harry, the external champion, had completely dropped out of sight on the project. Elizabeth didn't know the reason for this, and it concerned her. Perhaps he had sensed impending failure and wanted to distance himself. Perhaps he had simply been consumed by the day-to-day demands of managing Bucksburg Bank and Trust. Perhaps his attention had been diverted by another crusade. Or perhaps he was still very much involved in the Bucksburg 2000 initiative, exerting his considerable influence and accomplishing his personal agenda from behind the scenes.

Over the next year momentum was lost and the Bucksburg 2000 initiative died a slow, quiet death. The internal change agent, Ellen, had focused her efforts on a domain of responsibility she could understand (inside the city infrastructure exclusively), and the overall community effort disintegrated. Selected teams continued to meet, but in the absence of any real sponsorship or any Phase 7 (reinforcement) activity, they, too, eventually faded away.

Elizabeth thought back to the inception of Bucksburg 2000. Would anything of value come from the Center's efforts? It appeared on the surface as if Paul and Ken had been right when they advocated against accepting the project.. Kurt and Elizabeth both felt the domain of improvement was so large and sponsorship for change so inconsistent that these were the root causes of failure. They still both believed, on the basis of what they were reading in Weisbord's recent work on Future Search Conferences and in Peck's work on Community Building, that this could be done but not unless certain key requirements of success were met and maintained. They both now knew they had failed to do this.

Needless to say, Elizabeth was surprised several weeks later to receive a phone call from Frank, the superintendent of Bucksburg Public Schools. Tom, the School Board chairperson who had been a member of the Bucksburg 2000 design team, had urged Frank to contact OQPC for assistance in helping the Bucksburg School System integrate total quality and strategic planning. Elizabeth and Kurt met with the Superintendent to establish expectations and requirements, then scoped out a proposal for presentation to the executive committee for the Schools.

Kurt presented the proposed method and approach, leaving ample time for questions and concerns. During the next several months the proposal was refined, details worked out, and issues resolved. Eventually, a three-year effort was agreed to, and the project to build, implement, and deploy a plan of improvement was initiated.

The public school system leadership was clearly challenged by "A" and "C." They were extremely aware of the difficulties they would encounter trying to squeeze even a little "B" into their lives but were willing to try. They were primarily interested in building a strategic plan that had widespread involvement from the community, students, and teachers. Integrating TQM or "Quality Schools" into the effort also was an emphasis of the Superintendent. So, Kurt and Elizabeth suggested adopting the center's Strategic Performance Improvement Planning process and system. They, as mentioned, were successful in convincing the school system leadership that it would take three years to get past start up and past the false learning curve. A planning team was formed, comprised of wide representation from the total system. The agenda for the strategic planning session is shown in Figure 17.

Realizing that the Bucksburg 2000 effort, although not successful as success had originally been defined, represented the seed from which many other efforts could grow, Elizabeth decided to seize another opportunity. She had in the past made several attempts to establish a continuous improvement effort inside her own university. She had repeatedly tried to get the President and Provost interested in an improvement effort but had met with benevolent resistance. However, it seemed that the Bucksburg community effort had sensitized the leaders of Bucksburg Tech to the need for such an effort.

Additionally, significant budget cuts over the previous five years had left Tech in a situation of having to do the same or more with less resources. Although the President was uncomfortable with "programs," he clearly realized the need to take some sort of action.

Elizabeth had been reading about a program called The University Challenge TQM Partnership, involving a consortium of companies attempting to lead universities toward the integration of Total Quality into their academic and/or administrative processes. The University Challenge effort had been initiated in 1992 by Robert Galvin, chairman of the Executive Board of Motorola, Inc. During the spring and summer of 1992, business and education partnerships involving eight universities and five corporations had been piloted successfully. Participating corporations had hosted up to 163 faculty and administrators from their partnering universities for an intensive education and training program about the practice of Total Quality Management. After the education and training session, plans were jointly developed for integrating TQM into partnering universities.

To Elizabeth, it seemed an opportunity to participate in a Challenge partnership would provide the impetus needed to move Bucksburg Tech forward with continuous improvement. However, Elizabeth knew she needed a sponsor if this effort were to succeed. She met with Wayne, Dean of the College of Engineering, to learn more about his ideas for how Tech should proceed with continuous improvement and assess his interest in the Challenge partnership program. Wayne stepped forward as a strong and enthusiastic sponsor of the Challenge effort. He realized the potential benefits and was an effective communicator and motivator. Rich, the Dean of Business, got on board as well (although reluctantly at first), and this caused a critical mass of support that was crucial to obtain President and Provost endorsement. The President and Deans tasked Elizabeth with leading the development of Tech's Challenge proposal.

Elizabeth, with assistance from others at OQPC, wrote Bucksburg Tech's proposal and ensured its timely submission to Procter & Gamble, the University Challenge corporate coordinator. Approximately six weeks later, Elizabeth received official notification that Bucksburg Tech had been selected as a Challege partner by Westin, Inc., a leading corporation in the East.

In addition to Elizabeth, several change agents had for some time been working behind the scenes at Bucksburg Tech to create awareness and enlightenment on the part of the top management team. Bob, a professor from the Business College, had exposed Tech leaders, in a nonthreatening and effective way, to TQM. Anne and Wayland, change agents within administration, had initiated pilot improvement projects using TQ tools. So in a sense the University Challenge partnership culminated several years of foundation laying.

Wayne and Rich chartered a team of these internal change masters to lead the Challenge effort, and Elizabeth was designated as team leader. The group, calling

AGENDA II
Strategic Planning Session

Day 1

7:30	Continental Breakfast
8:00	Power of Vision videotape - Joel Barker
8:45	Kick-off/Welcome
	Ground rules
	Introduction to Strategic Planning Process
	Current Performance Levels
10:00	Break
10:15	Input /Output analysis
11:45	Lunch
1:00	Assumption Generation
1:30	Small Group Activity
	Develop Vision, Mission, Guiding Principles
2:30	Working Break
3:00	Group presentations
3:45	Wrapup/Integration of Day 1
5:00	Adjourn

Day2

7:30	Continental Breakfast
8:00	Review of Day 1
8:45	Upline Planning
9:30	Strategic Goal Setting
10:00	Working Break
10:15	Continue Strategic Goal Setting
11:45	Lunch/Video Tape - Abilene Paradox
1:00	Continue Strategic Goal Setting
2:30	Working Break
4:00	Wrapup/Integration of Day 2
5:00	Adjourn

Day 3

7:30	Continental Breakfast
8:00	Tactical Objective Setting
10:00	Working Break
10:15	ContinueTactical Goal Setting
11:45	Lunch/Video Tape - Paradigm Pioneers
1:00	Tactical Object Scoping proposals
2:30	Working Break
3:00	Next Steps
4:00	Adjourn

Figure 17. A sample agenda for a public school's strategic planning session.

themselves the Challenge Steering Committee, agreed to meet bi-weekly to plan for the Challenge program and also to begin thinking through how to continue to move forward beyond the time frame of the Challenge. Elizabeth's immediate challenge (she was beginning to understand how the program got its name) was to coordinate the efforts of the Steering Committee and the Westin team to design an agenda for a four-day TQM training session. This training session, a requirement set forth under the Challenge guidelines, would involve up to 100 faculty and administrators from Bucksburg Tech and would be facilitated by a team of trainers from Westin. The agenda for the four-day, off-site educational session is shown in Figures 18 and 18A.

The session went very well, considering that convening a heterogeneous group of personnel from across a major university for four days to concentrate on improving things is extremely rare. One hundred Bucksburg Tech faculty, staff, administrators, and the top leadership and administration, in addition to fourteen Westin facilitators, were brought together in round tables of between ten and twelve each. As the four days progressed, the Westin facilitators revealed their process improvement methodology. Each table was assigned a unique key process within the university and worked through the methodology, step by step, stopping periodically for instruction and debriefs. The energy and enthusiasm rose gradually over the four days. People who had never worked together as a team began to do so and gained a greater appreciation for the interdependencies within the larger system. It seemed to Elizabeth that a pent up demand to surface these system issues was being addressed, and, for the most part, it appeared to be quite satisfying.

The Challenge Steering Committee met after the four-day session and began to map out strategies for expansion of the effort within the university. They were cognizant of the importance of leadership involvement and support and were pleasantly surprised by the extent to which this had occurred (with some prodding on their part) during the four-day training session. There was a strong demand to hold another four day session with yet another 100 personnel from across campus, so plans were initiated with Westin staff. For this session, the Steering Committee wanted to utilize in-house facilitators as opposed to Westin facilitators for each roundtable workshop. Westin agreed to provide a facilitator training session two months prior to the larger four-day session.

Approximately forty volunteers from within the university emerged to be trained in Westin's process improvement methodology, a far greater number than the Steering Committee had anticipated. From this group, ten were selected to facilitate the round tables at the next training session.

These two training sessions sparked numerous improvement efforts in the academic and administrative support areas within the university. These efforts ranged from reducing the cycle time and improving the quality of the bi-ennium budget request to improving the quality of instruction. Other focuses were integrating Total Quality into the curriculum, re-engineering two major business processes in the Research Division, facilities improvement, classroom quality, enrollment services, academic advising, and personnel services. An outside Dean of a major college (Business for the first session and Engineering for the second), who was an articulate advocate of reform and total quality improvement in universities, was invited to keynote the sessions. This provided some benchmarking and external legitimacy to Bucksburg Tech's effort.

Elizabeth gradually was weaned from this effort inside the university as ownership grew within the ranks of leadership and the Steering Committee. At first, this was difficult to

---

Bucksburg Tech/Westin - University TQM Challenge Boot Camp Agenda

DAY 1

When: 8:30 - 8:45
What: Welcome
Who: University President

When: 8:45 - 9:15
What: Current University efforts (phase II) and the case for continuous improvement and the need for change
Who: Provost and Westing Vice President

When: 9:15-10:15 (break)
What: Introduction, agenda review & overview of TQM at Westin
Who: Director, Westing Productivity Center

When: 10:45 - 12:00 (lunch)
What: TQM Table Exercise and Table reports of output
Who: TQM Facilitators

When: 1:00 - 2:45 (break) 3:15 - 4:30
What: Implementation of Change
Who: TQM Educators

When: 4:30 - 5:00
What: Wrap up - prepare for tomorrow
Who: Director, Westin Productivity Center

When: 5:00 - 9:00
What: Happy Hour, Keynote Speaker, Banquet

DAY 2

When: 8:30 - 8:45
What: Review of Day 1 and Day 2 overview
Who: Director, Westin Productivity Center

When: 8:45 10:00 (break)
What: Explore/Discuss UT Proism - Who does Bucksburg Tech server?
Who: TQM Facilitators

When: 10:30 - 12:00 (lunch)
What: Examine University processes and expectations
Who: TQM Facilitators

When: 1:00 - 2:45 (break)
What: Process Improvement Methodology
Who: TQM Educators

When: 3:15 - 4:30
What: Applying Process Improvement to University processes
Who: Director, Westin Productivity Center

When: 4:30 - 4:45
What: Wrap up and homework for Day 3
Who: Director, Westin Productivity Center

Figure 18. A sample agenda for a four-day educational session (bootcamp).

Bucksburg Tech/Westin - University TQM Challenge
BootCamp Agenda - cont'd

DAY 3

When: 8:30 - 8:45
What: Review of Day 2 and Day 3 overview
Who: Director, Westin Productivity Center

When: 8:45 10:00 (break)
What: Overview of other University Challenges in North America
Who: Corporate Coordinator for University Challenge,

When: 10:30 - 12:00 (lunch)
What: Discovering the Future - Paradigms videotape

When: 1:00 - 2:45 (break)
What: University Paradigm Identification and Exploration Exercise
Who: TQM Facilitators

When: 3:15 - 4:30
What: Analysing current processes and redesign
Who: TQM Educators

When: 4:30 - 4:45
What: Wrap up and homework for Day 3
Who: Director, Westin Productivity Center

DAY 4

When: 8:30 - 8:45
What: Review of Day 3 and Day 4 overview
Who: Director, Westin Productivity Center

When: 8:45 10:00 (break)
What: Continuation of Redesigning University Processes
Who: TQM Facilitators

When: 10:30 - 12:00 (lunch)
What: Implementing the Redesigns
Who: TQM Educators

When: 1:00 - 2:45 (break)
What: Group Exercise and reports on Implementation Strategies
Who: TQM Facilitators

When: 3:15 - 4:30
What: Next Step Discussion with President, Provost and Deans
Who: Vice President, Westin, Inc.

When: 4:30 - 4:45
What: Closing Remarks
Who: Vice president of Westin, President of Bucksburg Tech

When: 5:00 - 7:00
What: Closing reception, Offsite lounge

Figure 18A. A sample agenda (continued) days 3 and 4.

accept, and she felt a bit rejected. But as she stood back and examined the bigger picture (this initiative in the context of the community effort begun over three years ago), she felt a sense of accomplishment. Things certainly hadn't played out the way she had envisioned—detours, blind alleys, dead ends, brick walls, and setbacks were much more common and unpredictable than expected. The political front was much more prominent within the community and in the university setting than she had expected. It had become even more clear that leadership (sponsorship) involvement and commitment were central to getting past startup and maintaining momentum; it was certainly not overstated in the literature, as Elizabeth had seen firsthand. It seemed this one factor caused the decline of the community effort and was, at least at this point, helping the forward progress in both the Public Schools and the University.

Whether the Design and Development Team in the Public Schools and the Challenge Steering Committee were knowledgeable and skilled enough to navigate the transformation and maintain momentum for the next two to three years remained to be seen. Both Kurt and Elizabeth were somewhat skeptical that a full appreciation of phases of change and modes of professional functioning were internalized enough for the two groups to avoid major problems. They could only hope they would be able to influence these two teams as they continued to craft a strategy for improving their organizations.

SOME PREMISES

We will use both offshoot improvement efforts in the previous case example as ways of bringing to life the professional modes of functioning over the course of an improvement project. Here, we begin our discussion by presenting some fundamental premises upon which we have developed research and experience-based hypotheses about change mastering for quality and productivity improvement. It may be helpful to recall that the term "client" is being used to refer to individuals, groups, and organizations, and that the change master may be either an insider or an outside consultant. The premises are as follows:

1. Change process design involves at least the professional activities of situation appraisal, information gathering, and application of methods based on mathematics, statistics, engineering, the behavioral and social sciences, and systems design.

2. We assume the change master's objectives are not problem solving or report production but planned and intended changes in the behavior of clients. We assume the change master wants to build capacity and competency for sustainable performance improvement on the part of the client.

3. Practicing change masters always face the problem of "keeping three balls in the air at once." To reiterate, the three-ball problem consists of:

   A. Dealing with the client's focal problem and creating the new system;

   B. Allocating all scarce resources (e.g., professional time, client time, project budget) in ways calculated to maximize the mutual satisfaction of client and change master;

   C. Executing an implementation strategy designed to assure a high probability that intended behavior changes will actually occur.

4. There is a strong relationship between the ways in which the phases of a project are executed and the probability that the intended behavior changes will actually occur.

5. Experienced, practicing change masters behave in ways that can be characterized as

personal styles. Style tends to reflect one's self-image, competencies, and reinforced experiences. Education should, therefore, openly and explicitly aim at the development of personal styles. Students should experiment with professional behaviors and be self-consciously concerned with the development of their own personal style.

6. Other people's paradigms of professional functioning have a low probability of guiding or influencing one's behavior. This statement includes, of course, the paradigm developed in this chapter. Change masters should explicitly develop their own paradigms of professional functioning since these will have a much higher probability of guiding their behavior.

SOME BASIC HYPOTHESES

We are now in a position to raise basic hypotheses which may be of some help in understanding the development of personal styles:

1. The findings of the behavioral sciences suggest a way of looking at alternative modes of professional functioning that is useful in the development of one's personal style. Sometimes, for example, the change master operates in a facilitating mode, helping clients work out their own problems, and sometimes in an expert mode, recommending changes based on a high degree of professional knowledge and skill.
2. Professions engaged in helping to change behavior use a relatively common model or sequence of phases in moving their clients toward these changes. It is also the case that phases of group and organizational development and evolution are identified in the literature.
3. A helpful "first cut" at developing a personal style is to attempt to create a contingency theory which focuses research and experience on this double question: *What mode of professional functioning should I use in each phase of the client change process, and how much effort (in the general sense) should I allocate to each phase?*
4. It has been suggested that team building requires members of the team to know themselves and to know the other members of the team (McManus 1983). Bennis and Nanus (1985), Covey (1991), and Peck (1993) have all suggested that effective leaders are self-aware, conscious as to strengths, weaknesses, likes, dislikes, etc. The change master must create significant consciousness of self, others, situation (past and present), environment, technology, content, and process to be effective.

SEVEN MODES OF PROFESSIONAL FUNCTIONING

To argue the plausibility of these hypotheses, we begin by laying out some modes of professional functioning which have been found useful.

Inquiry Mode (Acceptant and Active Listener)

The change master encourages client expression, listens effectively, and makes no evaluative responses. The change master exhibits the clinical skill of concerned listening without being judgmental, thus encouraging the client to clarify problems and to relieve anxieties and frustrations. The change master is an active listener, probing unobtrusively for meaning, searching to understand. This mode can be passive (the acceptant listener) or active (practicing inquiry with the aim of better understanding).

Data/Fact Gatherer (Information System Designer)

The change master undertakes to collect, or plan the collection of, information believed by either the client or the change master to be useful in some phase of the client change process. Note that in this mode the change master is acting as a data gatherer only, leaving the analysis and interpretation of the data to the client or to some joint effort involving both client and change master. The change master may, in this mode, play the role of measurement system designer and developer—again, not getting into evaluation but assisting with the enhancement of measurement systems. The change master may be leading the architecture and engineering of the measurement front.

Collaborator (Team Member)

The change master becomes a member of the client team, working on some fairly well-defined task. He or she may bring special skills and experience to the work of the team but is careful to recognize the knowledge and experience of other team members as well. The change master avoids leading or dominating the work of the team, seeking consensus decisions. The change master demonstrates good followership in this role, accepting other emergent leadership.

Structure Provider (Structured Group Process Coordinator)

The change master coordinates and facilitates clients working on well-defined tasks by using structured group processes such as brainstorming, brainwriting, the Nominal Group Technique, or the Delphi Technique. The change master is careful to stay out of substantive considerations and play the low-profile role of structuring an efficient and effective group process. The change master focuses on process, not on task or content. In this mode, the change master is most directly in the stereotypical role of facilitator. The change master manages group behavior and process.

Teacher and Skill Developer

The change master seeks to enhance the competence of clients by teaching tools, techniques, methods, and skills which have direct application to immediate client concerns. The change master also may teach principles, theories, or bodies of knowledge which are expected to increase client competence in a much longer term sense. The change master architects and engineers and provides leadership for the education, training, and development front.

Expert (Solution Provider)

The change master functions in the traditional mode of the expert with special knowledge and experience, solves the client's problem, and produces a recommended solution or design for a new system. The change master architects and engineers and provides leadership for the planning, culture, communication, political, technology, infrastructure, motivation, measurement, and education/training/development fronts. In some cases, the change master may simply broker experts in a given area or field, not providing the expertise personally but ensuring that the right talent is brought to bear on the situation.

Challenger

The change master challenges or confronts the client with data, information, standards, comparisons, and "tough" questions. The change master seeks to make the client "face up" to opportunities, shortcomings, inconsistencies, and evidence which may suggest unfavorable interpretations. The change master seeks to make the client intellectually honest. The change master confronts and manages conflict rather than attempting to smooth it over or ignore it. The change master is a conflict manager.

These, then, are the seven basic modes of professional functioning. Clearly, there are other modes and other ways to characterize or structure them. For example, the role of honest broker is frequently discussed in some literature. The role of broker, where the change master obtains appropriate resources or expertise for the client, also is common. The notion of leadership, in general, is perhaps cross-cutting in this taxonomy. The small-group behavior literature presents common behavioral roles of participants in group meetings: opinion seeker, opinion giver, process observer, critic, reflective thinker, information giver or seeker, chronic malcontent, restater (sometimes of the obvious), and clarifier, to name the most common. These are refinements to the professional modes of functioning we are presenting in Figure 19.

So, the personal styles of experienced change masters may include other modes of professional functioning, some of which may be complex and subtle mixtures of those outlined above. The experienced change master may shift back and forth quickly among these modes as the contingencies of the situation suggest. These basic building blocks can, however, clarify and serve as the basis for developing a personal style of change process design.

Figure 19. Professional modes of functioning are leadership/behavior styles the change master can use situationally to lead and manage improvement efforts.

CHAPTER 6

PROFESSIONAL MODES OF FUNCTIONING: A CLOSER LOOK

I n the following pages, we expand the description of the different types of professional action, illustrate them with typical change master methods, discuss common difficulties associated with each mode, and relate the mode in the context of this section's case study participants.

INQUIRY MODE: ACCEPTANT LISTENER, ACTIVE LISTENER, DIALOGUE CREATOR

Expanded Description

 The change master makes it easy for clients to talk about their situation, problems, frustrations, and conflicts. To do this, the change master listens with interest and encouragement, avoids arguing, demanding justification, or making value judgments. The change master facilitates expression by repeating the client's thoughts, by asking for clarification, and by direct questioning. In this sense the change master, in this mode, may well be working to build what Peck (1993) calls community. The intent is to get the client to deal with their "affects" and to create intellectual openness and honesty.

The objectives of the acceptant mode include the following:

1. Establishing a comfortable, trusting, mutually respecting relationship between the change master and client people;
2. Allowing clients to become aware of their own thoughts, attitudes, sources of difficulty, and views of the situation;
3. Permitting the change master to obtain a large amount of information which will be useful and even essential to the design of the change process;
4. Permitting the client to make the change master fully aware of the importance, difficulty, and history of the problems at hand;
5. Permitting the client to communicate to the change master personal and departmental interests, objectives, and constraints relative to the area of potential change;
6. Allowing the client to see that the change master is genuinely interested in the problem, is open to and accepting of the client's advice and experience, and does not immediately take the stance of an uninformed expert insisting on solutions ill-adapted to the local situation.

Change Master Methods Associated with Inquiry Mode

Inquiry, reflection, echoing, restatement, passive but attentive listening, note taking if not obtrusive or offensive, appropriate body language, ensuring equality of participation (in a group setting), giving ample time for people to finish thoughts, and use of silence are examples of behaviors and styles useful in this mode. It is important to note here that inquiry questions are not answerable by yes or no. Nor are they leading questions which reveal the change master's preferences or opinions.

Allowing affect to be exposed in the context of a discussion is also important. Here, the change master must allow the client to express emotions in a way that doesn't make them feel guilty or embarrassed. If someone wants to vent or even cry, it may be best to let that happen before moving on.

The change master should be knowledgeable about diversity (e.g., cognitive styles, personality types, sex differences, cultural differences) in order to be effective in this mode. We provide several references at the end of this chapter that will serve as a starting point to establishing this sensitivity and skill.

Case 2B in the Context of Inquiry Mode

Kurt's initial meeting with Frank, the Superintendent of Schools, and Elizabeth's initial meeting with Wayne, the Dean of Engineering, were both situations where the change master had to be an acceptant and active listener. Kurt needed to collect enough information to be able to prepare a scoping proposal and to determine next steps. This is part of the situation appraisal phase of change. Elizabeth's aim was to explore Wayne's position and determine whether he would support Tech moving forward as a participant in the TQM Challenge Partnership.

In later meetings with the Deans of Business and Engineering, and the Provost and President of Bucksburg Tech, Elizabeth again had to be an acceptant listener, moving to active listening only when she felt the Deans weren't obtaining enough information or making the right and necessary decisions to facilitate next steps. Elizabeth had to think through what information and decisions were needed in each early meeting to set the stage to move to next phases of the effort.

Common Difficulties Encountered

If you are, as am I (Scott Sink), a highly dominant, assertive, strong leader, if (like me) your Meyers-Briggs Type Indicator is INTJ (introversion, intuition, thinking, judging), if you are direct and tend to be quick tempered (again, like me), then this mode may be very difficult for you. Strong intuitive types who are also judging tend to rush to conclusions on the basis of their instinct or intuition. As they get more experienced, they begin to trust that instinct and intuition to an even greater extent. They become fast reads and able to appraise a situation very quickly. However, this means that they may cut off active listening prematurely. It may be very difficult for them to inquire. They may seek to judge and evaluate, forming closure prior to truly understanding. They may often be right, but that is irrelevant to the client. The client often seeks to be understood.

Several good books have been written on the male/female dimensions of this mode (Rubin 1983 and Tannen 1990). It is not clear to me that the construct here is male/female as much as it is other dimensions of cognitive style (e.g., how we prefer to collect information and how we prefer to process it) and personality type (Briggs and Myers 1987,

Myers and Myers 1986, and McManus 1983). Nevertheless, we know that there are dimensions of our personalities that may make certain modes more difficult to accommodate than others. Certain actors are better suited for certain roles. The mark of a great actor, as well as a competent change master, is when they can perform outside the realm of a preferred role.

FACT AND DATA GATHERER MODE: DATA COLLECTOR, INFORMATION SYSTEM ENHANCER, MEASUREMENT SYSTEM DESIGNER AND DEVELOPER

Expanded Description

 In this mode, the change master undertakes to: plan experiments, design information, create data collection systems, enhance the measurement system–producing systems, or simply collecting data which the client feels would be useful. The change master assists the client in understanding how to move from measurement, to data, to information. The change master may, for example:

1. Diagram and describe the present system;
2. Survey the attitudes of client people about various issues;
3. Document past performance;
4. Design experiments to contrast the effectiveness of alternative methods or systems;
5. Create data collection logs and other record-keeping forms for the client to use;
6. Teach/educate on the importance of facts and data in problem-solving, teach understanding of variation;
7. Work to enhance measurement systems;
8. Work to enhance the systems aimed at converting data to information.

We distinguish here the function of producing the data from that of interpreting them (i.e., measurement, which creates data, vs. evaluation, which attempts to convert data into information and eventually into decisions and actions). Since the change master often wishes to make the interpretation and conclusion in a collaborative effort with the client, we speak here of the data production mode first and of the information portrayal and perception mode second.

This mode calls on the change master to contribute:

1. Time and effort to get the data, a job the client may have little time for;
2. Skill in the recognition and resolution of measurement problems (e.g., measurement errors, proxy measures);
3. Skill as an experimental designer to create effective information production methods;
4. Skill as a statistician to suggest what messages may be hidden in the data and what inferences can reasonably be made from them.

Change Master Methods Associated with Fact and Data Gatherer Mode

In this mode, the change master is called upon to understand measurement system design, information systems design, the requirements of success of the focal system and what information is required to support managing the system, the relationship between decisions and actions aimed at improving performance, and information to support those decisions and actions. It is impossible to operate in this mode without first understanding what information is required to assist with the task of quality and productivity improvement. If this mode is performed in a vacuum, then the change master runs the risk of perpetuating data rich, information poor (DRIP) organizations.

Understanding methods for measuring and collecting data, how to maintain data collection, and data storage and retrieval is important in this mode. Survey feedback, structured group processes, and instrumentation are all examples of specific methods that may be useful in this mode. Data is gathered in one or more of three ways: (1) ask people in the system for data, (2) observe the system to obtain data, and (3) utilize system documentation and data. Typically, it is wise to use all three approaches when collecting data to support self-awareness and evaluation and to support self-designed change and improvement.

The change master will need to understand how to explore data for meaning, how to perform both exploratory data analysis and confirmatory data analysis. She or he will need to know the differences between data and information. Methods for measurement will need to be understood in the context of methods for evaluation.

Fact and Data Gatherer Mode in Context of Case 2B

The change master's data gatherer mode is directed and focused by the particular methodology being employed. During situation appraisal and catharsis phases of change, the change master is using observation, asking, and system documentation as modes of data gathering. In the case of Kurt's work with the Bucksburg public schools, the Strategic Performance Improvement Planning Process, Step 1, calls for specific data collection regarding trends in performance over time. Kurt and Elizabeth were engaged in individual interviews and small group meetings where data was being gathered during start-up of both projects. Logs were kept from all these meetings, and data collected was reviewed with the OQPC teams working on the projects. Previous plans from both the University and the Public Schools were obtained and studied as a way of understanding what had happened in the past, what had worked, what hadn't worked, and stage of evolution relative to quality and productivity improvement.

The central question is what data was collected and then "fed back" to the clients with the intent of facilitating progress through future phases of change (awareness, evaluation, self-design, and trying out new behaviors)? In this regard, particularly in the University, there was not enough work done in this respect.

In the case of the Public Schools, the planning process called for a thorough and comprehensive "state of the school system" overview. The Superintendent and his staff did an excellent job presenting data to prepare the planning team to build a good plan for improvement. The problem encountered was that certain members of the planning team were compelled to jump from measurement and data to evaluation and actions. Kurt had to keep reminding them of the purpose of Step 1, Organizational Systems Analysis, and the sub-step focusing on current and past performance levels. Kurt had to become almost challenging to get them to inquire from the data presented rather than advocate and jump to conclusions and actions. This is a common difficulty that the change master will have to manage.

Common Difficulties Encountered

Different disciplines and different types (cognitive style and personality) of people acquire preferences for data collection methods. Learning to use a more complete spectrum of data collection methods is a common difficulty. For example, an industrial psychologist may have acquired a preference for "asking" as a way of collecting data. An industrial engineer may have acquired a preference for "observing." An accountant may have acquired a "system documentation" preference. None are wrong; they will, however, probably be incomplete. The same can be said for methods of data-to-information conversion. Strong intuitive types with considerable experience in the system will tend to leap from data to actions. Those who are stronger at sensing, thinking, and perceiving will tend to be more cautious in moving from data to actions. Those well versed in statistics and understanding variation will be less subject to classic errors in interpretation (e.g., special cause versus common cause, tampering, cyclical variation).

Data gathering is tedious, attention-to-detail type work. It requires that the change master be able to "zoom in," focus, converge, and then quickly "zoom out," see the big picture, diverge. A change master as data collector has to be consistent at keeping the forest in mind even when working among the trees.

It is easy to begin a data collection hunt. It is harder to plan and be reflective about what data are needed to support improvement. Data gathering has to be done in the context of decisions, actions, and required information. Data gathering should be system and user/customer driven.

COLLABORATOR MODE: TEAM MEMBER

Expanded Description

In this mode, the change master becomes a member of a task force or project team and may serve in various roles, such as leader, organizer, meeting manager, agenda builder, facilitator, technical resource, or the person responsible for support, leg work, continuity, and reporting. In sum, the change master serves to help in whatever capacity is necessary and appropriate. The change master seeks, while acting as a team member, to involve others in such a way that they form a commitment to the team output as a result of satisfying participation. Without dominating the team, the change master:

- Works toward problem definition;
- Helps the team clarify its function;
- Suggests next steps;
- Challenges, evaluates, listens;
- Poses alternatives for group decision;
- Records, reports, builds the team's agenda;
- Makes major technical contributions.

In many situations, the change master acting as team member is the basic element of the change process design. It is perhaps the most widely accepted and used mode for large problems and changes of some complexity. Often, this role evolves from other roles during a large-scale and long-term change/improvement effort. Evolving from other roles/modes to this one can be a challenge in and of itself.

Change Master Methods Associated with Collaborator, Team Member

Perhaps the most important method is that of being a situational team player. Understanding the necessary roles for healthy groups and teams to have fulfilled is important so that the change master can, working with the group leader, make sure key roles are not unfulfilled. Group process observation thus becomes a method to be applied. This requires the simultaneous ability to stay up with content of the meeting or situation while at the same time maintaining process awareness.

Understanding what it means to be a good follower will also be important in this mode. Again, good followership means playing roles that are not fulfilled, bringing your special talents and skills to the group, and working with the group leader to build teamwork necessary for success with the improvement project.

Collaborator Mode in the Context of Case 2B

Once the infrastructure for both efforts was solidly established, this mode became more predominant for Kurt and Elizabeth. Kurt, while being a member of the public schools' design team, worked to develop collective and individual knowledge and skills for that team. He also worked hard to move the team into the self-designed change phase, building ownership and understanding for how to implement and deploy their strategic plan while integrating principles and methods of total quality.

Elizabeth got Tech's University Challenge effort past start-up, got the Steering Committee firmly established and to the perform stage, then passed the baton to another member of the Steering Committee. However, Elizabeth remained a member of the Steering Committee, switching modes when appropriate with that group, this time from a team member position rather than a lead change master position.

Common Difficulties Encountered

Change masters may most often find themselves in a leadership position (e.g., guiding a meeting, leading a discussion). Being able to fall back into a more reflective, follower role may be difficult. I find that I have to concentrate on taking notes, writing down what I would (am tempted) to say or do in order to switch from active leadership to more passive followership.

Diagnosing unfulfilled roles is a skill that takes practice. First, it is necessary to have a firm understanding of the research on small group behavior. This allows the change master to stand back from behaviors in meetings and understand them in the context of theory. Helping groups and teams get unstuck is an almost endless task and is mentally fatiguing, but it is also highly rewarding when the change master begins to see evidence of self-management on the part of the team.

STRUCTURE PROVIDER MODE: STRUCTURED GROUP PROCESS PROVIDER, AGENDA BUILDING, STRATEGY PROVIDER, METHOD PROVIDER

Expanded Description

Participation by clients in the change process often takes place in small groups, and it is of considerable importance that the change master design the methods by which these groups operate effectively. The change master designs and brings to the group a process for accomplishing its tasks. The change master, then, serves as a facilitator, coordinator, or process consultant. Facilitating a brainstorming group is a familiar example.

Research and design of structured group processes have come a long way since brainstorming, however. For example, the Nominal Group Technique(NGT), extensively utilized by change masters, involves a series of steps which include:

1. Presentation of a problem or task by the change master;
2. Silent, individual generation of solutions;
3. Sharing and listing of the solutions;
4. Clarification of the solutions;
5. Voting to evaluate the solutions.

For more information on NGT, see the Plan of Study section at the end of this section.

Groups are used in change process design for several reasons:

1. Groups bring together knowledge and skills not possessed by an individual.
2. The product of a group is more likely to be accepted by those who must act on it than is the product of an individual.
3. If the members of the group must themselves act on the basis of their group efforts, not only are they more likely to accept the group's findings, but they are also likely to be more effective and productive in the ensuing actions.
4. There is a "group effect" through which group members learn from each other, stimulate each other, and supplement each other's knowledge and skills. The product of the group is thus in a sense greater than the sum of the individual contributions.

In the experience of many managers, the validity of these reasons is such as to make participative strategies appealing. Group processes, however, are not without their shortcomings. These group process losses make participative strategies involving unstructured groups expensive and, at times, seriously ineffective.

The structured group process approach gives the change master a low-profile role as a provider of methodology or strategy rather than as a substantive resource for the group. In this approach, however, there is little that is casual or unplanned about the group process. It typically consists of a set of clear, well-defined activities which the participants are asked to undertake at specific times. Structured group processes suggest themselves, for although they are among the newest professional modes to be explicitly recognized, there is considerable evidence to testify to their effectiveness. They have the virtues of being:

- Robust, user-proof;
- Teachable;
- Efficient and effective;
- Highly rewarding and satisfying to the client participants.

Structured group processes have found a variety of important applications in change process design:

- Planning
- Forecasting
- Value clarification
- Goal setting, prioritizing
- Ideation and evaluation
- Alternative generation
- Catharsis

- Consensus reaching
- Information gathering
- Information and opinion exchange
- Measurement
- Community building
- Grand Strategy development
- Guiding Principle development

Change Master Methods Associated with Structure Provider Mode

Knowledge of small-group behavior research and literature is necessary for the change master to fully operationalize this mode. Reference material for associated techniques and for small group behavior knowledge can be found at the end of the section.

A method for learning how to facilitate a technique such as the Nominal Group Technique is as follows: (1) read about the technique and small-group theory in the references included at the end of this chapter, (2) participate in an NGT session (training or otherwise) led by a skilled facilitator who will explain the basic technique as he or she is doing it and point out any modifications or variations that are being made (make sure you understand the pure model), (3) create or take advantage of an opportunity to lead an NGT session, planning carefully and doing a post-session assessment of what worked and what didn't, (4) practice, practice, practice.

Structure Provider Mode in the Context of Case 2B

In the case of the public school system in Bucksburg, Kurt conducted a modified Nominal Group Technique at the strategic planning session. It was used for Steps 2 and 3 of the Strategic Performance Improvement Planning Process. It created consensus on the highest priority performance improvement objectives for the school system. This technique was not used to develop a mission or vision because it didn't fit the task. However, a very simplified and modified NGT was used in a subset group to develop guiding principles for the school system. Kurt employed multivoting, several rounds of voting to attempt to ensure stronger consensus, since the planning team for the public schools was heterogeneous.

Structured group processes were used only informally in the University Challenge effort. Agenda building, meeting management, and strategy mapping for multiple sequential meetings were the basic methods employed in this effort. The Challenge partnership did involve several very large sessions that were structured by agenda, learning objectives, exercises, etc. Structure in large improvement efforts such as these two (the university and the public schools) is crucial to progress.

Common Difficulties Encountered

It seems that many people get stuck knowing when to use this mode and techniques within the mode. Developing the skills to run an NGT, for example, seems more difficult for some than others. The clarification step requires patience, thinking on your feet, logic skills, diplomacy, knowing when to cut off discussion, etc. This step, in particular, is the most complex and difficult of all the steps in the NGT. By contrast, the Delphi Technique, which just moves information and not people, does not require as much behavioral skill, since the change master is basically just a survey designer and implementer. Providing some structure to group meetings as an informal, "armchair" facilitator may require the most art and skill, since there is less technique and simply application of knowledge of group behavior to help a group move forward.

Structured group techniques are used when the change master wants to shape group consensus, convergence, and focus, and when there is a task that is appropriate for a particular technique. They are not particularly appropriate when dealing with too large or too small a group or when dealing with ambiguity, a perplexity, premature convergence, or a multifaceted problem requiring many stages of consensus.

TEACHER MODE: EDUCATOR, KNOWLEDGE AND SKILL DEVELOPER, MENTOR, COACH, COUNSELOR, TRAINER

Expanded Description

 As mentioned earlier, the industrial engineering profession is evolving from one of "doing" methods engineering and process improvement to one of teaching people the techniques with which to improve their own work methods, processes, and systems. Change masters in general are finding the mode of educating and training to be a significant portion of their responsibilities. There is a more recent history of the effective approach to engineering economic analysis, quality control, and cost reduction through teaching client personnel the necessary methods rather than by having the change master carry out the projects. Indeed, industrial engineering change masters have been involved in teaching clients everything from basic management to risk analysis, short interval scheduling, and how to improve the maintenance function.

The change master in the teaching mode should not be seen only in the role of traditional classroom instructor. In fact, this mode will be most effectively viewed in the context of on-the-job, individualized, just-in-time, informal instruction. We have long known that adults learn best when they have a need to know and are coached and counseled in the knowledge and skills necessary to solve problems. Many adults have little tolerance for theories and concepts, yet, as Dr. Deming said, examples in the absence of theory are useless. Therefore, the challenge to the change master is how to make education, training, and development palatable and effective, how to synthesize what we feel and think the people involved in improvement need to know to be successful.

A major theme of this book is that the change master has to be technically competent and well versed to be effective in this mode. The change master cannot broker everything and maintain credibility.

Teaching people to diagnose problems and design and test new methods is done in all sorts of both obvious and subtle ways to enhance the effectiveness of change processes. Teaching and skill development fit in when:

1. It is useful to build client competence to deal with problems rather than to continue to rely on the change master or their staff, especially when the client seeks this self-reliance.
2. The techniques involved can be taught effectively and applied widely throughout the

client organization, as is the case with most of the tools of quality and productivity improvement.
3. Clients can free themselves from immediate pressures to deal with problems.
4. Clients can effectively adapt general techniques and methods to the specific aspects of their own jobs and situations.
5. There is sponsor support for pushing the education, training, and development front, there is a desire to become a learning organization on the part of top management, and they back up that desire with resources.

The special nature of the teaching done by the change master distinguishes it from conventional classroom instruction. The primary objectives are for the client to:

1. Master a specific method or technique;
2. See some real examples of uses of the specific method or technique, both to build confidence in its usefulness and to suggest the variety of its possible adaptations and applications;
3. Have an opportunity to test his or her own mastery of the method in a situation where failure is without cost;
4. Make some specific plans for adapting the methods in his or her own potential application.

Change Master Methods Associated with Teacher Mode

The change master needs to develop knowledge relative to theory and methods of learning. We provide references at the end of this chapter to assist you in learning more about learning. Specifically, the change master must understand the five levels of knowledge and how they work together: (1) theory, concepts, principles; (2) operational definitions; (3) methods; (4) skills; and (5) profound. He or she must know how to integrate learning into the change process at the appropriate time and in the appropriate fashion.

Specific questions the change master as teacher must address include:

• Who has to gain certain knowledge and skills for this improvement effort to succeed?
• When do they need specific knowledge and skills?
• How can we best help them acquire what they need to know to move forward?
• How do we move back and forth between levels of knowledge 1, 2, 3, and 4 to ensure they truly acquire the knowledge and skills to succeed with this improvement project and with others in the future?
• How does the change master acquire Level 5 knowledge and then apply it to help the client succeed with this improvement effort?
• What is the difference between education, training, and development?

To be effective as a teacher and skill developer will require the change master to understand how to develop and deliver good presentations and written summaries. Communication skills are crucial: There is a science to communication, and the change master must be exposed to this in the context of education and training. Storyboarding presentations, papers, and handout materials is an important method to practice and develop. Storyboarding develops the skills of logic and orderly, efficient presentations.

Designing and developing off-site sessions, workshops, and training sessions (one to five days in length) using the agenda-building process described in a later chapter and alluded to earlier also is important. Developing the ability to integrate or synthesize learning materials into work sessions associated with improvement projects is a key skill as well.

The change master must be able to educate, train, and develop "on the fly," in a serendipitous fashion. If a team is working on some aspect of an improvement project and the change master sees they need a lesson on cause-and-effect diagrams, then she or he must be able to teach cause-and-effect diagrams on the spot, with the intent of moving the team from Level 1 to Level 4 quickly.

Expand this example to the full spectrum of group situations in which the participants aren't employing a tool, technique, or method that would help them move forward. They might not be employing a specific tool because they aren't aware of it; this creates one type of educational intervention. They might not be employing a specific tool because they haven't developed the skill to diagnose when to use which tools; yet another educational intervention is required. They might not be employing a specific tool because they haven't developed Level 4 knowledge; they know the tool exists, sense it might help, but no one is confident enough to suggest the group use it and to lead its use. The change master will be confronted with a tremendous range of situations with respect to a reasonably predictable set of tools of improvement. We can predict the tools, suggest ways for the change master to move to at least Level 3 with respect to the tools, provide ample additional references and resources to support change master development, but we cannot actually move you to Level 5 with the spectrum of technologies of improvement or even with one. You must move yourself through the phases of change to accomplish this.

Teacher Mode in the Context of Case 2B

Elizabeth and Kurt were forced to think through carefully what they did and how they did it with respect to educational interventions in these particular settings. Educators and administrators in educational systems, as might be expected, have perhaps even less tolerance for being lectured to than do most adults. The change masters were forced to concentrate on very short, effective educational interventions that made the appropriate point in the context of the application.

Although there is a growing level of awareness about total quality and productivity improvement in this sector, there still is widespread lack of knowledge about certain fundamentals. For example, in the private sector and in areas in the defense community, reference to Dr. Deming's fourteen points is commonplace. Juran and Deming are household names. In education, this is still not the case. So, TQM had to be boiled down to a short overview that was presented in a way that broke down resistance rather than built it up. Bob, the Business College professor, had done an excellent job at this with the top management team at Bucksburg Tech. Kurt had to do this with the planning team for the Bucksburg Public Schools.

One approach that OQPC had tried with some degree of success was to ask their audiences what they thought the components of total quality and continuous improvement included. The OQPC change masters had found that, surprisingly, groups typically were able to list most of the principles and elements of TQ. The change masters would then fill in any omissions (this requires profound knowledge and the ability to think on one's feet). Once this was done and the groups could see what "the transformation" means in toto, the change master would then get the participants to do a simple "start, stop, continue" exercise (McManus 1992): On the basis of what they said TQ/CI involves and means, what would they do individually and as a group to improve?

We provide this little scenario to trigger thinking outside the box on how one does education and training. The traditional alternative to this approach would be to develop a "TQM 101" presentation and then do a canned pitch. We're suggesting that this didn't and probably can't work in the setting Kurt and Elizabeth were in or with the people with whom they were working. The nontraditional alternative is to ask leading questions and then teach from their responses — teaching the client what they need to know and what they appear not to know, as opposed to what they already know and may have internalized. This approach is more difficult but often much more effective.

This is how Kurt and Elizabeth approached the teacher and skill developer mode in these two educational settings. They had modules of overheads on given subjects they felt were appropriate at any given point in time. They "pulled" overheads or handout material as appropriate and as the situation presented itself. They kept track of what had been done with whom to avoid repetition. They pushed certain methods, tools, and techniques as they felt appropriate, then did on the spot training, just enough to apply the tool. Kurt and Elizabeth used pre-work assignments and reading liberally as a way of continuing to get their groups to think about what they were trying to do and to spark desire to learn more about improvement. They planned what handouts to provide at various stages of the efforts as a way of increasing common language and common understanding. Their strategies for education and training were different for the design and development teams, the sponsors, the champions, the targets, the improvement teams, the internal coordinators, and the change masters. The different needs and roles of these various individuals and groups had to be thought through carefully.

Common Difficulties Encountered

Becoming an effective teacher, skill developer, and change master requires you to be a continual learner, ever expanding your knowledge base with respect to quality and productivity improvement. We've already covered the five levels of knowledge. There also are some guidelines about how people learn. As we progress toward profound knowledge in a given dimension, we remember (Glasser 1990):

- 10% of what we read;
- 20% of what we hear;
- 30% of what we see;
- 50% of what we both see and hear;
- 70% of what we discuss with others;
- 80% of what we experience personally;
- 95% of what we teach to someone else.

It is harder to teach right than to teach wrong. It is easy to fall into traditional, sloppy, ineffective modes of education, training, and development. This is why there is an old saying suggesting that perhaps "the most unprofessional profession is the profession of being a professor." This statement was made because many who teach in higher education never took a course in learning or in teaching adults. They have mimicked the behaviors of those who taught them. It is worker training worker, as Dr. Deming would say.

EXPERT MODE: CONSULTANT, SOLUTION PROVIDER

Expanded Description

 This is the traditional image for most professionals in the position of change master — the technical expert, taking responsibility for the targeting, diagnosis, solution, and perhaps the implementation of the expert-produced solution to the client's problem. The change master acting as expert must depend on the client's acceptance of his or her high level of technical knowledge, broad experience, and special intellectual skill. This is the professional mode that is implied in most industrial engineering education, as well as that of other professions engaged in change mastering.

The process is usually represented as: Define the problem → Build the model and collect the data → Obtain the optimal solution →"Sell" the solution to the client. This stance, this self-image, comes very naturally to many in the field of change mastering, whose training has placed great emphasis on the tools, techniques, methods, and models that are the technical core of a profession or discipline.

In thinking about this mode of professional functioning, it is useful to distinguish between:

• the *expert only change process*, in which virtually all of the change master relations with the client are characterized by the change master in the role of expert;
• the *expert mode in the context of a change process*, in which the change master makes significant scientific and technical contributions but does so in the context of other modes of professional functioning.

In attempting to rely on the expert mode, the change master usually listens to what the client has to say about the problem and then conducts an independent investigation to determine the nature of the "real" problem. Once the diagnosis is complete, the change master proceeds to collect and analyze data, create models, do surveys, impose personal paradigms of "the one best way," and so on. The change master tries to function like a physician diagnosing an illness and prescribing a cure. The result is recommended (and perhaps "sold") to the client, carrying the weight of the change master's reputation, experience, and expertise.

This *expert only change process* presumes that:

1. The change master is capable of assembling the data and the insights needed to solve the problem.
2. The client is without the time, skills, or situational knowledge to contribute to the development of improvements.
3. The client respects the expertise of the change master and is prepared to accept the recommended changes.

The *expert only change process* is typically used under conditions such as the following:

- The problem is very complex.
- Time is short; a quick fix is needed.
- The client is frustrated and gives up.
- The client feels ineffective and helpless.
- A high-quality solution is needed.
- There is not a great need for wide acceptance of the solution; it can be imposed.

Using the *expert mode in the context of change processes* involves other professional functions to bring the client toward self-awareness and self-designed change and rests on different presumptions:

1. The change master has a central role in the development of new methods and systems by virtue of education and training, experience, and skill in a variety of improvement techniques.
2. By embedding it in a collaborative process with the client, this expertise can be utilized in ways which maximize the probability of improvement actually occurring.
3. The change master's expert contribution works most effectively when the client sees the need for it in the context of a client-directed change process.

Change Master Methods Associated with Expert Mode

The tool kit of the change master is eminent in this mode. The ability to prescribe in a wide range of situations is key, just as a general practitioner must have a wide range of knowledge about diseases and disorders. Typically, a consultant is called in as a specialist to focus on a given domain of problems or opportunities. However, a change master often is confronted with "a mess." The situation is often not as well focused as one the typical consultant faces. The change master must be able to sort through the mess and focus on specific problems or opportunities.

This mode of professional functioning then, as discussed in more detail in Chapters 8 and 11, often requires knowledge and skill in the following areas:

- Planning;
- Project management;
- Problem solving and decision making;
- Motivation;
- Financial analysis;
- Methods engineering, business process re-engineering;
- Measurement.

Expert Mode in the Context of Case 2B

Once Kurt completed the initial situation appraisal with the public schools, he, with the assistance of others in the OQPC, had to craft a proposal. Similarly, Elizabeth led the writing of Bucksburg Tech's University Challenge proposal. The development of these proposals required the integration of prescriptions and technical competencies in such areas as TQM, strategic planning, and management of change. In a sense, proposals reflect the change master inserting strategy and solutions into the change process. Strategies are revealed, decisions and actions are implied, and these, of course, have to be sold to the client.

In the case of the public schools, first the Superintendent and his executive cabinet had to be sold. Then his Board had to be sold and budget implications thought through. In the case of the University, the Deans had to be convinced that the proposal for proceeding was reflective of their level of sponsorship and commitment. They had to sign the cover page. Then they had to obtain signatures by the President and the Provost. Signatures represent a level of commitment to do what the proposal spells out.

The solutions revealed in the proposals reflect the change masters biases, experience, and beliefs in cause-and-effect relationships. They represent the change master articulating expert, solution provider behaviors in words. The change master often has to defend (respond with advocacy not inquiry) his or her proposal. It may be impossible to avoid this role in the proposal development and submission process. The difficulty lies in getting the client to understand the notion of "living plan." The change master may need to provide solutions in the way of strategies and then get the client to understand that the specifics of the strategies are what must be thrashed through with the constituents in the system. This occurred in both scenarios in the case example.

Common Difficulties Encountered

As mentioned, this is the most common mode in the field of consulting. Knowledgeable people, particularly in a specific field, will find this to be the most comfortable and natural of modes. As mentioned earlier, the traditional role of the industrial engineer was to do industrial engineering. This has changed in recent years. The need and requirement is now for the industrial engineer to train others to be industrial engineers. This has forced the industrial engineer out of the expert mode and into the teacher, skill developer mode. Unfortunately, many have been unable to make the transition. The saying that "Those who can, do and those who can't, teach" is obsolete. Those who can do performance improvement must teach this to others while maintaining their skills at doing. The change master must maintain this mode while at the same time developing the teacher, skill developer mode. This is the challenge of the '90s and beyond.

Maintaining technical competence in a wide range of areas is a challenge. In Chapter 12 we discuss how you can develop your own personal and professional plan of study and development for acquiring more knowledge in various technology and method areas. Learning is a never-ending process for the change master.

CHALLENGER MODE: HONEST BROKER, CRITIC, "RED TEAM," JUDGER/EVALUATOR

Expanded Description

In this mode the change master seeks to:

1. Force the client toward evaluation of past practices and existing methods;
2. Confront the client with comparisons, standards, and goals with which the client may make self-evaluations (benchmarking);
3. Confront the client with data, surveys, audits, and attitudes which suggest that all is not well;
4. Suggest to the client the order of magnitude of improvements which might be expected if the client would become involved in a change process

5. Force the client to clarify goals, objectives, underlying assumptions, and things taken for granted
6. Stimulate the client to justify, explain, and examine existing methods and systems and keep asking, "Why do we do this?" "Why do we do it this way?"
7. Draw the client's attention to evidence which suggests opportunities for effective change
8. Encourage the client to be open to change, not threatened by it, and to consider alternatives
9. Challenge to spark intellectual honesty, play devil's advocate, play the role of critic
10. Use a "red team," a group of external experts who are brought in by the change master to critique and evaluate the need for improvement and positive change or a plan for improvement
11. Create and manage conflict as a way of forcing catharsis, sparking thinking outside the box, forcing dissatisfaction with the status quo, creating a challenging vision, forcing discipline, or forcing the client to "pay the price" of improvement.

This mode is usually considered a high-risk one, for it involves basic difficulties:

• Challenge may be interpreted as threatening or critical and be resented and rejected.
• Challenge may cause a negative client reaction since it appears to give the initiative to the change master, tending to remove the process of change from the client's control.
• Challenge may cause "transference" on the part of the client. The client may transfer the conflict or dissonance created by challenge to the change master. The downside risk is that the change master is rendered completely ineffective due to the negative affect created by the challenging strategy. Change masters with a style that is comfortable with challenge may need to be leery of overusing this mode.

The mode of challenger typically is selected when:

• The client is unwilling to devote time and resources to change.
• The problem is very low on the client's agenda.
• The client feels powerless and ineffective.
• A dramatic, "hard-sell" approach to change is warranted.

In certain cases, the challenger mode represents a last ditch effort on the part of the change master to salvage positive change. I have personally been helped to understand how to use this mode effectively through the works of M. Scott Peck.

Change Master Methods Associated with Challenger Mode
There exists a wide range of challenging behaviors and styles. What we say, when we say it, how we say it, intonation, and body language all play a part in the challenger mode. Certain questions can be asked in a nonchallenging way and still challenge. There is a difference between challenging and threatening or putting on the defensive. It certainly may be a fine line, and there may be times when the change master wants or needs to cross over the line.

Often, challenging is an act. The change master is playing a role that only he or she can play and is trying to evoke some behavior or emotion in a given situation. The change master must learn to be a challenger. It is clear, however, that each change master will challenge a little differently. That's okay, as long as it gets the job done. A change master who is unable or unwilling to challenge when appropriate will fail in the long run, in my opinion. The world of quality and productivity improvement is filled with conflicts not confronted and managed, concerns and fears unspoken, trust untested, and barriers not broken down. These roadblocks to improvement must be confronted and challenging is often the only way to do that.

Challenger Mode in the Context of Case 2B

Challenging with the school system came at several points. Kurt had learned well from his experience with the Bucksburg 2000 initiative, and although he still wasn't comfortable in the challenger mode, he knew it was far better to risk temporary discomfort than ultimate project failure. Early in his work with the public schools, Kurt challenged Frank the Superintendent regarding resource allocation to the project. Kurt defined the requirements of success and then attempted to get Frank and his leadership team to clearly understand the amount of effort and commitment that was going to be needed from them. During the planning session itself, Kurt challenged the planning team in various ways on vision, on need for change, on method, and on their role in the overall effort.

In the case of the University Challenge effort at Bucksburg Tech, challenging was much more subtle. As director of the OQPC, Elizabeth was an internal change master, so her bases of power shifted substantially. She had to finesse challenging much more in this context than when she played the role of an external change agent.

Although it didn't involve Elizabeth, a critical incident did occur during the University Challenge training session that represents the challenger mode. Tech's President, Provost, and Chief Financial Officer had committed to attend most of the four-day workshop as a show of support for this improvement effort. During lunch on the first day of the session, Jay, the Westin coordinator, learned that the top leadership of the University would not be attending the banquet that evening, during which a very important external speaker would deliver the session's keynote address. Jay directly challenged the President, Provost, and CFO on this, suggesting that if they did not attend that evening, he would call the dinner speaker and tell him not to travel to Bucksburg. This didn't make Jay very popular with the top leadership of the university. But Jay believed that the top leadership's attendance at the capstone dinner was a crucial symbol of their support. As a change master, Jay was willing to sacrifice being "liked" to get the job done. He could have played acceptant and compromised on the situation, but he chose not to.

Common Difficulties Encountered

Challenging can place the change master in a role of "bad guy" as opposed to "good guy." Clients typically look for support and encouragement; however, challenging often places the change master in a situation that may be perceived as, "I'm OK, you're not OK." It's the same dilemma an advisor has with an advisee, that of balancing encouragement and nurturing while at the same time being a critic, challenger, and prodder. The solution is to separate sessions in which you are challenging from the sessions in which you are being the counselor, the developer, the coach, the mentor, the supporter. Making sure the client knows what "hat" you are wearing is central to this working. If the client confuses "role" with "self," then the change master can, in fact, become the "bad guy" and effectiveness in other modes will be at risk.

As mentioned, certain personality types are more predisposed to this mode than others. They may overuse and abuse the mode, while others will underuse the mode. Certain situations may prompt abuse of the mode. If the change master is tired, on edge, loaded with too much caffeine, etc. he or she may revert to a preferred mode and slip out of planned acting. If the preferred mode is inappropriate or inappropriately delivered it can jeopardize the success of the phase.

CONCLUSION

It is not common for professionals engaged in quality and productivity improvement to be aware of professional modes of functioning. Most tend to develop a style of behavior and interaction with client people and simply lock into that style. They exhibit some variation in style and behaviors depending on the situation, but it is not common that this is a planned or systematic effort. What is being suggested here is that the change master consider these seven modes of functioning in the context of their specific and individual styles. Think about these modes of functioning in the context of your efforts to help individuals, groups and organizations improve quality and productivity. The hypothesis, of course, is that there are certain modes that have a higher probability of supporting positive change in given situations. To be even more specific, there are mode and phase combinations that are likely to be required or experienced as you attempt to implement and deploy improvement efforts. The more you, the change master, become familiar and comfortable with these mode and phase associations, the more effective you will be. The next section examines this notion of mode and phase combinations in detail.

DEVELOPMENT WORK

INQUIRY QUESTIONS

These are questions you have for yourself or for others to help you better understand what was covered in this section.

Inquire First

What didn't you understand, what do you want to know about, what assumptions or beliefs do we posit that you want us to explain, what do you want clarification on?

Advocate Second

What did you disagree with, what do you want to argue about, what didn't you like, what do you want to challenge, in what areas do we appear to have different assumptions, data bases, beliefs, or attitudes?

LEARNING EXERCISES

LE 3.1 Rank the various modes of professional functioning in order of:
   A.   Increasing substantive professional involvement of the change master;
   B.   Assertiveness and directiveness on the part of the change master;

C. Appropriateness for a client who is eager for improvement;

D. Appropriateness for a client who is not ready for improvement and is resisting the whole idea;

E. Appropriateness for a client who is willing but not able, not past the false learning curve;

F. Appropriateness for a client who has enlightened and championing leadership but inadequate internal change masters.

LE 3.2 Enhance the list of professional modes of functioning.

LE 3.3 Evaluate your knowledge and skills relative to each professional mode of functioning. What are your preferences for modes? Why? Which modes are most difficult for you? Why? Evaluate your use of modes in the context of information you have relative to your cognitive style and your personality style.

LE 3.4 The three-ball problem suggests that a change master needs to handle at least three tasks in quality and productivity improvement efforts: (1) solve the focal problem, (2) do traditional project management and allocation of resources, and (3) manage implementation and deployment effectiveness. We have now addressed phases of change clients pass through in improvement efforts and professional modes of functioning. If you put these two concepts together in the context of the third ball, what do you have?

LE 3.5 Consider an improvement effort you have experienced or read about. Think about the change agent behavior in that effort. How did it vary over time? Was it planned out, thought through? Did it appear there was a strategy for how to behave and when to exhibit different behaviors? Do the change masters you know seem to be reflective and conscious about their behaviors and how they affect improvement efforts? How might the concept of professional modes of functioning help change masters become more purposeful and effective in their efforts? How would you design a change effort aimed at getting change masters or yourself to adopt a more conscious strategy of behaviors in improvement efforts?

LE 3.6 There is an acting aspect to professional mode of functioning adoption. Our "self" is who we are and how we behave when we are just being ourselves; we aren't overly conscious of how we are behaving, we just are ourselves. Our "role" is how we behave on the job. Often our "role" is more formal, more conscious, than our "self." Professional modes of functioning is about increasing the range of behaviors we can exhibit in "role." As you have discovered, some professional modes of functioning are more natural and preferred than others. Developing professional mode of functioning flexibility and range requires willingness to practice other roles. Practice in a low threat, low risk environment the key professional modes of functioning that are not natural and common to you. How did you feel doing this? As you practiced them more, did they become more natural? Did you have difficulty operationalizing them at first? Did the audience detect your awkwardness, or were you able to disguise it? Can you deal with the anxiety of behaving in other roles long enough to get to a comfort level with these new roles?

FEEDBACK QUESTIONS

FBQ 3.1 What professional mode or modes do the following types of professions tend to use most?

- Teachers
- Doctors
- Accountants
- Adminstrators
- Vice-presidents
- Presidents
- Executive directors
- High ranking military officers
- Staff personnel
- Support staff
- Industrial engineers, industrial psychologists and sociologists
- Consultants
- Spouses, your spouse
- Parents
- Your children or your students.

We know there is variability. If you separate your analysis, looking at those people in positions or roles listed above who are more successful in comparison to those who are less successful, do you see a trend in terms of professional modes of functioning flexibility and range? What would your conclusion be? What are the situational and temporal factors that cause professional mode of functioning appropriateness to change?

FBQ 3.2 Operationally define the following:

- Professional mode of functioning
- Acting
- Role
- Self
- Situational leadership
- Contingency, contingency theory
- Leadership
- Change master
- Mentor, protege
- Intellectual honesty
- Technical competence
- Content versus process.

PLAN OF STUDY DEVELOPMENT

What follows is a list of resources that support, in general, the material introduced in this section. Scan the list, indicate which you have read (R), studied (S), attempted to use (U), and which you would like to become acquainted with (TBD).

LITERATURE CITED

Belasco, J. A. 1990. *Teaching the Elephant to Dance*. New York: Crown Publishers.

Belasco, J. A., and R. C. Stayer. 1993. *Flight of the Buffalo: Soaring to Excellence, Learning to Let Employees Lead*. New York: Warner Books.

Bennis, W., and B. Nannus. 1985. *Leaders*. New York: Harper and Row.

Briggs, K. C., and I. B. Myers. 1987. *Myers-Briggs Type Indicator*. Form G. Palo Alto, Calif.: Consulting Psychologists Press.

Covey, S. 1989. *Seven Habits of Highly Effective People*. New York: Simon and Schuster.

Covey, S. 1991. *Principle Centered Leadership*. New York: SummitBooks.

Covey, S. R., A. R. Merrill, and R. R. Merrill. 1994. *First Things First*. New York: Simon and Schuster.

Glasser, W. 1990. *The Quality School*. New York: Harper Perennial.

Hersey, P. 1984. *The Situational Leader*. New York: Warner Books.

McManus, L. F. 1983. *Self-Perception: A Profile Analysis*. Worcester, Mass.: L. F. McManus Co.

Myers, I. B., and P. B. Myers. 1986. *Gifts Differing* (9th edn.). Palo Alto, CA: Consulting Psychologists Press.

Peck, M. S. 1978. *The Road Less Traveled*. New York: Simon and Schuster.

Peck, M. S. 1993. *A World Waiting to be Born: Civility Rediscovered*. New York: Bantam Books.

Rubin, L. B. 1983. *Intimate Strangers: Men and Women Together*. New York: Harper & Row.

Scholtes, P. R. 1988. *The Team Handbook*. Madison, Wis.: Joiner Assoc.

Sink, D. S. 1983. Using the nominal group technique effectively. *National Productivity Review*. Spring: 173-184.

Sink, D. S., and T. C. Tuttle. 1989. *Planning and Measurement in Your Organization of the Future*. Norcross, Ga.: Industrial Engineering and Management Press.

Tannen, D. 1990. *You Just Don't Understand*. New York: Ballantine Books.

Thomas, K. W., and R. H. Kilmann. 1974. *Thomas-Kilmann Conflict Mode Instrument*. Tuxedo, N.Y.: XICOM.

Westinghouse Corporate Productivity and Quality. 1993. University Challenge Partnership with Virginia Tech. WesTIP® Workshop, Aug. 15-19, Blacksburg, Va.

Weisbord, M. R. 1991. *Productive Workplaces: Organizing for Dignity, Meaning, and Community*. San Francisco: Jossey-Bass.

Weisbord, M. R. (ed.). 1992. *Discovering Common Ground: How Future Search Conferences Bring People Together to Achieve Breakthrough Innovation, Empowerment, Shared Vision, and Collaborative Action*. San Francisco: Berrett-Koehler.

BIBLIOGRAPHY

Argyris, C. 1970. *Intervention Theory and Method: A Behavioral Science View*. Reading, Mass.: Addison-Wesley.

Blake, R. R., and J. S. Mouton. 1976. *Consultation*. Reading, Pa.: Addison-Wesley.

Block, P. 1978. *Flawless Consulting*. San Diego: Pfeiffer & Co.

Bobbitt, H. R., R. H. Breinholt, R. H. Doktor, and J. P. McNaul. 1974. *Organizational Behavior Understanding and Prediction*. Englewood Cliffs, N.J.: Prentice-Hall.

Corey, M. S., and G. Corey. 1993. *Becoming a Helper* (2nd edn.). Pacific Grove, Calif.: Brooks/Cole.

Kanter, R. M. 1983. *The Change Masters*. New York: Simon and Schuster.

Kennedy, E. 1992. *On Becoming a Counselor: A Basic Guide for Non-Professional Counselors*. New York: Crossroad Pub.

Margulies, N., and A. P. Raia. 1972. *Organizational Development; Values, Process, and Technology*. New York: McGraw-Hill.

Schon, D. 1983. *The Reflective Practitioner: How Professionals Think in Action*. New York: Basic Books.

Skovholt, T. M., and M. H. Ronnestad. 1992. *The Evolving Professional Self: Stages and Themes in Therapist and Counselor Development*. New York: John Wiley.

Tichy, N., and M. Devanna. 1987. *The Transformational Leader*. New York: John Wiley.

Walton, R. E. 1969. *Interpersonal Peacemaking: Confrontations and Third Party Consultation*. Reading, Mass.: Addison-Wesley.

INTEGRATING PHASES OF CHANGE AND MODES OF PROFESSIONAL FUNCTIONING WITH METHODS OF IMPROVEMENT

Simply stated, the basic question of change process design is: *Which modes of professional functioning should be used for each phase of client change to maximize the probability that improvement will occur?* We can begin to answer this question by bringing together the phases of the client change model discussed in Section Two with the modes of professional functioning presented in Section Three. We can suggest the relationships among these concepts by picturing the alternative modes of professional functioning in association with the rows of a matrix, and the phases of the client change process in association with the columns. Depending upon the situation, each row element (professional mode of functioning) maps qualitatively to a given stage of client change. However, there are certain professional modes that appear to more closely "fit" with specific phases of change (e.g., acceptant listener and catharsis). While each of the forty-nine cells in our matrix could be described in some detail, we have chosen only to highlight those that we have found to be particularly useful, likely to be used, or problematic.

In Chapter 7, we present the matrix, highlighting important row-column combinations. Chapter 8 introduces the notion of core competencies commonly of use to the change master, particularly as related to phase/mode combinations. Chapter 9 provides a more detailed description of key cells in the matrix.

OPERATIONAL DEFINITIONS

Appreciation of a System: A system is comprised of processes, processes are comprised of steps, and techniques or methods are used to accomplish steps. We improve steps to improve processes to improve systems. Appreciation for a system—systems thinking—means that when we improve a step using a technology, we do so with the goal of the system in mind. We do not optimize a step, subsystem, or a process at the expense of the larger or perhaps the largest system.

How is the larger or largest system, the system we are trying to optimize, defined? We suggest you first define your unit of analysis, the subsystem you are focusing on improving. Complete an input/output analysis for this subsystem. Draw a hierarchy diagram defining levels in the system (see Figure 9). Keep defining and drawing the next larger system until you get to the point that it becomes unrealistic to assume this is the system you are trying to optimize. At this point, you have defined the system within which you are working. Your aim is to improve the subsystem but ensure that improvement interventions will translate into improvements at the system level. Of course, this decision will almost always be based on beliefs in cause-and-effect relationships not on knowledge of cause-and-effect relationships. At the very least, you will be considering linkages and relationships in planning your improvement efforts.

Consensus: General agreement, enough agreement to move forward with decision making, problem solving, and implementation. Consensus does not necessarily mean unanimity; rather, it means that we have enough agreement to move forward successfully.

Elegant Variation: As we understand it, elegant variation is when we overuse and abuse synonyms. We're probably guilty of elegant variation to a large extent in this book, although we have tried to avoid it where possible. Examples are target system, unit of analysis, and domain of responsibility. These concepts are not necessarily synonymous; however, they could be, and using all three terms causes confusion. One indication of the maturity of a science is the level of agreement in use of terms. Clearly, the science of quality and productivity improvement is immature in that regard, thus there exists a great deal of confusion about operational definitions, which means there is more than the desired amount of elegant variation. We bring this up to caution you against doing this in your writing and in your speaking. Each organization should create (many already have) an operational dictionary of terms and concepts utilized in quality and productivity improvement.

The worst form of elegant variation is when a given technique is not consistently understood and consequently becomes many things to many people. For example, we often have heard someone say, "Yes, we do the Nominal Group Technique." Yet, when they are pressed to operationally define NGT and depict the method, we find they are not doing what they thought. Again, techniques and processes are operationally defined by steps, and often the steps have associated techniques for accomplishing them. The Nominal Group Technique has five steps, with a very specific methodology for doing each step. Delbecq, Van de Ven, and Gustafson designed it carefully and specifically (1986). Variation on the themes, of course, is fine, but let's make sure we call things by their right names. Emerging disciplines require discipline.

Hoshin Kanri: *Ho* means method or form, *Shin* means shiny needle or compass. Taken together the word "hoshin" means a "methodology for strategic direction setting" (*Hoshin Kanri*, Akao 1991, p. xxi). Hoshin Kanri is a methodology for deploying strategic planning and policies for quality and productivity improvement throughout the organization. It is a very disciplined set of tools that are used to create visible linkages for all units within the organizational system; linkages between policies (The word policy in Hoshin Kanri really means a key performance area or indicator and includes an indication of a target for performance which is translated into specific measures and actions at all appropriate levels in the organization.), strategies, and actions at all appropriate levels in the organization.

TLA: Three-Letter Acronyms, a phenomenon of the recent management era that involves a propensity to abbreviate concepts by first initials only. A new physical principle was discovered in doing this; more often than not the abbreviations have three letters. The three letters often have a "ring" to them (e.g., JIT, MRP, TQM), so people begin to use them rather than the long description or title. This became so widespread in the '90s, particularly in government organizations, that a ban was enacted and anyone inventing a new TLA was subject to severe public mockery and admonished not to use these in their writings or speech. Upon further consideration, those in the field of management realized that acronyms are attempts to create efficiencies in communication and are common to most maturing disciplines; thus, it was decided that they would follow a more rational path such as is followed by the medical discipline.

Tool and Technology: A way of accomplishing something, a means to an end; method, process, model, blueprint, equipment, software, technique, protocol. We use the terms in their broadest sense.

CHAPTER 7

THE MATRIX

In Chapter 4, we discussed seven distinct phases clients pass through in the change process. In Chapters 5 and 6, we discussed seven professional modes of functioning that change masters, as helpers, can fulfill as they assist with managing the change process and the implementation and deployment of improvement efforts. In this chapter, we bring professional modes of functioning and phases of client change together. This is done to set the stage for discussion of phase and mode combinations that are likely and useful as change masters go about their work.

When portrayed as a matrix, with the phases of change as the x-axis and the modes of professional functioning as the y-axis, phase and mode relationships can be conceptualized (see Figure 20). The change master can begin to think of cells in the matrix as representing situations where a mode is matched to a phase. Within each cell are core competencies and tools that are appropriate for a phase and mode combination. For example, most readers are familiar with the tools of quality (e.g., cause-and-effect diagrams, process flow diagrams, Pareto diagrams, histograms, run charts). There are certainly additional tools for quality and productivity improvement available to the change master, and we introduce these in Chapter 8. For now, however, let it suffice to suggest that certain cells will be likely to require certain specific competencies and tools.

The matrix is arranged as follows. The phases are presented in general sequence of occurrence. However, it is important to remember that there is wide variation in client behaviors during the process of change. Certain phases may be passed through almost imperceptibly or skipped altogether. In some cases, there may be significant gray areas, and exactly what phase the client is in becomes unclear to the change master. There may even be regression. Certainly, reality is not as neat and clear as the matrix may make it appear.

The professional modes of functioning are arranged in ascending order of "obtrusiveness." By obtrusiveness, we mean the extent to which the change master is intervening, providing structure and leadership in the change process. At the bottom of the axis, the change master is relatively unobtrusive; in fact, the client may even wonder what value the change master is adding to the improvement effort. At the top of the axis, the change master is significantly more involved, visible, and directing in the improvement effort. The client may wonder at times if the change master isn't overstepping his or her bounds.

Let's begin to dissect the matrix, examining specific cells. We'll do so by moving from left to right relative to phases of change and up, vertically, in the matrix to those professional modes of functioning that are most commonly utilized, appropriate, or problematic for the respective phase of change.

Figure 20. The matrix of phases of change (as situations) and professional modes of functioning (as behaviors) creates a framework for planning and development for the change master.

SITUATION APPRAISAL

The situation appraisal phase of change represents the foundation for successful improvement efforts. It is an attempt on the part of the change master to ensure the right problem is being solved, that root causes rather than symptoms are being addressed, and that a systems view is being considered as the client enters the improvement project. It is an opportunity for the change master to confirm the extent to which there is:

• Widespread commitment to the change;
• A sufficient level of dissatisfaction with the status quo;
• A clear understanding of the need for improvement;
• General agreement about what to improve.

It is often the case that the sponsor will have this improvement effort high on his or her agenda but that it is a relatively lower priority for the change target. The client (sponsor and target) often will lack the time and resources necessary to obtain the data which will confirm or deny strongly held beliefs about what is wrong. Or it may be the case that the client (sponsor or targets, or both) is inexperienced, and has little information relative to the particular improvement effort, although considerable general experience.

The change master serves to provide structure to the situation appraisal phase of change. The intent is to get the client to focus, to converge on specific improvement problems or opportunities. The fact that the client does come to understand the situation does not necessarily mean that they will have moved through denial, anger, and confusion regarding how to solve the problem or capture the opportunity. Just as in structured problem solving, situation appraisal through scouting and targeting simply clarifies the "mess," it doesn't solve the problem. This phase will more often than not lead into and overlap with the next phase: catharsis and stress relief over goals and paths.

It may be that a structured group process will be useful to assist with focus and convergence. However, it is often the case that there is not enough systematic understanding at this point to use a structured technique. Consensus at this phase of change is much different than consensus at the self-design phase. To help shape convergence, we may use some of the steps of the Nominal Group Technique or Delphi (see Development Work section for references on these techniques) but not use the complete technique. For example, we might not use the voting and ranking step as a technique for creating consensus. It is possible, perhaps quite common, for a change master to try to force convergence prematurely. We believe that the rate at which convergence and consensus can be achieved is a function of a number of factors, for example: homogeneity of the group, complexity of the situation, amount of prediscussion or pre-exposure to this situation by the group, amount of data available, and sense of urgency. If time is not crucial and the situation is new or complex, it may be dysfunctional to force convergence rapidly at this phase.

Creating an environment and a situation where people from the total system to be improved can share data, affects, assumptions, and beliefs is important to this first phase of change. The change master in this case is creating a search conference (Weisbord 1992), where key stakeholders and targets meet with the sponsor and change agent to merge data, information and knowledge bases. The change master's job is to structure dialogue, inquiry, and small-group and large-group activity such that the organizational system is postured to plan for improvement.

The change master, of course, also is posturing the targets for the catharsis, stress-relief phase of change. It is not the intent of the situation appraisal to create conflict and stress-relief, rather it is the intent to lay the foundation for this to occur. The change master can utilize the situation appraisal phase as a way to identify specific individuals who may have a greater need for stress relief. This phase also serves as an opportunity to target key individuals or groups for focused data collection and processing.

I tend not to use the challenger, teacher, or expert mode much in this phase. The aim is to get enough consensus and agreement on the situation, the problems, and the opportunities to move forward. We want to make sure we are tackling the "right" (in a Pareto sense, in statistical variation sense, in a root-cause versus symptom sense, in a benefit to cost sense, in an intuitive sense, in a politically astute sense, in a customer driven sense, from a total system perspective sense) problems or opportunities. The discovery of common ground, as discussed by Weisbord, is the intent. Sharing enough information and data is often the key to discovering this common ground. This step often is not pretty. It is time consuming, frustrating, often evokes emotion, and requires a tolerance for ambiguity.

Description Of Key Cells (1,1), (1,2), and (1,4)

During the Situation Appraisal, Scouting, Targeting, Diagnosis Phase, the change master will find the Inquiry; Data Gatherer, Information Systems Designer and Developer; and, possibly, the Structure Provider Modes most useful.

Situation Appraisal — Scouting, Targeting-Inquiry Mode (1,1)

The change master has been contacted by the client to provide assistance with a quality and productivity improvement initiative. The change master has developed a procedure for entry and contracting (Block 1981) and has a set of data and information that he or she feels is necessary to determine whether and how to proceed. To reiterate entry and contracting is the process of gaining entry to an organizational system, being legitimized, establishing relationships with the clients, and developing clear and agreed upon requirements and expectations. Dr. Deming would suggest that the change master might be invited from the outside.

Once entry and contracting have been completed, this phase of the change process can begin in earnest. Again, the change master has developed a routine or procedure for collecting data and information from the client. Interviews, surveys, focus groups, observation, and system documentation are all sources of data and information which will be helpful to both the change master and the client. The change master is acting as data gatherer in an acceptant fashion.

Being an active listener, asking follow-up questions, seeking to understand in more detail, and exploring meaning is the focus. Creating dialogue through inquiry versus advocacy (Senge 1990 and Weisbord 1991) will be central to this phase and mode combination. Sparking dialogue among targets and sponsors will be necessary in this phase.

The change master seeks meaning and understanding and avoids forcing the client to defend. He or she avoids judgment and evaluation, seeking to bring forth and share data and information relevant to the situation. The change master is striving to help the client focus and converge to more clearly define the situation.

Situational Appraisal — Data Gatherer (1,2)

The change master collects information, which is presented to the client as the basis for the client's own diagnosis. The effective use conditions are similar to those for the inquiry mode. In addition, the data gatherer mode is applicable in this phase when: change is low on the client's agenda; the client lacks the time and resources to get the data that will confirm or deny strongly held beliefs about what is wrong; or the client is new, inexperienced, or has little information relative to the particular situation at hand but considerable relevant general experience.

The change master will find the mode of data gatherer is quite important in this phase. It may be useful to work with the client as a team member and collaborator (1,3) to gather data and information regarding:

• The past, including: performance against key indicators (five-year trend data), critical incidents, previous improvement efforts (successes and failures), lessons learned, and relevant shifts in the environment (external and internal)
• The present, including: current performance levels against key indicators, current perceptions of problems and opportunities, current ongoing improvement efforts, readiness for change relative to this improvement effort, and sponsors/targets/stakeholders for the improvement effort
• Expectations for the improvement effort, including desired results to be achieved and preferred or preconceived notions regarding how, when, who, and resources to be applied
• Assumptions about what needs to be improved, the environment, the future, cause-and-effect relationships, the problems, the opportunities, and other relevant factors.

Situation Appraisal — Structure Provider Mode (1,4)

Structured group processes are particularly effective in bringing together a considerable range of client knowledge, identifying problems, and reaching some consensus about the priorities associated with various problem areas. Structured group processes involve clients early in the change process in ways that are satisfying, highly motivating, effective in the production of valid diagnoses, and efficient in the use of client time. Structured group process educates, sensitizes, and creates a high readiness to accept changes which will follow.

Other Phase/Mode Combinations

Situation Appraisal — Collaborator, Team Member (1,3)

The change master works as a member of a client team charged with diagnosis and targeting, usually as the initial step in a complete change process. The collaborator, team member mode is useful when the diagnostic phase: requires considerable widely dispersed client information and judgment, requires a high level of professional and technical skill which can be supplied by the change master, or is to be used to achieve wide acceptance of the diagnosis and subsequent changes.

Formal, explicit diagnosis and problem definition most often are done with "mild" problems. Intense problems and crises produce pressures that discourage the use of this phase and cause the team to rush toward solutions. The change master can be particularly effective in maintaining some degree of "problem mindedness" before the team moves to solutions. Again, it is a matter of trying to ensure that all of the phases of the change process receive the team's attention.

Situation Appraisal — Teacher, Skill Developer (1,5)

The change master teaches diagnostic skills, techniques, and methods. The material taught must have some reasonable relation to the technical abilities and motivation of the learners. In this phase, the teacher/skill developer mode works particularly well when widespread and repeated situation appraisal, targeting, and diagnosis will be required, the client is interested in learning diagnostic skills and has a strong preference for doing their own diagnosis, or clients have the ability, resources, and access to change master support that will permit them to complete the change processes likely to follow the diagnostic stage.

Situation Appraisal — Expert (1,6)

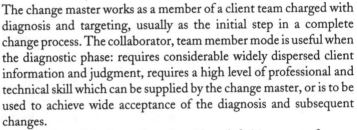

In this mode, the change master studies the client situation independently and tells the client what the problem is and where change efforts should be targeted. The change master is willing to take full responsibility for the diagnosis. In situation appraisal, this mode is useful when the client is in a hurry, has no time to participate, believes the change master is competent to diagnose, and is frustrated with unassisted efforts to find the problem. This mode is effective when the client has low diagnostic ability, when the diagnosis and resulting change need not be accepted by a large number of people, and when few people will find their behavior impacted by the change.

It is important that the change master have confidence in the expert mode for making the diagnosis based typically on considerable relevant experience. It is very useful to elicit at least a basic participative commitment from the client by presenting some alternative expert diagnoses among which the client is asked to choose.

Situation Appraisal — Challenger (1,7)

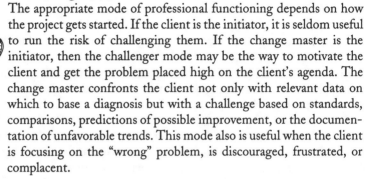

The appropriate mode of professional functioning depends on how the project gets started. If the client is the initiator, it is seldom useful to run the risk of challenging them. If the change master is the initiator, then the challenger mode may be the way to motivate the client and get the problem placed high on the client's agenda. The change master confronts the client not only with relevant data on which to base a diagnosis but with a challenge based on standards, comparisons, predictions of possible improvement, or the documentation of unfavorable trends. This mode also is useful when the client is focusing on the "wrong" problem, is discouraged, frustrated, or complacent.

CATHARSIS, STRESS RELIEF

This phase of change is one that is often skipped for any number of reasons (e.g., perception of not enough time, fear of dealing with anger and emotion, lack of skill in dealing with emotion, perception or belief that smoothing over is better than confrontation, disdain for the "soft stuff"). There is ample support in the literature to suggest that this is a mistake. Significant efforts to improve performance will always involve emotion and often conflict. Fear—of losing resources, losing jobs, exposing poor performance, loss of face, losing power—is the primary reason for this. Resistance to change occurs because people fear the consequences of change more than they fear the consequences of not changing. This is called the burning platform phenomenon. At what point will someone jump from a burning platform? In either case there is a probability of death. At what point does the fear of death by staying on the platform become greater than the fear of death by jumping? This is the "level of dissatisfaction with the status quo" variable in the readiness for change model presented in Section II.

Many people become quite proficient at hiding their fears and affects regarding change. The result is that improvement efforts are embarked upon with compliance rather than commitment. Ultimately, this single issue may spell the difference between success and failure. The change master must develop the artful skill of moving clients through this phase of change.

The catharsis, stress relief phase of change is filled with conflict, emotion, anger, frustration, anxiety, and fear. This is clearly a difficult phase of change to learn to move through and help with. Often, transference occurs, and the client projects these negative emotions onto the change master. This puts the change master at risk and must be carefully navigated to save the overall effort. Significant improvement efforts always involve this phase of change and if the phase is skipped, the price must always be paid later. Using the matrix requires understanding when to move back and forth between modes relative to a given phase; it may take the change master moving back and forth among acceptant listener, teacher, expert, solution provider, and challenger to get the client through this phase.

We have found that the change master often must challenge (2,7), just a bit, to spark catharsis; then he or she moves to a more inquirer, acceptant listener mode (2,1), and then, more often than not, the client gets impatient with the confusion and ambiguity and the change master must add some structure by playing the role of expert and providing clear next steps (2,4).

Think about this in the context of the change model presented in Section II. This phase of change is creating a dissatisfaction with the status quo which then has to be directed to a clear understanding of next steps and a reaffirmation of the vision. This phase may require some just-in-time education or training to help clients understand what is happening to them. The change master provides a bit of theory, and the client reflects on the theory in the context of what they are feeling (2,5).

This discussion is not to suggest that Modes 2, 3, and 4 are not salient. In one way or another, these modes may well come into play entering this phase, during the phase, or exiting the phase and preparing for the next. As you may be beginning to realize, it is the development of instinct and intuition about when to switch modes during a phase that is the key to change master development. One could also suggest that developing the instinct about when to move from one phase to the next also is crucial in the development process.

Certain methods of managing through this phase might include the following:

1. The change master may arrange a series of individual interviews with those clients whose behavior ultimately is most likely to be influenced by the change process. The change master listens effectively, avoids judgmental remarks, and encourages the expression of frustrations and past roadblocks that have prevented change and improvement.
2. The change master may seek the same opportunities on a casual, unscheduled basis.
3. Client personnel may be invited to write an anonymous letter to the change master expressing their frustrations or conflicts. These data are later summarized for discussion at a group session.
4. Leadership of the organization can be convinced to hold all-hands meetings where people are invited to write questions anonymously on cards. Leaders of the organization are then, in an open fashion, required to respond to any and all questions regarding the improvement initiative (Monetta 1991).
5. A structured group process may be used to bring out frustrations and conflicts in a depersonalized and efficient way. The Nominal Group Technique has been used to do this effectively as well as to test for consensus among clients in this regard. Here, the change master really is combining the inquiry mode with the structured group process coordinator mode. The change master may hold the front end of a search conference or the early steps of the Strategic Performance Improvement Planning Process.
6. An external change agent skilled at interviewing, focus groups, and stress relief might be brought in. In this case the change master is serving as a broker.

Another use of the matrix in this mode and phase combination would encourage the change master to come to grips with the question of what resources should be devoted to the inquiry mode-catharsis aspect of the performance improvement effort. Here, the matrix begins to provide a structure for planning the full program for bringing positive change to a client organization. Determining how much time to spend in each stage of change and what level of resources to devote to each phase is more an art than a science at this point.

It is, however, very worthwhile to formulate some rough hypotheses such as the following:

• The greater the client's history of frustration and conflict associated with an area of potential change and improvement, the greater the urgency of such change; the longer client people have worked together, the greater the effort allocated to the inquiry-catharsis aspect of the consulting engagement. This may be simply another way of recognizing the forming, norming, storming phases of group development as a prelude to group performance. If the group is mature, then they may well be comfortable and experienced at this phase of change.

• However, it will be common that the change master is forming cross-functional groups and planning teams for the total system and that these teams and groups often will never have worked together. Therefore, it is reasonable to suspect that storming and norming (somewhat analogous to this phase) will be necessary.

Description Of Key Cells (2,1), (2,4), and (2,7)

During the Catharsis, Stress Relief phase of change, the change master will find the Inquiry and Dialogue Creator Mode (2,1); the Structured Group Process Coordinator Mode (2,4); and, for certain situations, the Challenger Mode (2,7) useful.

Catharsis — Inquiry Mode (2,1)

This is the natural and most widely used mode for catharsis. The change master listens effectively and nonjudgmentally in an attempt to encourage the client to express past frustrations, anxieties, and conflicts. This mode is especially useful when clients have a long history of trouble, failure, blame casting, and bitterness in the problem area. It is useful also when there is a low degree of trust among client people and mutually conflicting objectives. The inquiry mode is effective when clients have a low regard for the effectiveness of the change master and the change master wishes to build an informal and trusting relationship, and it is important when the client has a long history with the problem which may be useful to the change master in designing the change process.

To the extent there appears to be no history of frustration, failure, conflict, and mistrust, the catharsis phase may be suppressed. However, this condition should not be assumed too easily. If stresses are present they will eventually come out, and the change process will be more effective if they come out early in an atmosphere designed by the change master. Some opportunity should always be made available to express:

• Previous negative experiences;
• Efforts that have failed;
• Antagonism;
• Distrust of the change master;
• Feelings of powerlessness;
• Differing priorities, objectives, or perceptions.

The inquiry mode is one which most practicing change masters, particularly those with strong technical expertise in some dimension of quality and productivity improvement, immediately acknowledge as a part of their style that is most difficult to operationalize. They often quickly grasp the situation, quickly close on a solution, and immediately try to sell the solution (Expert, Solution Provider Mode). However, this does not allow sufficient time for the client to work through the affective dimensions of improvement and change.

Those change masters with strong backgrounds in psychology, sociology, and counseling may find inquiry a very comfortable mode. They may not have a preferred solution and may, in fact, need the client to work through that. We suspect cognitive style and personality type also may play a role in level of skill and comfort with this mode. For example, one would suspect that ISFP (Introversion, Sensing, Feeling, Perceiving dimension on the Meyers-Briggs type indicator) types might find this mode quite natural.

Catharsis — Structure Provider (2,4)

The change master coordinates a structured group process with the objective of bringing out and sharing past stressful experiences with the problem area. The process may be designed to utilize the members of the group as acceptants, to express anger and frustration in a psychologically safe way, and to depersonalize blame casting and accusation. This can be an extremely effective and widely useful mode for accomplishing catharsis. Participants generally will express organizational or institutional difficulties first. It is useful to prolong the process to assure that personal difficulties are eventually brought out. Using the Nominal Group Technique, for example, to expose roadblocks, obstacles, and hurdles preventing the organization from performing as well as it could or should is an effective approach.

Catharsis — Challenger (2,7)

The change master confronts the client with data and symptoms indicating the presence of stresses and strains and challenges the client by interpreting the data in this way. If the client is reluctant to express stresses, the change master presses this interpretation of the data, pushing the client to be open and to "let it come out." As previously indicated, this is a high-risk mode, but it may be effective with some particularly reluctant clients.

Confrontation in a different sense often is used by change masters as an effective way of resolving conflicts among client people or client subunits. When conflicts arise over the nature of the problem or the acceptability of proposed changes, the change master may structure a conflict-resolution process known as confrontation. In managed confrontation, the parties are brought together, data are exchanged, feelings are aired, and resolution can be sought in some orderly way.

Many change masters avoid this phase of change due to the emotions involved. They may be uncomfortable in the challenger mode even though it may be necessary to spark this phase of change. They may be unskilled at the challenger mode and may execute it in a fashion that inflicts more damage than progress. They may feel or believe that smoothing over is better than confronting and managing conflict associated with this phase. Of course, the research suggests just the opposite, but they may not be aware of the research.

Other Phase/Mode Combinations

Catharsis — Data Gatherer (2,2)

The change master brings the client data which tend to reflect the sources and symptoms of possible failures, frustrations, anxieties, and conflicts and then simply gives the client the opportunity to react to the data. This is particularly useful for clients who are: (1) not particularly self-aware, (2) not convinced (explicitly or implicitly) of the usefulness of catharsis, (3) reluctant to express stressful experiences or unwilling to discuss them, or (4) strongly motivated to move toward the solution without adequately exploring the problem.

Catharsis — Team Member, Collaborator (2,3)

The change master seeks to assure that catharsis is among the team's early activities, perhaps modeling it with his or her own behavior. The change master tries to create an atmosphere in which the team members can act as acceptants and stresses can be brought out without excessive personal bitterness or damage to relationships among team members. Structured group process coordination may be an especially effective method for doing this.

Catharsis — Teacher, Skill Developer (2,5)

The change master teaches and demonstrates the importance of catharsis and some of the techniques for achieving it. While this may increase client effectiveness in management and problem solving in the long run, it is likely to do little to advance the immediate change process.

Catharsis-Expert (2,6)

The change master tells the client to forget the past, overlook past stressful experiences, and concentrate on the future and on changing things. The change master indicates that there is usually a history of anxiety, frustration, and conflict but that this plays no role in the constructive solution of the problem. Interpreted in this way, the expert mode is seldom effective if stresses are present.

SELF-AWARENESS

Self-awareness requires intellectual honesty. We become self-aware through the use of self-exploration, individually, in groups, and in the organizational system. The change master must help the client separate facts from fiction. Data and facts are central to creating valid self-awareness that can be used to guide our improvement efforts. We find that many improvement-oriented decisions and actions are based on beliefs in as opposed to knowledge of cause-and-effect relationships. We are, as Weisbord and colleagues would say, searching for "common ground," for consensus as to what needs to be improved, why, how, when, and by whom. The change master must manage individual, group and organizational system self-awareness. It is self-awareness of the sponsor and targets we strive to create during this phase.

The change master must be sensitive to situations where there is a lack of willingness or ability to be intellectually honest and to situations where the measurement and motivation or culture subsystems do not reinforce positive self-awareness. The client may have the ability to be self-aware, but the system within which they operate may not make it feasible to utilize this self-awareness for the purpose of improvement.

Description Of Key Cells (3,2), (3,5), (3,6), and (3,7)
During the Self-Awareness Phase of Change, the change master will find the Data-Gatherer, Information System Developer; the Teacher, Skill Developer; Expert; and the Challenger Modes useful.

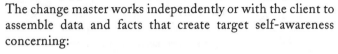

Self-Awareness — Data Gatherer (3,2)

The change master works independently or with the client to assemble data and facts that create target self-awareness concerning:

- The need for improvement;
- The reason for improvement;
- The consequences of not improving;
- The vision of desired levels of performance;
- Improving understanding of alternative paths for improvement.

The change master is attempting to improve the quality of the performance measurement systems such that the targets understand past and current levels of performance (thinking statistically and understanding variation) and linkages (appreciation for systems), and they are learning and improving their knowledge of cause-and-effect relationships.

Self-Awareness — Teacher, Skill Developer (3,5)

The change master teaches the importance of attaining a clear view of the present system and basic methods such as process charting, measuring, modeling, and performance evaluation. This mode is very useful when widespread and frequent change processes will be undertaken independently by clients and when clients have access to the resources and change master support that will permit them to complete the change processes that should follow from this phase.

Self-Awareness — Expert (3,6)

The change master conducts an independent, expert-designed investigation using professional resources such as process flow charting, layout diagrams, models, simulations, and the full range of measurement techniques designed to capture performance and cost-benefit relationships. Using the expert mode for this phase is robust and widely effective, does not generally carry with it the disadvantages of the expert mode in other phases, and does not prejudice the use of other modes for later phases of the change process. The change master as a technical expert often can provide the client with a revealing and even surprising picture of operational reality and current conditions.

Self-Awareness — Challenger (3,7)

Here, the change master operates much as in the expert mode to design and execute a description of existing methods and systems but goes somewhat further and is somewhat more forceful. The client is challenged to recognize current reality, acknowledge at least partial ignorance, question the change master's description of existing operations, and move toward self-evaluation for which this phase provides the basis.

Other Phase/Mode Combinations

Self-Awareness — Inquiry Mode (3,1)

The purpose of the self-awareness phase is for the client organization to reach a clear and explicit appreciation of the existing methods and systems. This serves as the basis for self-evaluation and the self-designed change process. It is essential to recognize that simply having experience with present ways of doing things may not be the same as self-awareness. Change masters often have the experience of charting, measuring, modeling, or simulating an existing system for a client only to have the client express very considerable surprise at what has been going on.

For describing and measuring the performance of a system, the change master has a variety of tools and techniques that are especially useful in making the client organization self-aware. There may, of course, be situations in which clients already have a usefully high degree of self-awareness and appreciation of existing methods and systems. The inquiry mode, particularly in conjunction with leading and probing questions by the change master, may lead clients to express their understanding of the existing system and by this expression to become explicitly self-aware. To listen to the client describe the situation is often to see the client go through an experience of heightened appreciation and self-discovery. The listener mode is, at the very least, an opportunity for the change master to gauge how much effort may be required to facilitate self-awareness through other modes.

Self-Awareness — Team Member, Collaborator (3,3)

Given the appropriateness of the team approach to a variety of client situations, the change master functions to: assure that the team includes this phase, avoiding the tendency to assume that what is presently being done is clearly understood; provide professional and technical support with change master techniques and methods; and provide staff support, very often from the change master or his or her group. A team involved in describing an existing operation often is involved in a highly reactive measurement and description process. Describing existing operations may in itself be enough to bring about change and will almost certainly increase the motivation toward change.

Self-Awareness — Structure Provider Mode (3,4)

The structure provider mode is not very useful for putting together a complex and detailed view of the existing operations and methods. Structured group processes may, however, be used to: (1) bring together some of the information needed from a group of client people; obtain specific information on problems, attitudes, and priorities connected with existing activities; respond to specific inquiries structured by the change master; and evaluate and criticize a description created by the change master.

SELF-EVALUATION

Self-awareness is the process of converting data to information. It is heavily reliant upon the measurement process and measurement systems. Self-evaluation is the process of moving from information and awareness into knowledge, decisions, and actions. We analyze and evaluate information about the situation, problem, opportunity, and performance of the organizational system we are trying to improve. Judgment now becomes crucial to improvement.

We evaluate data and information formally and informally. Statistical methods and other analytical tools may play a heavy role in this phase of change. However, the change master should not underestimate the value of instinct, intuition, and informal evaluation. The blending of the quantitative with the qualitative is vital to this phase of change. The engineer and scientist will emphasize the rational, logical, scientific method of evaluation. Those trained in and preferring the "art" side of management and leadership will emphasize, not necessarily the obverse, but different aspects of evaluation. The affect of those in the system must be considered. The change master must, over time, strive to develop balance in this phase of change. Just as Luke Skywalker had to know when to "trust the force," so the change master must know when to use technology for evaluation and when to trust instinct, intuition, and less formal methods of evaluation.

The key in this phase/mode combination, of course, is the word "self" in front of evaluation. The change master is attempting to internalize, on the part of the client, the conversion of data-to-information-to-knowledge-to-decisions and actions. The conversion of data to information occurs during self-awareness. The conversion of information to knowledge occurs in self-evaluation. Knowledge to decisions and actions occurs in the next phase of self-designed change and improvement. The change master is "teaching how to fish, not giving the client a fish." The change master should avoid doing the data-to-information-to-knowledge-to-decisions and actions for the client. Rather, he or she information-to-knowledge-to-decisions and actions for the client. Rather, he or she should work with the client to teach them how to go through this process (Figure 21).

Description Of Key Cells (4,2), (4,4), (4,5), and (4,7)
During the Self-Evaluation phase of change, the change master will find the Data Gatherer/Information System Developer and Enhancer; Structure Provider; Teacher, Skill Developer; and the Challenger Modes useful.

Self-Evaluation — Data Gatherer (4,2)
In some ways, this mode is similar to the expert mode, but here the change master encourages the client to take a larger role in the actual explication of goals, establishment of standards, development of criteria, and application of these to the existing situation. This is effective where there is a need to obtain wide acceptance of the evaluation, bring to bear implicitly held client standards, goals, and criteria, and avoid threatening the client or arousing resentment of criticism.

Self-Evaluation — Structure Provider (4,4)
This is an especially effective mode for self-evaluation when a number of client people have interests in the change process, when differing goals and objectives must be compromised, and when threats, power, and politics may endanger the evaluation process. Structured group processes are particularly effective since they make it possible for the change master to take advantage of the group's greater effectiveness as an evaluation mechanism without paying the price of the shortcomings common to unstructured groups. Care should be taken in designing group tasks that involve the exploration of high-level goals of an organization. It is almost always more effective to have the group deal with the problem of how to measure performance.

Self-Evaluation — Teacher, Skill Developer (4,5)
A change process in which the teaching mode has been used for the previous phases of stress relief and self-evaluation will rather naturally continue the use of this mode.

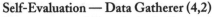

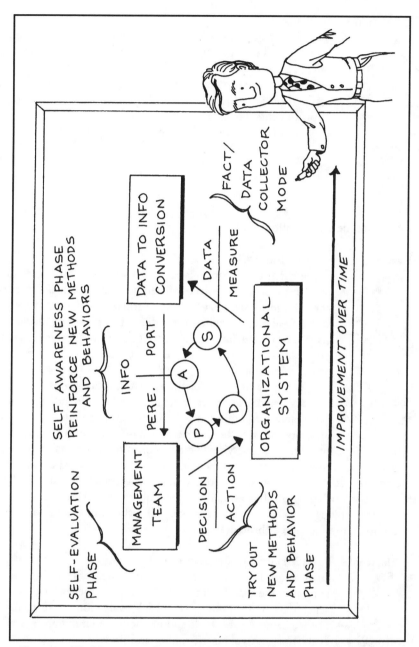

Figure 21. The Management Systems Model can highlight the interaction between the phases of change and the professional modes of functioning (adapted from Kurstedt).

Self-Evaluation — Challenger (4,7)

The advantages and risks outlined previously for this mode most probably will emerge here. The change master challenges the client organization to undertake a self-evaluation, an act which is often resisted. The change master then strongly suggests goals, standards, comparison with others and with past experience, and possible improvements. He or she confronts the client organization with the evaluative conclusions which result from applying these methods.

Other Phase/Mode Combinations

Self-Evaluation — Inquiry Mode (4,1)

If the client organization is equipped with a useful degree of self-awareness, then some effective listening, probing, and questioning by the change master may be both sufficient and most effective in bringing about an explicit evaluation. The client organization will have to be reasonably objective about its effectiveness, clear about its goals, and sufficiently successful and confident to see self-evaluation as nonthreatening.

The change master functions in this situation as an effective, nonjudgmental listener, reflecting to client people their own views of the organization's differences between aspirations and achievements. The importance of the change master as listener is to serve as a person (other than a supervisor) who responds to the clients' statements of self-evaluation in such a way as to make them active motivators toward change for the client. Once the client has made an evaluation explicit to another, it is far more likely that the change process will progress. In all situations, the inquiry mode should be used to help the change master judge to what degree this mode will suffice and to what degree self-evaluation needs to be achieved through the other modes.

Self-Evaluation — Team Member, Collaborator (4,3)

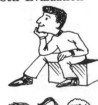

In the wide variety of client situations that yield effectively to the team approach, the change master works to: assure the team explicitly and separately attends to the phase of self-evaluation; make available all of the change master tools and methods which might be useful for evaluation and goal clarification; and provide support, continuity, and structure to see that closure is reached in the self-evaluation phase.

Self-Evaluation — Expert (4,6)

While using the expert mode for client self-evaluation seems almost like a contradiction, the change master may function effectively this way in situations where: the client lacks the time, resources, and motivation to accomplish a self-evaluation; the client wants the objectivity of the change master; or the client finds that evaluation requires professional techniques and methods which the change master can supply. The change master, in these cases, carries out an evaluation of the client's methods and systems but tries to offer the client more than a single evaluation from which to choose. Applying different standards or criteria of performance, looking at the data in different ways, considering alternative objectives are all ways of generating alternative evaluations. The client, given the opportunity to make this choice, then becomes involved in the evaluation, and it begins to become a self-evaluation.

The change master can function as expert with considerable effectiveness when the evaluation process is complex, technical, and requires a major effort. Of special importance are those situations in which client goals are not particularly clear and measurement, multiple-criterion decision analysis, utility analysis, cost-benefit analysis, and cost-effectiveness analysis are highly valued expert contributions.

SELF-DESIGNED CHANGE

Self-designed change is, to some extent, the payoff phase. The first four phases of change lay the foundation for the client to become involved in the design and development of solutions to problems, ways to capture improvement opportunities, and actions to be taken to improve performance. If the first four phases have been successful and have not drug out too long, then this phase will be uplifting, exciting, and motivating for the client. Typically, clients have pent up energy, enthusiasm, and desire coming into the self-design phase. They all have strong beliefs in what should be done and how. The change master needs to harness this energy and focus the group on coming up with the most satisfactory (not necessarily optimal) solution.

More often than not, the change master will struggle with client discipline, knowledge, and skill during this phase. Methodology for design, problem solving, and project management and planning often will be deficient. This is why cell (5,5) is an important cell during this phase.

Many organizations find resources such as *The Team Handbook* useful; as they provide guidance on how improvement teams can use prescribed methods for designing, developing, implementing, and evaluating improvement efforts. The change master becomes a resource person, networking the client to the right resources for specific improvement projects.

Description Of Key Cells (5,3), (5,4), (5,5), and (5,6)

During the Self-Designed Change Phase, the change master will find the Team Member, Collaborator; Structure Provider; Teacher, Skill Developer; and Expert Modes useful.

Self-Designed Change — Team Member, Collaborator (5,3)

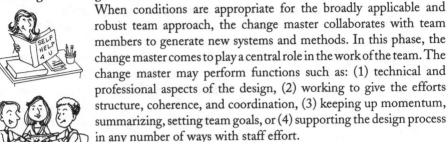

When conditions are appropriate for the broadly applicable and robust team approach, the change master collaborates with team members to generate new systems and methods. In this phase, the change master comes to play a central role in the work of the team. The change master may perform functions such as: (1) technical and professional aspects of the design, (2) working to give the efforts structure, coherence, and coordination, (3) keeping up momentum, summarizing, setting team goals, or (4) supporting the design process in any number of ways with staff effort.

However, in spite of the change master's central role, considerable efforts are made to keep team members involved, make use of their special knowledge and skills, have them make key design decisions, and keep them constantly evaluating, criticizing, and improving the designs that are developed.

Self-Designed Change — Structure Provider (5,4)

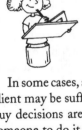

The change master wants to provide enough structure so that the client can continue to move forward with this phase of change and improvement. It is important not to lose momentum here. Structured group processes may be useful for assisting the client in identifying and prioritizing improvement objectives, improvement methods, or criteria for evaluating performance or improvement alternatives. Structured processes also may be useful to assist the client with the process of problem solving, decision analysis, and design. This structure often takes the form of a method depiction or description, forms, checklists, or written procedures. Designing and developing ways to improve performance often is difficult for clients, and they often require a method to help reduce ambiguity.

In some cases, a "cookbook," step-by-step approach may be required. In other cases, the client may be sufficiently skilled and knowledgeable to proceed. The proverbial make or buy decisions are always an issue in this phase. Do we do this ourselves or search for someone to do it for us? Often, the change master must assist with these decisions.

Self-Designed Change — Teacher, Skill Developer (5,5)

The change master teaches, coaches, or demonstrates design methods and techniques to enhance the client's level of competence. Previous comments on the teaching mode also apply here. One very effective use of this mode involves the presentation by the change master of a number of solutions, systems, methods, or alternative ways of doing things strictly as examples, models, or suggestions to the client. The client is cautioned not to copy these models but rather to let them simply become stimuli and guides to help the process of self-designed change. Clients often are far more effective at adapting general solutions to their specific situations than they are at creating solutions "from scratch."

Self-Designed Change — Expert (5,6)

In its conventional form this mode is a contradiction; the solution cannot simultaneously be self-designed and have the change master function as an expert. In its more effective form, the change master functions as expert to design changes and improvement in methods and systems but produces alternative designs among which the client must choose. Thus, the work of the expert forms a starting point for self-designed change in which the client makes key decisions and modifies and adapts the product of the expert.

This mode is effective when there exists: (1) need for a high-quality solution, (2) need for considerable change master technical skill in the design, (3) low need for acceptance of the change, (4) severe constraints on the effort that the client can devote to designing change, or (5) a sense of frustration, powerlessness, and urgency on the part of the client.

Other Phase/Mode Combinations

Self-Designed Change — Inquiry Mode (5,1)

In this mode the change master is an effective listener while clients work out and express their own ideas for change. Clients who are successful, open, confident, and innovative will have numerous concepts for new methods and systems. If, in addition, these clients are highly motivated to place change near the tops of their agendas and if they are technically strong, the change master may be most effective as a constructive listener. The client, in such situations, welcomes the change master in the role of acceptant because the change master can be trusted to avoid ridicule, expected to be constructive in probing and questioning, and relied upon to treat clients' ideas as confidential. The change master performs the valuable functions of letting the client "bounce off" new ideas, clarifying and confirming the client's design concepts, and being willing to help the client find out which ideas are best but not trying to change the client's mind forcefully.

Self-Designed Change — Data Gatherer (5,2)

The change master gathers data which support the design process, serve as inputs to design choices and illustrate design possibilities. The data gatherer mode is not widely used or particularly effective in this phase. It implies that the alternatives are already identified and accepted and that data are being obtained at the specific request of the client organization. In this mode, the change master is primarily performing a data-gathering service for the client rather than playing a central role in the change process. It may, in fact, be an example of a number of ancillary services that change masters often perform for clients. These ancillary services may include the following: (1) "quick and dirty" answers to client questions, (2) obtaining a variety of types of information, (3) getting the attention of top management, (4) taking the heat for unpleasant

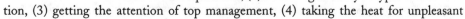

changes which the client must make, or (5) helping the client to justify a course of action already decided upon.

Self-Designed Change — Challenger (5,7)

The change master challenges the client to "shoot down" solutions and designs proposed by the change master, to come up with reasons for not accepting a new method or system. The change master presents solutions in the expert mode and then confronts the client with specific predictions of savings, improvements, and benefits. Once again, all the risks and payoffs of the challenger mode are present in this phase in a particularly crucial way. This mode is sometimes used by outside consultants with a predetermined solution to offer the client.

TRYING OUT THE NEW BEHAVIOR

This represents the implementation and possibly deployment phase of the improvement effort. It is the DO in the PDSA improvement cycle. Individuals and groups are being called upon to alter behaviors and to complete tasks and objectives that have been identified as integral to the improvement effort. This phase requires attention to detail, maintenance of momentum, and individual and group responsibility. The change master must work with the client to ensure individuals and groups are held accountable for timely and quality execution of tasks and objectives. It is in this phase that we often find "A" and "C" squeezing "B" out. The change master must work with the client to manage this.

There is an old saying that, "We are much more likely to act our way into a new way of thinking than to think our way into a new way of acting." We know that more often than not, behavior is a function of its consequences. Therefore, the change master must ensure the consequences of not moving through this phase and the consequences of moving through this phase are clearly maintained. Accountability mechanisms must be built in to ensure that new methods, new behaviors, and improvement actions actually occur.

We believe peer pressure can be a powerful reinforcer in this case. Periodically, we hold review sessions with targets, sponsors, and improvement teams. Those responsible for trying out new behaviors, for implementing tasks, are required to provide periodic progress and performance updates. It becomes clear who is allowing "A" and "C" to squeeze "B" out, and these individuals or teams often are sanctioned by the group.

During these sessions we evaluate:

1. Effectiveness — are we doing what we said we would do, on time?
2. Efficiency — are we under resourcing or over resourcing the task or objective?
3. Quality — are we doing a good job, are our cause-and-effect relationships still valid?
4. Impact — as we implement and deploy, are we seeing the positive impact on performance indicators we thought we would see?

Time management and often stress management may become essential in this phase, and the change master will want to provide training in these areas on a situational basis when appropriate. Individuals and groups find themselves challenged, even frustrated, by the addition of "B" tasks and activities, often without a corresponding reduction in existing workload. Immature individuals may be overwhelmed at the prospect of doing more with the same resources.

Reinforcement and encouragement must occur regularly in this phase. Making sure that the sponsor continues to articulate the vision and the importance of the improvement effort is crucial. The change master also will want to encourage the targets to accept that this is difficult and that others are facing the same challenges. Encouraging individual responsibility for solving these related problems is important. The change master may want to be empathetic (not sympathetic) with those who are struggling to adopt new behaviors.

Ultimately, in the environment most organizations are in today, those who can cope and adapt must be rewarded and encouraged and held up as role models. Those who cannot or will not do this should be helped to find opportunities where they will be able to contribute more appropriately. This may seem harsh, but in today's competitive environment individuals and groups must develop the willingness and ability to participate actively in improvement or find other ways to make a living. These are the hard realities of the '90s.

Description Of Key Cells (6,1), (6,5), and (6,6)

During the Trying Out New Behavior phase of change, the change master will find the Inquiry, Acceptant Listener; Teacher, Skill Developer; and Expert Modes most useful.

Trying Out New Behavior — Inquiry Mode (6,1)

Moving toward an actual test of new methods and systems is a crucial point in any change process. This is the point at which the client must make a major commitment to action and often take appreciable risks. Generally, there is a low probability of an actual test taking place if this phase is left entirely to the initiative of the client. There are exceptions, of course, when there is very high motivation for change and a serious need to improve an ineffective system. Most often, however, the change master must play a strong role, facilitating and encouraging the movement toward an operational trial of the new methods. This is much easier if top management commitment to a test is obtained very early in the change process, and, likewise, if plans for the test are begun early on. In every situation the change master frequently should act as a listener to determine the client's commitment to an actual trial and the expectations currently held about the results of a trial.

Trying Out New Behavior — Teacher, Skill Developer (6,5)

Under previously described contingencies for the use of the teaching mode, this may be an effective way to function. However, this step is one at which many change processes fail. It is, therefore, risky to be content with simply teaching the client about the need for a test and the techniques of measurement, experimental design, and data analysis. The teacher, skill developer mode also includes mentoring, role modeling, coaching, and counselor behaviors. The change master will be

called upon to "hand hold," to coach, to encourage instructionally, to help the client get unstuck as they try out new behaviors and methods. Just-in-time training and coaching often is required. This may be difficult for the change master because he or she may not be available to be this responsive. Nevertheless, teaching, coaching, and training will be required during this phase, and the change master must address this need.

Trying Out New Behavior — Expert, Solution Provider (6,6)

The change master plans the actual testing of the changes, supplying technical solutions to problems of measurement, experimental design, and data analysis. The change master undertakes a considerable portion of the field work necessary to train clients in choosing among alternative experimental plans, thus including the client as a creator of the test program. At this advanced point in a change process, relationships between change master and client are well established, the stimulus that can be provided by the change master is much needed, and the change master's technical and administrative contribution is particularly crucial. Thus, the disadvantages associated with the use of the expert mode in previous phases are likely to be absent. The expert mode will enhance the probability of change process success in a wide range of client situations.

Other Phase/Mode Combinations

Trying Out New Behavior — Data Gatherer (6,2)

The data gatherer mode is similar to the expert mode for this phase, possibly allowing the client to take a leading role in the interpretation of the data on the effectiveness of the change test. The change master may need to collect data to support awareness of whether or not the plans for new behaviors or methods are, in fact, being followed. Data gathering serves the purpose of implementation assessment during the implementation itself.

Trying Out New Behavior — Team Member, Collaborator (6,3)

In this phase the change master becomes a strong stimulus to moving ahead with the test, a central technical resource, solving the problems of measurement, experimental design, and data analysis, and an effective but subtle director of the group's deliberations, taking advantage of the group effects indicated above under the structured group process mode. As always, the change master seeks to keep team members fully involved in decision making for test planning and in the interpretation of test results. The team members also may be the key actors in the administration and conduct of the trial.

Trying Out New Behavior — Structure Provider (6,4)

A structured group process may be designed to involve clients in the planning of some specific aspects of the test and in fixing responsibility of carrying it out. While this mode is not especially effective here, it does play a strong role in cases where client people are hesitant about going ahead. In the context of the group process, clients may share the responsibility for the trial, the process may be designed to have participants reinforce each others' determination to make a trial, and the well-known effect of the willingness of a group to assume more risk than an individual comes into play.

Trying Out New Behavior — Challenger (6,7)

The change master operates in two ways. First, he or she challenges (almost dares) the client to have the courage to conduct a test. The change master uses examples of others who have made trials, predictions of results to be expected, and reflections on the amount of effort that has already gone into the change process. Second, when data on the effectiveness of the changes begin to become available, the change master interprets them and confronts the client with this interpretation. The hope is that the client will be moved to continue the testing, modify the changes, and make them a routine part of the organization's operations.

REINFORCING NEW BEHAVIOR

Reinforcement of new behavior can come in the form of feedback (self or externally provided, formal or informal), change master reinforcement, peer recognition and support, supervisor feedback, key performance indicator improvements, and intrinsic reinforcement. This phase represents the "refreezing" phase in the Kurt Lewin three-phase change model. The clients are thinking their way and acting their way into a new way of performing because they believe that positive consequences will result. The change master must ensure that evaluation and reinforcement are occurring so the improvements will be sustained. In the PDSA model, this phase would represent the Study and Act steps. Additionally, theory of psychology (one of Dr. Deming's four elements of profound knowledge) comes into play. We are promoting study and action, but we also are promoting constancy of purpose. We want to ensure that the clients give things time to work, sustain discipline, and stick with the improvements long enough to evaluate whether they, in fact, have worked. If the improvements are working, then we want to ensure that the improvements will "stick." We want to reinforce the new behaviors and methods so they become the new way of doing business.

Description Of Key Cells (7,3), (7,5), and (7,6)

During the Reinforcing New Behavior Phase, the change master will find the Team Member, Collaborator; the Teacher, Skill Developer; and the Expert Modes most useful.

Reinforcing New Methods and Behaviors — Team Member, Collaborator (7,3)

The change master may find it necessary to work at getting the team to consider the design of support and reinforcement procedures when the members feel that their work has already concluded. Team members form a natural group for mutual support and reinforcement, processes which may be effectively undertaken in the format of the structured mode. Team members often consider this final phase a minor detail, necessitating both leadership and staff support by the change master.

Reinforcing New Behavior — Teacher, Skill Developer (7,5)

This is a necessary but seldom sufficient step when the teaching mode is being used in change processes. It is useful to communicate the importance of reinforcement and support together with the techniques for accomplishing these things, but experience suggests a more directive mode for the change master will be required. The change master will find that telling or teaching the clients that rewards and recognition (extrinsic and intrinsic) are important to ensuring that improvements become a way of doing business is necessary but clearly

not sufficient. It will be necessary to go beyond teaching motivation theory and help the clients understand how to put those theories to work to ensure that change and improvement is lasting.

Reinforcing New Behavior — Expert (7,6)

There are a variety of ways in which the change master can design and execute reinforcement and support. These include: (1) top-management notice and review; (2) advisory committee reporting; (3) simple encouragement from superiors; (4) feeding back to those involved measures of performance improvement, results, attainment of change-process goals; (5) bringing those involved together for mutual support and reinforcement in meetings, conferences, seminars on the progress and effects of the change; (6) regular reviews at staff meetings, operating meetings, supervisory conferences, all-hands meetings; (7) using the change as a springboard for further changes; and (8) using the change as a demonstration program for others who may face similar opportunities.

These events are unlikely to occur at the initiative of most clients, and the change master can function effectively as an expert to bring them about. Again, this late in the change process, relationships between the change master and the client are fully determined and disadvantages associated with the early use of the expert mode are unlikely to occur. It is at this last stage, when the client's attention is very likely to turn to other things, that the change master can be somewhat directive in bringing about support and reinforcement to solidify change.

Other Phase/Mode Combinations

Reinforcing New Behavior — Inquiry Mode (7,1)

The function of this final phase of the change process is to prevent new systems and methods from being tested once or twice and then allowed to fade from use. The concept is based on one of the most fundamental laws of human and organizational psychology: the probability that a behavior will be repeated is proportional to the degree to which it is reinforced.

This is the phase of the change process that is perhaps least appreciated by most clients, with the evident result that many carefully designed and tested changes are simply lost through eventual neglect, lack of reinforcement, and the absence of some sort of support system. Reinforcement, support, and motivation to continue and improve further can seldom be effectively accomplished in the inquiry mode. The change master will usually need to take a more stimulative and directive role because clients may tend to conclude that when the test has been completed the change process has been completed. Simply acting as a listener will seldom suffice to cope with frustration, disappointments, disapproval, and the need to support and reinforce new ways of doing things to prevent a gradual reversion to the old ways. As always, the change master should provide ample opportunity for the client organization to express itself on reinforcement and support, but it will be rare that this alone will be effective.

Reinforcing New Behavior — Data Gatherer (7,2)

Progress reporting and post-auditing by the change master are useful, but other modes (expert, structure provider) are usually needed to truly accomplish reinforcements and support. The use of visibility, measurement, and evaluation is a particularly powerful mechanism for reinforcement. Feedback is crucial to reinforcement and sustained improvements. The change master can ensure that the feedback systems are adequate by challenging, teaching, designing, assisting with implementation (team member), etc.

Reinforcing New Behavior — Structure Provider (7,4)

Groups involved in the change and concerned with its effects form natural mechanisms for mutual support and reinforcement. Structured group processes, with tasks involving the assessment of progress and the planning of next steps (described above under the expert mode), can be particularly useful and a natural way to ensure that implementation and evaluation is completed and that improvements will be sustained and maintained.

Reinforcing New Behavior — Challenger (7,7)

The change master may confront the client organization with the results of the change trial and challenge those concerned with the threat that, unless support and reinforcement are provided, what has been accomplished may be lost. As previously discussed, this mode has predictable risks. The clients may be in a somewhat fragile state at this point; they may need encouragement not challenging. Challenging may cause them to become disheartened and may, in fact, serve to unreinforce. This mode is often tricky and in some cases not well advised. Having said this, if the change master feels that the client

 is not stressing evaluation, recognition, rewards, and feedback sufficiently to ensure that improvements are sustained and maintained, it may be necessary to challenge or confront this in a tactful fashion to cause appropriate actions.

DEVELOPING A PERSONAL CONTINGENCY PLANNING BASIS

The most effective way to summarize this chapter is to review its underlying principles:

1. At this time there is a limited amount of systematic evidence on which to base a contingent or situational method of change-process design. We must rely on case experience and professional judgment.
2. Other people's models or theories are unlikely to have a major influence in guiding our design activities. Models and theories we put together for ourselves have a much higher probability of actually influencing our professional performance.
3. The process of constructing a contingent basis for change-process design is in itself an extremely valuable learning experience which cannot be matched by simply reading a chapter such as this.
4. For these reasons and because of the prominent roles of individual professional styles, experience, professional judgment, and common sense, any useful contingency approach to change-process design will, for now at least, necessarily be a personally developed approach.
5. Finally, a personal contingency approach provides a method and structure for assimilating all types of professionally relevant knowledge, whether from the research literature, from experience, or from a developing judgment and common sense.

The present state of the art and the necessity for acting in the absence of systematic bases for allocation of change master effort may lead one to formulate the following, possibly dangerous, hypothesis, which is plausible to some practicing consultants:

> *Given an explicit recognition of the alternative modes of professional functioning, and given an explicit recognition of the phases in the client change process, the probability of achieving change is not very sensitive to rather wide variation in consulting effort allocations.*

We believe, to the contrary, that the art and science of planning change and improvement efforts, particularly determining time and resource allocation relative to mode-phase issues, is crucial to success of TQM-type efforts. We discuss this in more detail in later chapters and, of course, will have some thought provoking feedback questions and learning exercises in this regard at the end of this section.

CONCLUSIONS

The matrix suggests three tentative conclusions which seem to shed some light on understanding the design of change processes:

1. Don't insist that the design of change processes is either totally artistic or totally scientific and operational. Change masters should develop their own styles through explicit planning, self-perception, experimentation, and practice.
2. It is easy in the academic world to achieve pseudo-generality by saying everything is related to everything and it all depends. This represents contingency theory at its worst. For the change master faced with the need for action, it is more helpful to raise explicit hypotheses about first-order dependencies to emphasize what we have and what we lack in the way of systematic evidence. Our goal is reduction to practice not elegant theories or rigorous research. We have chosen to use the elegant theories and rigorous research to improve the quality of our reduction to practice.
3. What we are attempting might be characterized as providing insights and experiences that will alter the change master's self-image from "I am the doctor with the cure" or "I am the problem solver with the tool kit" toward "I am a change process designer."

The notion of explicating the relationships among modes of professional functioning and phases of the client change process is a useful one for change masters. We emphasize once again, however, that there is a low probability that learning about someone else's matrix will influence one's own behavior. A matrix created for oneself and which serves similar functions may, on the other hand, have a much higher probability of influencing professional behavior. The functions that might be ascribed to such a conceptual map include:

1. Providing a basis for planning the strategy for a particular project;
2. Providing a means for the self-conscious development of one's style and for the accumulation of experience in a systematic way;
3. Characterizing the styles used by others for comparison. It may be helpful to suggest which cells receive the major allocation of effort by the stereotypical practicing consultant, social scientist, industrial and systems engineer (human factors, operations research, management systems, or manufacturing systems), or academician.

To reiterate, the change master of the future must deal with the 3^n-ball problem:

- Solving the focal problem or capturing the opportunity: **effectively implementing and deploying, if appropriate, the performance improvement project(s)**
- Bringing to bear and allocating the right amount and appropriate type of resources to succeed with the improvement projects: **resource management, project management**
- Successfully designing, developing, and implementing strategies for these improvement projects such that results are achieved at the appropriate system levels: **implementation and deployment strategies of the change master.**

We would argue that it is the combination of these three balls that must be mastered to address the challenges and problems discussed in Chapter 1. **Change masters will be more successful if they employ the matrix as a guide in planning improvement projects; this is our** hypothesis. If change masters are more successful, rate of improvement will increase over time and the organization will be more successful. If the organization's rate of improvement increases, particularly if the organization's capacity and capability to improve increases over time, then it will be postured to compete, survive, and thrive in the future. "B" will become a way of doing business throughout the organization, and there will be less "C" and more time to do both "A" and "B." This is the cycle of relationships that the change master is attempting to establish.

CHAPTER 8

CORE COMPETENCIES AND TOOLS
OF THE CHANGE MASTER

We have discussed the phases of change individuals, groups, and organizations generally tend to pass through when engaging in improvement efforts of any size or magnitude. We have presented and discussed professional modes of functioning that change masters employ as they help clients improve performance. Chapter 7 combined these two dimensions in the form of a matrix and discussed numerous phase/mode combinations. To this point, we have minimized an emphasis on core competencies and tools that the change master or change target must personally, or through other resources, apply to quality and productivity improvement efforts. However, this is another dimension crucial to change master success. In this chapter, and in Chapter 11, these topics are the focus of our discussion. As we proceed, please continue to internalize the phase/mode matrix as we address core competencies and tools that relate to phases of change.

In order to avoid elegant variation, we wish to clarify what we mean by the terms core competency and tools. A core competency represents a key area of knowledge and skill we believe must be brought to bear on large-scale improvement efforts. Core competencies can be mapped to cells in the matrix presented in Chapter 7. A tool is a process, technique, or method. A given tool can be mapped to a core competency, as we illustrate later in this chapter. Core competencies are, in a sense, clusters of tools. Having presented those definitions, we now turn to a more detailed discussion of core competencies for the change master.

EXPANDING THE MATRIX

What are the core technical areas that change masters must be familiar with to perform effectively in the organizational system of the '90s and beyond? We have been studying this problem at Virginia Tech for the past eight years, and I have struggled with this issue since the late seventies. It is clear to us that this subject is of increasing importance and interest. Universities are being challenged to apply TQM, to research TQM, to teach TQM, to become more customer driven. Engineering programs are being challenged to integrate TQM into their curriculum. Some are choosing the analytical approach, creating courses specifically devoted to TQM, while others, like Virginia Tech, have chosen to attempt to synthesize TQM into all or most of our courses. The synthesis approach, of course, is the most complex, difficult, and yet potentially rewarding.

During the summer of 1992, I had the opportunity to host a joint meeting of the Council of Industrial Engineering (CIE—practicing leaders and managers of industrial engineering or related functions), Council of Industrial Engineering Academic Department Heads (CIEADH—chairs and heads of academic industrial engineering departments), and the Institute of Industrial Engineers (IIE—the professional society for industrial engineers worldwide). Several key leaders from each of these three groups participated in a strategy session relative to our profession. One of our more significant discussions centered around the life-long learning process and the relative roles of the university, the company, and the professional society in this endeavor. We also spent quite a bit of time discussing business, industry, and government satisfaction with the industrial engineering education provided by academia.

When the CIE representatives spoke, they discussed customer and end-user requirements and expectations for graduate industrial engineers such as team building, problem solving, facilitation, and leadership. In other words, they tended to focus a great deal on what we have called professional modes of functioning. They rarely mentioned engineering economic analysis, operations research, quality control, or measurement as requirements not being met. It wasn't that these weren't important, it's just that, in practice, this isn't where their IEs and change masters are struggling.

We have been paying close attention to several organizations, one of them being Eli Lilly. They have developed a very successful performance improvement engineering department. The department is filled with internal change masters. We also have been fortunate to have had sponsors and supportive advocates, such as Dominic Monetta, who believe in our research and our visions and have been willing to provide grants and contracts that have supported continuing development of the Management Systems Engineering and Performance Improvement Engineering and change master training and development efforts. We have been attempting to do some reverse engineering. If we know what a successful change master looks like in practice, then can we create a plan of study that would create one "from scratch"? We think we are close to having at least an initial, feasible solution to that problem; we still have a lot of bugs to work out, but we're close.

We have taken a fairly disciplined curriculum design approach, identifying skill, knowledge, and information requirements, and background prerequisites, all driven from an attempt to understand customer and user requirements and expectations. Based on our analysis, we believe change masters will have to be technically competent in the following areas:

- **Planning:** Strategic planning, implementation, deployment, Hoshin-Kanri;
- **Problem-solving:** Analytic, creative, individual and group;
- **Project and Program Management:** Managing the "three-ball" problem and the "3^n-ball" problem;
- **Financial Decision Analysis:** Engineering economic analysis, corporate finance, accounting, the ability to speak the language of management and translate improvement alternatives into bottom-line numbers;
- **Measurement:** Statistical thinking, extreme proficiency in statistics, exploratory data analysis, understanding variation, understanding the process of deciding what to measure, how to get data, how to store, retrieve, and process data, how to convert data into information, and how to convert information into knowledge are the key aspects of this area. Theory of knowledge is somewhat related, as is philosophy of science.
- **Motivation:** Theory of psychology, basic motivation theories (job characteristics theory, expectancy theory, equity theory, reinforcement theory), individual, group, and organizational behavior. Related core competencies include: meeting management, small-group behavior, time management, stress management, conflict management, management of participation, team building, and management of change.
- **System and Process Improvement (Methods Engineering, Systems Engineering, Process Engineering, Design and Development):** Business process re-engineering, process improvement, organizational alignment, organizational redesign.

Figure 22 attempts to integrate the core competency areas into the matrix.

These core competencies, then, represent what we believe are the minimum requirements for change masters. It may well be that we have left some critical competencies off our list; clearly, our taxonomy will be challenged. Our intent is to cluster areas of knowledge that have tools associated with them that will be called upon frequently by change masters. Our presentation and discussion focus not so much on how to apply these competencies and tools as on ensuring that the reader has adequate direction for further study. In Chapter 11, we provide additional developmental guidance and address key application issues. The aim in this chapter and in Chapter 11 is to guide readers in their efforts to come up to speed in these areas.

To reiterate, the individual change master may not always personally provide the expertise in a given situation, rather he or she may broker the applicable competence; the important thing is that the appropriate knowledge or skill is applied at the right time to ensure success in the improvement effort. Thus, the challenge for the change master is not necessarily to apply the technical skills, but to ensure that the appropriate competency is brought to bear on the problem or opportunity at hand. In some cases, the change master may be applying the particular expertise, in other cases teaching it, in other cases working to locate and obtain (broker) an internal or external source of that particular competency. This represents "situational competency application" as applied to the art and science of change mastering.

AN OVERVIEW

Planning

We begin here because if an organizational system isn't ensuring it is doing the right things first, then nothing else matters. The improvement cycle (plan-do-study-act) begins with planning. Planning, to us, involves the organization's entire planning system or front, including strategic planning, short-interval scheduling, daily controls, tactical planning, operational planning, individual/group/organizational planning, implementation and deployment, budget planning, market and sales planning, and time management.

Perhaps first, strategic planning is important to understand. We have found since strategic planning is clearly in the domain of top management and leadership it is crucial a change master be knowledgeable. This does not mean that the change master must be the strategic planner, just that the change master should be technically competent in this area. Lack of top management involvement is the most often cited roadblock to quality and productivity improvement. If the change master is able to get top leadership and management involved in their form of P (plan), then a lot of the common problems associated with TQM, CI (continuous improvement), and "B" will disappear. The secret, it seems, is how to integrate TQM, CI, "B" in with the "A," and strategic planning—how to get top leadership and management to see total quality and continuous improvement in the context of what they do and how they do it.

Top leadership almost always is unhappy with the quality of their strategic planning methods. They are almost always searching for an improved way to ensure implementation and deployment. If the change master could provide a technology for doing this, then other improvement initiatives would logically drive from this effort. All improvement interventions throughout the organization, vertically and horizontally, should be driven from the

	SITUATION APPRAISAL	CATHARSIS	SELF EVALUATION	SELF AWARENESS	SELF DESIGNED CHANGE	TRYING NEW BEHAVIORS	REINFORCING NEW BEHAVIORS
CHALLENGER	1.7	BEF 2.7	EF 3.7	ABDE FG 4.7	5.7	6.7	EF 7.7
EXPERT	EG 1.6	BEDF 2.6	3.6	ABC DEG 4.6	ABC DEG 5.6	6.6	EGBA C 7.6
TEACHER	GEB 1.5	B 2.5	3.5	BE 4.5	ABDG 5.5	BAC DEG 6.5	FEC 7.5
STRUCTURE PROVIDER	BE 1.4	2.4	3.4	EBD 4.4	AB 5.4	GBA 6.4	AFC DE 7.4
COLLABORATOR	BEF 1.3	F 2.3	EBF 3.3	FEDB 4.3	ABC DEG 5.3	F 6.3	E 7.3
DATA/FACT GATHERER	EB 1.2	EB 2.2	EBF 3.2	EFDB 4.2	BCED 5.2	6.2	EFCB 7.2
INQUIRY	EBF 1.1	F 2.1	F 3.1	F 4.1	F 5.1	F 6.1	F 7.1

Figure 22. The matrix shows the relationships between the Phases of Change (Figure 14), Professional Modes of Functioning (Figure 19), and Core Competencies of the Change Master (Figure 22A).

AREAS OF CHANGEMASTER TECHNICAL COMPETENCE

A = PLANNING

B = PROBLEM SOLVING

C = PROJECT MANAGEMENT

D = DECISION ANALYSIS (FINANCIAL)

E = MEASUREMENT

F = MOTIVATION

G = SYSTEM AND PROCESS IMPROVEMENT

DEGREE OF MATCH

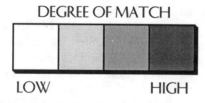

LOW   HIGH

Figure 22A. The matrix becomes a more powerful and versatile tool for the change master when tools and areas of technical competence are identified for each cell of the matrix.

organization's strategic plan. In this sense, we feel that Hoshin Kanri appears to be something very worthy of change master study. This done in the context of the Strategic Performance Improvement Planning Process (SPIPP) presented by Sink and Tuttle provides a solid foundation for thinking about the planning system component of an organization.

Measurement, Analysis, Evaluation, Assessment

Perhaps the best way to understand the role of measurement in improvement is to review Kurstedt's Management Systems Model in the context of the improvement cycle (PDSA). Figure 23 depicts a modified Management Systems Model (MSM). To elaborate a bit more on the MSM, a management system has three components: (1) who manages—manager, leader, management team, employees, process owner, etc., (2) what is being managed—an organizational system, a process, a project, a program, and (3) what we manage with—broadly speaking, "tools"—the conversion of data to information, to include mind/intuition/judgment, software, models, etc. A management system has three interfaces: (1) the decision-to-action interface, (2) the information portrayal-to-information perception interface, and (3) the measurement-to-data interface.

Measurement creates data, data is converted into information, information is evaluated by who is managing, decisions are made on the basis of information, actions are taking on the basis of these decisions, the organizational system is affected by these actions, we measure the effects, and the cycle continues. Planning occurs in the decision phase, Doing occurs in the action phase, Study occurs in the data-to-information-to-portrayal and processing phase, Acting occurs in rounding the corner and replanning.

The SPIPP also can be fit into this model (Figure 24). Steps 2 through 4 represent the Plan phase, the decision-to-action interface. Step 5 is the Do phase or the action portion of the decision to action interface. Step 6 is the Study phase or the measurement-to-data-to-information portrayal portion of MSM. Step 7 is the Act phase or the recycle of the process.

Every management team has a domain of responsibility for "A," "B," and "C." Their job is at least threefold: (1) ensure that "A" is getting accomplished in a fashion that meets or exceeds requirements and expectations and that periodically delights the customers, (2) ensure that the organizational system they are responsible for is continually improving at a rate that is competitive and in such a way as to optimize the performance of the larger system, and (3) effectively and efficiently solve the endless stream of crises and problems that will arise as they attempt to do 1 and 2. It is clear that management teams cannot succeed without effective, high-quality measurement systems, yet this is truly the weak link in most organizations.

In many respects, our measurement problems are information system problems—getting appropriate information to people in a timely fashion such that problem solving and decision making relative to improvement are supported. The key question is what information is required to support problem solving, opportunity capturing, and decision making/action taking aimed at doing "A," "B," and "C"? Measurement systems are required to provide data that then will be converted to information, evaluated, and used.

We don't mean to oversimplify measurement, but these are the basics. This isn't all there is, but it's a start. References at the end of the chapter are intended to solidify your foundation and to provide a basis for your study plan in this area.

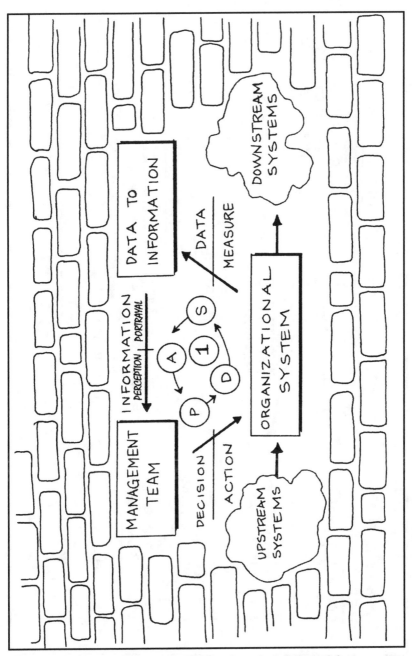

Figure 23. The Management Systems Model can be used as a framework for understanding measurement and its engineering (adapted from Kurstedt).

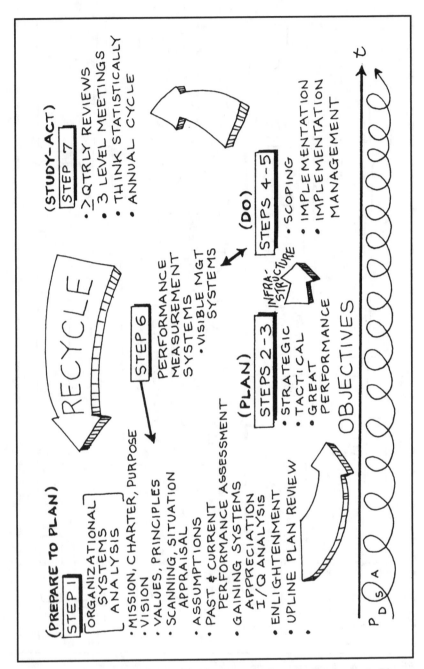

Figure 24. The steps in the strategic planning process can be mapped to the steps in Plan-Do-Study-Act (PDSA).

Problem Solving

Most people aren't exposed to something as "ordinary" as problem solving in college or high school. That's interesting, because as M. Scott Peck (1978) suggests, life is an endless stream of problems. Every time we solve one problem, we create another. Life in organizations is surely filled with problems and crises. It seems that this era of increasing pressures for improvement has created a predictable generator of problems and that problem-solving skills are at a premium. We all solve problems, but the key question is, "By what method?" The variation in methods for problem solving is tremendous among individuals, yet next to planning, problem solving may be the most written about subject in management.

The change master must be a skilled individual and team problem solver. He or she must have to have a core methodology that they understand and can teach in helping teams and organizations develop methods for more effective problem solving. We will have more and more problems to solve, so the method by which we solve them must improve significantly. This is a key technical requirement for the change master that we feel is often overlooked but relatively easy to acquire.

Motivation

Understanding individual, group, and organizational motivation is at the heart of positive change and improvement. Why would people want to change, to participate in improvement efforts? What makes people want to contribute to making things better? Again, theory of psychology is one of Dr. Deming's four elements of profound knowledge. How do we operationalize this aspect of profound knowledge? Perhaps most simplistically, theory of psychology begins with an understanding of four basic theories of motivation:

- Expectancy Theory
- Equity Theory
- Job Characteristics Theory
- Reinforcement Theory.

References for each of the four theory areas are provided at the end of this chapter and application issues relative to these theories will be discussed in Chapter 11. These four theories present different, though not necessarily mutually exclusive, angles on motivation at the individual level.

Expectancy theory suggests that we choose what to do on the basis of expectations of time and ability to perform, relationship to performance and consequences, and values we place on consequences. It suggests our force to perform is most influenced by expectations that we can perform, expectations of consequences being tied to performance, and the values we place on these consequences.

Equity theory suggests that we compare ourselves to others and this influences our level of effort and the quality of our effort. It suggests our motivation is most influenced by these social comparisons and our perceptions of equity.

Job characteristics theory focuses on the dimensions of jobs that have motivational potential (task identity, task significance, skill variety, autonomy, and feedback). Job enrichment is based upon this theory. It suggests that we are most motivated by the characteristics of the job.

Reinforcement theory could be considered to be integral to expectancy theory. It focuses on the action-consequence linkages. It simplistically posits that people seek "sugar" (positive reinforcement) and avoid "shock" (negative reinforcement); therefore we should provide sugar for those behaviors and performances we want, and withhold it when we don't observe those behaviors and performances or observe behaviors we don't want. Reinforcement theory and research concludes that punishment is not an effective mechanism for positively influencing performance.

These four basic theories help the change master understand individual motivation and behavior. Unfortunately, there are not, to my knowledge, equally well articulated theories of motivation and behavior at the group and organizational level. Theories exist but not in quite the same "closed forms" that exist for the I-level theories. One could argue that group motivation and performance is simply the sum of individual-level motivations and performance, but we know that is overly simplistic. In its simplest form, group performance would be the sum of individual performances plus a synergistic component. The greater the interdependencies in the group the greater weighting the synergistic component will have, which means that the synergistic component must be managed for it to occur.

Perhaps most fundamental to understanding group and organizational motivation, behavior, and performance is an understanding and commitment to purpose. Barnard (1939) stated that there are at least three functions of the executive: (1) establish and maintain organizational purpose, (2) provide a system of communication, and (3) maintain a willingness to cooperate. Understanding organizational purpose, ensuring that individuals and groups understand their role in the organization, involving individuals and groups in the improvement cycle, providing a vision that all individuals can buy into, sharing information and knowledge on a consistent and ongoing basis, sharing power and rewards when appropriate, maintaining coordination, ensuring that the conditions of success for the business are understood, shared, and followed, inspiring and promoting learning individuals and groups—these are the essence of group and organizational motivation, behavior, and performance.

As the change master tackles the motivation front, he or she will be required to convert knowledge about motivation theories into interventions at the individual, group, and organizational levels to influence behaviors positively. We will discuss this more in Chapter 11.

Project and Program Management

We have introduced the three-ball problem and the 3^n-ball problem. Clearly, solving the focal problem, allocating resources on improvement projects, and developing and managing implementation strategy represent a project management challenge. In a sense the change master is a program and project manager. The program is the transformation; the projects are the variety of improvement efforts that will take place over time to make the transformation happen.

What can be said about project management that hasn't been written already or that isn't intuitively obvious? Again, the challenge for the change master with respect to project management may be in going from knowledge to skill. If this is the case, then "perfect practice makes perfect." We'll assume you have ability and willingness, and if you really are in a change master role you certainly have opportunities; therefore, performance should follow if you work at it.

Techniques or tools to aid project management abound: PERT (project evaluation and review technique) and CPM (critical path method); Gantt charts; budget software for projects to monitor efficiency; most Day-Timer-type products (personal planners) include hard-copy templates designed to aid project management. In short, the tools of project management range from very complex and software supported to very simple, almost intuitive aids.

Financial Decision Analysis

It has been said that the language of managers is money and finance. Improvement projects, most at least, will be decided upon and evaluated in terms of results to the organizational system. Benefits and costs will be assessed at some point in the life cycle of a project. The change master must be able to use accounting systems, understand corporate finance, and perform engineering economic analysis on specific projects. We refer the reader to examples of texts that can be utilized to gain foundational knowledge in these three areas at the end of this chapter.

Uncertainty and risk are other dimensions of decision making that will need to be incorporated by the change master. Decision analysis is a term given the study of improving rational decision making. It includes models for how decision makers deal with uncertainty and risk. Probabilities of success can be incorporated into decisions leading to expected value enumeration. The change master can assist decision makers by helping to weight alternatives or criteria of evaluation and by assisting with assessments of probabilities associated with outcome accomplishment (see Morris for a good treatment on this subject).

Projects spanning many years may require analysis incorporating the time value of money. Revenues and expenses in the future are less valuable than in the present. We want to defer expenses and move revenues closer to the present. There are straightforward formulas for evaluating cash flows over the life of a multiyear project and creating a present worth. Tax considerations may become a part of the analysis.

Methods Engineering, Systems Engineering, Process Improvement, Business Process Engineering/Re-engineering

The Japanese did not invent the study and improvement of work. They did not invent most of the tools of quality; the founders of industrial engineering, Frederick Taylor and Frank and Lilian Gilbreth, and their followers did. The productivity revolution was sparked by the application of industrial engineering. The current knowledge revolution will likely be driven by the application of change master principles and methods to knowledge work.

What industrial engineers and others have failed to do over the past forty years is to innovate and improve implementation effectiveness of these tools of improvement. The Japanese largely deserve credit for that. Most, if not all, traditional industrial engineering innovation in the study and improvement of work and work systems is being driven by the Japanese today, in my opinion. Industrial engineers in this country have lost sight of the ends and have focused on the means, and the result is perfection of means and confusion of end. Our "end" is quality and productivity improvement. We are perfecting the means, creating elegant models that can't be reduced to practice.

Business process engineering isn't new; it is methods engineering being applied at the organizational systems level. Yet, it is being hailed by some as the next wave, the approach that will displace TQM. We've got a lot of confused people today.

Methods engineering is the systematic application of key principles associated with work. We are engineering methods so that performance is optimized. Notice we didn't say efficiency is optimized. Again, systems thinking teaches us that optimizing a subsystem (in this case a method) may not always translate into improved performance of the larger system. We saw this in *The Goal.* Optimizing the performance of one piece of equipment did not translate into better performance of the plant because the piece of equipment was not a bottleneck. This is the tricky part of applying methods and process improvement today; we have to balance elements of performance, and we must do it in the context of the system. We can't always assume that optimal methods in terms of efficiency will translate into better performance. In the past we focused on efficiency only; now we must focus on total performance. It makes the job of an industrial engineer much more complex and important.

Figure 25 includes just a partial listing of tools and techniques for methods engineering and business process engineering we find being documented in case examples of Japanese quality and productivity improvement efforts (referenced at the end of this chapter). It makes our current work measurement and methods engineering text books look somewhat obsolete. I'm not convinced we have many, if any, people in this country who can write the work management textbooks for the '90s. It is not in vogue to teach work measurement and improvement courses in industrial engineering. Few if any young industrial engineering professors are researching this, let alone writing about it. Some departments are even discontinuing the course in favor of TQM-oriented courses. The study of work, how to improve it at the individual, work center, and group levels and in both blue-collar and white-collar settings is important for us to continue the productivity revolution, particularly in developing countries, and for us to progress in the knowledge revolution.

Change masters will need to play a role in maintaining the productivity and knowledge revolutions through innovation in methods and process improvement and application of quality and productivity improvement tools. The use of tools to facilitate consensus building, decision making, implementation, problem solving, planning, data analysis, information portrayal, and any number of tasks will accelerate in the '90s and beyond: the change master will need to lead the organization in a more systematic use of the tools of quality and productivity improvement. This clearly is a crucial technical component for a change master.

THE TOOLS OF THE CHANGE MASTER
A detailed discussion of all tools and technologies, at the method description or "how to" level, is beyond the scope of this book and beyond our ability. Recall that core competencies represent clusters of tools. Figure 26, 26A and 26B are our attempt to portray the relationships between Figure 25 and Figure 22A.

Clearly, there is a broader set of tools than we have identified that are at the disposal of the change master and the client for the purpose of performance improvement. Here, we provide a "shopping list" or "menu" of tools with which we are familiar. Our goal is not to teach you how to use these tools or describe them comprehensively because this has been done elsewhere. Rather, we want to make you aware of these tools and, we hope, spark your desire to broaden and deepen your knowledge and skill in applying them.

Recall that earlier in the chapter we indicated that tools mapped to core competencies, and core competencies could be mapped to cells in the phases of change/professional

Figure 25. The change master has many standardized tools available for use in leading improvement efforts.

A=PLANNING

Nominal Group Technique
Strategic Performance Improvement
  Planning Process (7 step)
Visioning Exercise, Field of Dreams
"Prouds and Sorries"
Assumptions, Importance/certainty Grid
Past and Present Analysis (structured)
Input/output Exercise
Guiding Principles (Man from Mars Exercise)
Enlightenment, Mental Preparation

B=PROBLEM SOLVING

Situation Appraisal
Problem Identification
Problem Analysis
Design, Development
Decision Analysis
Decision Making
Implementation Analysis
Implementation
Evaluation
Kepner-Tregoe
Creative Problem Solving
Imaginization
Utility Theory
Multi-attribute Decision Analysis

C=PROJECT/PROGRAM MANAGEMENT

PERT (Project Evaluation and
  Review Technique)
CPM (Critical Path Method)
GSS Mapping
Gantt Charts
Plan of Action and Milestone Charts (POAM)
All-hands Meetings
Organizational, Group, and
  Individual Development

Figure 26. Each area of technical competence identified in the matrix has a set of tools/ skills/methods available.

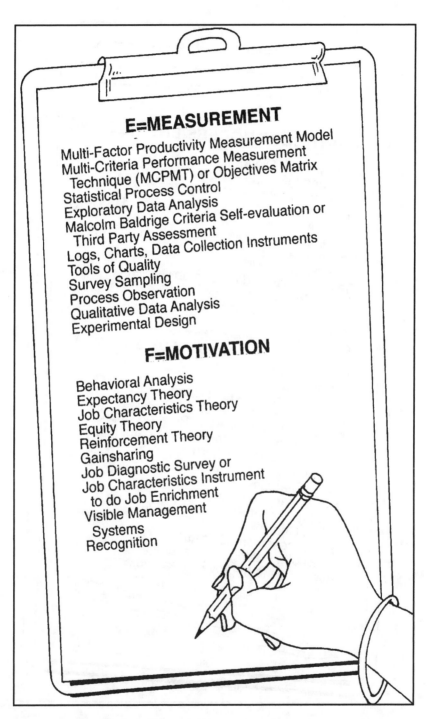

Figure 26 A. Each area of technical competence identified in the matrix has a set of tools/ skills/methods available.

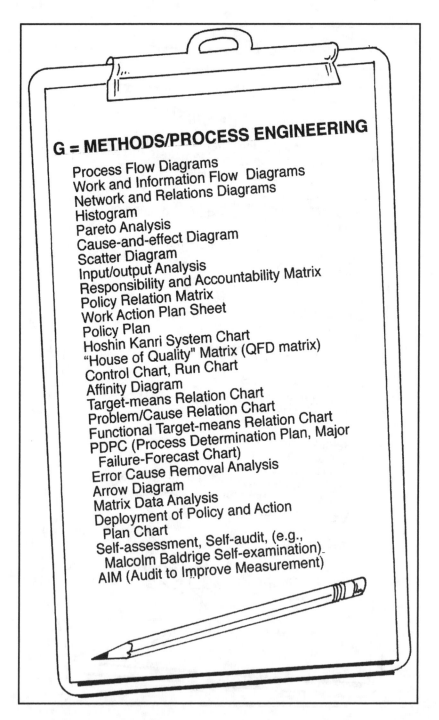

G = METHODS/PROCESS ENGINEERING

Process Flow Diagrams
Work and Information Flow Diagrams
Network and Relations Diagrams
Histogram
Pareto Analysis
Cause-and-effect Diagram
Scatter Diagram
Input/output Analysis
Responsibility and Accountability Matrix
Policy Relation Matrix
Work Action Plan Sheet
Policy Plan
Hoshin Kanri System Chart
"House of Quality" Matrix (QFD matrix)
Control Chart, Run Chart
Affinity Diagram
Target-means Relation Chart
Problem/Cause Relation Chart
Functional Target-means Relation Chart
PDPC (Process Determination Plan, Major
  Failure-Forecast Chart)
Error Cause Removal Analysis
Arrow Diagram
Matrix Data Analysis
Deployment of Policy and Action
  Plan Chart
Self-assessment, Self-audit, (e.g.,
  Malcolm Baldrige Self-examination)
AIM (Audit to Improve Measurement)

Figure 26 B (continued). Each area of technical competence identified in the matrix has a set of tools/skills/methods available.

modes of functioning matrix presented in Chapter 7. We conclude this chapter by providing guidance for the change master regarding which core competencies and corresponding tools will be most appropriate for specific phase/mode combinations. It may be helpful in this discussion to refer back to the matrix in Figure 22.

CORE COMPETENCIES AND TOOLS MAPPED TO THE MATRIX

Planning
Planning tools are most commonly applied during situation appraisal, self-designed change, and trying out new methods and behaviors. Mode relationships are strong with structure provider, data gatherer, inquiry mode, teacher, and expert (in that the change master often may bring a planning process to the client), and team member collaborator. Cells (1,1), (1,2), (5,1), (5,2), (5,4), (5,5), and (5,6) are most active in the context of the phase, mode, and competency combination.

Measurement, Analysis, Evaluation, Assessment
Measurement tools are most commonly applied during the situation appraisal, self-awareness, self-evaluation, and reinforcing new behavior phases of change. Mode relationships are strong with data gatherer, team member, teacher, and expert solution provider. Cells (1,2), (1,5), (1,6), (3,2), (4,2), (4,5), (4,6), (7,1), (7,2), (7,5), and (7,6) are most active in the context of the phase, mode, and competency combination.

Problem Solving
Problem-solving tools, when considered to include or encompass these broad areas, map very nicely to all phases of change: situation appraisal, issue identification and analysis, problem identification, problem analysis, design and development, decision analysis, decision making, implementation analysis, implementation, and evaluation. In fact, in some sense, the full problem-solving model parallels the phases of change. Likewise, the change master will find most modes useful and active at some point in full-scale problem solving. Specific cells of importance are: (1,1), (1,2), (1,3), (1,6), (2, 7), (2,1), (3,2), (3,5), (4,2), (4,3), (4,5), (5,3), (5,5), (5,6), (6,3), (6,6), (7,1), and (7,5).

Motivation
Motivation tools are most commonly applied during the situation appraisal, catharsis, self-designed change, trying out, and reinforcing new methods and behaviors phases. Mode relationships are strong with inquiry mode, data gatherer, team member, structured group process provider, and teacher. Cells (1,1), (2,1), (5,3), (5,5), (5,6), (6,5), (7,1), (7,2), and (7,5) are most active in the context of the phase, mode, and competency combination.

Project and Program Management
Project and program management tools are most predominant during the self-designed change and trying out new behavior phases. Mode relationships are strong with data gatherer, team member, teacher, and expert. Cells (5,2), (5,3), (5,5), (5,6), (6,2), (6,3), (6,5), and (6,6) are most active in the context of the phase, mode, and competency combination.

Financial Decision Analysis

Financial decision analysis tools are most commonly applied during the situation appraisal, self-evaluation, self-designed change, and reinforcing new methods and behavior phases. Mode relationships are with data gatherer, teacher, and expert. Cells (1,2), (1,6), (1,5), (4,2), (4,5), (4,6), (7,2), (7,5), and (7,6) are most active in the context of the phase, mode, and competency combinations.

Methods Engineering, Management Systems Engineering, Process Improvement, Business Process Engineering/Re-engineering

These types of tools are commonly applied during the self-awareness, self-evaluation, self-designed change, and reinforcing new methods and behaviors phases. Mode relationships exist with data gatherer, structure provider, teacher, and expert. Cells (3,2), (3,5), (3,6), (4,2), (4,3), (4,5), (4,6), (5,2), (5,5), (5,6), (7,2), (7,5), and (7,6) are most active in the context of the phase, mode, and competency combinations.

CONCLUSION

In the earlier work by Morris, the client change phase and professional mode of functioning matrix was introduced as an attempt to integrate bodies of knowledge from counseling, psychotherapy, implementation, evaluation, public administration, industrial engineering, organizational development, group development, and industrial psychology and to bring this knowledge to bear on the problem of implementation. Since that time not much has changed; we still face significant implementation and deployment challenges relative to quality and productivity improvement. However, there have been significant strides made in the area of broader utilization of industrial and systems engineering tools for quality and productivity improvement. The productivity revolution of the '70s and '80s created a solid foundation for the quality revolution of the '90s. TQM has become almost a household term as a result of the Malcolm Baldrige Award visibility, regional and local quality councils, state quality and productivity centers and award processes, and, of course, the unrelenting dedication of Dr. Deming. Attempts to utilize quality tools to improve performance are still in an early stage of development, but deployment is far greater than in the '70s and '80s.

It seems to us that the relationship between areas of technical competency, phases of change, and professional modes of functioning is crucial to the success of quality and productivity improvement efforts. Our experience suggests that change masters who fail typically do so because they lack one or more of the following:

• Technical competence in at least a set of key areas;
• Intellectual honesty;
• Social skills;
• Political astuteness;
• Planning and project management skills;
• Positive self-regard;
• Unrelenting dedication, proper work ethic;
• Communication skills;
• A network within the organization and outside the organization;
• Desire to learn;

• Ability to envision, to think big, to think systems;
• A servant, service mentality;
• Learned optimism.

So we see that success as a change master is a function of a number of factors in addition to understanding phases of change, being able to situationally call upon a number of professional modes of functioning, and having a set of technical competencies. What we have attempted to do in Sections I through IV is present and explore, in some detail, the three basic variables of phases of change, professional modes of functioning, and areas of technical competencies and tools. The additional variables listed above should be considered during Section VI as you develop your personal and professional plan of study and development.

Next, we move to the application of the phase/mode/tool model to large-scale quality and productivity improvement efforts. A clear trend has emerged in the past several years of making systemwide (implied in large-scale) improvements. Business Process Engineering, for example, is large-scale by definition. TQM, if done properly, is large-scale. What we are finding is that our small-scale productivity and quality improvement intervention approaches are failing us. Transitioning from a small-scale improvement project to a large-scale program is difficult. So, Section V is devoted to presenting a method for approaching these ambitious improvement efforts we all seem to be a part of today.

DEVELOPMENT WORK

INQUIRY QUESTIONS
These are questions you have for yourself or for others to help you better understand what was covered in this section.

Inquire First
What didn't you understand, what do you want to know about, what assumptions or beliefs do we posit that you want us to explain, what do you want clarification on?

Advocate Second
What did you disagree with, what do you want to argue about, what didn't you like, what do you want to challenge, in what areas do we appear to have different assumptions, data bases, beliefs, or attitudes?

LEARNING EXERCISES
LE 4.1 The following sequences of cell numbers suggest possible descriptions of change processes relative to the matrix for a variety of disciplines and experiences. To what degree do these descriptions match your experience? What would you predict about the relative effectiveness of these phase mode combinations? Again, remember the numbers are x-axis first (phases of change) and the y-axis second (PMOF).

Traditional industrial engineer: 1,2; 1,6; 6,6; 7,2
Academic consultant: 1,5; 1,6; 4,6; 6,6

Short course, seminar:	1,5; 3,5
Social scientist:	1,2; 1,3; 2,1; 7,1
Private sector consultant:	6,6; 1,2
TQM coordinator:	7,7; 7,3; 2,7

Think about how our disciplines in effect restrict how we operate as change masters. Think about how broadening these "preferred" cells or domains of behavior would improve implementation and deployment effectiveness.

LE 4.2 Obtain a case study from Harvard Business School, or other source, or from your own experience as long as your data are complete enough for analysis, or from some journal, and interpret what was done in terms of the matrix. What does this suggest in the way of modifications to the matrix? Does the use of the matrix suggest any insights about the way the project was accomplished or its outcomes?

LE 4.3 Try to find as many case examples of failures as possible either from personal experience or from the literature. You may want to do some interviews with people who have worked on a number of improvement projects. Do a root-cause analysis of the failures. What did you find, and how does it match with what has been presented to this point in the book?

LE 4.4 Try using the matrix to plan your next improvement project. Each time you plan to make an intervention think through cells you want or need to be in and then, once you have made a client contact, assess the effectiveness of your strategy.

LE 4.5 Use the matrix to do a professional assessment or audit of your change master breadth and depth. Take a sheet of paper and list the fourteen categories for the two dimensions (seven categories for each dimension or axis).
First, evaluate your understanding of, your ability to sense the need for, your ability to identify, your ability to behave in a given phase of change. For example, do you recognize when catharsis is needed, and can you behave accordingly?
Next, evaluate your level of skill in behaving in each of the seven behavioral modes of functioning. You might want to rank these in terms of your preference based upon your style and your skill.
Next, rate your LOK (level of knowledge, from 1 to 5) in each of the core technology areas. If you want to subdivide the areas into specific technologies that is even better, the more specific you can be the better. What does your tool kit look like?
Now, identify cells in the matrix and the technologies that you feel are most critical to success as a change master. For example: Cell 1,1 is obviously a critical cell. Cell 4,5 also is going to be critical on a real-time basis, the ability to teach the right thing at the right time or get access to it quickly. Of the forty-nine possible cells only a subset will be used commonly and only certain technologies will be utilized; what do you think this subset is? Once you have identified the cells you think will be most in demand, rank and rate your skill level and knowledge level relative to those.
Save this assignment; we will be using it again in the last section.

LE 4.6 From your own personal experience, write up a case example of an improvement project you led or in which you participated closely in the form we have been following in our case examples. What did you learn in writing down your experience? What could have been done differently to improve implementation and deployment?

LE 4.7 One of the most successful and well-developed contingency models of management decision making is that of Vroom and Yetton (Ivancevich 1977). Show how the structure of this model might be adapted to change-process design.

FEEDBACK QUESTIONS

FBQ 4.1 Explain the relationship between phases of change, professional modes of functioning, and core competency areas.

FBQ 4.2 What core competency areas have been left out of our discussion?

FBQ 4.3 What are your areas of technical competence?

FBQ 4.4 How much do you know, what is your level of knowledge, about the following:

A. Quality Function Deployment
B. Hoshin Kanri
C. ISO-9000
D. Malcolm Baldrige Award
E. Business Process Engineering or re-engineering
F. Benchmarking
G. Strategic Planning
H. Statistics (regression analysis, sampling, nonparametric, statistical process control, experimental design, exploratory data analysis)
I. Seven Basic Tools of Quality
J. Seven New Tools of Quality
K. Measurement
   — Total Factor Productivity Measurement Model
   — Multi-Criteria Performance Measurement Technique
   — Objectives Matrix
   — Psychometrics
L. Problem solving (group, structured, creative)
M. Group Behavior
N. Expectancy Theory, Equity Theory, Job Characteristics Theory, Reinforcement Theory, Behavioral Analysis
O. Organizational Development
P. Nominal Group Technique and Delphi Technique
Q. Engineering Economic Analysis
R. Time management
S. Counseling
T. Stress management

U.   Goal setting
V.   Longitudinal data analysis, theory of variation
W. PERT, CPM, Gantt Charts, Milestone Charts
X.   Meeting management
Y.   POAM's (plans of action and milestone charts)
Z.   Life-cycle systems engineering and management.

FBQ 4.5 What technologies, tools, methods, and techniques have you found useful over your years of experience? What are your preferred tools? Do you tend to overuse a given tool just because it has worked in the past and you are comfortable with it? What are you doing to increase breadth and depth of tools related to performance improvement?

FBQ 4.6 Discuss which cells (mode, phase, tool) make the most sense to you. Which are you most familiar with? Which are you most skilled with? How would you map out a phase, mode, tool overall strategy for an improvement effort? What would this strategy look like if you were to formalize it, make it explicit? How could you develop one that would be a useful tool for you? Relate the three-ball problem to the phase, mode, tool model.

FBQ 4.7 Operationally define:
  • Phases of change
  • Professional modes of functioning
  • Tools
  • Phase, mode, tool combinations/cells
  • The three balls in the three-ball problem.

FBQ 4.8 If you were to identify core competency areas relevant for change masters, what would the categories be? What specific techologies/tools/techniques would you put in these categories that are particularly relevant for change masters?

PLAN OF STUDY
What follows is a list of resources that support, in general, the material introduced in this section. Scan the list, indicate which you have read (R), studied (S), attempted to use (U), and which you would like to become acquainted with (TBD).

LITERATURE CITED
Akao, Y. (ed.). 1991. *Hoshin Kanri: Policy Deployment for Successful TQM*. Cambridge, Conn.: Productivity Press.
Barnard, C. I. 1938. *The Functions of the Executive*. Cambridge, Mass.: Harvard University Press.
Block, P. 1981. *Flawless Consulting*. San Diego, Calif.: University Associates.
Deming, W. E. 1993. *The New Economics*. Cambridge, Mass.: MIT Center for Advanced Engineering Study.
Delbecq, A. L., A. H. Van de Ven, and D. H. Gustafson. 1986. *Group Techniques for Program Planning: a guide to nominal group and delphi processes*. Middleton, Wis.: Green Briar Press.
Kurstedt, H. A. 1993. *The Industrial Engineer's Systematic Approach to Management*. MSL Working Draft and articles and responsive systems article. Blacksburg, Va.: Management Systems Laboratories.

Lewin, K. 1947. Frontiers in group dynamics: concepts, method and reality in social science. *Human Relations*. 1(5): 5-42.

Lewin, K. 1951. *Field Theory in Social Sciences*. New York: Harper and Row.

Lewin, K. 1958. Group decision and social change. In *Readings in Social Psychology*. Edited by E. E. Maccoby, I. E. Newcomb, and E. L. Hartley. New York: Holt.

Monetta, D. J., and D. S. Sink. 1991. Continuous improvement: implementing a grand strategy system at the office of new production reactors. *Quality and Productivity Management*. 9(3).

Morris, W. T. 1977. *Decision Analysis*. Columbus, Ohio: Grid.

Peck, M. S. 1978. *The Road Less Traveled*. New York: Simon and Schuster.

Peck, M. S. 1993. *A World Waiting to be Born: Civility Rediscovered*. New York: Bantam Books.

Scholtes, P. R. 1988. *The Team Handbook*. Madison, Wis.: Joiner Assoc.

Sink, D. S. 1983. Using the nominal group technique effectively. *National Productivity Review*. Spring, pp. 173-184.

Sink, D. S., and T. C. Tuttle. 1989. *Planning and Measurement in Your Organization of the Future*. Norcross, Ga.: Industrial Engineering and Management Press.

Weisbord, M. R. (ed.). 1992. *Discovering Common Ground: How Future Search Conferences Bring People Together to Achieve Breakthrough Innovation, Empowerment, Shared Vision, and Collaborative Action*. San Francisco: Berrett-Koehler.

Weisbord, M. R. 1991. *Productive Workplaces: Organizing for Dignity, Meaning, and Community*. San Francisco: Jossey-Bass.

BIBLIOGRAPHY
Management of Participation

Belasco, J. A., and R. C. Stayer. 1993. *Flight of the Buffalo: Soaring to Excellence, Learning to Let Employees Lead*. New York: Warner Books.

Davidson, W. H. 1982. Small group activity at Mushashi Semi-conductor Works. *Sloan Management Review*. Spring.

Hackman, J. R. 1986. The psychology of self-management in organizations. *Psychology and Work: Productivity, Change and Employment*. Edited by M. S. Pallack, and R. O. Perloff. Washington, D.C.: American Psychological Association.

Hackman, J. R. (ed.). 1990. *Groups That Work (and Those That Don't)*. San Francisco: Jossey-Bass.

Hackman, J. R., and G. R. Oldham. 1980. *Work Redesign*. Reading, Mass.: Addison-Wesley.

Kanter, R. M. 1982. Dilemmas of managing participation. *Organizational Dynamics*. Summer.

Kanter, R. M. 1983. *The Change Masters*. New York: Simon and Schuster.

Kanter, R. M. 1989. The new managerial work. *Harvard Business Review*. November-December.

Kilman, R., and T. J. Covin. 1989. *Corporate Transformations*. San Francisco: Jossey-Bass.

Klein, J. A. 1984. Why supervisors resist employee involvement. *Harvard Business Review*. September-October.

Lawler, III, E. E. 1986. *High Involvement Management*. San Francisco: Jossey-Bass.

Lawler, E. E. III. 1988. Transforming from control to involvement. In *Corporate Transformation* (R. Kilmann and T. Covin, editors). San Francisco: Jossey-Bass.

Lawler, E. E. III. 1992. *The Ultimate Advantage: Creating the High-Involvement Organization*. San Francisco: Jossey-Bass.

Semler, R. 1989. Managing without managers. *Harvard Business Review*. September-October.

Sink, D. S. 1982. The ABC's of theories X, Y, and Z. *IE Fall Conference Proceedings*. Norcross, Ga.: Industrial Engineering and Management Press.

Sink, D. S., and L. K. Swim. 1983. Participative problem solving techniques: when are they appropriate? *Fall Industrial Engineering Conference Proceedings*. December.

Sink, D. S., L. Shetzer, and D. Marion. 1986. Performance action teams: a case study. *National Productivity Review*. Summer, pp. 233-251.

Walton, R. 1985. From control to commitment in the work place. *Harvard Business Review.* March-April, pp. 77-84.

Walton, R. E., and L. A. Schlesinger. 1979. Do supervisors thrive in participative work systems? *Organizational Dynamics.* Winter.

Waterman, R. H. 1987. *The Renewal Factor.* Toronto: Bantam.

Waterman, R. H. 1990. *AdHocracy: The Power to Change.* Knoxville, Tenn.: Whittle Direct Books.

Measurement (exploratory data analysis, statistics, decision making, evaluation)

Adam, E. E., J. C. Hershauer, and W. A. Ruch. 1986. *Productivity and Quality: Measurement as a Basis for Improvement* (2nd edn.). New York: Prentice-Hall.

American Productivity Center. 1978. How to measure productivity at the firm level. *Short Course Notebook and Reference Manual.* Houston, Tex.

American Productivity Center. 1987. Chemical plant tests "family of measures" approach to productivity improvement and gainsharing. *The Productivity Letter.* 6(8).

Anderson, D. R., D. J. Sweeney, and T. A. Williams. 1981. *Introduction to Statistics: An Applications Approach.* St. Paul, Minn.: West Publishing.

Aragon, G. A. 1989. *Financial Management.* Boston: Allyn and Bacon.

Bain, D. 1982. *The Productivity Prescription: The Manager's Guide to Improving Productivity and Profits.* New York: McGraw-Hill Book Co.

Balm, G. J. 1992. *Benchmarking: A Practitioner's Guide for Becoming and Staying Best of Best.* Scharumburg, Ill.: QPMA Press.

Box, G.E.P., W. G. Hunter, and J. S. Hunter. 1978. *Statistics for Experimenters.* New York: John Wiley & Sons.

Bruns, W. J., Jr. 1992. *Performance Measurement, Evaluation, and Incentives.* Boston: Harvard Business School Press.

Buehler, V. M., and Y. K. Shetty (eds.). 1981. *Productivity Improvement: Case Studies of Proven Practice.* New York: AMACOM.

Camp, R. C. 1989. *Benchmarking: The Search for Industry Best Practices that Lead to Superior Performance.* Milwaukee, Wis.: Quality Press.

Christopher, W. F., and C. G. Thor (eds.). 1993. *Handbook for Productivity Measurement and Improvement.* Cambridge, Mass.: Productivity Press.

Churchill, N. C. 1984. Budget choice: planning vs. Control. *Harvard Business Review.* July-August, pp. 150-164.

Cosgrove, C. V. 1986. How to report productivity: Linking measurements to bottom-line financial results. *National Productivity Review.* Winter.

Craig, C. E., and R. C. Harris. 1973. Total productivity measurement at the firm level. *Sloan Management Review.* 14(3): 13-29(Spring).

Davis, H. S. 1978. *Productivity Accounting.* Major Study No. 37. University of Pennsylvania, The Wharton School Industrial Research Unit. Originally published in 1955.

Dixon, J. R., A. J. Nanni, and T. E. Vollmann. 1990. *The New Performance Challenge.* Homewood, Ill.: Dow Jones Irwin.

Duncan, A. J. 1986. *Quality Control and Industrial Statistics* (5th edn). Homewood, Ill.: Irwin.

Feinberg, S. E. 1991. *The Analysis of Cross-Classified Categorical Data.* Cambridge, Mass.: The MIT Press.

Gollop, F. M. 1986. Corporate earnings and productivity analysis. *Working Paper.* Boston: Boston College Department of Economics.

Hall, R. W., H. T. Johnson, and P.B.B. Turney. 1991. *Measuring Up: Charting Pathways to Manufacturing Excellence.* Homewood, Ill.: Business One Irwin.

Hayes, R. F., and K. B. Clark. 1986. Why some factories are more productive than others. *Harvard Business Review.* September-October.

Hoaglin, D. C., F. Mosteller, and J. W. Tukey (eds.). 1983. *Understanding Robust and Exploratory Data Analysis*. New York: John Wiley & Sons.

Hollander, M., and D. A. Wolfe. 1973. *Nonparametric Statistical Methods*. New York: John Wiley.

How to Measure Productivity at the Firm Level. 1978. Short Course Notebook and Reference Manual. Houston, Tex.: American Productivity Center.

Institute of Science and Technology, Industrial Development Division. 1980. *Productivity and Cost Control for the Small and Medium-Sized Firm*. Ann Arbor: University of Michigan.

Japan Productivity Center. 1984. *Measuring Productivity: Trends and Comparisons from the First International Productivity Symposium*. New York: Unipub.

Johnson, H. T. 1992. *Relevance Regained: From Top-Down Control to Bottom-Up Empowerment*. New York: The Free Press.

Johnson, H. T., and R. S. Kaplan. 1987. *Relevance Lost: The Rise and Fall of Managerial Accounting*. Boston, Mass.: Harvard Business School Press.

Kaplan, R. S. 1983. Measuring manufacturing performance: a new challenge for managerial accounting research. *The Accounting Review*. 58(4).

Kaplan, R. S. 1984. Yesterday's accounting undermines production: efforts to revitalize manufacturing industries cannot succeed if outdated accounting and control systems remain unchanged. *Harvard Business Review*. July-August.

Kaplan, R. S. 1986. Accounting lag: the obsolescence of cost accounting systems. *California Management Review*. 28(2).

Kaplan, R. S. (ed.). 1990. *Measures for Manufacturing Excellence*. Boston: Harvard Business School Press.

Kaplan, R. S. 1993. Measuring manufacturing performance: a new challenge for managerial accounting research. *The Accounting Review*. 48(4).

Kaplan, R. S., and D. P. Norton. 1993. Putting the balanced scorecard to work. *Harvard Business Review*. September-October, pp. 134-147.

Kearney Inc., A. T. 1984. *Measuring and Improving Productivity in Physical Distribution*. Oak Brook, Ill.: National Council of Physical Distribution Management.

Keeney, R. L., and H. Raiffa. 1976. *Decisions with Multiple Objectives. Preferences and Value Tradeoffs*. New York: John Wiley.

Kendrick, J. W., and D. Creamer. 1965. Measuring company productivity: handbook with case studies. *Studies in Business Economics*, No. 89. New York: Conference Board.

Kendrick, J. W. 1984. *Improving Company Productivity: Handbook With Case Studies*. Baltimore: The John Hopkins University Press.

Khadem, R., and R. Lorber. 1986. *One Page Management: How to Use Information to Achieve Your Goals*. New York: Morrow.

Kinlaw, D. C. 1992. *Continuous Improvement and Measurement for total Quality*. Homewood, Ill.: Business One Irwin.

Kizilos, T. 1984. Kratylus automates his urnworks. *Harvard Business Review*. May-June.

Mali, P. 1978. *Improving Total Productivity: MBO Strategies for Business, Government, and Not-for-profit Organizations*. New York: John Wiley.

Meyers, H. N., N. E. Kay, and J.R.P. French. 1965. Split roles in performance appraisal. *Sloan Management Review*. January-February.

Miller, D. 1984. Profitability = productivity + price recovery. *Harvard Business Review*. 62(3).

Monetta, D. J. 1981. *PAM: A Research and Development Project Appraisal Methodology*. Doctoral dissertation. University of Southern California, School of Public Administration.

Morris, W. T. 1977. *Decision Analysis*. Columbus, Ohio: Grid.

Lehrer, R. H. (ed.). 1983. *White Collar Productivity*. New York: McGraw-Hill.

Nagashima, S. 1973. *100 Management Charts*. Tokyo: Asian Productivity Center.

Neter, J., and W. Wasserman. 1974. *Applied Statistical Models*. Homewood, Ill.: Irwin.

Ohio State University Productivity Research Group (William T. Morris and George L. Smith). 1977. *Productivity Measurement Systems for Administrative Computing and Information Services.* An Executive Summary and User's Manual. Columbus, Ohio: NSF-RANN research grant.

Olson, V. 1983. *White Collar Waste.* Englewood Cliffs, N.J.: Prentice Hall.

Riggs, H. E. 1981. *Accounting Survey.* New York: McGraw-Hill.

Riggs, J. L., and G. H. Felix. 1983. *Productivity by Objectives.* Englewood Cliffs, N.J.: Prentice Hall.

Senju, S., T. Fushimi, and S. Fujita. 1980. *Profitability Analysis: For Managerial and Engineering Decisions.* Tokyo: Asian Productivity Organization.

Shewhart, W. A. 1980. *Economic Control of Quality of Manufactured Product.* Milwaukee, Wis.: American Society for Quality Control

Sink, D. S., and J. B. Keats. 1983. Using quality costs in productivity measurement. *ASOC Quality Congress Transactions.* Boston: ASOC.

Sink, D. S., T. C. Tuttle, and S. J. DeVries. 1984. Productivity measurement and evaluation: what is available? *National Productivity Review.* Summer.

Sink, D. S. 1985. *Productivity Measurement: Planning, Measurement and Evaluation, Control and Improvement.* New York: John Wiley and Sons.

Sloma, R. S. 1980. *How to Measure Managerial Performance.* New York: MacMillan Publishing Co.

Smith, G. L. 1978. *Work Measurement: A Systems Approach.* Columbus, Ohio: Grid.

Spendolini, M. J. 1978. A yardstick for measuring productivity. *Industrial Engineering.* 10(2).

Stewart, W. T. 1978. A yardstick for measuring productivity. *Industrial Engineering.* 10(2).

Sumanth, D. J. 1984. *Productivity Engineering and Management.* New York: McGraw-Hill.

Thor, C. 1986. Capital productivity within the firm. *National Productivity Review.* Autumn.

Tukey, J. W. 1977. *Exploratory Data Analysis.* Reading, Mass.: Addison-Wesley.

Tuttle, T. C., R. E. Wilkinson, W. L. Gatewood, and L. Lucke. 1981. *Measuring and Enhancing Organizational Productivity: An Annotated Bibliography.* Air Force Systems Command, AFHRL-81-6, July.

van Loggerenberg, B. J. 1988. *Productivity Decoding of Financial Signals.* Pretoria, South Africa: Productivity Measurement Associates.

van Loggerenberg, B. J., and S. J. Cucchiaro. 1981. Productivity measurement and the bottom line. *National Productivity Review.* Winter.

Vroom, V. H., and P. W. Yetton. 1973. *Leadership and Decision Making.* Pittsburgh: University of Pittsburgh Press.

Wheeler, D. J. 1993. *Understanding Variation.* Knoxville, Tenn.: SPC Press.

Wheeler, D. J., and D. S. Chambers. 1992. *Understanding Statistical Process Control* (2nd edn.). Knoxville, Tenn.: SPC Press.

Wheeler, D. J., and R. W. Lyday. 1989. *Evaluating the Measurement Process* (2nd edn.). Knoxville, Tenn.: SPC Press.

Wilson, P. F., L. D. Dell, and G. F. Anderson. 1993. *Root Cause Analysis: A Tool for Total Quality Management.* Milwaukee, Wis.: ASQC Quality Press.

Motivation (individual, group, organizational behavior, compensation management, organizational development, management of participation)

American Productivity Center. 1986. Gainsharing promotes employee involvement at Motorola. *The Productivity Letter.* 6(1).

American Productivity Center. 1986. Ongoing revision key to gainsharing at Knoll International. *The Productivity Letter.* 6(4).

Bion, W. 1961. *Experiences in Groups.* New York: Basic Books.

Blumberg, M., and C. D. Pringle. 1982. The missing opportunity in organizational research: some implications for a theory of work performance. *The Academy of Management Review.* October.

Bradford, L. P. (ed.). 1978. *Group Development.* La Jolla, Calif.: University Associates.

Bullock, R. J., and P. F. Bullock. 1982. Gainsharing and Rubik's cube: solving systems problems. *National Productivity Review*. 1(4).

Dar-el, E. M. 1986. *Productivity improvement: employee involvement and gainsharing plans*. Amsterdam: Elsevier.

Doyle, R. J. 1983. *Gainsharing and Productivity: A Guide to Planning, Implementation, and Development*. New York: AMACOM.

Fein, M. 1974. *Rational Approaches to Raising Productivity*. Norcross, Ga.: Industrial Engineering and Management Press.

Fein, M. 1981. *Improshare: An Alternative to Traditional Managing*. Norcross, Ga.: Institute of Industrial Engineers.

Fein, M. 1983. *Improved Productivity through Worker Involvement in Gainsharing: A collection of Papers*. Norcross, Ga.: Industrial Engineering and Management Press, Institute of Industrial Engineers.

Frost, C. F., J. H. Wakely, and R. A. Ruh. 1974. *The Scanlon Plan for Organization Development: Identity, Participation, and Equity*. East Lansing: The Michigan State University Press.

Geare, A. J. 1976. Productivity from Scanlon-type plans. *Academy of Management Review*. July.

General Accounting Office. 1981. *Productivity Sharing Programs: Can They Contribute to Productivity Improvement*. GAO/AFMD-81-22, March.

Henderson, R. I. 1985. *Compensation Management: Rewarding Performance* (4th edn.). Reston, Va.: Reston Publishing Co.

Huseman, R. C., and J. D. Hatfield. 1989. *Managing the Equity Factor: or "After All I've Done for You..."*. Boston, Mass.: Houghton Mifflin.

Kanter, R. M. 1987. The attack on pay. *Harvard Business Review*. 65(2): [?PAGE?].

Kerr, S. 1975. On the folly of rewarding A, while hoping for B. *Academy of Management Journal*.

Kohn, A. 1993. Why inventive plans cannot work. *Harvard Business Review*. September-October, pp. 54-63.

Lawler, III, E. E. 1971. *Pay and Organizational Effectiveness: A Psychological View*. New York: McGraw-Hill.

Lawler, E. E., III. 1973. *Motivation in Work Organizations*. Belmont, Calif.: Wadsworth Publishing.

Lawler, III, E. E. 1981. *Pay and Organization Development*. Reading, Mass.: Addison-Wesley.

Lawler, III, E. E. 1985. *Gainsharing Research: Findings and Future Directions*. University of Southern California, Center for Effective Organizations.

Lawler, E. E., III. 1990. *Strategic Pay: Aligning Organizational Strategies and Pay Systems*. San Francisco: Jossey-Bass.

Lesieur, F. G. (ed.). 1958. *The Scanlon Plan: A Frontier in Labor–Management Cooperation*. Cambridge, Mass.: MIT Press..

Locke, E. A., *et al.* 1980. The relative effectiveness of four methods of motivating employee performance. *Changes in Working Life*. New York: John Wiley and Sons.

Masternak, R. L. 1993. Gainsharing boosts quality and productivity at a BF Goodrich plant. *National Productivity Review*. 12(2): 225-238.

Mitchell, T. R. 1982. Motivation: new directions for theory, research and practice. *Academy of Management Review*. 7(1).

Moore, B. E., and T. L. Ross. 1978. *The Scanlon Way to Improved Productivity: A Practical Guide*. New York: John Wiley.

Moore, B. E., and T. L. Ross (ed.). 1983. *Productivity Gainsharing: How Employee Incentive Programs Can Improve Business Performance*. Englewood Cliffs, N.J.: Prentice-Hall.

O'Dell, C. S. 1981. *Gainsharing: Involvement, Incentives, and Productivity*. New York: AMACOM Management Briefing.

O'Dell, C. S. 1987, with J. McAdams. *People Performance and Pay: A National Survey on Non-*

traditional Reward and Human Resource Practices. Houston, Tex.: American Productivity Center.

Patten, T. H., and M. G. Damico. 1993. Survey details profit-sharing plans: is revealing allocation formulas a performance incentive? *National Productivity Review*. 12(3): 383-294.

Ringham, A. J. 1984. Designing a gainsharing program to fit a company's operations. *National Productivity Review*. 3(2).

Ritti, R., and G. R. Funkhouser. 1977. *Ropes to Skip and Ropes To Snow: Studies in Organizatonal Behavior*. Columbus, Ohio: Grid Publishing.

Ross, T. L., and W. C. Hauck. 1983. *Gainsharing in the United States* in: *Motivating people to work*. Norcross, Ga.: Industrial Engineering and Management Press.

Ross, T. L., and R. A. Ross. 1984. Productivity gainsharing: resolving some of the measurement issues. *National Productivity Review*. 3(4).

Rossler, P. E., and C. P. Koelling. The effect of gainsharing on business performance at a papermill. *National Productivity Review*. 12(3): 365-382.

Sims, H. P., and A. D. Szilagyi. 1976. Job characteristic relationships: individual and structural moderators. *Organizational Behavior and Human Performance*. 17.

Steers, R. M., and L. W. Porter. 1983. *Motivation and Work Behavior* (3rd edn.). New York: McGraw-Hill.

White, K. J. 1979. The Scanlon plan: causes and correlates of success. *Academy Management Journal*. 22(20).

Organizational Development

Adizes, I. 1979. Organizational passages—diagnosing and treating lifecycle problems of organizations. *Organizational Dynamics*. Summer.

Adizes, I. 1988. *Corporate Lifecycles: How and Why Corporations Grow and Die and What to Do About It*. Englewood Cliffs, N.J.: Prentice-Hall.

Adler, P. S., and R. E. Cole. 1993. Designed for learning: a tale of two auto plants. *Sloan Management Review*. Spring, pp. 85-94.

Argyris, C., and D. Schon. 1978. *Organizational Learning: A Theory of Action Perspective*. Reading, Mass.: Addison-Wesley.

Garvin, D. A. 1993. Building a learning organization. *Harvard Business Review*. July-August, pp. 78-91.

Hatch, M. J. 1993. The dynamics of organizational culture. *The Academy of Management Review*. 18(4): 657-693.

Isaacs, W. N. 1993. Taking lfight: dialogue, collective thinking, and organizational learning. *Organizational Dynamics*. Autumn, pp. 24-39.

Kilmann, R. H. 1975. Designing and developing a "real" organization in the classroom. *Academy of Management Journal*. 18(1): 143-148.

Kim, D. H. 1993. The link between individual and organizational learning. *Sloan Management Review*. Fall, pp. 37-50.

Kofman, F., and P. M. Senge. 1993. Communities of commitment: the heart of learning organizations. *Organizational Dynamics*. Autumn, pp. 5-23.

Leonard-Barton, D. 1992. The factory as a learning laboratory. *Sloan Management Review*. Fall, pp. 23-38.

McGill, M. E., J. W. Slocum, and D. Lei. 1992. Management Practices in learning organizations. *Organizational Dynamics*. Summer, pp. 5-17.

Plovnick, M. S., R. E. Fry, and W. W. Burke. 1982. *Organization Development: Exercises, Cases, and Readings*. Boston: Little, Brown, and Co.

Ryan, K. D., and D. K. Oestreich. 1991. *Driving Fear Out of the Workplace: How to Overcome the Invisible Barriers to Quality, Productivity and Innovation*. San Francisco: Jossey-Bass.

Schein, E. H. 1993. On dialogue, culture, and organizational learning. *Organizational Dynamics.* Autumn, pp. 40-51.

Planning

Akao, Y. (ed.). 1991. *Hosin Kanri: Policy Deployment for Successful TQM.* Cambridge, Conn.: Productivity Press.

Bandrowski, J. F. 1985. *Creative Planning throughout the Organization.* New York: American Management Association Membership Publication Division.

Below, P. J., G. L. Morrisey, and B. L. Acomb. 1987. *The Executive Guide to Strategic Planning.* San Francisco: Jossey-Bass.

Bennis, W. G., K. D. Benne, and R. Chin. 1985. *The Planning of Change* (4th edn.). New York: Holt, Rinehart, Winston.

DeGeus, A. P. 1988. Planning as learning. *Harvard Business Review.* March-April.

Gray, D. H. 1986. Uses and misuses of strategic planning. *Harvard Business Review.* January-February.

Hayes, R. H. 1985. Strategic planning—forward in reverse? *Harvard Business Review.* November—December.

Juran, J. M. 1988. *Juran on Planning for Quality.* New York: The Free Press.

Kami, M. J. 1988. *Trigger Points.* New York: McGraw-Hill.

Lenz, R. T. 1987. Managing the evolution of the strategic planning process. *Business Horizons.* January-February.

McGinnis, M. A. 1984. The key to strategic planning: integrating, analysis and intuition. *Sloan Management Review.* Fall.

Mintzberg, H. 1987. Crafting strategy. *Harvard Business Review.* 64: 66-75.

Mintzberg, H. 1990. The design school: reconsidering the basic premises of strategic management. *Strategic Management Journal.* 11(3): 171-195.

Mintzberg, H. 1994. The fall and rise of strategic planning. *Harvard Business Review.* January-February, pp. 107-114.

Morrisey, G. L, P. J. Below, and B. L. Acomb. 1988. *The Executive Guide to Operational Planning.* San Francisco: Jossey-Bass.

Pfeiffer, J. W., L. D. Goodstein, and T. M. Nolan. 1986. *Applied Strategic Planning: A How to Do it Guide.* San Diego, Calif.: University Associates.

Pfeiffer, J. W. (ed.). 1986. *Strategic Planning: Selected Readings.* San Diego, Calif.: University Associates.

Schoemaker, P.J.H. 1992. How to link strategic vision to core cpabilities. *Sloan Management Review.* Fall, pp. 67-81.

Sink, D. S. 1983. Using the nominal group technique effectively. *National Productivity Review.* Spring, pp. 173-184.

Sink, D. S., and T. C. Tuttle. 1989. *Planning and Measurement in Your Organization of the Future.* Norcross, Ga.: Industrial Engineering and Management Press.

Steiner, G. A. 1979. *Strategic Planning: What Every Manager Must Know.* New York: The Free Press.

Taylor, B. 1984. Strategic planning—which style do you need? *Long Range Planning.* 17(3).

Quality Management

Aguayo, R. 1990. *Dr. Deming: the American Who Taught the Japanese About Quality.* New York: Carol Publishing.

Albrecht, K. 1988. *At America's Service.* New York: Warner Books.

Albrecht, K. 1990. *Service Within: Solving the Middle Management Leadership Crisis.* Homewood, Ill.: Irwin.

Albrecht, K., and R. Zemke. 1985. *Service America.* Homewood, Ill.: Dow Jones Irwin.

Baker, E. M. 1985. Quality performance system: producer-customer interface. *Quality Progress.* June.

Bishop, L., W. J. Hill, and W. S. Lindsay. 1987. Don't be fooled by the measurement systems. *Quality Progress.* December.

Blackburn, R., and B. Rosen. 1993. Total quality and human resources management: lessons learned from Baldridge Award-winning companies. *The Academy of Management Executive.* VII(3): 49-66.

Burnstein, C., and K. Sedlak. 1988. The federal quality and productivity improvement effort. *Quality Progress.* October.

Conway, W. E. 1992. Quality management in an economic downturn. *Quality Progress.* XXV(5): 27-29.

Crosby, P. B. 1979. *Quality Is Free.* New York: McGraw-Hill Book Co.

Crosby, P. B. 1984. *Quality Without Tears.* New York: McGraw-Hill.

Davis, T. 1993. Effective supply chain management. *Sloan Management Review.* Summer, pp. 35-46.

Deming, W. E. 1981. Improvement of quality and productivity through action by management. *National Productivity Review.* Winter, pp. 12-22.

Deming, W. E. 1982. *Quality, Productivity, and Competitive Position.* Cambridge, Mass.: MIT Center for Advanced Engineering Study.

Dobyns, L., and C. Crawford-Mason. 1991. *Quality or Else: The Revolution in World Business.* A companion to the IBM-funded PBS series. Boston: Houghton-Mifflin.

Duncan, A. J. 1965. *Quality Control: Industrial Statistics.* Homewood, Ill.: Richard D. Irwin.

Dyer, J. H., and W. G. Ouchi. 1993. Japanese-style partnerships: giving companies the competitive edge. *Sloan Management Review.* Fall, pp. 51-63.

Easton, G. S. 1993. A Baldridge examiner's view of U.S. total quality management. *California Management Review.* 35(3): 32-54.

Feigenbaum, A. V. 1961. *Total Quality Control.* New York: McGraw-Hill Book Co.

Gabor, A. 1990. *The Man Who Discovered Quality: How W. Edwards Deming Brought the Quality Revolution to America—The Stories of Ford, Xerox and GM.* New York: Penguin Books.

Garvin, D. A. 1988. *Managing Quality: The Strategic and Competitive Edge.* New York: The Free Press.

Gehani, R. R. 1993. Quality value-chain: a meta-synthesis of frontiers of quality movement. *The Academy of Management Executive.* VII(2): 29-42.

Gitlow, H. S., and S. J. Gitlow. 1987. *The Deming Guide to Quality and Competitive Position.* Englewood Cliffs, N.J.: Prentice-Hall.

Glasser, W. 1990. *The Quality School.* New York: Harper Perennial.

Gluckman, P., and D. R. Roome. 1990. *Everyday Heroes: From Taylor to Deming: The Journey to Higher Productivity.* Knoxville, Tenn.: SPC Press.

Harrington, H. J. 1987. *Poor-Quality Cost.* New York: Marcel Dekker.

Hauser, J. R. 1993. How Puritan-Bennett used the house of quality. *Sloan Management Review.* Spring, pp. 61-70.

Hiam, A. 1992. *Closing the Quality Gap: Lessons from America's Leading Companies.* Englewood Cliffs, N.J.: Prentice-Hall.

Hosotani, K. 1992. *Japanese Quality Concepts: An Overview.* White Plains, N.Y.: Quality Resources.

Hudiburg, J. J. 1991. *Winning with Quality: The FPL Story.* White Plains, N.Y.: Quality Resources.

Hunt, D. V. 1992. *Quality in America: How to Implement a Competitive Quality Program.* Homewood, Ill.: Irwin.

Ishikawa, K. 1985. *What is Total Quality Control? The Japanese Way.* Englewood Cliffs, N.J.: Prentice-Hall.

Jacobsen, G., and J. Hillkirk. 1986. *Xerox American Samurai: The Behind-the-Scenes Story of How a Corporate Giant Beat the Japanese at Their Own Game.* New York: Collier.

Juran, J. M. 1988. *Juran on Planning for Quality.* New York: Free Press.

Juran, J. M. 1989. *Juran on Leadership for Quality: An Executive Handbook.* New York: The Free Press.

Juran, J. M. 1993. Made in U.S.A.: a renaissance in quality. *Harvard Business Review.* July-August, pp. 42-50.

Juran, J. M., and F. M. Gyrna. 1988. *Juran's Quality Control Handbook* (4th edn.). New York: McGraw-Hill Book Co.

Juran, J. M, and F. M. Gyrna. 1989. *Quality Planning and Analysis From Product Development Through Use.* New York: McGraw-Hill Book Co.

Kano, N. 1993. A perspective on quality activities in American firms. *California Management Review.* 35(3): 12-31.

Kanatsu, T. 1990. *TQC for Accounting: A New Role in Companywide Improvement.* Cambridge, Mass.: Productivity Press.

Kilian, C. S. 1992. *The World of W. Edwards Deming* (2nd edn.). Knoxville, Tenn.: SPC Press.

Lawler, E. E. III, S. A. Mohrman, and G. E. Ledford. 1992. *Employee Involvement and total Quality Management: Practices and Results in Fortune 1000 Companies.* San Francisco: Jossey-Bass.

Luther, D. B. 1992/93. Advanced TQM: measurements, missteps, and progress through key result indicators at Corning. *National Productivity Review.* 12(1): 23-36.

Levi, A. S., and L. E. Mainstone. 1987. Obstacles to understanding and using statistical process control as a productivity improvement approach. *Journal of Organizational Behavior Management.* 9(1).

Mann, N. R. 1987. *The Keys to Excellence—The Story of the Deming Philosophy.* Los Angeles: Prestwick Books.

McCabe, W. J. 1989. Examining processes improves operations. *Quality Progress.* July.

Miller, R. I. (ed.). 1991. *Applying the Deming Method to Higher Education: For More Effective Human Resource Management.* Washington, D.C.: College and Personnel Association.

Mizuno, S. 1988. *Management for Quality Improvement: The Seven New QC Tools.* Cambridge, Mass.: Productivity Press.

Pirsig, R. 1974. *Zen and the Art of Motorcycle Maintenance.* New York: Bantam Books.

Propst, A. L. 1989. In search of a new process. *Quality Progress.* June.

Ranney, G., and B. Carlson. 1988. Deming's Point Four: a study. *Quality Progress.* December.

Scherkenbach, W. W. 1988. *The Deming Route to Quality and Productivity: Road Maps and Roadblocks.* Washington, D.C.: Ceep Press.

Scherkenbach, W. W. 1991. *Deming's Road to Continual Improvement.* Knoxville, Tenn.: SPC Press.

Seymour, D. T. 1992. *On Q: Causing Quality in Higher Education.* New York: Macmillan.

Shewhart, W. A. 1986. *Statistical Method: From the Viewpoint of Quality Control.* New York: Dover Publications. Original work 1939.

Shiba, S., A. Graham, and D. Walden. 1993. *A New American TQM: Four Practical Revolutions in Management.* Portland, Ore.: Productivity Press.

Sink, D. S. 1989. TQM: the next frontier or just another bandwagon to jump on? *Quality and Productivity Management.* 7(2).

Sink, D. S. 1990. Total quality management is .... *Quality and Productivity Management.* 8(2).

Sink, D. S., and D. D. Acker (eds.). 1988. *Managing Quality and Productivity in Aerospace and Defense.* Fort Belvoir, Va.: Defense Systems Management College.

Statistical Methods Office Operations Support Staffs. 1985. *Ford: Continuing Process Control and Process Capability Improvement.* Detroit: Ford Motor Co.

Steele, J. 1993. Implementing total quality management for long- and short-term bottom-line results. *National Productivity Review.* 12(3): 425-441.

Steeples, M. M. 1992. *The Corporate Guide to the Malcolm Baldrige National Quality Award.* Milwaukee, Wis.: ASQC Press.

Sullivan, L. P. 1986. The seven stages in company-wide quality control. *Quality Progress*. May.

Sullivan, L. P. 1986. Quality Function Deployment. *Quality Progress*. June.

Taguchi, G., E. A. Elsayed, and T. Hsiang. 1989. *Quality Engineering in Production Systems*. New York: McGraw Hill Book Co.

Townsend, P. L., and J. E. Gebhardt. 1992. *Quality in Action*. New York: John Wiley.

Townsend, P. R. 1986. *Commit To Quality*. New York: John Wiley & Sons.

Wallace, T. F. 1992. *Customer Driven Strategy: Winning Through Operational Excellence*. Essex Junction, Vt.: Oliver Wight.

Walton, M. 1986. *The Deming Management Method*. Dodd, Mead, & Co.

Walton, M. 1990. *Deming Management at Work: Six Successful Companies that Use the Quality Principles of the World-Famous W. Edwards Deming*. New York: C. P. Putnam's.

Zeithaml, V. A., A. Parasuraman, and L. L. Berry. 1990. *Delivering Quality Service: Balancing Customer Perceptions and Expectations*. New York: The Free Press.

Quality Principles, Deming's Fourteen Points

Kanter, R. M., and D. W. Brinkerhoff. Appraising the performance of performance appraisal. *Sloan Management Review*. 21(3): 3-16.

Meyers, H. N., N. E. Kay, and J.R.P. French. 1965. Split roles in performance appraisal. *Sloan Management Review*. January-February.

Mintzberg, H. 1986. The manager's job: folklore and fact. *Management Classics* (3rd edn.). Edited by M. T. Matteson and J. M. Ivancevich. Plano, Tex.: Business Publications.

Pirsig, R. 1974. *Zen and the Art of Motorcycle Maintenance*. New York: Bantam Books.

Pirsig, R. 1991. *Lila: An Inquiry into Morals*. New York: Bantam Books.

Rosander, A. C. 1991. *Deming's 14 Points Applied to Services*. Milwaukee, Wis.: ASQC Press.

System and Process Improvement (systems thinking, organization development, process improvement, problem solving, methods engineering)

Archer, B. L. 1970. *Technological Innovation: A Methodology*. London: Royal College of Art.

Barnes, R. M. 1980. *Motion and Time Study: Design and Measurement of Work*. New York: John Wiley & Sons.

Imai, M. 1986. *KAIZEN—The Key to Japan's Competitive Success*. New York: Random House Business Division.

Kaufman, R. S. 1992. Why operations improvement programs fail: four managerial controdictions. *Sloan Management Review*. Fall, pp. 83-93.

Karger, D. W., and F. H. Bayha. 1987. *Engineered Work Measurement*. New York: Industrial Press.

Konz, S. 1990. *Work Design: Industrial Ergonomics*. Worthington, Ohio: Publishing Horizons.

Kepner, C. H., and B. B. Tregoe. 1965. *The Rational Manager*. New York: McGraw-Hill.

Lawrence, P. R., and J. W. Lorsch. 1967. *Organization and Environment*. Cambridge, Mass.: Harvard University.

Mundel, M. 1985. *Motion and Time Study: Improving Productivity*. Englewood Cliffs, N.J.: Prentice-Hall.

Niebel, B. W. 1982. *Motion and Time Study*. Homewood, Ill.: Irwin.

Short, J. E., and N. Venkatraman. 1992. Beyond business process redesign: redefining Baxter's business network. *Sloan Management Review*. Fall, pp. 23-28.

Tools/Methods of Quality and Productivity Improvement

Akao, Y. (ed.). 1991. *Hoshin Kanri: Policy Deployment for Successful TQM*. Cambridge, Conn.: Productivity Press.

Akao, Y. (ed.). 1990. *Quality Function Deployment: Integrating Customer Requirements into Product Design*. Cambridge, Mass.: Productivity Press.

Akiyama, K. 1991. *Function Analysis: Systematic Improvement of Quality and Performance.* Cambridge, Mass.: Productivity Press.

Bendell, T., J. Kelly, T. Merry, and F. Sims. 1993. *Quality: Measuring and Monitoring.* London: Century Business.

Bossert, J. L. 1991. *Quality Function Deployment: A Practitioner's Approach.* Milwaukee, Wis.: ASQC Press.

Brassard, M. 1989. *The Memory Jogger Plus.* Methuen, Mass.: Goal/QPC.

Byrne, D. M., and S. Taguchi. 1987. The Taguchi approach to parameter design. In *Quest for Quality* by M. Sepehri. Norcross, Ga.: Institute of Industrial Engineers.

Carr, L. P. 1992. Applying cost of quality to a service business. *Sloan Management Review.* Summer, pp. 72-77.

Competitive Benchmarking: What It Is and What It Can Do for You. Stamford, Conn.: Xerox Corporate Quality Office, Reference No. 700P90201.

Feigenbaum, A. V. 1983. *Total Quality Control* (3rd edn.). New York: McGraw-Hill.

Gitlow, H., S. Gitlow, A. Oppenheim, and R. Oppenheim. *Tools and Methods for the Improvement of Quality.* Homewood, Ill.: Irwin.

Grant, E. L., and R. S. Leavenworth. 1988. *Statistical Quality Control* (6th edn.) New York: McGraw-Hill.

Hauser, J. R., and D. Clausing. 1988. The house of quality. *Harvard Business Review.* May-June, pp. 66-73.

Harrington, H. J. 1987. *The Improvement Process: How America's Leading Companies Improve Quality.* New York: McGraw-Hill.

Harrington, H. J. 1991. *Business Process Improvement: The Breakthrough Strategy for Total Quality, Productivity, and Competitiveness.* New York: McGraw-Hill.

Ishikawa, K. 1982. *Guide to Quality Control.* Tokyo: Asian Productivity Organization.

Ishikawa, K. 1985. *What is Total Quality Control? The Japanese Way.* Englewood Cliffs, N.J.: Prentice-Hall.

Ishikawa, K. 1990. *Introduction to Quality Control.* Tokyo: 3A Corporation.

Imai, M. 1986. *Kaizen: The Key to Japan's Competitive Success.* New York: Random House.

Japan Quality Control Circles: Quality Control Circle Case Studies. Tokyo: Asian Productivity Organization.

Juran, J. M. 1992. *Juran on Quality By Design: The New Steps for Planning Quality Into Goods and Services.* New York: The Free Press.

Kaizen Teian 1: Developing Systems for Continuous Improvement Through Employee Suggestions. Cambridge, Mass.: Productivity Press.

Kaizen Teian 2: Guiding Continuous Improvement Through Employee Suggestions. Cambridge, Mass.: Productivity Press.

Krismann, C. 1990. *Quality Control: An Annotated Bibliography* (through 1988). White Plains, N.Y.: Quality Resources.

Mills, C. A. 1989. *The Quality Audit: A Management Tool.* New York: McGraw-Hill.

Mizuno, S. (ed.). 1988. *Management for Quality Improvment: The 7 New QC Tools.* Cambridge, Mass.: Productivity Press.

Mizuno, S. 1990. *Company-wide Total Quality Control.* White Plains, N.Y.: Quality Resources.

Nemoto, M. 1987. *Total Quality Control for Management: Strategies and Techniques from Toyota and Toyoda Gosei.* Englewood Cliffs, N.J.: Prentice-Hall.

Ozeki, K., and T. Asaka. 1990. *Handbook of Quality Tools.* Cambridge, Mass.: Productivity Press.

Robson, G. D. 1991. *Continuous Process Improvement: Simplifying Work Flow Systems.* New York: The Free Press.

Quality Control Circles at Work. Tokyo: Asian Productivity Organization.

Scholtes, P. R. 1988. *The Team Handbook.* Madison, Wis.: Joiner Assoc.

Sullivan, L. P. 1986. Quality function deployment. *Quality Progress.* June.

Taguchi, G., E. A. Elsayed, and T. Hsiang. 1989. *Quality Engineering in Production Systems.* New York: McGraw-Hill.

Talley, D. J. 1991. *Total Quality Management: Performance Cost Measures, the Strategy for Economic Survival.* Milwaukee, Wis.: ASQC Press.

Watson, G. H. 1992. *The Benchmarking Workbook: Adapting Best Practices for Performance Improvement.* Cambridge, Mass.: Productivity Press.

PLANNING AND LEADING LARGE-SCALE QUALITY AND PRODUCTIVITY IMPROVEMENT EFFORTS

Peter Drucker (1993) suggests we are in the midst of a knowledge revolution. Clearly, rapid advances in technology and the shift to a global market economy are two root causes. We can't eliminate the root causes; we can only adapt accordingly. This growing revolution has been a stimulus causing many responses, some effective and others ineffective. Increasingly, we have seen the quick fix approach fail. Approaches that are strategically thought through, comprehensive and well integrated, approaches that have continuity of leadership, constancy of purpose, and consistency of method are proving to be the most successful.

The ability to integrate re-engineering with continuous improvement is the learning challenge of the '90s. Indeed, becoming a learning organization may not be sufficient; we may need to become an organization with profound knowledge. Ultimately, quality jobs, quality products and services, quality of work, quality of work life, quality of life, and long-term survival and success are the bottom lines. Market share, achieving customer satisfaction, return on assets and stockholder equity, profits, new product and service introductions, and cost reductions are all impact indicators, milestones representing progress. There isn't an end, of course, but we must still strive not to confuse the ends with the means.

We have spent four sections presenting a piece of the puzzle and solution for you and your organization. If you are a top manager, and your domain of responsibility is extremely large and complex, you may argue that this is but a small piece of a big, big puzzle. You might see yourself solely as the change master in your organization; your view might be that a formal leader is the change master. This view presumes that change masters must be in positions of formal power. However, it has been suggested that, in fact, leaders can't lead; they have been paralyzed by an increasingly diverse set of stakeholders with wide-ranging special interests.

In an era of evolution to self-managing teams, it would appear that formal leaders need to broaden their view of change masters. Leaders in your organization will need to assemble a critical mass of change masters and empower them to assist with the demanding task of transforming the organization. We believe that creating teams of change masters is a very large piece of the very large puzzle, and it is an important task of top management to establish this piece and fit it properly into place.

Your organization is probably already moving beyond the quick fix of small, independent improvement interventions. It is likely that your organization is in the midst of trying to figure out what TQM is, what it means to your organization, and how to do it. We suspect that you now know TQM is more than teaching everybody the tools of quality and hoping for a miracle, or just re-engineering, or just process improvement, or just customer satisfaction, or just quality circles and self-managing teams — or just any single intervention.

Those who are past the false learning curve (Scholtes 1988) know that TQM is a system of improvement interventions executed over time that ultimately will result in success. Orchestrating these interventions over time is the key. Involving leadership in this orchestration process and then making sure that the system of improvements is deployed effectively is what is required. You probably have begun to learn that the integration of planning, measurement, training, empowerment, and other initiatives—putting the pieces of the puzzle together—is difficult but critical to success. Getting the pieces of this large, complex puzzle laid out and then put them together takes time.

If your organization's top leaders have been at all serious about the transformation, about really surviving and thriving in the '90s and beyond, you now realize that the "flavor of the month or year club" won't get it. You now realize that top management being sold by consultants on quick fixes, "blessing" the quick fixes, and then empowering the consultants to do the quick fixes to the masses won't work. Top management must be a part of laying out the puzzle; they have to learn enough to become contributors to the architect and engineering team for the organization. They must alter their habits so they have the time to participate meaningfully in the development of strategies for improvement that will yield immediate results but that also will build capacity for long-term improvement. They already know that large-scale organizational change is what is needed, but they seldom know how to orchestrate it; this is where the design and development team (or the architect and engineering team) becomes important. The architect and engineering team is a group of change masters established to build a grand strategy for the organization.

OPERATIONAL DEFINITIONS

Affinity Groups: An affinity group is a collegial association of peers which meets on a regular basis to share information, capture opportunities, and solve problems that affect the group and the overall organization(Van Akin, Sink, Monetta, 1994). An affinity group must share these seven characteristics:

1. Affinity groups members have the same job position.
2. Group roles are formalized.
3. Affinity groups meet on a regular and frequent basis.
4. The charter defines group mission.
5. The group is self-managing.
6. Off-site retreats (periodic)
7. A facilitator's conclave shares key learnings.

Alignment: The degree to which everyone works toward common goals. All arrows or vectors of activity are pointing in the same direction but the distance between them can be great. The degree that intentions and purposes are similar; the degree of focus and consensus; coordinated effort toward the same goals (implies accuracy).

Attunement: To work in harmony cooperatively and looking out for the welfare of the whole system rather than just individual subsystems; the mutual supporting activity of each element through a sense of mutual responsibility, caring, and love. All arrows or vectors of activity are close together, the relationships/distances between them are well understood and acknowledged. For attunement the system needs to maintain harmony among its elements (implies precision).

Your quality and productivity improvement efforts should be both aligned (in the same direction, accurate) and attuned (close together, precise).

Bases of Power: Power has been defined, in an organizational setting, as the ability to influence behavior. We might extend this to suggest that it is the ability to influence behaviors, attitudes, commitment, performance in an individual, group, and organization unit of analysis. We can influence performance improvement by demonstrating a method, coercing people to follow a method, rewarding people for following a method, or rewarding results by making it clear what we want and need and what the consequences are for those involved.

There are generally thought to be the following fundamental bases of power:

• Legitimate (legitimate in that it flows from the follower to the leader): position, power granted by virtue of position; charismatic, power granted by virtue of some characteristics of the leader; traditional, power granted by virtue of some accepted status such as king or queen.
• Coercive: power coming from the ability to punish, to create negative consequences for doing something or not doing something.
• Reward: power coming from the ability to provide positive consequences for doing something or not doing something.
• Expert: power coming from the basis of what one knows and can do, knowledge and skills and reputation.
• Referent: power coming from the basis of connections, who we know, who we can influence.

Clearly, the change master must understand these and be able to utilize bases of power in order to succeed.

Boot Camps: Intense educational sessions held off-site from the company. The sessions are intended to "condition the mind" and prepare the participants to rethink or reconsider how they think and do when working within the organization or "cook" the participants in the technology and methods of quality and productivity improvement.

"B" Leadership Group (ESG/SC): This group of leaders and managers sponsors the overall improvement effort. They are known by different names including Executive Steering Group, Quality and Productivity Improvement Council, and Steering Council. They represent a collection of sponsors, target organization leaders, and "A" infrastructure leaders from across the system being improved. This group sets policy, makes decisions or solves problems when appropriate, adjudicates cross-functional issues, ensures that appreciation for system is being maintained, provides situational leadership. They also ensure the quality of the overall strategy being designed and developed by the DDT, maintain involvement and visibility for implementation and deployment, provide overarching strategy, champion and sponsor positive change, and provide a unified sense of alignment and attunement. They provide continuity of leadership, constancy of purpose, and consistency of method. This group "owns" the Grand Strategy. They lead it. They ensure that fronts are moving forward, are aligned, and are being integrated. They provide big picture perspective. They have a partnership with the DDT. They are the "owners and operators" in the construction management metaphor sense. They represent linking pins to the next level in the system and in this respect are the initiators of deployment. If they don't perform effectively as linking pins, then deployment cannot occur.

There will be a network of "B" leadership groups in the organization. Each major subsystem will have a "B" leadership group. The top "A" leader in each group is the linking pin. They are conduits of information and knowledge and policy sharing. They must portray continuity of leadership, constancy of purpose, and consistency of method from level to level in order for deployment to be successful.

Grand Strategy System (GSS): The learning challenge of the '90s is how to integrate re-engineering (step-function, or new S-shaped curve inmprovements) with continuous improvement ("baby steps," incremental improvements) to achieve large-scale positive change. The aim of the Grand Strategy System is to ensure that your organization's improvement efforts are strategically thought through, comprehensive, well integrated, and that they build on lessons learned from the past and present. The Grand Strategy System is one method for accomplishing this integration through studying the past and present, outlining the future, and defining, categorizing, coordinating and integrating quality and productivity improvement efforts through fronts to aid in our understanding and accomplishment of how individual actions affect the entire organization system.

Infrastructure: Defined in Webster's Dictionary as "sub-structure or underlying foundation; esp. the basic installations and facilities on which the continuance and growth of a community, state, organization, etc. depend." We focus on the latter portion of the definition. Specifically, we are interested in the infrastructure for "B" (building the business and continuous performance improvement). The infrastructure for "A" (administering the business) is normally depicted by an organizational chart which portrays relationships, often in a reporting or responsibility sense. The "B" infrastructure is the framework for continuous improvement. Each "B" infrastructure component (or group) has a domain of responsibility within the continuous improvement function.

Key Performance Indicator (KPI): A well defined, specific measure that is derived from quality and productivity improvement efforts. It is an indication of progress towards completing performance improvement objectives. It is a means to demonstrate belief or knowledge in cause-and-effect relationships between strategy, actions, and measures.

Large scale: System-wide, comprehensive, complex.

Performance Action or Improvement Teams (PATS/PITS): The planning process (steps 3 and 4) create specific performance improvement objectives (PIOs) that will be implemented. These PIOs tend to fall into several domains of responsibility:

- Someone's individual responsibility, someone's job;
- A functional responsibility of an "A" infrastructure unit;
- Outside established domains of responsibility.

The third category calls for establishment of an ad hoc PAT to solve the problem, capture the opportunity, or accomplish the objective. PATs are normally 6–12 people in size. They are assembled on the basis of their willingness and ability to work the PIO. They will be chartered by the planning team, take the scoping proposal from the planning team and enhance it for review by the planning team at a quarterly review session, develop an implementation proposal and plan, seek approval in an appropriate fashion, either delegate implementation, coordinate implementation, or do it, and, finally, they will evaluate the success of the PIO for at least six months prior to disbanding. They are problem-solving teams; they engage in the PDSA cycle. They must be required to complete the study and act stages of the improvement cycle. Again, they are ad hoc, not standing.

Planning Team: A planning team is created to develop the improvement plan for the organization. The "Plan" in the improvement cycle (PDSA) for the organizational system is crucial. Infrastructure, communications, education/training/development, and measurement are key startup and enabling fronts. Once the foundation is laid for the transformation effort, the planning front is pushed forward. We utilize a seven-step Strategic Performance Improvement Planning Process as the method for moving the planning front forward. The planning team is the "B" leadership group augmented with significant customers, providers, and significant others. The planning team is normally 25–50 people. It is constructed to ensure that the plan is comprehensive, strategically thought through, and integrated from a systems perspective. We build the team with people from the total system (vertical and horizontal representation) to ensure the highest quality plan is created. A successful planning session with a planning team of this diversity and size requires a good method and skilled facilitation. The planning team is an ad hoc group, clearly part of the "B" infrastructure.

Red Teams: A team of critics charged with finding the gaps/holes in the Plan for quality and productivity improvement. Those designing the quality and productivity improvement Plan (usually the DDT) must present and justify the Plan to this panel of "experts" and use the feedback/comments from the panel to make the Plan comprehensive and seamless.

S-Shaped Curve: A representation for how learning and performance can change over time. As we learn, use and improve current processes, methods, or technological advancements; the rate of change of our performance is slow or flat at first, then becomes exponential. Any method/process/technology has limitations in how much we can improve its performance, and we reach a point where the rate of change in our performance tapers off, stabilizes, and becomes ingrained in the organization and is well understood and used (see Figure 5, page 8, for a graphical representation).

Task Forces: It is common for organizations to have standing committees, part of the "A" infrastructure. Certain "A" or "B" aspects of the organization require a longer-term and in some cases more intense effort. Often there are "frontal" task forces established to plan and develop strategies and actions aimed at moving a given subsystem or front forward. These task forces are often cross-functional, system-wide, major efforts. They are less ad hoc in character; there is a beginning and end to what they do, but it is less clear. In this respect task forces are working on programs or key processes rather than projects. PATs are clearly working on projects with beginnings and endings. Task forces can be chartered by the DDT, by the "A" and "B" leadership group, or by the Planning Team (if necessary). A Business Process Re-engineering effort would probably require chartering a task force rather than a PAT due to the scope of the effort. Frontal improvement often requires a task force. Coordination of task force work with PAT work is the duty of the DDT and the Leadership Team.

Three-level Meetings: A meeting to share information between upline and downline groups within an organization. The group/level sponsoring the meeting would include representatives from the sponsor's parent level and from the sponsor's daughter level.

Version 1.0, 1.5, etc.: In a culture of continuous improvement it is useful to create a mechanism for deferring judgment, to create a condition of unconditional acceptance at the same time we are aiming for improvement and having high standards. We have adopted the software convention of versions for strategic plans, for GSS plans, for proposals. It allows people to get things down on paper and not have to worry about them being perfect. Now we know you "zero defects" advocates will be screaming "what happened to do it right the first time?" We believe that doing it right the first time makes sense in some situations and not in others. When it comes to plans we want to create a spirit of continuous improvement, a living plan atmosphere. This doesn't mean we lower our standards; it means that we accept that our ability to think through plans varies or improves over time. It is more important to get an imperfect plan down on paper and get working on improvement than to be paralyzed by analysis and a sense that we must to have it perfect. It has worked pretty well for us; we encourage you to play with the idea.

CHAPTER 9
GRAND STRATEGY SYSTEM: A METHOD
FOR LEADING THE TRANSFORMATION

As introduced in the operational definitions in Section One and referred to throughout the previous chapters, there are different types of improvement. The dimensions characterizing improvement efforts are well understood and documented, for example: breadth and depth (scope), horizon or period of performance, level of involvement/range of targets, focus of the improvement, intensity, sense of urgency/conditions under which improvement is being made, driving forces/restraining forces. Increasingly, we are finding that a system-wide orientation is required to assure that our efforts don't create more dysfunctional consequences than functional consequences.

As has been said before, our contribution to the field can best be seen as integration and synthesis of multidisciplinary methods for improving performance. It is in this chapter that we attempt to bring together, in a reduction-to-practice fashion, appropriate concepts and methods from various fields to help change masters learn how to lead, manage, and participate in large-scale improvement efforts.

Large-scale is, of course, relative. Often, however, change masters are called upon to guide efforts that are beyond their domain of responsibility. The change master may suddenly be called upon to focus on a unit of analysis significantly larger than in his or her past experiences. When this occurs in the absence of any substantial body of knowledge for large-scale organizational change, they are left to flounder. Although the vision may be clear, the change master doesn't know how to proceed.

We have seen many situations where a change master has been given a large-scale change assignment without adequate knowledge, skills, resources, or top management involvement. They invariably fail, "willing workers" (Deming 1986) who become victims of the system. They are not to blame, their leadership is. Leadership often is unenlightened and unwilling to take the time to understand the requirements of success for system-wide efforts to improve performance.

One word of advice to those finding themselves in situations where they are willing but unable: be intellectually honest. Life is too short to go on crusades that may be momentarily blessed by the "Pope" but will not be supported for the duration. Large-scale improvement efforts aren't even marathon-type crusades; they have no ending; improvement is ongoing and should be pervasive.

We suggest you think through the requirements of success. Barnard calls these "strategic factors" — factors that, if you manage them successfully, will significantly enhance your probability of overall success, as well as factors that, if not managed successfully, will almost assuredly cause failure. After identifying requirements for success, you must demand that leadership fulfill their obligation and help you manage these factors. If they are unwilling or unable, we suggest you decline the opportunity to lead the crusade.

The majority (90%) of the productivity and quality improvement efforts we have observed over the past twenty years have not met the requirements of success and have predictably failed. Quality Circles did not, and they failed. MRP and JIT have significant failure rates. TQM failure rates are soaring because TQM has been allowed to become just another fad. Change masters cannot allow themselves to be "victims." You must be intellectually honest with yourself, with your sponsors, and with your clients. With that caveat, we turn now to the Theory of Grand Strategy Systems.

THE THEORY OF GRAND STRATEGY SYSTEMS

Large-scale, total-system improvement efforts are programs, not just projects. Again, programs contain multiple projects. Many change masters are deficient in project management knowledge and skills, let alone program management skills. The 3-ball problem associated with an improvement project becomes a 3^n-ball problem with a program. System-wide improvement efforts, such as business process re-engineering, cut across the functional organization. They require a multidisciplinary approach because there is a bit of industrial engineering, accounting, finance, psychology and sociology, organizational behavior, and counseling involved.

Improvement efforts of this magnitude require, in our opinion, a framework to make something that can appear overwhelming seem manageable. In a way, the Malcolm Baldrige Award criteria provide this structure for many organizations. These criteria reduce a perplexity to seven areas of effort and performance: senior executive leadership, information and analysis, strategic quality planning, human resource development and management, management of process quality, quality and operational results, and customer focus and satisfaction. They focus our attention. Kilmann's (1989) five tracks (culture, management skills, team-building, strategy-structure, and reward) also provide a structure for improvement efforts. He suggests that managing these five tracks leads to a "completely integrated program for creating and maintaining organizational success."

Anyone who has been involved in a single dimension, small-scope improvement effort has experienced failures they would attribute to a larger system interdependency left unmanaged: they change the plan but ignore the measurement and reward system and then are surprised when the plan isn't accomplished; they change the measurement system for the better, but don't do anything to the reward system or the education and training system and consequently find that the measurement system is sabotaged; they make an educational intervention, hope for a miracle, and are discouraged when "nothing takes." These are general examples that most experienced change masters can add to in substantial and specific detail.

The point is that there are subsystems (made up of processes) within the organization that are heavily interdependent. Improving one has a ripple effect on others (Figure 27). If the ripples bounce up against a solid wall (unchanging system), then they invariably wave back and alter the improvement made in a given subsystem.

Components of the Grand Strategy System

Fronts are an integral piece of a Grand Strategy System, which consists of four components (Figure 28):

1. Documenting and Understanding the Past—Improvement initiatives, performance levels and trends, problems, critical incidents, opportunities captured or not captured, key personnel changes, milestones, lessons learned;
2. Documenting and Understanding the Present—Current performance levels, current improvement initiatives, plans, opportunities, etc.;
3. Strategic Performance Plan for the Future—Benchmarks for future performance levels,

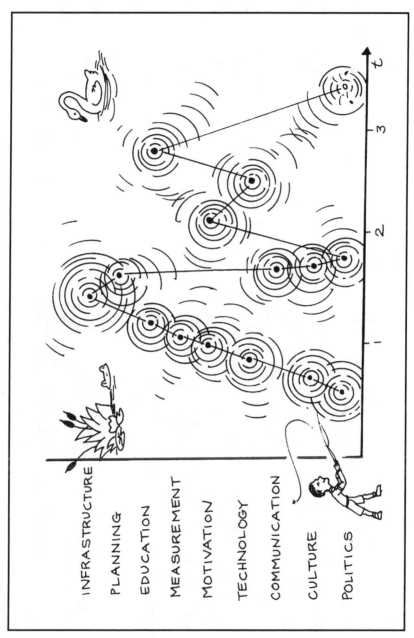

Figure 27. Interventions on a particular front create "ripples" across the organization affecting other fronts. These interrelationships, over time, are central to the progress of improvement efforts.

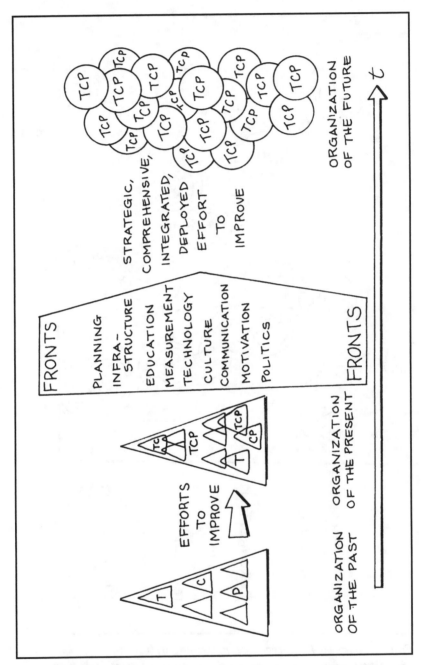

Figure 28. A grand strategy system contains these basic components: thinking (T), controlling (C), and performing (P).

long-range goals, visions, strategies, objectives, tactics, opportunities;
4. Frontal Plans and Strategies—We have identified nine fronts or subsystems that must be pushed forward for an organization to drive the rate of improvement necessary for success and survival in the `90s and beyond. They are:
   * Planning;
   * Education, Training, Development (knowledge and skill sharing);
   * Infrastructure ("B" infrastructure in context of "A" and "C");
   * Culture;
   * Measurement (to support improvement);
   * Motivation;
   * Technology (ways of getting things done);
   * Politics (internal and external, boundary spanning, alliances);
   * Communication (information sharing).

We won't spend a great deal of time defending the nine subsystems we have identified. Indeed, there are many different paradigms regarding the exact nature of these key fronts or subsystems. We encourage you to compare and contrast these subsystems to Kilmann's five tracks and the Malcolm Baldrige criteria introduced earlier, in addition to the variables Mohrman, *et al.* suggest (1989), the eight common attributes of successful American firms presented in *In Search of Excellence* (Peters and Waterman 1982), and other such models for system-wide improvement.

We have attempted to integrate what we see in the literature into a model that makes sense to us. We have attempted to ensure that the fronts make sense to leaders and change masters. Our data to this point suggest this is the case.

So, these are the subsystems that our experience and research suggest change masters can manipulate and improve over time. In improving these subsystems we increase the organization's capacity to improve, adapt, solve problems, and capture opportunities. Most, perhaps all, of the improvement initiatives that you and your organization have worked on in the past five years can be mapped to one or more of these fronts.

As we inferred earlier, the reason for developing categories (fronts) of improvement interventions is that it is easier to strategize for nine or so areas than for the hundreds of individual initiatives going on in an organization at any given time. This seems to help change masters as they construct their future plans: they easily can think about movement across nine fronts. This seems so simple on the surface, yet this approach is rarely taken in TQM or similar efforts.

The aim of the Grand Strategy System, then, is to ensure plans for improvement are strategically thought through, comprehensive, well integrated, and that they build on lessons learned from the past and present. We, of course, can't change the past, but we can learn from it, reflect on it, and evaluate the extent to which we have had constancy of purpose, continuity of leadership, and consistency of method. Most organizations today are not improving the quality of their plans for improvement, specifically their ability to ensure plans are implemented, deployed, and achieve the desired results. The Grand Strategy System is one method for solving this problem.

The Fronts Described
Let's review the nine fronts for further clarification.

Planning. The planning system represents how the organization plans, how implementation is assured, how deployment is assured, who is involved in planning, what the planning methods and processes are, how the organization ensures that method variation is controlled, the planning calendar, planning document specifications, how plans are used, and assurance that the improvement cycle (plan-do-study-act) is done throughout the organization and that these cycles are coordinated so that the system is optimized.

In the Hoshin Kanri sense, it is the systematic approach to management of improvement throughout the organization. Hoshin Kanri is more than strategic planning; it is strategic management. It includes deployment and implementation considerations. It links performance improvement initiatives from top to bottom and links strategic planning to daily planning and control. It is a much larger, more comprehensive system of planning than is traditionally managed in most American organizations. It is what will be required to make the transformation. Past planning methods and practices will not suffice in the future.

The planning front, then, represents the entire system of plan-do-study-act at all levels in the organization. In most organizations, this system needs to be re-engineered because it is so deficient. The biggest problem we have had on this front is establishing discipline and consistency in method. There is a real resistance to formal, disciplined methodology when it comes to planning; there is a tendency to want to "wing it." We think there is a need for balance. Inconsistent methods is the single biggest problem the change master will face on the planning front. Consistent, predictable performance is not possible without consistent methods in planning. Even the most disciplined of managers and leaders struggle to accept this.

Infrastructure. This front represents how the organization is structured and organized to do "A" and "B." It is not clear that organizations have infrastructures for "C" and "D," although emergency preparedness might be an example of a "C" infrastructure. The organizational chart represents one portrayal of how to organized to do "A." We all know, of course, that the organizational chart doesn't portray all of the interdependencies and interrelationships that exist in the organization. Recently we have seen the emergence of parallel or shadow organizational structures primarily for the purpose of doing "B." The challenge has been in figuring out how to integrate the "A" and the "B."

Most organizations today utilize ad-hoc teams, many routinely utilize process action and improvement teams. Self-managing teams are becoming more common as "high involvement" management approaches are evolving. These all entail infrastructural changes in sharing information, sharing knowledge, who is empowered to solve problems, make decisions, etc. In short, we are seeing the shoving of responsibility and authority for solving problems, making decisions, and improving performance to the lowest appropriate levels. Formal and informal structures for doing this are being established. These efforts are forcing us to rethink how we are currently organized, levels in the organization, paradigms about roles and responsibilities, and even how we portray infrastructure. Portrayal of infrastructure is going beyond simple organizational charts, and we are innovating with ways to portray new decision making, problem solving, and empowerment accountabilities. The old organizational chart is beginning to look like a pretty crude and ineffective tool for portraying how we are organized to do "A," "B," and perhaps "C."

Measurement. The measurement subsystem includes the entire cycle of measurement-to-data-to-information-to-knowledge-to-decision-to-action; it represents the study-act portion of the improvement cycle. The measurement front is inextricably tied to the communication front because it involves sharing information and knowledge such that empowered individuals and teams at all levels can make the appropriate decisions and take the appropriate actions. It incorporates the design and development of more comprehensive and effective information systems to support decision making and problem solving aimed at improvement. It includes the design and development of visible management systems throughout the organization. It entails converting all areas where teams meet into visibility and control rooms; our conference rooms will become information centers, hubs of information that teams use to support improvement activities.

All this requires that we re-engineer our information systems, adopting a user- and customer-driven approach to their development. We will have to move from being data rich and information poor (DRIP) to having timely, accurate, appropriate information necessary to support improvement decisions and actions. We must move from a control orientation to an improvement orientation, making all employees team members in the improvement cycle. This will require greater openness to information than heretofore practiced in most organizations.

The measurement front also includes incorporation of statistical thinking, which requires longitudinal data. There should be no more cross-sectional snapshots in time leading to tampering; no more comparing this month only to last month or this year to last year. Understanding statistical cycles and trends, not tampering, not micro managing, understanding process and system capability, and not exhorting people to do better when they already are doing their best and are simply constrained by the process or system—all these things must be accomplished through work on the measurement front.

Education/Training/Development. This subsystem focuses on ensuring that individuals and groups are constantly improving personally and professionally. It will require training in your organization to be re-engineered. It will require that the strategy of selecting the low-cost provider of training be abandoned and that it be replaced with selection of the highest value provider. It will require that you abandon the provider-driven approach to training and adopt a customer-driven approach.

A customer-driven approach to education, training, and development means that we would observe the customer at work and come to understand their needs and expectations. We would find the highest value (quality and cost) way to improve customer performance in response to their needs. We would more rigorously evaluate our in-house education and training courses, not just administer "smile sheets" at the end of each session. This, I think you will agree, will require re-engineering. Your current training system is probably not designed to achieve these aims.

Motivation. What combination of strategies and approaches does your organization use to maintain appropriate levels of effort to sustain competitive performance at the individual, group, and organizational levels? Do you routinely monitor your employees' satisfaction with pay, benefits, work, working conditions, communication, co-workers, leadership, supervision, growth opportunities, etc.? Do you have a system for sharing rewards when the organization wins? If so, do you share rewards with all employees or just with a select few? Do you train managers and leaders to apply job characteristics theory, equity theory, expectancy theory, or reinforcement theory (gainsharing, compensation management, behavior analysis) when dealing with motivational problems or opportunities? Is your total motivation front designed in an integrated fashion, or do you have motivational initiatives that are serving at cross purposes (e.g., individual suggestion systems attached to rewards and recognition simultaneously operating with team based improvement approaches)? What is your formal and informal reward and recognition system? Do you have good "line of sight" (strong cause-and-effect relationships between performance and rewards and recognition)? Do you reward and recognize the team? What is the ratio of total compensation from the highest paid employee to the lowest paid employee in your organization? How do you maintain cooperation through your motivation system? How do you motivate and maintain acceptable performance levels (APL)? How do you motivate and maintain motivated performance levels (MPL)? (Where MPL > APL by a significant margin, say 10-30% consistently over time)? MPL is the type of performance achieved when you have real commitment, people understand that if the organization wins they will win too, rewards are commensurate with performance, inducements balance with contributions, and contributions are high. How do you ensure that you don't pay extra for APL? How do you determine what to pay for MPL?

These are the types of questions and issues that must be addressed in the motivation front. The motivation front may well be the most complex front. Individual differences vary greatly. If your employees (managers included) are the customer of the motivation front, then the voice of the customer has large variation. What motivates one will not necessarily motivate another.

The motivation front is the entire system of base compensation, variable pay, benefits, gainsharing, recognition, pay for performance, job enrichment, team building, consequence management, etc. It links tightly to the communication, education/training/development, and infrastructure fronts because, as Lawler (1992) has indicated, sharing rewards must be preceded by sharing of information, knowledge, and power. Too often our motivation fronts get overdriven by the base compensation system; this is understandable because it is complex in and of itself. But to have a world-class organization, to truly make the transformation, the motivation front must better integrate a full complement of motivational strategies and approaches. These initiatives must be deployed successfully so that the motivational system is consistently applied throughout the organization. This seems to be the biggest problem facing this front. Too often the motivation system is largely left up to the individual supervisor or manager. Variation in how these individuals "motivate" is tremendous; therefore motivation to perform is highly variable and unpredictable. Making the system more consistent, improving the design and execution of the motivation system, is central to progressing on this front.

Communication. How does your organization share information? Do you have a control orientation, or do you have a commitment orientation? Are your information sharing approaches diverse to ensure you meet the varying requirements and expectations of all the customers of the communication system? Do you share the right information with the right people at the right time? Do you view your employees (all of them) as customers and users of information that have requirements, needs, and expectations? Are you data rich and information poor? Do you have all-hands meetings regularly? How much time do you spend designing agendas for these meetings? Is meeting management a fine tuned art and science in your organization? Do you overly rely on newsletters as the main mechanism for sharing information? Are people free to ask any and all questions, anonymously if necessary, in meetings? Do you apply quality function deployment to the communication front? Have you confronted the variation that exists throughout the organization in terms of what is shared, with whom, and when? Have all your conference rooms been converted into visibility rooms? Have you successfully integrated the measurement front with the communication front? Do you work hard enough at understanding information requirements throughout your organization or simply take the easy way out? Do your managers truly understand the relationship between sharing information, sharing knowledge and sharing of power? Do you empower in the absence of sufficient information and knowledge? Is this a form of exhortation? Are the results therefore predictable? If we can predict performance, can we improve it? How would a cause-and-effect diagram be useful in this situation?

These are just a sampling of the questions and issues associated with the communication front. It focuses primarily on the sharing of information. Key issues include who needs what information and when and how we portray the information so it can be converted into decisions and actions aimed at improvement. Here again, as was the case with education/training/development, a customer orientation is required. Too often information technologists (e.g., programmers) have driven the requirements for the system; we start in the data to conversion/tool box portion of the management systems model rather than with customer and user requirements.

Learning how to improve the communication front will require experimentation, it will require more meetings rather than fewer, and it will require better managed meetings. Many will be impatient with your efforts to improve communication; they may feel you are wasting their time. This is often because they do not really understand the cause-and-effect relationship between information, knowledge, decisions, and actions. They may not really want to participate in performance improvement and therefore don't understand the need for more information. They want to be left alone, to continue to optimize their little part of the world regardless of its impact on the larger system. The change master must understand this and manage it.

Technology. As mentioned earlier, technology is defined as a way of getting something accomplished. It would include hardware, equipment, software, methods, procedures, protocols, policies, processes, techniques, and tools. The technology front, therefore, includes the constant search for a better way to accomplish things: innovation, methods engineering and improvement, process improvement, reduction to practice, technology transfer, value engineering, re-engineering, continuous improvement, etc.

The relationship between changes in technology and performance improvement may be more direct than with other fronts. In this respect, other fronts are often considered to be enablers while technology could be considered, in some cases, to be a direct driver. Communication, education/training/development, planning, and infrastructure enable us to perform better, whereas in some cases technology improvements directly drive improvement. The secret, it seems, lies in managing the balance between the enablers and the more direct drivers of performance improvement.

Politics. Politics plays an important role in complex organizations. The informal organization is often at least as powerful as the formal. Selling large-scale organizational change is often as much a game of politics as it is ensuring that the quality of the solution is high. Effective implementation is a function of at least two basic variables: acceptance and quality. The political front and the communication front are interwoven. Playing politics in an organization often is driven by sharing information with the right people at the right time. The political front also is interwoven with the culture front — the values and the identity of the organization. The culture of an organization thus is made up of a complex combination of individual values and identities. Lining up support for improvement efforts clearly is an art. Making sure data and facts support the improvement is, of course, the first priority. But we all know that just because something makes sense on paper doesn't always ensure its success. Balancing the quality of the solution with acceptance of the solution is important.

Often the political front involves work with upline systems and managers and leaders within. Also, it often includes ensuring you have identified all significant stakeholders and have considered their inputs. Often, the change master is viewed as an outsider, so taking the time to become accepted and trusted is an important political consideration. In this sense, managing psychological distance is important—we can be too psychologically distant or too close to our clients and to the people in the system we are trying to help. This is a political consideration in a sense.

Understanding where the bases of power are in the organization and who controls them is key. If you are an external change master and do not align yourself with someone in a pivotal position of power, then your chances of success are limited. Having their commitment is as central to success as is a good solution to a problem. In organizations that have predictable changes in leadership, you will have to adopt a strategy for maintaining positioning. This may be one of the more difficult dimensions of the political front.

The political front is always present; however, in some organizations it is more pronounced than in others. Change masters must understand and manage politics if they are to be successful with large-scale organizational change.

Culture. Culture is shared values and beliefs. It is what you want, desire, value, and believe, but it is also what you have, your identity (Kurstedt 1993). Identity is comprised of rites, rituals, policies, procedures, motivation front, communication front, political front, habits, and traditions. Types of cultures have been identified and labeled (e.g., "work hard, play hard;" "country club;" "laissez faire"), but it is clear we all have slightly different impressions of our culture depending upon where we sit in the organization.

When there is a large gap between what we desire, what we value, what we believe in, and what we have there are usually problems. Recent interest in explicating guiding principles has revealed significant differences between the "talk" and the "walk," particularly in the context of TQM. We think there will always be gaps. When the gaps remain consistently large, then we need to examine our beliefs in the context of our identity.

Improvement occurs within the context of culture just like it occurs within the context of politics. The change master must understand and accept this. When solutions challenge or conflict with culture or politics, then the change master will face resistance. When solutions seek to change culture, there will be resistance that must be managed. The identity part of culture is rooted in habits, and habits die hard. The phases of change take longer to move through when dealing with established cultural patterns of behavior.

The culture front does not represent culture the noun; it represents the system by which culture is managed in a way that supports performance improvement. How do we continually shape our culture so it supports continual improvement? How do we drive out fear of improvement? How do we create a culture that accepts change as the norm? How do we close gaps between our values, beliefs, guiding principles, and behaviors? How do we ensure that our culture supports our survival? How do we develop a culture management system? These are the central questions associated with the culture front.

Thinking Multiple Fronts

Appreciation for a system is one of Dr. Deming's four elements of profound knowledge. What does it really mean? Deming defined a system as "a network of interdependent components that work together to try to accomplish the aim of the system" (Deming 1993). He stated further that, "a system must have an aim. Without an aim, there is no system. The aim of the system must be clear to everyone in the system... Management of a system therefore requires knowledge of the interrelationships between all the components within the system and of the people that work in it." Dr. Deming suggested that the aim is for everyone to gain. He taught us that optimization is management's job and that optimization is the process of orchestrating the efforts of all components toward the achievement of the stated aim.

There are many ways to view the components of a system. One way is to consider management subsystems as key components, as independent variables in a research sense. The fronts or subsystems are the things that leaders and managers improve to optimize the overall system. In improving these fronts, everyone doing their very best becomes good enough because they are working in a system that is designed to ensure this. The subsystems that cause suboptimization are the fronts we have identified. If we improve the fronts, then the best efforts of all within the system come closer to optimization of the system than previously was the case. If we are systematic and consistent in our efforts to improve the fronts, we will move towards optimization. The secret, as Dr. Deming suggested, is how we orchestrate our efforts across all the fronts.

An aspect of appreciation for a system, then, is thinking multiple fronts. Leaders, managers, and change masters must view improving the performance of these fronts as an important aspect of their jobs. They must become technically competent in understanding how to improve frontal performance. They must accept ownership for continually improving the performance of these fronts, which requires understanding how to redesign, in some cases re-engineer, them. Most leaders and managers do not see themselves as front managers. However, they can't fix the problem or capture the opportunities unless or until they fix the systems and processes. The design of the fronts causes levels of performance or lack thereof. Until this is understood, no systematic, sustainable improvement will be possible.

As mentioned earlier, conceptual acceptance of multiple fronts is not that difficult. However, operationalizing this understanding is more difficult. One way to assist management teams to move toward operational understanding of fronts is to get them to simply generate lists of current activities within each front, then ask critically introspective questions about these lists. By what method do we plan? How many plans do we have in our system? How are those plans generated? How are they used? Do they cause or promote improvement? What are we doing to maintain motivation? Are any of our motivational initiatives conflicting? What is our education/training/development plan? Are people really learning how to learn, learning how to improve performance? Do we have a formal, explicit strategy for improvement in this front? If not, what is the implied strategy from the list of things we are doing? How do we feel about this implied strategy?

We have found this exercise is a good way to help management teams operationalize a Grand Strategy System (GSS). We use templates to structure the exercise. We build a Grand Strategy System Wall in a visibility room. Figure 29 is a somewhat generic example of a GSS wall chart.

Thinking multiple fronts only requires the use of a few tools—input/output analysis, GSS wall chart, explicating initiatives within fronts, and understanding explicit or implied strategy—and a little bit of practice. They key is to stick with it. The change master will have to work hard with the management team on the education/training/development front and on the planning front to get them comfortable with the concepts and the tools.

Our operational definition of Total Quality Management is "the measurement and management of performance of each of the five quality checkpoints and of each of the nine fronts, over time, so as to optimize the performance of the overall system." Doing this by building on the past and present, by planning future interventions across fronts so that fronts move forward in a concerted effort, is what the Grand Strategy System approach is all about. Leadership and management for the Grand Strategy System clearly is a 3^n-ball problem. Assembling a team of people that can deal with the conceptual complexity of the Grand Strategy is a first step.

GRAND STRATEGY SYSTEM INFRASTRUCTURE

Our infrastructure for GSS calls for the following components: a design and development team (DDT), a steering council or executive steering group, a planning team, performance action teams (PATS), and front teams and front leaders. Each of these components has its own role in managing the implementation and deployment of the Grand Strategy System. Role clarification is what we are striving for.

We introduced the concept of Design and Development Teams (Architect and Engineering Teams) earlier. To elaborate, the DDT designs, develops, and leads Grand Strategy System planning, implementation, and deployment. The DDT is comprised of nine to twelve individuals who have knowledge of the organizational system targeted for improvement and the willingness and ability to lead organizational learning with respect to change and performance improvement.

Together, DDT members are responsible for moving the fronts forward in an integrated fashion across time and across the organizational system. During GSS start up, the DDT meets on a regular and frequent basis to plan and to engage in rigorous education and training. Core knowledge and experience to "cover" all the fronts must reside within the DDT; often DDT members are selected because of their expertise with respect to a particular front.

In that vein, the design and development team typically assigns front owners or front teams to plan for and manage implementation of specific interventions within a particular front. A front owner or front team is responsible for ensuring consistent coordination between their assigned front and the other fronts, measuring frontal progress, and reporting status to the DDT.

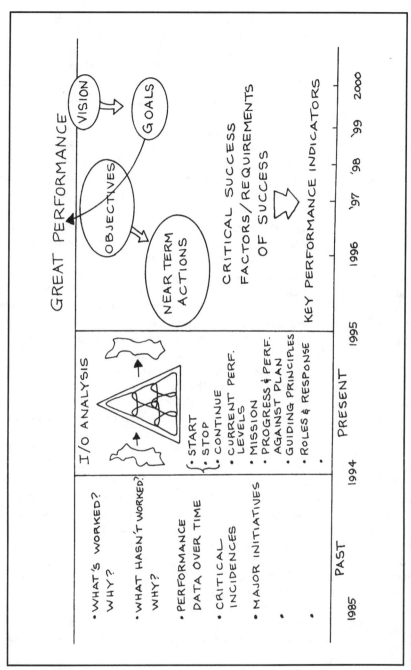

Figure 29. A grand strategy system wall chart helps the design and development team see the forest despite the trees.

The Steering Council is comprised of sponsor(s) and champions of the improvement effort. The steering council includes the top management team of the organizational system and selected others. Members of the steering council hold legitimate and position power in the organization. They establish policy, oversee and advise on strategy and action development, are involved and visible in this improvement endeavor but not intimately or on a day-to-day basis. The most important role the steering council plays is that it brings a larger systems perspective to the improvement effort. It ensures that the GSS design and development, as initiated by the design and development team, is congruent with the organization's vision and strategic direction. The steering council serves as a conduit for information sharing between the DDT and the organization. Its members are significantly involved in learning and improving their knowledge and skills to lead and participate in the transformation; however, they cannot be expected to be architects and engineers of the transformation.

A fourth component of the GSS infrastructure is the Planning Team. The DDT is a subset of this team. A Planning Team is an extended top management and leadership team for the system or subsystem. It will include, for example, key customers, key upstream system representatives, key personnel from down inside the system, key upline representatives, and the change master. The planning team may be up to fifty people but normally is six to twenty core members making up the top management team from the organization, another five or so from "down inside" the organization, five or so upstream and downstream participants, and a small group of upline representatives. The planning process methods developed to accomplish each step are robust enough to accommodate groups with from six to fifty or so members. The purpose of the planning team is to create a high-quality **plan for improvement** that is strategically thought through, comprehensive, incorporates a system perspective, and will be well integrated. These planning teams are ad hoc in that they come together for about five to seven days during a planning cycle (fifteen months), and the planning team composition may, in fact, be somewhat dynamic over time.

Additionally, the GSS infrastructure calls for **Performance or Process Action Teams**. These PATs are formed to accomplish specific performance improvement objectives (*i.e.*, solve a problem, capture an opportunity, improve a process, implement a decision or design, evaluate an improvement). They are chartered by the planning team. They periodically report progress and performance to the planning team and the steering council. They disband only when they have completed the improvement cycle (plan-do-study-act). They must complete the study, act, or evaluation phase to disband.

COMMONLY ASKED QUESTIONS ABOUT THE THEORY
AND METHOD OF GRAND STRATEGY SYSTEM

To conclude this chapter, we address a number of key questions that we are commonly asked when presenting or initiating the start up of a Grand Strategy System. We realize at this point that you probably have several questions of your own, and we hope to address them below.

Q1: This seems too academic to sell to my top management group. How do top management teams respond to this and how do you present it?

A1: Again, we find that this model has a great deal of face validity with top management groups—they find the concept of fronts easy to grasp, and this operationalizes TQM for them. However, paradoxically, Grand Strategy System both simplifies and complicates things for top managers. They relate easily to the analogy of waging a war and fronts. They can better understand TQM with the Grand Strategy System model. But they now see they have a bigger problem or task ahead of them than they thought previously. Many thought they could just work the infrastructure front, set up parallel structures of process improvement teams, do a little training, and that was TQM. After being presented the GSS model, they understand linkages and interdependencies better. They are a bit overwhelmed.

When introducing the concept of Grand Strategy System to a management team, I always start by presenting the Management Systems Model and then overlay the nine fronts on it, at the decision/action interface (Figure 30). This helps management understand GSS in the context of the management process, the plan-do-study-act improvement cycle, and in the context of a dynamic, open-system model of the organization (over time and in interaction with its environments). I recently made a presentation to Steelcase and AT&T jointly using just these two models. These managers wanted to work on the measurement front. Within ten minutes of my explanation of the interrelationships between the measurement front and other fronts, they grasped the approach and were very comfortable with it. It takes practice to completely internalize these models so you are comfortable and skilled at presenting them, but once you do this they are very powerful ways of explaining the transformation.

Q2: How is Grand Strategy System different from strategic planning? We already do strategic planning, and a lot of the things you discussed here should be included, shouldn't they?

A2: If your strategic planning system is designed properly, has improved over time, and focuses effectively on implementation and deployment, then there might not be much difference. However, if your strategic planning approach is like most we have seen, there are many significant differences. This does not suggest you should throw away your strategic planning approach; it might simply suggest you should expand, improve, perhaps re-engineer it.

First, most strategic planning efforts do not spend enough time in the "preparation to plan" phase. Understanding where the organization has been, what has worked, and what hasn't is an aspect of preparing to plan that often is not addressed in traditional strategic planning. By explicitly addressing this, we can operationalize continuity of leadership, constancy of purpose, and, perhaps most importantly, constancy of method. Studying the past and present before creating improvement plans for the future is a step often left out of strategic planning.

Second, most strategic planning does not really ensure a systems view; it does not ensure that our improvement efforts are comprehensive or integrated. Often, strategic planning methods and processes allow planning teams to fixate on current problems out of the context of problems of the past and future. The result is that many strategic plans are very temporal, very focused on today's problems rather than future opportunities or fronts that are lagging behind. It is the total management system that must be enhanced over time. Most strategic planning processes do not focus planning teams on system improvements. Often they fixate on what we do, what we produce, on what we would call the business plan. The business

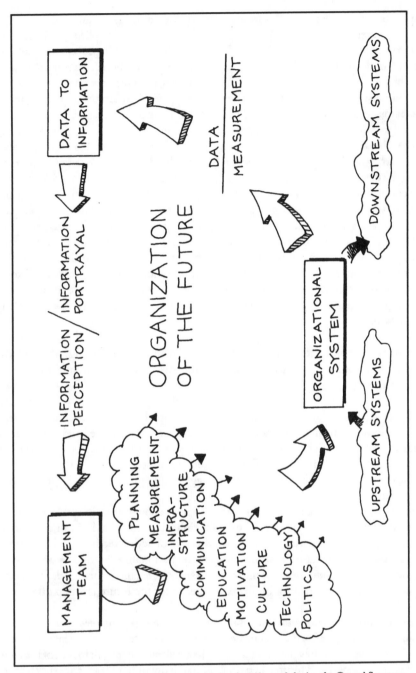

Figure 30. The management systems model helps describe and depict the Grand Strategy system (adapted from Kurstedt).

plan is important but so is the performance improvement plan. The performance improvement plan has been neglected in most strategic planning efforts. It focuses on improving what we do and how we do the things we do. It focuses on improving process and system capacity and capability. The strategic performance improvement plan and the business plan must be integrated to be successful. In a sense the business plan focuses on "A" and the performance improvement plan focuses on "B." Oddly, most strategic plans don't really focus on "B."

Finally, the method by which most strategic plans are built is not well defined or consistently executed in organizations. If the method is variable, then the results will be variable. Grand Strategy System requires consistent execution of planning methodology over time to succeed. The planning front requires a disciplined, systematic planning methodology (the PDSA cycle) that is deployed throughout the organization. This is not the case in most organizations and as a result improvements are inconsistent and unpredictable.

Q3: I don't understand the infrastructure front. In particular, I don't understand the concept of the architect and engineering team.

A3: The infrastructure front includes the organizational structure for "A." It also contains how the organization is structured to accomplish "B" and even "C." Many organizations are experimenting with parallel, or shadow, organizations (e.g., Executive Steering Groups, Quality Management Boards, Process Action Teams, ad-hoc improvement teams). The challenge is how to interface and integrate the "A" infrastructure with the "B" infrastructure, how to ensure that the "A" and the "C" don't drive out all the "B." Perhaps advanced stages of maturity with respect to TQM would render the differentiation between how we are organized to do "A" and how we are organized to do "B" unnecessary. In many self-managing team, green-field organizations we are seeing evidence that this might be the case.

There are certain standard elements of infrastructure for "B," particularly during startup, that we have come to understand. The design and development team, or architect and engineering team, is one of those elements. During start up of the Grand Strategy System, we have found it necessary to create a small (nine to twelve people) team that is knowledgeable about the transformation. This team represents a critical mass of change masters. The group will probably be multi-disciplinary and functional in educational background as well as organizational experience. One or more members of top management should be on the team in addition to some technical experts in key fronts (e.g., planning, measurement, motivation, technology). Critical mass implies that there are enough members and that their knowledge base is sufficient to lead the design and development of the grand strategy. This doesn't mean they do the design and development; it means they lead the effort.

Phases of change, professional modes of functioning (group and individual), and core competencies to be applied all will be topics of discussion as the design and development team orchestrates the grand strategy. They perform the way an architect and engineering (A&E) firm would in a large construction project. They are not the construction management firm (CM) or the owners/operators/managers (O&M), they are architecting and engineering on the basis of change master knowledge and skills. Over time, their relationship with the CM and the O&M groups changes and evolves. At some point they may adopt only a maintain and monitor role since the grand strategy ownership has been transferred to the "A" infrastructure, and "B" has become a way of doing business. This may ultimately define success for the design and development team. Of course, a great deal of work on the education/training and development front is required to achieve this.

Q4: I'm beginning to see the connection between the 3^n-ball problem and the design and development team. This design and development group will have to grapple with strategizing across multiple fronts first, then teach the CM group how to manage improvement projects across multiple fronts. Someone must maintain visibility and coordination on all this improvement activity. Is this the job of the CM group or the A&E group?

A4: Initially, the A&E group has to do this because the specific improvement project managers have their hands full with the 3-ball problem. They often can't handle the 3^n-ball problem until they have mastered the 3-ball problem. So, during startup, the A&E group usually establishes front owners. These front owners accept responsibility for the strategy design, development, and implementation in a single front. They become the integrator to the larger grand strategy. They are technically competent in the front (advancing their learning faster then others), and they are responsible for being knowledgeable regarding the status of the front at any given point in time. They may establish front teams they work with, at times bringing in profound knowledge (invited and from the outside, Deming 1992) when appropriate. As the organization's grand strategy evolves, the top management and leadership team may accept ownership of these front strategies. Again, this evolution is driven by the rate of progress on the education/training/ development front with the top management and leadership team.

Q5: How do we pull all this together? I understand this conceptually but don't see how it is operationalized. What tools are used to operationalize this concept of GSS? By what method do we do GSS?

A5: Unless there is awareness of the need to change and a search for methods to make the transformation, this won't get started. So, top management commits to moving forward, a high-level strategy is mapped out and sold, infrastructure is set up, and then work on the planning front begins. Our experience suggests that planning is interwoven with education/training/development. The measurement front is activated to establish a baseline, to understand differences between system and process capability and requirements and expectations of customers and stakeholders.

Regarding specific tools we used to manage GSS, we can list a number of examples. For the planning front, we utilize the Strategic Performance Improvement Planning Process (the seven-step model presented earlier and detailed in Sink and Tuttle 1989). In addition, "boot camps" are utilized periodically to push plans for fronts forward. These boot camps usually establish enough work for six to twelve months on a given front, then another boot camp is held. We further explain boot camps in the next chapter.

All-hands sessions (these are called three-level or multiple-level meetings in Hoshin Kanri) are held periodically to maintain the communication front and ensure that information is being shared adequately to keep efforts coordinated. The measurement system design and development process outlined in Sink and Tuttle (1989) is followed to move the measurement front forward. We also are stressing the increasing use of visible management systems (as in Hoshin Kanri) in GSS development.

On the technology front, we rely on those with technical competence in the technologies of the trade or business and of improvement tools. "Red teams," teams of outside experts in a given area, often are brought in to critique and improve frontal strategies. These outside experts can be honest brokers; they can assist with benchmarking; they can help you get unstuck; they can chide you if "A" and "C" are driving out "B;" they can kick you in the seat of the pants if you are dilly dallying, etc. If you pick the right "red team" members, this tool can be quite effective in keeping you moving and ensuring you don't get complacent.

On the motivation front, we force the team to learn the four basic theories of motivation (equity, expectancy, reinforcement, job characteristics) and to audit motivational tactics against these theories.

Perhaps our most important tools are the ones of fundamental planning, project management, and problem solving. Each front is expected to have a formal and written plan. These front plans are then integrated into an overall GSS written plan that is published and shared widely. The plan is a "living plan" so we use version numbers (e.g., v 1.0, 1.3, 3.0). Each year we increment the plan by one version number (e.g., 1.0 to 2.0.) Within years we increment by a tenth increment (e.g., 1.2 to 1.3). Milestone charts, Gantt charts, etc. for each front are integrated into an overall GSS program chart so initiatives within fronts can be viewed in the context of overall initiatives.

A "war room" or visibility and control room is established where the A&E team meets. This room contains the overall GSS program plan chart and is updated by front leaders periodically. Perhaps most importantly, the overall impact performance measurement system is displayed so the A&E team can monitor over time the impact of their efforts to improve performance across the multiple fronts. The GSS plan and the control and visibility room are perhaps the two most crucial tools associated with successful implementation of GSS.

To summarize, the change master has to manage: (1) phases of change, (2) professional modes of functioning, (3) technological applications as situationally appropriate, and (4) fronts to accomplish the transformation—a challenging assignment but vital to the success

CHAPTER 10

PHASES, MODES, AND METHODS
FOR IMPLEMENTING GRAND STRATEGY SYSTEMS

CASE EXAMPLE 3: THE START UP OF A GRAND STRATEGY SYSTEM
AT NATIONALE DISTRIBUTORS: 40% IMPROVEMENT IN 24 MONTHS!

The setting for this case example is Nationale Distributor (ND), a unionized distribution system consisting of nine warehouses geographically dispersed throughout a fairly large region in Mexico.

Nationale's information systems support division and the industrial engineering department have been two very important groups involved in improvement projects. Information systems support clearly has been recognized as crucial to success in distribution systems. The firm has created its own management college modeled after Motorola University in the United States and several other organizations' efforts to improve the quality of in-house education, training, and development. Their college works in conjunction with several local universities in addition to tapping internal expertise.

Most of ND's improvement initiatives over the past five years have been independent, unintegrated projects, such as consolidation, warehouse management system installations, operations research model applications, technology modernization, traditional layout improvements, development of standards, training on an ad-hoc basis, and small methods improvement projects.

CAST OF CHARACTERS

Dan — Vice President at Nationale. Dan is an industrial engineer in his mid-thirties, who has risen rapidly within the organization. He is dynamic, keenly intelligent, aggressive, demanding, innovative, politically astute, and an intelligent risk taker. Dan plans his improvement initiatives carefully and has achieved results. His firm and division are both doing very well in the market place and he wants this trend to continue. He benchmarks vigorously and challenges his division to improve in spite of their successes. His efforts over the years have been supported by external support organizations that bring new "technologies," new ideas—external change masters. He has smartly brokered these external services and been reasonably successful at using them to augment his own internal change master efforts. Education/training/development, planning, new technologies, and leadership have been the hallmarks of his efforts.

Dan has been following a range of developments in quality and productivity improvement: benchmarking, business process engineering, grand strategy systems and large-scale organizational change, breakthrough thinking, TQM and the concept of total performance, measurement system developments, strategic planning improvements, the learning organization etc. He is a visionary and understands mentally what a "great performance" will be for a distribution system in the '90s.

Angelo — **Nationale Senior Vice-President and Dan's boss.** Angelo lets Dan take a lot of the risks, sitting on the fence waiting to see whether an initiative will work. If it doesn't, he doesn't "punish" Dan; he protects him, if necessary, from the wrath of upper management (but doesn't identify himself with the project). When one of Dan's projects does work or is highly favored by management, then he becomes a visible supporter and champion. Dan accepts this phenomenon well and uses it to his advantage.

Miguel — **a Vice-President who reports directly to Dan.** Miguel has worked his way up through the distribution system, knows it well, and has been a buffer between the distribution managers, the union, the workers, and Dan. Miguel also is politically astute and has learned to be an early adopter of Dan's initiatives, even when he doesn't completely understand them. He's not a yes man; he thinks for himself, but he isn't a change master or a leader of change either. Dan and Angelo have a good relationship; in a sense they are both "coat tailing" each other. Miguel knows this and supports them in full knowledge that he will benefit.

Stephen — **Director of a QPC quality and productivity center in the United States.**

Tim — **Senior Associate at the QPC and Program Manager for ND.**

Deborah and Michael — **Members of the QPC project team.**

Dan sat at his desk on Monday at 6:30 a.m., appreciating the silence. He liked to arrive at the office early, not just to get a head start on the day, but also to have some concentrated, uninterrupted thinking time. This particular Monday morning, Dan was thinking hard about a potential problem which could have serious implications for Nationale: The union had successfully pressured increases in Nationale's labor costs to the point that a nonunion third party could take over the nine warehouses and run them for Nationale at significantly lower cost. Dan had facts and data to support the notion that the distribution system could and indeed must improve performance by a minimum of 40% within 24 months or run the risk of facing a major "make or buy" decision by the senior managers of the firm. Dan preferred the "make" strategy; he wanted to protect the jobs of his ND employees, but knew they were at risk.

Dan had communicated the need for this dramatic level of improvement and, perhaps not surprisingly, many in his division had seen this as a ploy on Dan's part to reduce wages or squeeze more profits out of the system to ensure another early promotion. But Dan knew the score on the basis of benchmarking and the acquisition of hard data and facts. The potential threat of a new entrant into the marketplace with a breakthrough system for distribution was growing in Dan's view. For example, Wal-Mart and a number of European distribution system organizations were breaking paradigms and challenging traditional thinking, resulting in dramatic improvements in market penetration and performance improvement. How could he portray and communicate these threats so people would develop the sense of urgency to take action?

Nationale's nine distribution managers, for the most part, had worked their way up through the system. They understood and excelled at distribution as it had existed for the past twenty years; they knew they were successful and that the company was successful and saw no reason to change. The distribution managers simultaneously respected and resented Dan. Dan didn't come up through the ranks, was a "fair-haired boy", and had a tendency to push his initiatives too hard.

In Dan's estimation, the ND industrial engineering group and others involved in improvement projects had an antiquated paradigm of change mastering. They saw themselves in one professional mode: the expert solution provider. They were "stuck" in that mode, therefore improvement wasn't increasing at an acceptable rate. The organization was not learning and developing the capacity to improve fast enough. "B" was not seen as an integral part of everyones' jobs and wasn't being done in a systematic, coordinated fashion.

Dan decided his best strategy was to obtain outside help. He contacted QPC, a quality and productivity center in the United States that he had worked with several times in the past to see if they would be willing to take on what was, at this point, a very ill-structured initiative.

Stephen, the director of the Center traveled to Nationale and conducted a situation appraisal, which formed the basis of a scoping proposal he presented for review by Dan, Angelo, and Miguel. In his scoping proposal, Stephen recommended to pilot test a modified application of the Grand Strategy System approach in two of the warehouses: one large and one small. Successes and lessons learned from the pilot test applications then would be replicated throughout the larger distribution system. He explained in the proposal the fit between that approach and the desired outcomes explicated by Nationale Distributors. The proposal outlined a multifront attack—coordinated interventions on the infrastructure, planning, education/training/development, technology, measurement, communication, and motivation fronts. Stephen explained that the fronts would be tackled in roughly that order, although once the project began there would be much parallel activity. Stephen suggested that, as a starting point, an initial design and strategy session be held at his Center with key leaders of this project.

In preparation for the session Stephen selected Tim, a senior associate, to be the project manager, and Tim in turn selected Michael, a graduate student from the "quality and productivity teaching hospital," and Deborah, an administrative professional, as support. Together, these individuals represented the Center's ND team.

The Center team spent several days prior to the session building the agenda, focusing on desired outcomes and outputs, sequencing agenda modules, and deciding who would lead the modules and how they would be executed. The day before the ND group arrived, they rehearsed the strategy session, going over who would do what, when, and how. Deborah concentrated on logistics and details with Michael, Tim prepared materials to be used during the session, and Stephen tried to keep the big picture in view and get mentally prepared for what was sure to be a grueling and mentally fatiguing two and a half days.

A twenty-foot Grand Strategy System Wall Chart was prepared in the meeting room (Figure 31). Space for documenting past, present, and future was allocated. The ND "A"

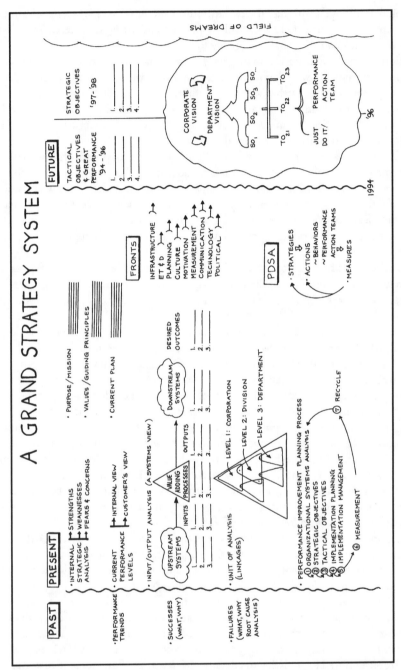

Figure 31. Structure providing for the Grand Strategy System includes the construction of a GSS wall chart.

infrastructure was posted on the time-line in the "present" position. Vertical and horizontal subsystems were identified to get a feel for the size and scope of the intervention; numbers of people in each subsystem were identified. Forms were prepared and had been assigned as pre-work to facilitate development of the GSS Wall Chart.

A last-minute call to Dan confirmed that all travel arrangements were coordinated and that the agenda looked fine. Stephen confirmed that all attendees were fluent in English and also that all attendees had completed the pre-work reading and data gathering.

Dan, Angelo, Miguel, and a representative from the Information System Support Division (ISSD) and the Industrial Engineering Division (IED) arrived on a Sunday evening, and the nine people participating in the strategy session had dinner together. For the first time, Stephen has a chance to see the ND personnel interacting and discussing the project. He sensed some resistance and skepticism on the part of Miguel and the other two project team members. These individuals were clearly not as enlightened and knowledgeable as Dan. Angelo was reserved, taking a wait and see attitude. He acknowledged this project had potential but was concerned about the complexity of the approach and by the academic orientation. Miguel also was very concerned about the complexity and sophistication of the approach; he knew his distribution managers and their employees and could envision their resistance. Stephen sensed all this but wasn't able to get these reservations and concerns out on the table that evening. He tried to manage the catharsis phase, but in a social setting it was tough to challenge enough to cause this to occur. Dan and Stephen talked after dinner, and Dan confirmed Stephen's intuition.

Monday morning, the five ND personnel and the four-member Center ND team met in the Center's previously prepared conference room. The goals of this working group were to: map out the project for at least the first nine months, clarify and lock in on desired outcomes, do some team building between the Center personnel who would be working on the project and the ND personnel, build the infrastructure for the improvement effort (the "B" infrastructure), finalize scope of effort and budget, establish key performance indicators against which the project's success would be evaluated, and educate the ND participants on the theory and application of the Grand Strategy System.

Stephen had used, intuitively, the change master matrix as he prepared for the strategy session. He realized that he probably would be able to jump directly to column 5 of the matrix (the self-designed change phase) and that rows 1 (Inquiry Mode), 4 (Structure provider mode), 5 (teacher), 2 (data gatherer), and 3 (collaborator) would be most appropriate and called upon. He would have to bring planning, measurement, motivation, problem solving, process improvement, and project management technologies to bear during this strategy session to succeed. In this respect, he would be called upon to, at times, be an expert and a teacher, using the technologies but also explaining where the technologies would come into play during the life-cycle of the project.

Stephen began the session in the inquiring mode to see if, in fact, the group from ND was ready to go to phase 5 (self-designed change). He inquired with the group, seeking to clarify and reach consensus on desired results from this project. He was surprised to find there were some hidden agendas that hadn't come out as he had prepared the proposal.

Although Dan had the vision fairly clear in his head, he hadn't consistently articulated it with this group, so Stephen facilitated this to occur. There was not a strong crystallization as to what the future levels of performance should be or the nature of the challenge. Stephen realized he was really back at Phases 3 and 4 (self-awareness and self-evaluation), so he processed this with the group. This took the entire morning, throwing the painstakingly designed agenda off by two and one-half hours. Tim, Michael, and Deborah were almost frantic at the slippage in schedule, but Stephen reassured them it would work out and that he knew what he was doing.

Over lunch that day, Stephen sensed that the ND team was ready to move to Phase 5 (self-designed change). He also now realized that Tim would be unable, at this point, to run much of the meeting. The group was tougher to work with than Stephen had thought they would be. Dan was quiet, not wanting to push too hard, and was deferring to Miguel a great deal because he knew that Miguel's acceptance and understanding were key to this project's success. Dan had told Stephen privately that if Miguel didn't buy-in they might as well not proceed. Knowing this, Stephen had spent time talking with Miguel, trying to establish a rapport. It had been slow going, but Stephen was beginning to see signs that his efforts were paying off.

After lunch, Stephen recapitulated the theory of Grand Strategy System and explained the GSS Wall Chart. Over lunch, Tim and Michael had taken the completed GSS data collection forms, integrated the input, and captured it on the wall chart. Stephen then was able to review the past and present in terms of improvement initiatives, successes, failures, lessons learned, ongoing initiatives, and critical incidents. As he did this, it triggered additional data, and Tim added it to the chart as appropriate.

By mid-afternoon, the group had a good grasp of where ND has been and what they were doing currently to improve quality and productivity. It was the first time they had seen all this together, portrayed in one location. Stephen's comment that their improvement efforts probably hadn't been strategically thought through, comprehensive, or well integrated hit home. Their efforts really did appear more like a "random walk" than any thoughtful strategy. Stephen asked them to see if they could articulate their "intended or inferred" strategy on the basis of this data; if it wasn't planned then what did it appear to be in hindsight? Each came up with a different interpretation, and this made it clear there was work to be done.

Dan commented that he was surprised, given that they had spent so much time and effort on strategic planning. Stephen asked Dan to explain Nationale's strategic planning approach and Dan did so briefly. Stephen said the problem was clear, the method they were using didn't focus on integrating "B," didn't focus on the issue of deployment, and also had no mechanism to ensure that their plans were comprehensive.

Stephen felt very good about the extent to which the GSS Wall Chart had helped him create a catharsis (Phase 2), of sorts, and had heightened self-awareness and evaluation. The ND team really was ready to move to Phase 5, but at mid-afternoon they were all a little "burnt" so they switched gears, took a tour of campus, watched a new video on the power of visions (Barker 1986), took time off for R&R, and then reassembled for a social hour at Stephen's house before an informal dinner at a local restaurant. Stephen opted not to join them for dinner, hoping that this would give Tim, Michael, Deborah, and a couple of other Center personnel time to develop rapport with the client. It also gave Stephen time to mentally recharge for the second day, which he knew he needed.

Tim kicked off Day 2 by asking the five ND people to reflect on what they had heard, learned, and reacted to the first day. The Center personnel wanted to hear, in the client's words, what had sunk in. This was a standard practice of the Center, to allow end of day and start of day reflection on what was heard. It was a way of confirming whether key points were getting across, and it helped them determine what to emphasize or re-emphasize that day. It was also a good way to sense where they were with the client in the matrix.

They then began by taking each of the fronts (they had decided to tackle seven fronts out of a possible nine) and identifying major activities or milestones within the front. They tackled them in roughly the order that Stephen suggested they must be dealt with over time, starting with infrastructure for the project. The "A" infrastructure was insufficient to support the project, so a parallel structure was established. This "B" infrastructure included a Design and Development Team (DDT), a Steering Council (SC), a Warehouse Leadership Team (WLT for each pilot warehouse), and Warehouse Improvement Teams (WIT). Figure 32 depicts the relationship between these "B" infrastructure components.

Each infrastructural element had a specific role and domain of responsibility that was specified by the group. The DDT was the architect and engineering group for the project. They would be this group of five, the two distribution managers whose warehouses were involved, and several functional or technical specialists, including Tim from the Center. They were to be a critical mass of change masters, and they were in charge of designing and developing the project over the next twenty-four months. The SC included all the distribution managers in addition to key top managers from other functional areas in the firm. The plan was to share information and knowledge with this group over time, not necessarily to empower them to supervise the project. Gaining understanding and eventual buy-in for the other seven distribution managers was crucial if this approach ultimately was to be replicated throughout the distribution system. The SC also was established to ensure that systems thinking was maintained over time and that the entire system was considered when any given improvement initiative was undertaken.

There were two WLTs, one for each of the pilot test warehouses. They included the distribution manager, his top management team, selected supervisors, union representation, the warehouse IE, and several elected employee representatives. In each case they were approximately twelve to eighteen people. Their role was to implement and deploy the project as the DDT intended.

The linking pin to both the DDT and SC was the distribution manager (DM). This linking pin responsibility meant that the DM was going to have significantly increased activities and would somehow have to off-load some traditional duties. This was an opportunity to see if the DMs could begin to do less tampering and micromanaging and evolve toward strategy development and deployment and "B"-type activities. The life of a DM at that time was one of lots of "C," plenty of "A," and almost no "B," adding up to 60-70-hour weeks. Dan and Miguel knew this had to change, but did the DMs? Maybe the more important question was whether they had the ability and willingness to change.

The WITs were designed to be ad-hoc improvement teams working on projects identified by the SC, DDT and WLT. From the outset, it was clear there was a lot of work to be done on the education/training/development, motivation, and communication fronts if they were going to be successful at empowering their workers to engage in "B." Stephen cautioned them (per Lawler 1986) to share information and knowledge before sharing power. Too many horror stories from the past twenty years associated with quality circles to mae it unnecessary for Stephen to have to reinforce this.

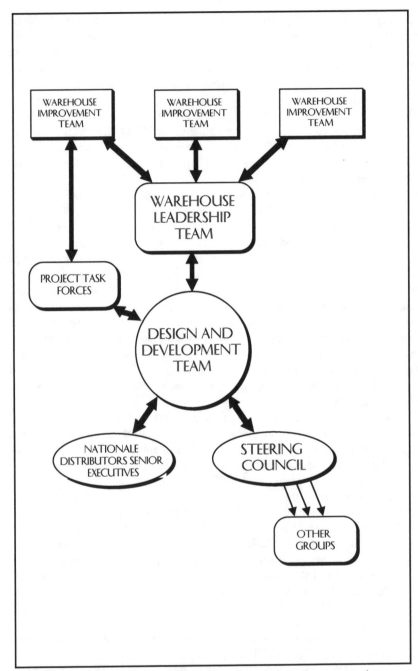

Figure 32. A sample infrastructure depiction for a warehouse improvement project.

Locking in the infrastructure took the better part of the day, so, again, they were behind schedule. To Tim and Michael, it seemed as if Stephen was letting them get side-tracked, but Stephen saw it as part of the data gathering mode (row 5) and forced Deborah and Tim to take copious and well organized notes, knowing that the information they acquired now would become invaluable in the near future.

Stephen realized that he would not be able to bring enough knowledge or technology to bear to do much project planning for measurement, technology education/training/development, or motivation so he deferred that till later. He did want to map out the start-up phase of the project in great detail. They scheduled meetings through January, created a communication plan, discussed how to implement the infrastructure, and managed to think through educational sessions needed to bring participants up to speed on what was going to be done, when, why, etc. Most importantly, they scheduled a planning/education and training session, or boot camp, as the Center called it, with the DDT. The intent was to create a project proposal and plan. The project proposal and plan would map out the strategy and specific initiatives that would be taken to improve performance by 40% in twenty-four months (the target that had been established on the basis of facts and data supplied by Dan and Angelo). It would be presented to the SC and the WLTs in January, along with a proposed budget. Recommendations would be reviewed by the SC and WLTs and opinions given to Angelo and Dan. Angelo and Dan then would have to sell the plan to their bosses for support. If the DDT and the Center succeeded then they could move from Phase I to Phase II of the project; if not, the effort would be abandoned.

By the end of the strategy session, everyone was tired and a little disappointed there wasn't more completed and more closure. Next steps were clear, and they were anxious to press on. Tim and Michael were overwhelmed. Dan and Stephen were confident and pleased with this first effort but had a healthy respect for what was next. Angelo had a little better feel for what this entailed but was sure he couldn't, at this point, articulate with any degree of confidence what this was all about to his management. He also wasn't confident at this point that the approach was pragmatic enough to achieve such significant improvement targets without laying off huge numbers of people, a tactic he knew would be difficult and very unpopular in the current economic situation. Miguel thought this was all too academic and complex but was willing to go along with Dan. He didn't have the foggiest idea how to tell somebody what he had done the last few days. The other two ND personnel (ISSD and IED) thought this was a crock. They were way over their heads, were not, at this point, able or willing to be change masters, didn't see the big picture, and would rather be working on some very small, tangible, easy improvement project that didn't stretch their technical skills too much. They contributed almost nothing during the strategy session. All they knew was that they were surrounded by the most powerful people in their division, so they played along. They had no idea what was in store for them in the future.

It took a full six months, one fourth of the project schedule, to get the GSS plan developed. At one point, Stephen used an external red team as a forcing function to get the Design and Development Team off dead center. They were not used to having to complete the planning phase of the improvement cycle before entering the Do portion. The culture was one of plan quickly, do, then get on to other projects. Study-Act was almost nonexistent in the organization. It was a "fire, ready, aim" culture. The red team was very critical of the plan that evolved from the strategy session. The technology interventions were fairly comprehensive but the red team wasn't sure that they were going to achieve the 40% improvement target in twenty-four months. The red team was unimpressed with the work on the other fronts; they were not sold on the Grand Strategy concept. Most were of the old school of thought—drive the technology front, everything else will come along in the slip stream. Stephen and Tim had worked hard to continue to educate the Design and Development Team, the Steering Committee, and the WLTs, and now also had to work politics with the red team.

Clearly, entropy was setting in at this point. Most ND project personnel had never been on a project this complex. They were like fighters who had never gone a full twelve rounds; they just didn't know how to pace themselves; they couldn't envision or anticipate what was next. The short lived highs from the strategy session, the project startup, and the boot camp evaporated on the breeze.

Stephen and Tim had motivation front problems of their own with the Design and Development Team. Teams were being established in the two pilot warehouses; there was initial excitement and enthusiasm, but even that was wearing out. The whole project seemed to be running into the "wall," bumping up against the false learning curve. Stephen and Tim, and even the DDT, sensed this and started to strategize how to address it. They had to have some small victories; the people involved in this project had to have a sense of success soon or entropy would fulfill its mission.

The secret seemed to be carving out some doable, small, technology front-related projects that the distribution system could implement and with which results could be seen. Stephen and Tim simultaneously considered other fronts and worked on identifying doable tasks for the measurement, motivation, and education/training/development fronts. In total, six small tasks in the overall plan were targeted for focus during the second six-month interval: three technology front projects and one project each for the other three fronts. In parallel, the communication front was maintained through the infrastructure that was set up; at the same time the political front was managed through the linking pins established in the organizational hierarchy.

Stephen and Tim increased their efforts to keep the Design and Development Team focused and clear on what the next steps were in the context of the overall plan.

This start-up scenario gives you some sense of how the matrix proved to be an effective tool for Stephen as he planned and executed his strategy for getting this very large and complex change project off the ground. Stephen had been involved in leading and researching large-scale organizational improvement for over twenty years. He had first been very systematic in his use of the matrix, writing down strategies (cells to be in at particular points in time), analyzing his strategies after the fact to learn how he could have been more effective and what to do differently next time; he even wrote up these implementation plans as part of his dissertation. Now, after years of practice and internalization, he had become very intuitive about the use of this tool. However, from time to time he found it useful to refer to the structure as a way of thinking through strategies and reflecting on experiences. He carried a copy of it with him in his Day Timer to ensure access at all times.

It had taken Stephen over eight years of formal education and well over twelve years of what he considered internship to get close to having enough knowledge and skill in most critical cells to be a complete change master in most quality and productivity situations.

Even now, his rate of learning was steady, a blend of reading, practice, study, teaching, and discussions with colleagues. His foundation was solid but refinement in specific areas was a never-ending process. So it is with the career of a change master.

Regardless of the type of improvement in which the change master is involved, the phase and mode concept applies. Clearly, application of the matrix becomes significantly more complex in the context of a GSS application. The 3^n-ball problem becomes a reality, and the change master is called upon to be a program manager, not just a project manager. The number of sponsors, targets, stakeholders, and critics increases, thus the number of relationships to be maintained increases. As a program manager, the change master is leading and coordinating specific project manager efforts, so the role of leader of a team of change masters is now added.

In a large-scale Grand Strategy System improvement effort, change masters will find themselves bouncing back and forth between projects and fronts; at any given moment, they may be called upon to switch modes and to operate at different phases of change. Indeed, this is challenging. One works up to developing the knowledge and skills necessary to succeed with this level of complexity. Good program managers were at one time good project managers. Good project managers were at one time good task managers.

Developing mode proficiency is similar to the process of developing situational leadership skill. It takes time and conscious practice. You must have a strategy, plan it out, execute it, process your execution, and make necessary adjustments—and do all this over and over again. The change master has to be able to switch back and forth between a "30,000 foot," total systems, multiple front perspective and a "close-up," attention to detail within a front perspective. We call this the ability to zoom in and out.

START UP OF A GRAND STRATEGY SYSTEM

It is possible to think of a large organizational system passing through phases of change, although clearly this is easier to envision with individuals and smaller groups and organizational systems. The difficulty in using the phase of change model with a large organizational system is that there probably is no such thing as a system that large, comprised of subunits and many individuals, moving from catharsis to self-awareness. However, we can speak of a critical mass of subunits and individuals as moving from one phase to another, and it is in this light that the model is useful.

The change master will find it necessary to work with key individuals and key subunits within the larger organizational system and to concentrate phase of change planning and interventions for these key individuals and groups. It is the orchestration and alignment of phase movement across key individuals and groups that becomes critical to GSS progress. Having said this, it is clear that identification of these key groups and individuals is an early step. During the situation appraisal phase, we model the total system being improved and even consider the system above it. Normally we start by drawing a simple pyramid and linking-pin model (Figure 33) to gain a visible understanding of system components and vertical and horizontal linkages.

Once this is completed, we identify key sponsor(s), target(s) (individuals and subunits), stakeholders, upstream and downstream systems, and upline systems. In short, we complete a fairly thorough input/output analysis for the organizational system to be improved. An audit of the past and present relative to each front and overall improvement efforts and performance is completed as thoroughly as is possible at this point.

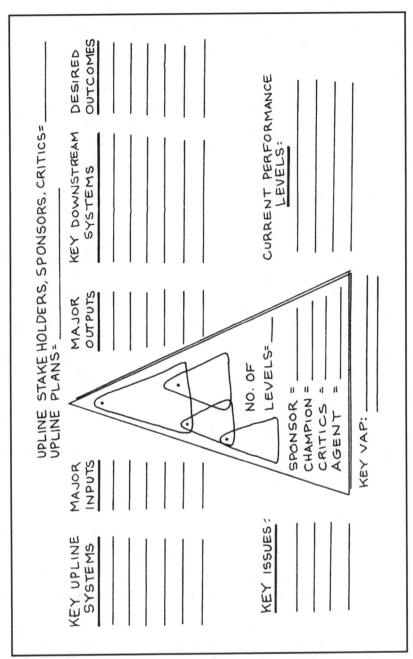

Figure 33. Modeling of the target organization aids the change master in gaining appreciation for the target system.

We lead large-scale quality and productivity improvement efforts with the planning front. To reiterate, most organizations do planning, but it is not well designed, not well executed, not well deployed. Implementation, follow-through, and results over time often are not good. Many organizations today are interested in linking plans to actions and measures, and they are interested in integrating continuous improvement and re-engineering into their planning efforts. We begin by developing a planning system.

The next six phases of change, catharsis through reinforcement of new and more functional methods and behaviors, surface at major milestones during the planning system. The change master literally will observe and experience phases of change for individuals and subunits as the planning system rolls out. Engaging an organizational system in a plan-do-study-act process or system as a lead front is a good way to synthesize total quality principles and the GSS approach into an overall effort. Our intent is to get individuals and groups acting right as quickly as possible; we want to balance the need for quick, positive results with the need to make longer-term improvements in the overall system. The education/training/development front can be woven into planning activities such that just-in-time, synthesized education is being done and is seen as a means to an end rather than an end in and of itself. We believe that improvements in the culture front will be a natural outgrowth of GSS implementation as other fronts, such as education, motivation, and communication, are worked.

Infrastructure for "B" is an intervention that closely parallels and may even precede initiating improvements in the planning system. Succeeding with large-scale quality and productivity improvement efforts is akin to building a large, complex building. As previously stated, there is a need for an "architect and engineering" (A&E) group; there is a need for a "construction management" group, and, there ultimately will be an "owner and operator" group. Doing TQM, making the transformation, succeeding with large-scale improvement efforts is a vast undertaking. Done in piecemeal fashion it is no better than a quick-fix approach. There must be a strategic, comprehensive, integrated effort. Building an infrastructure for startup of this undertaking is important but often neglected.

The infrastructure for "B" is often a parallel, collateral, or shadow infrastructure. That is, people have "A" jobs and they have ad hoc "B" jobs. The goal would ultimately be to have "A" and "B" integrated so well that there may not be a need for two infrastructures. However, we have found that the "A" and "C" roles often dominate. In the context of phases of change, learning to do "B" requires moving through the seven phases of change. It is not uncommon for individuals within an organization to pass through Phase 2 (catharsis, anger, denial, frustration) six to eighteen months, even years into a GSS effort. The frustrations of having "A" and "C" squeeze "B" out accumulate over time, and they often do not surface until people are well into trying out new behaviors. This is a good example of an individual, group, or organization regressing in phases of change. If this regression isn't managed properly, often with the expert mode (this happens, it is predictable, others experience it) and the challenger mode (you are not being individually responsible and intellectually honest, you are allowing yourselves to become victims), then the effort is in jeopardy.

BOOT CAMP FOR THE DESIGN AND DEVELOPMENT TEAM

The A&E team serves the sponsor(s), the Steering Council, and the Planning Team. They also have as targets the customers or users of their change initiatives. They often must learn and do at the same time, at an often unrelenting pace. Dedicated effort, especially during startup, is crucial. An early activity, introduced in this chapter's case example, is what we call a boot camp, an intense, learning and planning session off-site. The goal is to develop version 1.0 of the organization's Grand Strategy. At these boot camps, DDT members lock themselves behind closed doors in a retreat-like setting until they feel they have a GSS plan of sufficient quality to present to the Steering Council for review. During a boot camp session, there is a balance between education/training/development and planning out the next twelve to fifteen months, primarily for the infrastructure, planning, communication, education/training/development, and measurement fronts.

The A&E team also will want to discuss and address the issue of decision rules in the context of roles and empowerment. As the GSS effort progresses, management of participation becomes an increasingly significant issue, which can be addressed by the development of decision rules to operationalize empowerment and clarify roles and accountabilities. We adopt three types of decisions:

• Type I — Just do it
• Type II — Do it but let appropriate individuals or groups know
• Type III — Don't decide or take action until you have permission.

Examples of specific decisions are developed to anchor these types. Ultimately, it is likely that the organization will want to move the distribution of decisions from right to left (Figure 34).

The goal is to create an organization that is empowered in a predictable and controlled fashion, and that tends to seek forgiveness rather then permission, that acts on policies and principles, that is aggressive, proactive, flexible, and adaptive. This doesn't happen overnight. Ultimately the key test is one of downside risk. What's the worst that can happen if we make a Type I instead of a Type II or III decision? If the answer is that the downside risk isn't that great and the upside gain is good, then we should reward Type I decisions.

BEYOND THE BOOT CAMP: ESTABLISHING THE PLANNING SYSTEM

Once the A&E team has a version of the Grand Strategy documented and sold they have planned the work, and they then begin to work the plan. As indicated, our bias is to lead with the planning front. Many planning systems and processes are available to choose from in the literature. For purposes of illustration, we will use the Strategic Performance Improvement Planning Process described in detail in the Sink and Tuttle reference (Figure 35).

We distinguish between a planning system and the planning process in the following way. The planning process is the steps in proper sequence. Our model portrays a seven-step process. The planning system is the execution of these seven steps over a planning cycle (twelve to fifteen months). The planning system involves more than just the seven steps; it includes all the details of doing the seven steps over time, integration and interfacing with programming systems and budgeting systems, and, of course, the sequencing of planning (PDSA) vertically and horizontally within the organization over the planning cycle.

Planning Session Agenda Building

It is the responsibility of the Design and Development Team to build the agenda for

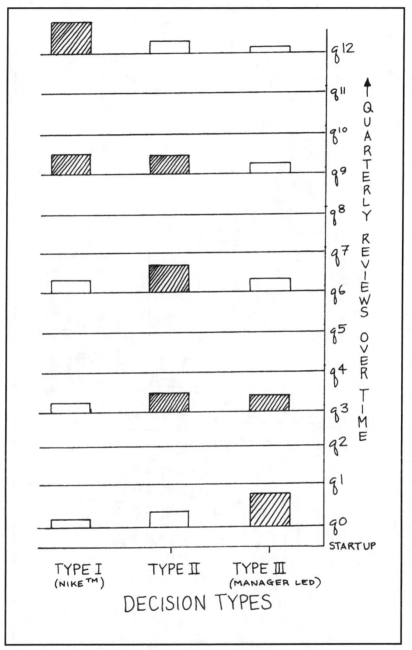

Figure 34. The types of decisions and the maturity of problem solving changes over time. Quarterly reviews are key points in its evolution.

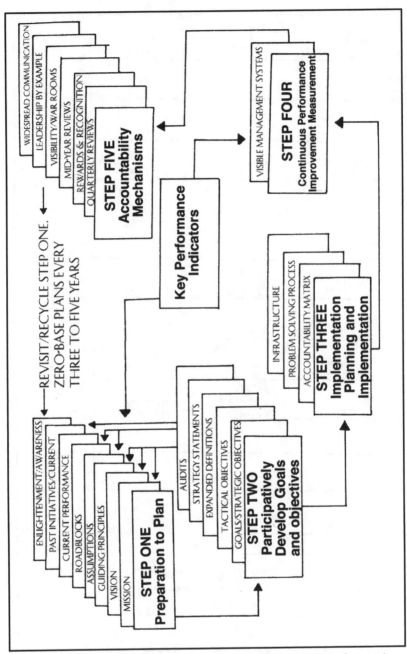

Figure 35. The strategic performance improvement planning process is the first step in creating a planning system.

planning off-sites. One or more members of the DDT will facilitate this agenda-building session, which includes: (1) identification of planning team participants, (2) identification of desired outcomes and outputs for the planning session, (3) discussion of specific agenda modules, some of which are standard to the planning process and others that are tailored modules deemed appropriate to facilitate accomplishment of particular desired outputs or outcomes, and (4) identification of key logistical issues such as preferences for location, length, evening sessions, special events, and pre-work.

The DDT team then takes the data from this agenda-building session and creates a version 1.0 agenda for review by the planning team or some subset. Several rounds of revisions may be necessary before an acceptable agenda is developed.

Pre-work

The planning team is almost always provided with pre-work approximately one to two months prior to the actual planning session. This pre-work may include: readings, videotape review, discussion groups, development of rough drafts of portions of the plan, and review of previous plans or upline plans. The intent is to prepare the planning team to come off-site ready to participate in a meaningful way.

Planning Off-site

Typically in a start-up application, the first four steps of the seven-step planning process are addressed during the off-site meeting. This includes, as shown in Figure 36:

• Step 1 — Mission, vision, guiding principles, input/output analysis, assumptions (to include internal and external strategic analysis), review of past and present initiatives, current performance levels, review of upline and downstream plans, frontal audit, educational sessions aimed to help the planning team do a better job planning
• Step 2 — Goals (horizon five to seven years)
• Step 3 — Objectives (horizon zero to three years), might also include development of "bold goals" or a great performance (horizon twelve months)
• Step 4 — Implementation planning.

These planning sessions are similar to what Weisbord (1992) calls search conferences. They normally take three to five days and are held in an off-site, retreat-type setting. It is important to hold these sessions in a familiar, comfortable, and predictable location that meets the necessary requirements.

During the planning session, the change master must maintain close coordination with key leaders, particularly the sponsor(s). The change master and the sponsor(s) must collaborate well during this session, "reading" each other and knowing when to rely on each other's judgments regarding when to call time-outs, make mid-course corrections, or make real-time adjustments to the agenda.

The change master will need two other people on-site to support the effort. Support personnel ensure room arrangements meet requirements, ensure the change master has the necessary "tools," assist the change master in recording and posting flip-chart data, record session notes, and do any number of tasks to "anticipate in support of" the needs of session participants. Planning sessions are mentally and physically fatiguing for both participants and change masters. It is important that the change master does not allow the process or

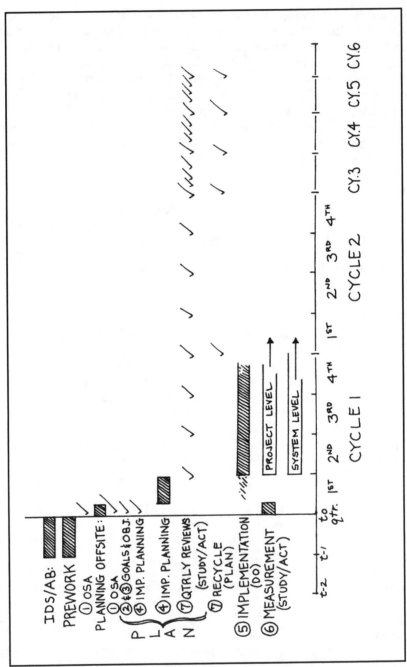

Figure 36. The sequence of events within the planning system stretches out over time.

the planning team to "get ahead of" of him or her. The change master has to be thinking ahead while processing the current step. Balancing content understanding without getting hooked on content is a key. The change master is managing process but must be cognizant of content enough to know when to help the team get unstuck. Competent support personnel relieve the change master from thinking about logistical details, allowing him or her to concentrate on the task at hand.

With large planning teams, there will inevitably be significant variation in personality types and cognitive styles. Much of the planning session, particularly in early portions, will exist in Phases 1-4 (situation appraisal, catharsis, self-awareness, and self-evaluation). There will undoubtedly, despite best preparations, be a few prisoners and tourists in the group. There will be individuals who transfer to the change master during the session and create a negative affect toward the change master. The dynamic nature of phases of change will become quite transparent to the change master over the course of the session. The aim is to move the group forward, recognizing that there will be inherent variation regarding where specific individuals may be at any given moment. For example, the group in general may be prepared for self-designed change (to get into Steps 2 and 3 of the planning process) while certain individuals may still be in a catharsis phase.

The final product of a planning session is a skeletal plan, enough data from which a version 1.0 plan can be crafted. The session ends with small groups briefing the larger planning team on scoping proposals for specific performance improvement objectives. A scoping proposal contains an expanded definition of the objective, a short strategy statement, a very brief outline of why, what, who, how, when, and a clear list of key performance indicators (KPIs) for effectiveness, efficiency, quality and impact. The impact KPIs focus on identifying the predicted cause-and-effect relationships. Next steps are prepared by the change master and reviewed by the sponsor, who presents these to the larger group as the closing activity of the planning session.

The change master will be stimulated and challenged by the execution of the agenda for this multiple-day session. Armed with the theory behind the matrix, the change master will see come to life the notion of phases of change and modes of functioning. Using the matrix to plan behaviors within modules will be developmental. I always begin the day at 6:00 a.m. reviewing or revising the agenda. I meet with the sponsor(s) and colleague change masters at 7:00 a.m. to review the agenda and have them give me last-minute reactions.

I am particularly conscious of maintaining the collaborator mode with the key leadership and sponsors during these sessions. At various points throughout the day, I consult with colleagues and sponsors to ensure the session is meeting expectations. If I find myself getting fatigued, I might call a time-out and consult with sponsors or colleagues on how to proceed. Nine times out of ten, they will come up with a way to get me unstuck that I never would have thought of. Again, I want to maintain ownership of the agenda, the process, and the product with the sponsor and with the DDT team, not just with me.

I rely on instinct, experience, and my ability to read situations and people when deciding to switch modes. If your personality type causes you to prefer the challenging mode, you must be ever conscious to avoid overusing this mode. If you have a tendency to be a strong judging type and a strong intuitive type, you may have a tendency not to be reflective at times and to jump to conclusions or be too decisive. You'll have to work, at times, to slow down, to "listen to your listening," to give the group time to process things. You'll fight filling the moments of silence prematurely.

Each change master has a unique style, personality, and preference for collecting and processing data. You must become self-aware to make strengths decisive, while remembering that any strength overutilized or utilized at the wrong time becomes a weakness.

TRANSITIONING FROM A PLANNING PROCESS TO A PLANNING SYSTEM
The end of the planning session marks the beginning of the implementation and deployment process, the transition from a planning process to development of a planning system. As mentioned, the product of a planning session off-site is data that can be used to assemble an initial version of a plan for improvement for the organizational system. The A&E team, working with the change master, has the responsibility of converting the output of the off-site session with the planning team into a version 1.0 plan. This should occur within two weeks after the planning session. Version 1.0 of this plan is then distributed to the planning team for review, modification, and enhancement. The A&E team then integrates all feedback and distributes a final product of the off-site session to the planning team within 30 days.

Now the hard work begins. Implementation of the specific objectives in the plan has to move forward. Each of the Performance Improvement Objectives (PIOs) needs to be assigned. Some of the objectives are Type I and can be implemented quickly; some may be Type II or III and may require substantial further decision analysis, design, or implementation planning. It is most often clear that they either are an individual responsibility, a functional responsibility, or a cross-functional and do not have clear owners, in which case an ad hoc team is comprised. The assigned individual or team creates a scoping proposal for their objective.

Progress and performance against the PIOs are monitored in periodic planning team meetings. It may be the case that the planning team does not reassemble and that only a subset of that team participates in these review sessions. If, in fact, the improvement effort is attempting to positively influence the total system, then it may be wise to keep the entire planning team involved.

Deployment also is initiated during the three-month period following the planning off-site. Performance Improvement Planning is triggered at the next level of the organizational system. These Level 2 subunits (Figure 37) go through a planning process similar to the one executed for Level 1. The goal is to establish policy deployment in the Hoshin Kanri sense: plans, information, guidance, and knowledge cascade down in the form of upline plan review. Level 2 subsystems are to be influenced by, not constrained by, the Level 1 plan. In many cases Level 2 personnel will be involved in implementation teams for Level 1 PIOs.

In the second month of the planning system initiative, all Level 2 subunits will have completed their version 1.0 plans. An all-hands meeting is held. We suggest that it be a three-level meeting. In other words, key Level 3 personnel would be included in this all-hands planning brief. The Level 1 plan is briefed, followed by Level 2 plan briefings.

The change master facilitates this session and must ensure that dialogue and inquiry are exhibited as opposed to advocacy. The intent is to share information and knowledge, to explore and understand meaning, to begin to understand integration and coordination opportunities. A careful log of decisions and actions must be kept. A report of output from this multilevel meeting identifies specific actions that need to be taken to ensure that plans at the first two levels of the organization are aligned properly. This all-hands meeting should last approximately one day.

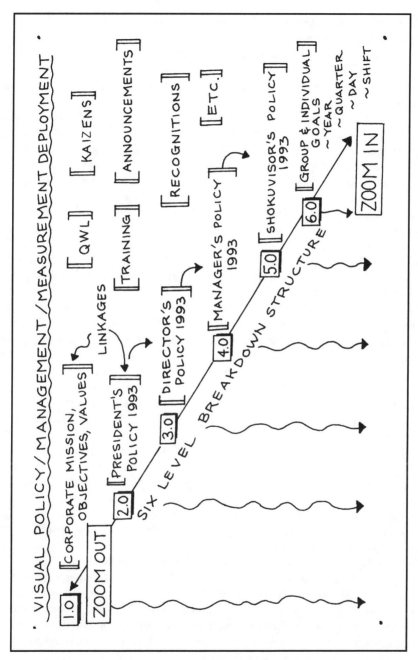

Figure 37. In Hoshin deployment, plans, information, and knowledge cascade down (Shokuvisor is akin to a supervisor).

The alignment and coordination of plans, moving from versions 1.0 to 2.0 for Level 1 and 2 plans, occurs in month three, when the planning teams (Levels 1 and 2) meet for a review session. The intent of these periodic review sessions is: (1) to maintain momentum; (2) to review progress and performance against PIOs; (3) to process the process; (4) to make decisions on how to move forward; and (5) to continue to work to establish linkages, at least between Levels 1 and 2 at this point.

The first periodic (in this case quarterly) review session encompasses a variety of phases of the change process. First, there will be a reasonable amount of enthusiasm and hope, as a growing number of people are engaged in self-designed change and improvement. There is typically a pent up need to participate, and the process will have tapped this need, causing a degree of satisfaction. However, if the organization has a history of stalled or failed improvement efforts, there may be significant cynicism and skepticism. Second, the review sessions themselves will demonstrate inherent variation in commitment to the improvement effort. Who is committed versus who is simply complying will become visible. It will be extremely obvious who has allowed "A" and "C" to squeeze the "B" out versus who has, in fact, been successful at trying out new behaviors and is succeeding with the problem of time management. In terms of quality, the range of variation of briefings updating progress and performance will be tremendous.

Management expectations play a large role in what the reaction will be to this variation. Our feeling is that the variation is predictable and should be accepted. Peer pressure will mount during this meeting. Leadership needs to recognize those making progress and performing and inquire only as to why others are not progressing. They should avoid sanctioning or being negative about lack of progress and performance. They should, however, consistently and clearly reinforce the requirements of success, the importance of this effort, and their expectations. They should be consistent in their articulation of the model or method being followed and reinforce sticking to the model, particularly during the first cycle.

To this point, we have consumed a great deal of change master and A&E team time and energy, approximately four to six days of planning team (includes top management) time, and a variable number of hours or days on the part of ad hoc Performance Action Teams. Top management will sense a great deal of enthusiasm and activity, they will sense improved focus and communication, but they will probably see no tangible results. This needs to be attended to by the change master during the next three months (second quarter) of planning system development.

The second quarter of Cycle 1 should focus on moving forward with increasing rapidity. Progress, performance, and results should be stressed. The change master, in cooperation with the A&E team, should "supervise" the PATs closely, making sure they maintain momentum, get unstuck if necessary, have the appropriate resources, have a plan and are working the plan, and are coached/mentored/trained when appropriate. It may be useful to develop an affinity group of PAT leaders so they can share problems, issues, dilemmas, progress across teams — a form of benchmarking.

The mid-year review is a bit more formal and lasts at least a day. It should represent the first time that the PATs are coming forward with significant progress — either their implementation plan is complete and approved, they are in the process of implementation, they have implemented and are in evaluation phase, or they have achieved results. This session should be a high spot in the process. People should be upbeat; they should be gaining confidence in the method and process. They have been in the midst of trying out new behaviors, and this meeting represents an opportunity to reinforce those new behaviors.

Immediately following the mid-year reviews for all planning teams at Levels 1 and 2, another all-hands meeting should be held. An executive summary-level brief will be given by key PATs for each planning team. Again, the change master must manage inquiry and dialogue, continue to work appreciation for a system by focusing on linkages vertically and horizontally, and strive to enhance integration, communication, coordination, and cooperation between subsystems.

By this point, an enhanced measurement system (visible management system for Level 1 and subsystems in Level 2) will be prototyped and in implementation. Improved portrayal of the total system's performance over time should be possible at this point. It is unlikely that significant results will be seen against Key Performance Indicators (KPIs), but at least the cause-and-effect relationships can be discussed, and predicted results and impact can be explored.

A third quarterly review is held, followed by another all-hands session. By this time it is possible that certain KPIs may be showing signs of changing. Run charts for these KPIs might begin to suggest that variation is being reduced or mean level of performance is improving, or both. The visible management system includes chartbooks that portray performance information and conversion of information to knowledge, decisions, and actions. Top leadership must be trained in terms of how to work with this component of the visible management system.

The change master and A&E team must be sensitive to regression relative to phases of change. Top leadership and management tend to have short attention spans. They may be tiring of this disciplined methodology, and their new behaviors may need reinforcing. Top management may be changing and new leaders may need to be informed, sold, and enlightened or educated.

A year-end planning recycle is held, during which the planning team:

• Updates and enhances the plans;
• Reviews progress and performance against the plans;
• Processes the process;
• Begins to move emphasis from Steps 1 and 2 of the planning process to Steps 3-6, more emphasis on implementation, deployment, results, and measuring results over time ;
• Continues to improve their ability to think about improvement across multiple fronts.

The recycle is preceded with agenda building process and pre-work. The session itself normally takes two to three days. The focus here is on updating and enhancing the plan and ensuring implementation, results, deployment, and frontal alignment. Better integration with the budgeting system can be concentrated on in this cycle. The plan is not zero-based unless drastic changes have caused this to be necessary.

THE START-UP PHASE

The first two to three cycles of the planning system represent startup. The aim is to introduce more discipline and consistency into performance improvement planning—to establish the method, process, steps, and techniques for steps. Hard work on the measurement and education/training/development fronts in parallel with planning system efforts is called for. The A&E team, in conjunction with the change master, must ensure that there is consistency of method during this phase. The tendency to tamper, to make adjustments before the process is stable, will be significant. You must warn against this and attempt to minimize this. The aim is to reduce variation, establish consistency, and establish discipline with the method. This does not infer that there will not or cannot be variations on the theme. If a subunit decides it has a better process, method, step, or technique for a step, it may be appropriate to allow them to try it. Again, self-designed change is the aim and increases ownership.

The A&E team and change master must guard against game playing, however. It is not uncommon for leaders and managers to argue that they want to do it their way. When pressed to document their way in writing, they often cannot. What they are really saying is that they don't want to "play." This is unacceptable. If they have a better way, it is documented, they are consistent, and, above all, produce results that meet the specifications of the overall system, then so be it. However, if they can't prove they have a better way that will produce acceptable results, they should be given the "voice, loyalty, exit" test: They voice and differences are adjudicated, they show loyalty to the existing approach, or they exit. It must be stressed that trying to improve performance before the variation is in control and predictable usually make things worse, not better.

Our experience is that in most organizations of any size and complexity, it will take three years to establish the planning system on a consistent basis and make it a way of doing business. This can, of course, be accelerated with more rapid movement on the culture, measurement, education/training/development, and motivation fronts. Learning-curve theory would predict that two years might be the minimum amount of time necessary. The most improvement in ability to take advantage of the process comes in the second cycle. We work to ensure that Level 1 leadership and management are forced to walk the talk. They must make the planning process work for themselves before expecting others to do the same.

TRANSITIONING FROM PLANNING SYSTEMS TO GRAND STRATEGY SYSTEMS

By the third cycle, perhaps the fourth, the organization should have significantly improved the planning front. "B" planning should be well integrated with "A" planning, "C" should be reduced and in control, TQM should be well integrated with planning systems, and implementation and deployment should be working well in the organization. Progress on the education/training/development, communication, and measurement fronts should be visible. As a result, the culture and motivation fronts should have "slip streamed" progress on these other fronts. The technology front also will have moved forward as many of the Performance Improvement Objectives (PIOs) will have focused on technological improvements. In fact, if the total system is involved in some way in planning, then we would assume that the political front has shown signs of improvement also.

The A&E team and the change master roles and requirements will have shifted dramatically, from start-up work to more of a maintenance and monitoring process. In many respects, they focus on continuing to reinforce new behaviors, sparking continued desire to learn, grow, and improve. The organization will be mature with respect to the planning front and will be becoming more knowledgeable and skilled in moving other fronts forward and maintaining alignment among fronts.

During this period, the A&E team and change master will be challenged to determine when it is necessary to zero-base or re-engineer the plans (not the process). Ongoing innovation relative to what we are doing and how will have occurred; however, it may be necessary to search for new S-shaped curves.

Turnover will, of course, be a continuing challenge with respect to maintaining constancy of purpose and method. There will simultaneously be significant demands just to maintain frontal progress in addition to challenges to go back to work on fundamental issues that are part of Step 1 in the planning process. At some point, there will be a sense that vision, perhaps even mission, guiding principles, and assumptions need to be revisited. This will be driven by several factors: (1) the leadership team and the planning team will have increased their level of maturity and sophistication with respect to planning, improvement, measurement, implementation and deployment, and systems thinking; (2) at some point there is a need to do more than update and enhance the plan; (3) the environment, competition, technology, internal culture, and staffing will have changed so much that the plan and Grand Strategy are out of touch with those variables; and (4) the change master and A&E team have grown to the point where they realize there are greater levels of performance that can be achieved and want to stimulate the organization to achieve them.

At this point, the organizational system has climbed several stairs in the staircase, has developed the ability to stay at that level, and is ready to begin in earnest to think through the next five to seven years of stairs. The organization has gotten beyond seeing improvement programs as an end and sees the need to integrate them, where appropriate, as means to an end. They see improvement and rate of improvement as a journey, not a destination. They have laid a foundation for even further improvements and gains and are ready to, on a system-wide basis, process through the phases of change again.

If the organization has been successful and is, in fact, improving at desired rates, then the motivation front may become an area of needed emphasis. The organization is winning, the employees should share in the "fruits of labor." Shifting from all fixed pay to a combination of fixed and variable may be increasingly necessary. This will allow the organization, in revenue downturns or budget cuts, to shrink payroll to a lower fixed level and provide more job security, thus impacting the culture of the organization positively. Learning how to invest gains from the improvement created wisely will be increasingly challenging. Recognition, too, will have become increasingly important as part of the motivation front.

The technology front will have changed the most at this point, in that people at all levels are more empowered to change how they perform their jobs. The challenge at this point will be to continue to ensure that the process for continuous improvement is stable and expanding and that types of improvement beyond tuning or continuous improvement are being experimented with, when appropriate. Re-engineering will probably have been experimented with on a limited basis in the start-up phase. This next phase of evolution will clearly place more emphasis on re-engineering and thinking outside the box.

The ability to integrate and coordinate among these fronts still will be in the development phase at this point. A war room or GSS control room may exist in rudimentary form. The A&E team will be struggling to employ tools such as program Gantt charts and other program management tools to plan ahead. The A&E team, at times, will be behind the power curve, the organization or subunits will have gotten ahead of them during the start-up phase. This next phase will see an increased emphasis on training and learning on the part of the A&E team as it relates to planning, leading, managing, controlling, communicating, and coordinating the GSS. In a sense, the A&E team will need to jump to a new S-shaped curve, either by themselves or with assistance from the change master.

This next phase, in summary, will see improving movement within and among fronts. There will be more sophistication and maturity in these efforts. The integration, synergy, and coordination among fronts will improve. The A&E team will improve their ability to lead the GSS transformation. The enlightenment, knowledge, and skills of at least the top three levels in the organization will have improved to the extent that they are proactive and are driving innovation in "B" throughout the organization. New S-shaped curves are being looked for throughout the organization, and re-engineering is more pervasive than during startup. The organization as a whole is, in fact, moving to a new S-shaped curve of its own.

The organizational system's planning team will have changed composition, and they will process through the entire seven phases of change in the fourth recycle because they are re-engineering their GSS to some extent. The change master will once again move from primarily being a team member or collaborator to a fuller spectrum of modes of professional functioning.

Many external change masters are not able to survive with one client this long. It is extremely difficult for change masters to grow with the organization and to continue to fulfill the needs of a learning, dynamic organization. Sometimes the organizational leadership tires of the change master; they are looking for new "tricks," new "magic," even if they are consistent with the methodology the change master brought to them. Sometimes the organization simply outgrows the change master; this may be a desired outcome and is natural in that respect. Sometimes the organization regresses at this phase and loses constancy of method.

If, as the case should be, the change master is a true master and is growing with the organization they are helping, then these situations should not occur. I'd like to believe that a GSS change master is a partner with the organization and will be able to sustain a helping relationship with the organization through this second phase of evolution. On the other hand, the true aim of helping professions is to create independence. In this debate, I am reminded of Dr. Deming's point that change masters with profound knowledge come from outside the organization and are invited, that a system can't understand itself. This also reminds me of a quote from *Laws* by Plato at the end of Chester Barnard's classic, *The Functions of the Executive*.

Anyone who sees all this, naturally rushes to the conclusion of which I was speaking, that no mortal legislates in anything, but that in human affairs chance is almost everything. And this may be said of the arts of the sailor, and the pilot, and the physician, and the general, and may seem to be said well said; and yet there is another thing which may be said with equal truth of all of them.

What is it?

That God governs all things, and that chance and opportunity cooperate with Him in the government of human affairs. There is, however, a third and less extreme view, that art should be there also; for I should say that in a storm there must surely be a great advantage in having the aid of the pilot's art. You would agree?

So this is the context within which I choose to view Dr. Deming's wisdom regarding change masters. They are navigators; they help you steer through uncharted waters. They help you get unstuck. They learn with you. They provide professional modes of functioning that might be difficult for you or others in your organization to provide. It is our view that your A&E team will need the art of a change master during startup and for getting to prime phases.

CONCLUSION

Increasingly, organizations are being forced to tackle cross-functional, inter-organizational improvement. There is a body of literature on such large-scale organizational improvements from organization development and an emerging body of literature on TQM and, specifically, large-scale organizational transformation. There is, however, much less experience with such efforts. These efforts, specifically, are where we see tremendous implementation and deployment problems. Leadership for these efforts, the quality of it, is highly variable. Methods for accomplishing such large transformations are not well defined or documented. It is becoming clearer that these large transformations require work on multiple fronts. We have presented a proposal for considering nine fronts or subsystems as you strive to make an organizational transformation. Clearly, we are in the very early stages of the development of theory and reduction-to-practice methods for making a transformation of the scope suggested by Dr. Deming. Consider our work in the field as presented in this chapter as exploratory.

Large-scale transformations present a unique challenge to the change master that goes beyond the implementation and deployment problems encountered with smaller-scale improvement projects. The 3^n-ball problem comes into play. The change master is forced to become a program manager. Ensuring that fronts are aligned is a significant challenge that we have little experience with; certainly there are no closed-form ways to know whether there is frontal imbalance at this point. We believe that the phase/mode/tool model becomes even more salient when the change master is engaged in large-scale improvement efforts such as TQM and business process re-engineering. The "By what method?" question becomes necessary, yet not sufficient for success in these cases.

There is such little experience with and guidance for these efforts. How does one develop the knowledge and skills to lead large-scale quality and productivity improvement efforts? This is the subject of our sixth and final section.

DEVELOPMENT WORK

INQUIRY QUESTIONS
These are questions you have for yourself or for others to help you better understand what was covered in this section.

Inquire First
What didn't you understand, what do you want to know about, what assumptions or beliefs do we posit that you want us to explain, what do you want clarification on?

Advocate Second

What did you disagree with, what do you want to argue about, what didn't you like, what do you want to challenge, in what areas do we appear to have different assumptions, data bases, beliefs, or attitudes?

LEARNING EXERCISES

LE 5.1 Attempt to create a change strategy for a large organization that addresses each of the nine fronts. The strategy should be thought through for at least six months and preferably eighteen. After you have crafted one, on paper, reflect on the fronts with which you struggled. Were you able to think about specific initiatives you would take in each front, over time? Is your "tool kit" and understanding of what actions can be taken to move fronts forward complete enough to do Grand Strategy System development? Which fronts did you feel most comfortable with as you thought through this exercise? Did the 3^n-ball problem become clearer as you did this exercise? What kind of resources, knowledge, and skills would be required to pull of a grand strategy, large-scale organizational improvement effort in your organization? Are you actually doing a GSS but not thinking it through strategically, comprehensively, or in an integrated fashion? If so, what will you do about it? Are you resourcing the effort properly? Again, if not, what will you do about it? Is there enough learning going on to support large-scale organizational change? If not, what will you do about it?

LE 5.2 Apply the GSS model to your organization, your immediate domain of responsibilty, the one over which you have most control. This exercise, if you choose to do it, will stretch out over about eighteen months. Update your GSS plan every two to three months. Build a GSS plan that meets the level of knowledge that exists currently, that does not overextend the organization, that the individuals in the organization can buy into and have ownership for. As you work the education/training/development front, the capacity of the DDT and others in the organization to understand what you are doing and to integrate things will improve. Monitor the improvements in your ability to develop a more complete GSS as you advance. Keep copies of your GSS versions as you proceed and periodically go back and look at them. I think you will be surprised how much learning and capability develops over even a twelve-month period of time.

LE 5.3 Document and depict the infrastructure for your organization currently. Compare and contrast that with the infrastructure for "B" presented in this chapter. Can you create a "shadow organization," "parallel structure," "collateral organization" that uses the infrastructure presented in this chapter as a prototype? Would it help your organization perform better on "B"? How would you or will you go about doing this? If you already have a "B" infrastructure, of sorts, what is working and what isn't? What aspects of what was presented in this section might help improve your infrastructure? What is your operational definition for the word infrastructure?

LE 5.4 Describe your organization's implicit strategy for improving performance organization-wide over the past five years.

LE 5.5 Audit your organization's current efforts and current plan for performance improvement against the nine fronts. Which fronts are lagging? Which fronts are ahead of others? What can be done to better align or attune the fronts? What is your operational definition of alignment and attunement?

LE 5.6 A useful way to plan and describe a change process is to create a scenario in outline form. Plan a large-scale change process for:
A. A situation described in a professional journal;
B. A situation with which you are personally familiar;
C. A client situation in which you have worked or expect to work;
D. A typical project involving:
— A major downsizing effort
— A major reorganization
— An attempt to do TQM
— Introduction of a major new technology (e.g., computer system, production and inventory control, accounting system, measurement system, office automation system).

LE 5.7 Think of your professional style as a change master in terms of the way you function comfortably, confidently, and with experience. How would you characterize your professional style in terms of the matrix? Suggest several dimensions that would be more useful for describing your professional style. What aspects of your professional style would you like to alter? How are the breadth and depth of your professional style challenged as you move from small-scale improvement projects to large-scale projects? What are you doing or do you plan to do to improve your professional style with respect to larger-scale improvement efforts?

LE 5.8 Do a cause-and-effect diagram on TQM failures. What are the root causes you have uncovered? What can be done to address these root causes? Is TQM, by definition, a large-scale organizational change? If an organization did GSS guided by TQM principles, would they be doing TQM? TQM has come under fire, increasingly, in the past year. Why? What can be done to enhance the success of overall improvements to improve performance in an organization?

FEEDBACK QUESTIONS

FBQ 5.1 Operationally define Grand Strategy System and the components (past, present, future, fronts).

FBQ 5.2 What additional knowledge and skills are required when moving from leading and managing a performance improvement project to a performance improvement program? What additional knowledge and skills are required when moving from leading and managing a performance improvement program to a large-scale organizational improvement effort (GSS)?

FBQ 5.3 What does "large-scale organizational change" imply to you? Have you been involved in such a change? How was it different than a smaller-scoped improvement project?

FBQ 5.4 Has your organization attempted anything like GSS? If so, what are the lessons learned? If not, why not? If the GSS makes sense, what factors are inhibiting moving forward with a more comprehensive and integrated improvement effort? How can you help manage these factors?

FBQ 5.5 What does the 3^n-ball problem suggest to you? Discuss this concept in the context of GSS and a program versus a project.

FBQ 5.6 What special issues have to be considered during the start-up phase of a project or program or organization that are not as crucial when the project or program or organization is more stable? As a change master, do you alter your approach, style, emphasis, energy level, or attention to detail during start-up?

PLAN OF STUDY
What follows is a list of resources that support, in general, the material introduced in this section. Scan the list, indicate which you have read (R), studied (S), attempted to use (U), and which you would like to become acquainted with (TBD).

LITERATURE CITED
Barker, J. A. 1986. *The Power of Visions*. Minneapolis, Minn.: Filmedia.

Barker, J. A. 1988. *Discovering the Future: The Business of Paradigms*. St. Paul, Minn.: ILI Press.

Barnard, C. I. 1938. *The Functions of the Executive*. Cambridge, Mass.: Harvard University Press.

Belasco, J. A. 1990. *Teaching the Elephant to Dance*. New York: Crown Publishers.

Belasco, J. A., and R. C. Stayer. 1993. *Flight of the Buffalo: Soaring to Excellence, Learning to Let Employees Lead*. New York: Warner Books.

Camp, R. C. 1989. *Benchmarking: The Search for Industry Best Practices that Lead to Superior Performance*. Milwaukee, Wis.: Quality Press.

Deming, W. E. 1986. *Out of the Crisis*. Cambridge, Mass.: MIT Center for Advanced Engineering Study.

Deming, W. E. 1993. *The New Economics*. Cambridge, Mass.: MIT Center for Advanced Engineering Study.

Juran, J. M. 1988. *Juran on Planning for Quality*. New York: Free Press.

Juran, J. M., and F. M. Gyma. 1988. *Juran's Quality Control Handbook* (4th edn.). New York: McGraw-Hill Book Co.

Juran, J. M., and F. M. Gyma. 1989. *Quality Planning and Analysis From Product Development Through Use*. New York: McGraw-Hill Book Co.

Kaplan, R. S., and D. P. Norton. 1993. Putting the balanced scorecard to work. *Harvard Business Review*. September-October, pp. 134-147.

Kurstedt, H. A. 1993. *The Industrial Engineer's Systematic Approach to Management*. MSL working draft and articles and responsive systems article. Blacksburg, Va.: Management Systems Laboratories.

Kilmann, R., T. J. Covin, and Associates. 1989. *Corporate Transformations*. San Francisco: Jossey Bass.

Kilmann, R. H. 1989. *Managing Beyond the Quick Fix: A Completely Integrated Program for Creating and Maintaining Organizational Success*. San Francisco: Jossey-Bass.

Lawler, E. E. III. 1986. *High-Involvement Management: Participative Strategies for Improving Organizational Performance.* San Francisco: Jossey-Bass.

Mohrman, A. M., S. A. Mohrman, G. E. Ledford, T. G. Cummings, and E. E. Lawler. 1989. *Large-Scale Organizational Change.* San Francisco: Jossey-Bass.

Peters, T. J., and R. H. Waterman, Jr. 1982. *In Search of Excellence: Lessons from America's Best-Run Companies.* New York: Warner Books.

Scholtes, P. R. 1988. *The Team Handbook.* Madison, Wis.: Joiner Assoc.

Senge, P. 1990. *The Fifth Discipline.* New York: Doubleday.

Sink, D. S. 1985. *Productivity Measurement: Planning, Measurement and Evaluation, Control and Improvement.* New York: John Wiley and Sons.

Sink, D. S., and T. C. Tuttle. 1989. *Planning and Measurement in Your Organization of the Future.* Norcross, Ga.: Industrial Engineering and Management Press.

Skinner, L., and C. D. Johnson. 1993. Business process engineerig at Texas Instruments. *Quality and Productivity Management.* 10(3).

Spencer, K. 1992. Handouts and notes from TI BPE approach presented to the Council of Industrial Engineers.

Van Aken, E. M., D. J. Monetta, and D. S. Sink. 1994. *Affinity groups: the missing link in employee involvement.* Organizational Dynamics. Spring, pp. 38-54.

Weisbord, M. R. 1991. *Productive Workplaces: Organizing for Dignity, Meaning, and Community.* San Francisco: Jossey-Bass.

Weisbord, M. R. (ed.). 1992. *Discovering Common Ground: How Future Search Conferences Bring People Together to Achieve Breakthrough Innovation, Empowerment, Shared Vision, and Collaborative Action.* San Francisco: Berrett-Koehler.

BIBLIOGRAPHY

Adizes, I. 1988. *Corporate Lifecycles.* Englewood Cliffs, N.J.: Prentice-Hall.

Argyris, C. 1970. *Intervention Theory and Method: A Behavioral Science View.* Reading, Mass.: Addison-Wesley.

Argyris, C. 1982. *Reasoning, Learning, and Action: Individual and Organizational.* San Francisco: Jossey-Bass.

Argyris, C. 1993. *Knowledge for Action: A Guide to Overcoming Barriers to Organizational Change.* San Francisco: Jossey-Bass.

Argyris, C., and D. Schon. 1974. *Theory in Practice.* Reading, Mass.: Addison-Wesley.

Beckhard, R. 1986. *Organization Development: Strategies and Models.* Reading, Mass.: Addison-Wesley.

Beer, M., R. Eisenstat, and B. Spector. 1990. Why change programs don't produce change. *Harvard Business Review.* 67: 158-166.

Bennis, W. 1989. *Why Leaders Can't Lead: The Unconscious Conspiracy Continues.* San Francisco: Jossey-Bass.

Bennis, W. G. 1966. *Changing Organizations.* New York: McGraw-Hill.

Berquist, W. 1993. *The Postmodern Organization: Mastering the Art of Irreversible Change.* San Francisco: Jossey-Bass.

Block, P. 1978. *Flawless Consulting.* San Diego, Calif.: Pfeiffer & Co.

Bolman, L. G., and T. E. Deal. 1991. *Reframing Organizations: Artistry, Choice and Leadership.* San Franciso: Jossey-Bass.

Davis, S., and B. Davidson. 1991. *2020 Vision: Tranform Your Business Today to Succeed in Tomorrow's Economy.* New York: Simon & Schuster.

Davis, S. M. 1987. *Future Perfect.* Reading, Mass.: Addison-Wesley.

Deal, T. E., and A. A. Kennedy. 1982. *Corporate Cultures: The Rites and Rituals of Corporate Life.* Reading, Mass.: Addison-Wesley.

Duck, J. D. 1993. Managing change: the art of balancing. *Harvard Business Review.* November-December, pp. 109-118.

Eisenhardt, K. M. 1989. Building theories from case study research. *Academy of Management Review.* 14: 4.

French, W. L., and C. H. Bell. 1978. *Organization Development: Behavioral Science Interventions for Organizational Improvement.* Englewood Cliffs, N.J.: Prentice-Hall.

Galbraith, J. 1973. *Designing Complex Organizations.* Reading, Mass.: Addison-Wesley.

Goss, T., R. Pascale, and A. Athos. 1993. The reinvention roller coaster: risking the present for a powerful future. *Harvard Business Review.* November-December, pp. 97-108.

Hall, G., J. Rosenthal, and J. Wade. 1993. How to make reengineering really work. *Harvard Business Review.* November-December, pp. 119-133.

Hammer, M., and J. Champy. 1993. *Reengineering the Corporation: A Manifesto for Business Revolution.* New York: Harper Business.

Hellriegel, D., and J. W. Slocum, Jr. 1974. *Management: A Contingency Approach.* Reading, Mass.: Addison-Wesley.

Kanter, R. M. 1989. *When Giants Learn to Dance: Mastering the Challenges of Strategy, Management, and Careers in the 1990s.* New York: Simon and Schuster.

Kimberly, J. R., R. H. Miles, and Associates. 1980. *The Organizational Life Cycle: Issues in the Creation, Transformation and Decline of Organizations.* San Francisco: Jossey-Bass.

Lawler, E. E., III. 1992. *The Ultimate Advantage: Creating the High-Involvement Organization.* San Francisco: Jossey-Bass.

Michael, D. 1973. *Planning to Learn and Learning to Plan.* San Francisco: Jossey-Bass.

Mills, D. Q. 1991. *Rebirth of the Corporation.* New York: John Wiley.

Mintzberg, H. 1985. Of strategies, deliberate and emergent. *Strategic Management Journal.* 6: 257-272.

Mintzberg, H. 1986. The manager's job: folklore and fact. *Management Classics* (3rd edn.). M. T. Matteson and J. M. Ivancevich, eds. Plano, Tex.: Business Publications.

Mintzberg, H. 1987. Crafting strategy. *Harvard Business Review.* 64: 66-75.

Mintzberg, H. 1989. *Mintzberg on Management: Inside our Strange World of Organizations.* New York: Free Press.

Morgan, G. 1986. *Images of the Organization.* Newbury Park, Calif.: Sage.

Morgan, G. 1983. *Beyond Method: Strategies for Social Research.* Beverly Hill, Calif.: Sage.

Morgan, G. 1988. *Riding the Waves of Change: Developing Managerial Competencies for a Turbulent World.* San Francisco: Jossey-Bass.

Morgan, G. 1993. Imaginization: The Art of Creative Management. Newbury Park, Calif.: Sage.

Naisbitt, J., and P. Aburdene. 1985. *Re-inventing the Corporation: Transforming your job and your company for the new information society.* New York: Warner Books.

Nutt, P. C. 1992. *Managing Planned Change.* New York: Macmillan.

Schein, E. H. 1985. *Organizational Culture and Leadership: A Dynamic View.* San Francisco, Calif.: Jossey-Bass.

Scherkenbach, W. W. 1988. *The Deming Route to Quality and Productivity: Road Maps and Roadblocks.* Washington, D.C.: Ceep Press.

Scott Morton, M. S. (ed.). 1991. *The Corporation of the 1990s: Information Technology and Organizational Transformation.* New York: Oxford University Press.

Sullivan, L. P. 1986. The seven stages in company-wide quality control. *Quality Progress.* May.

Susman, G. I., and R. D. Evered. 1978. An assessment of the scientific merits of action research. *Administrative Science Quarterly.* 23: 582-603.

Tichy, N. 1983. *Managing Strategic Change.* New York: John Wiley.

Tichy, N., and M. Devanna. 1987. *The Transformational Leader.* New York: John Wiley.

von Bertalanffy, L. 1968. *General Systems Theory: Foundations, Development, Applications* (revised edition). New York: George Braziller, Inc.

Weick, K. E. 1979. *The Social Psychology of Organizing.* Reading, Mass.: Addison-Wesley.

Whyte, W. F. (ed.). 1991. *Participative Action Research.* Newbury Park, Calif.: Sage.

Woodward, J. 1965. Industrial Organization: Theory and Practice. New York: Oxford University Press.

Woodward, J. (ed.). 1970. *Industrial Organization: Behavior and Control.* New York: Oxford University Press.

DEVELOPING THE KNOWLEDGE AND SKILLS TO LEAD QUALITY AND PRODUCTIVITY IMPROVEMENT

Much is being written about learning organizations today. It need not be reinforced that rate of improvement will be driven by learning at the individual, group, and organizational levels. Peter Drucker speaks of the industrial revolution, the productivity revolution, the management revolution, and now the knowledge revolution. He describes this knowledge revolution as one where we learn to learn, we turn knowledge on knowledge. Simplistically, it is a period where individual growth, personally and professionally, will be at the heart of an organization's ability to survive and thrive. The capacity to solve ever larger and more complex problems, to move quickly to new S-shaped curves, and to capture opportunities proactively have become hallmarks of the emerging successful organization.

Improvement requires that the education/training/development front be pushed forward effectively and consistently and that training and development not be the first thing cut when times get tough. A team doesn't quit practicing or studying the opposition when they start losing games; they practice even harder.

We won't repeat all the good words being published and spoken of late about learning organizations. We won't replicate the logic and the theory. Let's keep this last section basic, pragmatic, and to the point.

The number of phone calls I get from people forty- or fifty-something who are out of work and now in the unenviable position of finding a new career seems to grow daily. In many cases, these individuals represent a significant percentage of the workforce simply passed over by technology and change. They don't represent good value for their organizations anymore. Their contributions are not in excess of the inducements the organization has to provide to keep them. And so they are let go.

Were these decisions sound financially, from a bottom-line business standpoint? Probably. Were they profound? Were they humane? Were they culture building? Did they drive our fear? NO!

Leaders and managers today are finding themselves faced with extremely difficult decisions, and the personnel decisions seem to be the most troublesome. Downsizing (rightsizing?) is rampant today as organizations seek to improve efficiency, productivity, and profitability. Rethinking who does what in order to survive consumes much managerial time and effort. The end result is that people who thought they had careers, were part of a family, are caught off-guard by stark operational realities. Their worlds have been turned upside down. In some cases, managers who once enjoyed six-figure incomes are now willing to take huge cuts in pay just to maintain cash flow and a semblance of the standard of living to which they have become accustomed. It's disheartening to them, and it's a dilemma for their prospective new employers, as they worry about the level of motivation these individuals will be able to sustain in a new career with considerably less perceived equity. "Can these people 'retread' themselves such they move from being managers to doers?" is a central question on the minds of new employer and new employee.

The impact on the cultures of organizations in the midst of downsizing is "unknown and unknowable" (Deming 1986). What will the levels of productivity, quality, effectiveness, innovation, and quality of work life really be after downsizing? What will be the capacity to improve? What will happen to rate of improvement?

Managers and leaders are so overwhelmed with the need to reduce costs that they are often not able to think strategically about the consequences of their decisions. In all fairness, many managers are simply executing orders; they don't have a great deal of control over whether downsizing is done or how it is executed.

What are the root causes? Why are certain people let go and others not? Why are organizations faced with downsizing? Why aren't organizations creating "jobs and more jobs?" (Deming 1986) There is, of course, the macro-economist's answer to the question: global recession, decrease in Gross National Product growth, monetary policy instability, etc. At the managerial level, the answer might be unfair competition, union pressures, increasing labor rates, lack of leadership, stockholder pressures, market pressures, etc. The sociologist and psychologist may cite lack of community, poor communication and coordination, no common ground, too much fear in the workplace, no real commitment, absenteeism and turnover, low morale, poor quality of work life, etc.. The industrial engineer might point to lagging technology, no deployment of methods and process improvement, poor layouts, human factors engineering problems, poor decision-making, no utilization of operations research, poor inventory control models, no quality assurance, etc.

They are all correct, of course. It is all of these factors, in one way or another. They all come together to comprise the challenge leaders and managers face. An answer, perhaps *the* answer, is that we all must learn to come to grips with these challenges and problems and become more proactive at leading and managing for improvement within our domains of responsibility. If we have covered all the right domains of responsibility within the organization, and we have technical competence and individual responsibility within those domains, then we will increase the probability of success. Again, we define success as "jobs and more jobs, job security, higher and higher levels of quality of work, quality of work life, quality of life" (Deming and others).

How does this happen? Simplistically, leadership learns how to manage Grand Strategy Systems. They learn how to lead and manage large-scale organizational improvement. They become experts at "B" in addition to "A" and "C." Right now, we have leaders who are adept primarily at "A" and "C." They aren't even cognizant of what "B" would look like for them. They are victims of a system in which they have performed and excelled for years, but it is a system of the past. We are truly in the midst of a revolution; yet many are trying to solve today's problems with yesterday's solutions. How do we learn to lead and manage successfully in this new world order?

Let's think back to how we learned to survive in the world as we have known it. Most managers and leaders, most change masters, have had twelve to twenty years of formal education. During this time, the program of study was all arranged. Each semester was fairly well laid out for us. For each course we had a syllabus that told us what to read, what to do, and when to do it. The implicit promise or assumption was if we followed the program of study, we would develop the knowledge and skills to succeed in a given career. So, we followed the plan; we graduated, got jobs, and moved on with our lives and our careers.

But once we completed our formal education, who gave us our program of study, who mapped out the syllabus, who told us what to read, what to study, how to continue to grow and develop? The answer, of course, is no one. Continuing personal and professional development is something we have to do for ourselves. But are we prepared to be both the instructor and the student? Do we truly understand that we must continue to learn and adapt or at some point in our lives there may be consequences? Do our managers and leaders understand that if their organizations are filled with individuals who either don't or can't continue to learn at some point there will be consequences for the organization as well as for the individual?

We think these answers are self-evident. Many, if not most, individuals stop learning and growing at a sufficient rate after they complete their formal education. Their informal education is often very haphazard, if it exists at all. We are not a nation of readers. Our attention is not on personal and professional development as much as it is on getting the "A" and the "C" over with so we can enjoy our weekends. And it's catching up with us.

The organizations that can spark a rebirth of personal and professional development will thrive and survive. Those that fail to do so will pay the ultimate price. In today's fast-changing world, the cycle time for this phenomenon will be much shorter than one might suspect. The consequences of not managing the education/training/development front for an individual or for an organization will be experienced in a period of a decade or less, an extremely small action-consequence time frame.

So, we arrive at our thesis for this section. The current revolution (late '60s to the present) has placed a premium on learning to support improvement. However, the culture in North America during this same period was not one that stressed continued personal and professional development. In fact, it has been a culture of satisfaction with the status quo. We get our degrees, enter a career, and are entitled to being "taken care of," either by our company or society in general. Many of us have assumed a passive role in our growth as human beings and as professionals. We have adopted an attitude that we are paid to do "A" and "C," and that "B" for ourselves and our organizations is someone else's job. We argue that this is a root cause of the malaise we are experiencing in North America; not the only root cause, but one of the mighty few.

Today, we are experiencing the consequences of maintaining the status quo: reductions in force, poor competitiveness, slow rates of innovation and improvement, fear and anxiety, high unemployment rates in specific sectors of the workforce, working harder and living poorer, and the first generation of North Americans in history whose standard of living will be higher than that of their children.

At this point, you may be questioning the logic in our argument. You may be in a bit of denial, offended by our implications about you and your leaders and managers. Our thesis for this section is based on our observations over the past fifteen years. It is based on casual research but not on limited data. We hope, however, that you are in agreement with this root cause analysis and at this point are waiting for an answer to the problem. Our solution is fairly straightforward—create a personal and professional plan of study that will keep you growing and developing to ensure your organization succeeds, you succeed, and you make the most of your life.

The final section of this book focuses on helping you better understand how you will develop breadth and depth as a change master. In Chapter 12, we present a method you can utilize to develop a personal and professional plan of study and improvement. In a sense this method provides the framework for your personal grand strategy. It includes a conceptual image document and a plan of development. We guide you through this important exercise. We continue to reinforce the phases of change and professional modes of functioning model, encouraging you to apply the matrix on yourself.

Chapter 11 expands upon material presented in Chapter 8 regarding core competencies and tools. We address specific tool application issues and provide additional guidance on what we believe are the more critical tools of the change master.

The aim of this section is to give you next steps, to help you answer the question, "What do I do now?"

OPERATIONAL DEFINITIONS

Confirmatory Data Analysis (CDA): CDA is the process of converging on "an answer" or an interpretation from data. We are attempting to "fail to reject hypotheses." We are running experiments. We are trying to get reliable and valid answers to questions.

Error Cause Removal: Error Cause Removal is what we do when we have uncovered root causes. We seek to remove the root causes systematically, study the results, and act on the basis of our study. If we find that we have, in fact, identified and removed a root cause of variation or poor performance, then we standardize to ensure that the root cause does not reappear.

Exploratory Data Analysis (EDA): EDA is a process of extracting meaning from data. We are exploring the data, massaging it, portraying it in a variety of ways, playing with the data, diverging rather than converging.

We have found that, in general, change masters and managers do not have well developed skills in this area.

Root Cause Analysis (RCA): A unique and valuable tool for meeting the need to identify and explore and display the possible causes of a specific problem or condition. The cause-and-effect diagram is a method for analyzing process dispersion. The diagram's purpose is to relate causes and effects. It is also known as the Ishikawa diagram and the fishbone diagram (because the completed diagram resembles the skeleton of a fish). It is invaluable for virtually any issue requiring attention, and it can be easily learned by people at all levels of the organization and applied immediately.

Tools of Quality: The tools of quality term is used to represent a set of methodologies or techniques that are commonly used to improve performance. There are the seven basic tools of quality and then the seven new tools that are discussed in more detail. Additional reading guidance is provided at the end of the chapter.

We attempt to expand your thinking a bit in terms of thinking about the "tools of performance improvement" in general. What tools are in you tool kit currently? What is your level of knowledge and skill relative to them? What new tools do you need to continue to succeed as a change master?

CHAPTER 11

DEVELOPING TECHNICAL COMPETENCE AS A CHANGE MASTER

We begin this chapter with an exercise for you. Figure 38 is a diagnostic inventory that will force you to identify which tools are in your "tool kit" and at what level of knowledge and skill you are with respect to each tool. Please take a few minutes now to complete "Version 1.0" of the inventory. You will be asked to develop a more thorough version at the end of this section (LE 6.2).

What have you learned about your tool kit? Is it complete enough? Are your knowledge and skills relative to key tools sufficient? What areas of development do you feel compelled to do something about at this point of self-awareness and analysis?

What is the most effective and efficient way for you to learn? You will have the opportunity to enhance your learning by ensuring you acquire knowledge and skills in a way that is consistent with your preferences. For example, some people learn best when they can do a quick read of the method, try it out in a low risk setting, go back and study the method, and then try it out in a higher risk setting (in a situation where their execution really counts). This would be indicative of an intuitive type; they learn best experientially. They must internalize what they're trying to do, and why, how, and when. Once this is done, they can usually develop a satisfactory level of competence in most tools.

If we don't get in touch with how we learn best and create opportunities to learn in that fashion, then learning isn't satisfying, and we stop doing it. Learning is satisfying when we see results within a reasonable time frame. This requires us to learn efficiently and effectively and to try out what we are learning to reinforce this new knowledge. The reason so much training is wasted is that it is often not "tried out" and therefore not reinforced. As a change master, you must take individual responsibility for positively reinforcing yourself for your growing body of knowledge and skills. Write, teach it, give presentations, practice, create opportunities to hone the tools.

During my first year of learning about the Nominal Group Technique (1976), I created many opportunities (some low risk, some high) to practice the technique. I practiced with church groups, with student groups, with the classes I was teaching, with consulting opportunities. I worried about whether I was overusing and abusing the tool—"a hammer looking for a nail to pound." But, I was careful to always view it as a means to an end rather than an end. I probably led 30 NGT sessions the first year I learned about the tool. That's about sixty-plus hours of training on the tool. By the end of the year, I had developed a whole repertoire of little "tricks" that would make the tool more effective and efficient and lead to a higher-quality product. I also began to see the tool as part of

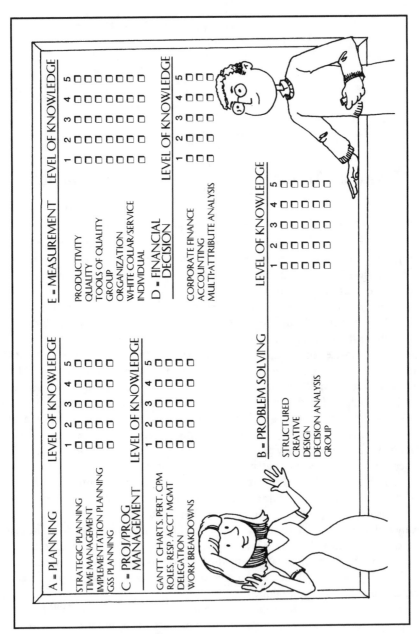

Figure 38. Understanding and acknowledging your level of technical competence, being intellectually honest, is crucial to the change master.

a process rather than an independent tool. In 1977, I developed the Strategic Performance Improvement Planning Process as part of my dissertation work, and the NGT was a key tool in that process.

This is the type of learning process you will have to think through for critical tools in which your knowledge and skills are insufficient. To reiterate, you must be individually responsible for your development as a change master; no one will do it for you. This will require that you identify what to learn, manage pace, try out these new tools, and reinforce your learning. You will have to, as suggested earlier, manage the phases of change for yourself; develop a personal and professional grand strategy. We give you an opportunity to do this in Chapter 12.

Let's turn our attention, once again, to the core competencies discussed in Chapter 8 and address critical application issues in this chapter as well as developmental guidance for the change master.

PLANNING

Application Issues
As stated in Chapter 8, there are many kinds of planning. The types of planning of most interest to the change master are: strategic planning, business planning, improvement planning, implementation planning, deployment planning, and the planning associated with time and meeting management. It can be useful to enter organizations from a strategic planning perspective. Most of our (VQPC) work in the past five years has been with top management and has focused on integrating TQM with strategic planning. Improved implementation and deployment, and measurement systems enhancement have typically been additional areas of emphasis. All the types of planning mentioned above become salient when the change master is involved in the integration of TQM and strategic planning for a given organizational system. In this respect, the change master has, if they can create this opportunity, the potential to influence much that takes place within the organization. This approach, strategic planning integrated with TQM, may be optimal in this sense; it provides tremendous leverage for the change master to work with people in pivotal positions of power.

We also have found that this entry approach can lead to an evolution into Grand Strategy Systems or larger-scale improvement interventions. GSS is a logical extension of a strategic performance improvement planning system. As indicated earlier, once a management team begins to think systems, focus on the customer, think statistically, and work through the seven steps and multiple substeps of the planning process, they quite naturally develop an appreciation for the concept of fronts and subsystems that must be managed over time in a coordinated fashion.

The SPIPP is actually a strategic management process in that it addresses planning (Steps 1-4), but also links that to action (Step 5), measures (Step 6), and follow-through (Step 7). In this regard, the process is more than strategic planning; it is the complete improvement cycle (PDSA). Our intent is not to sell you on this process; rather, it is to get you to think about planning in the context of PDSA. When planning is separated from doing, studying, and acting, then implementation and deployment will suffer predictably.

So many organizations unwittingly allow planning to become the end. They get caught up in an endless do-loop of planning. On the one hand, they are too action oriented: fire-ready-aim or fire-fire-fire. This most often occurs at the operational level. On the other hand, they are too planning oriented: ready-ready-ready-aim-aim or aim-ready-ready-aim-ready. This typically occurs at the top levels in the organization. The integration and balance among reflection, planning, and action are not managed well, as a general rule. The change master predictably will be confronted with this phenomenon. A method such as the SPIPP can help to break out of this vicious and destructive cycle.

When initiating a strategic planning process such as the SPIPP, you will find that the secret lies in getting a high-quality planning session agenda built with the help of the client. If you can succeed in ensuring you have the voice of the customer in your agenda, then the customer will own it, and the session will go much easier. If, on the other hand, they see something being "done to" them or question your intent, competency, or commitment, then you will have problems.

The agenda-building front work is absolutely essential. Make sure you understand the range of expectations from the planning team and, most importantly, from the top managers of the organizational system. Individual interviews followed by a group agenda-building session is preferable. This approach facilitates your understanding of existing phases of change at both the individual and group level. Always feed back what you heard them say, collectively, to confirm expectations, desired outcomes, and desired outputs for the session.

Next comes the art of preparing for a planning session. Sit down with the confirmed list of desired outcomes or outputs and brainstorm agenda modules that you think will lead to accomplishment of a particular expectation. Creativity is important in this process, so consult with others if necessary to help yourself think outside the box. Go to them with very focused questions that don't take up too much of their time. You also may rely on the literature, from which you may pick up countless ideas on agenda modules. Some organizations (e.g., University Associates in San Diego) even have handbooks that catalog agenda modules, any of which may be appropriate for specific needs.

Craft a draft agenda, indicating what will be done, how it leads to accomplishment of an output or will set the stage for accomplishment of an outcome, provide preliminary thoughts on who will lead the module and the method of implementation, and indicate estimated start and stop times, as well as sequencing. This is labeled agenda version 1.0.

Then share this version of the agenda with the client group and ask for feedback. Consolidate this input, make obvious changes to the agenda, and create version 1.5. At this point, meet face-to-face with the key decision makers in the organizational system and review the latest agenda version. Encourage them to project themselves mentally into the session, and take copious notes on their comments, reactions, and suggestions. Work hard to create their ownership of the agenda.

Many of the agenda modules are assigned at this point to leaders and others within the organization. Additionally, participant pre-work is thought through and assigned, and logistical details are discussed. These sessions are typically off-site and may last up to five days, so logistics are a significant issue. Most organizations have a preferred site, and in such cases we use that location. Always check out the details of the location to ensure that they meet the requirements of a session such as this. If the organization doesn't have a preferred site, try to have, in your hip pocket, some suggestions that you know meet your requirements. All this is happening about 30 days prior to the session itself. This ensures there is ample time to accomplish the pre-work activities and lock in site-specific details.

With respect to planning, the change master must be able to think at a 30,000-foot level and at the same time pay close attention to numerous details. Planning efforts often fail because of poor attention to detail rather than a flawed overall model. The change master is a helper; there is no task too menial or too small. This servant mentality is a key requirement for the change master.

Developmental Guidance for the Change Master

The change master should develop a study plan in the area of strategic and operational planning early on. The Strategic Performance Improvement Planning Process I developed evolved as a result of three things: (1) dissertation work, where I realized that working on the measurement front in the absence of working other fronts was futile; (2) working with and for Dr. Joe Mize at Oklahoma State (he exposed me to formal strategic planning); and (3) integrating as much literature and as many models as I could digest into a strategic management process that focused on improvement and on linking actions to strategies and measures.

The change master will be aided by the list of references on planning at the end of the section. We suggest that he or she also lead or help to lead a planning session, using the SPIPP or some similar methodology. Our recommendation is that you study the SPIPP, find an organizational system in need of planning, volunteer (with or without pay) to help, build an agenda with them, facilitate the session, and work with them to move through Steps 4-7 over the period of a year. This is the best way to develop skills in planning, implementation, deployment, and measurement. There are countless volunteer organizations in need of such help; there are numerous professional societies that would welcome some structured leadership, and there are probably organizational systems within your own organization that would be interested in experimenting with PDSA. Be bold; seek out an opportunity (low risk at first) and go through the process.

In summary, the change master needs to:

1. Read up on planning.
2. Lead a planning session (preferably using the SPIPP as your method) in a relatively low-risk setting.
3. Reflect on what you learned. Compare differences between what you read and what you experienced. Go back and study some of the better material on planning you have collected. You will find that reading it after you have experienced planning will be like taking blinders off; you will see things the author said that you didn't catch the first time.
4. Write down what you would do differently on the basis of what you have learned.
5. Repeat Steps 1-4 continually if this is going to be an area of true technical competence. Constantly read the planning literature, continually (at least four times a year) design and lead planning sessions of one type or another, constantly fine-tune the SPIPP (process and system) on the basis of what you learn from each new situation. The challenge for us is to learn how to continue to evolve planning (PDSA) over the years, from the first cycle to the nth. It is amazing how different the second or even third cycle is from the first. How do you keep the plan-do-study-act cycle at the organizational system level dynamic, progressing, effective, productive, and enjoyable? These are the challenges the change master faces as he or she develops planning as a core technical competency.

MEASUREMENT

Application Issues

As mentioned previously, the best way to understand the role of measurement in improvement is to review Kurstedt's Management Systems Model in the context of the improvement cycle (PDSA). Figure 39 depicts another modification to the Management Systems Model. This version stresses the development of a measurement system.

We design and develop measurement systems using a clock-wise process on the management systems model. What problems need to be solved? What decisions are made? What improvements need to be supported? Then, we identify information requirements to support decisions and actions. Once this has been done, data requirements are identified, and, finally, the data-to-information system requirements are determined. The naive change master often starts with our last step, searching for measurement tools and techniques. This is not a customer-driven approach; it is a hammer looking for a nail to pound and has a high probability of failure. Our method is more difficult and time consuming but is ultimately significantly more successful.

Crafting and enhancing a measurement system involves the following basic steps:

1. Gaining an understanding of user or customer problems, requirements, expectations, current information availability, purposes for measurement, decisions or actions that need to be supported or better supported by the measurement system;
2. Identifying key performance indicators that the user or customer would like information about;
3. Identifying data requirements for the required information;
4. The storing, retrieving, processing, and portraying of information;
5. Debugging and enhancing the information as the client or user attempts to use the measurement system. We build the measurement system in a clock-wise fashion, then use it in a counter-clockwise fashion.

To follow the model in Figure 39, measurement creates data, data are converted into information, information is evaluated by who is managing, decisions are made on the basis of information, actions are taken on the basis of these decisions, the organizational system is affected by these actions, we measure the effects, and the cycle continues. Organizational learning occurs when management teams become skilled at converting data to information, information to knowledge, and knowledge to decisions and actions. Confirmation that decisions and actions have or have not improved performance supports individual, group, and organizational learning. If the measurement system doesn't provide feedback to those who are planning for and implementing improvement, then they don't learn; they don't confirm whether their improvements have, in fact, caused improvement. This is happening today in most organizations; measurement systems are nonexistent in most cases and woefully inadequate in the rest.

One of your major tasks as a change master will be to correct this situation. You will undoubtedly be called upon to help your clients improve the quality of their measurement systems. This will require technical competence in the area of measurement. Herein lies a problem. Most change masters do not have sufficient education and training in the area of measurement. Often our measurement training is discipline-specific, very narrow in

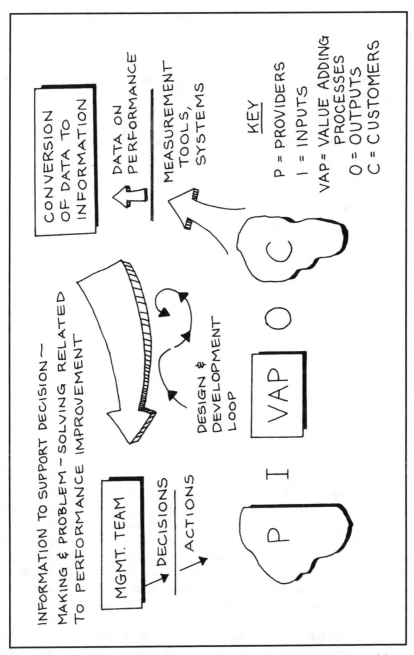

Figure 39. Building or enhancing the measurement system is done in the context of the management systems model (adapted from Kurstedt).

perspective, and not well grounded in theory or practice. We come at measurement from an accounting perspective, or from an industrial psychology or sociology perspective, or from a work measurement perspective. None of these perspectives is wrong; they are just not complete.

In most organizations, all too often measurement systems are not owned by anyone or any function. The responsibility for improving measurement systems typically is delegated to the unable and the unwilling, who approach the assignment by looking for a recipe. These practices must be addressed and resolved by the change master.

First, measurement systems to support improvement should be owned by a measurement front team. This team should be comprised of specialists in statistics, industrial psychology, industrial engineering, industrial sociology, accounting and finance, and in the business of the organization itself. The front team's job is to systematically and continuously improve the quality of the measurement systems in the organization. This team must be comprised of people who have an affinity for measurement, are willing to pay the price it takes to become a measurement master, understand the role of measurement in the PDSA cycle, and who will demonstrate unrelenting dedication to the continuous improvement of the measurement front in the organization. The measurement front team must approach their task from a systems perspective. They cannot fall into the trap of seeing measurement as a box to check, as an end in itself. They must understand the measurement system development process and the relationship between measurement and planning, strategies, and actions.

What have we learned in doing these things with organizations like yours over the past seventeen years?

• Performance is multi-dimensional, made up of a vector, or family, of criteria. We think Level 1 criteria are: effectiveness, efficiency, quality, productivity, quality of work life, innovation, and budgetability (cost center) or profitability (profit center). These are the major categories of indicators for performance.

Within each of these categories will be specific indicators (Level 2 measures) that will be somewhat unique to each organization. There are an infinite number of measures or indicators that are possible candidates; even for a given type of organization there are a greater number of potential indicators than can be utilized. The challenge facing the change master lies in helping the users or customers of the measurement system decide what indicators are truly important in their efforts to manage and improve performance. Once the users have been forced to think through what specific indicators would be useful, the change master works with them or the measurement front team to collect data, develop portrayal mechanisms, and put this to use.

• Creating visibility for the measures and indicators is crucial. Every management team in your organization should turn its conference rooms into visibility or control rooms.

You should build a "cockpit" of instruments (Figure 40) conveying vital information about the organizational system for which they are responsible. Visible management systems throughout your organization, at all levels vertically and horizontally, will be necessary in the future. These visibility rooms will need to depict information from Level

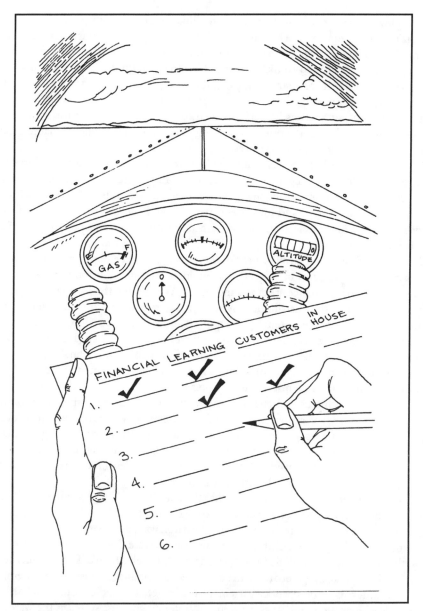

Figure 40. The cockpit and balanced scorecard concepts are useful when deciding how to build or enhance performance measurement systems.

1 so employees in your system can understand linkages between the performance of your organizational system and the larger system. The visibility system must provide adequate information so that at any point in time someone can assess the health of the organizational system. It is impossible to think statistically without longitudinal data, so this will be required. The "cockpit" or instrument panel for the organizational system will need to be as comprehensive as possible (you can have too many instruments and too few). It is crucial that an input/output analysis be performed so that the boundaries of the system being measured are clear. Not doing this is the leading cause of confusion about what to measure and leads to having too many measures.

We recently completed a visible management system project for a large distribution organization. It took us three months to get the visibility boards and chartbooks designed and developed, three months to debug them, and then six months to stabilize the utilization of them as a management and improvement tool. We believe this cycle time of twelve months can be reduced to less than six and are attempting to do this presently in another warehouse.

During the design and development of these visible management systems, we worked with users (employees and managers), stakeholders, and distribution system leaders to uncover the key performance areas and indicators. We audited the list against our input/output analysis for the distribution system, making sure we included measures of performance for the entire system (q1—suppliers and vendors, through q5 — customers) and ensuring that our measures were not q3 — warehouse dominated (Figure 41). We did not want to have this measurement system focus on the wrong unit of analysis (warehouse system versus distribution system). This is a common mistake made when building a measurement system, as mentioned in Chapter 8.

We began to architect and engineer our visibility boards for display in prominent locations within the warehouse. To reinforce linkages, we portrayed firm-level or corporate goals, strategies, performance measures, and improvement initiatives in the first row of the visibility board. On row two, we displayed distribution system-level measures. And on row three, we displayed warehouse and subsystem-level measures. We made no overt attempts to demonstrate the linkages initially.

Employees were involved in ensuring that the data for the key performance indicators were kept current. Daily meetings were held to review trends, both current and longer term. Shift transition meetings were held to ensure the baton was passed smoothly from one shift to the next, and that shift-to-shift performance trends were discussed and analyzed.

At the same time we developed a performance visibility chartbook. The audience for the fixed visibility management boards is the employees and managers inside the system; they come to the information and work with it in the workplace. The audience for the chartbooks is higher level managers and other distribution system managers, stores of the warehouse (customers), and even vendors to the warehouse. In this case the information goes to the user.

The chartbook contains: a table of contents with page numbers (Figure 42); an executive summary of the distribution system, prepared monthly by the leadership team (in this case a joint labor-management team) that summarizes their conversion of data-to-information-to-knowledge-to-decisions and actions; and key performance indicator charts in priority order, longitudinal data in all cases. We spent three months fine tuning what was portrayed and how. Once we got this locked in, we did not change the character of the chartbook for six months.

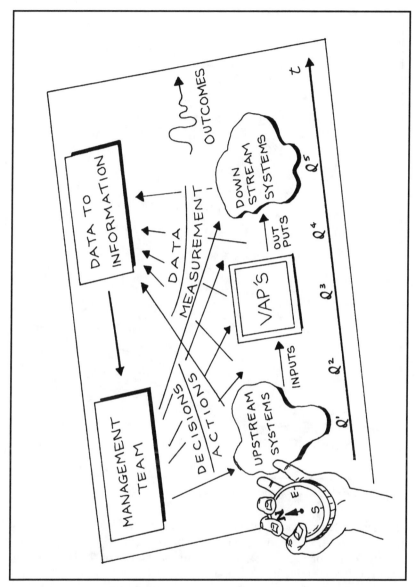

Figure 41. The five quality checkpoints map the management systems model and input–output analysis. Recall that TQM is the measurement and management of performance at each of the five checkpoints over time.

Figure 42. A chartbook contains four core chapters.

We focused, in that six-month period, on teaching the leadership team how to convert the data into information, the information into knowledge of cause-and-effect relationships, and the knowledge into decisions and actions. We taught the labor-management team how to explore meaning in the data and information and how to write the executive summary. The executive summary contains the leadership team's conclusions and interpretations of how the warehouse is performing, where there are areas in need of further analysis, where there are areas in need of intervention, what specific interventions will be made in the next month, and the corresponding performance improvement expectations. This executive summary is drafted in a team meeting where the entire team is attempting to process the data and information provided in the chartbook. The chartbook comes out on the 10th of every month, the team meeting occurs on the 15th, and the chartbooks are distributed to their intended audience on that day (the 15th).

Attention to detail, discipline, and linking of plans to actions to measures once again comes through in this measurement discussion as it did in the planning discussion. Notice how the steps in measurement system design are being carried out in this short scenario describing the development of the visible management system. In actual practice, it may not be quite as neat and clean as it appears in the method description. It takes planning, a critical mass of resources during startup, and follow through, but it can be done.

We are in the rudimentary stages of understanding cognitive styles, but we know enough to understand that the "how" is as important as the "what" when it comes to information portrayal. Often, meaning in data is obscured by poor portrayal. There exists a growing number of good books on information portrayal, and we reference these at the end of this section.

One technique that can be applied in this area is to take data portrayal and have people write the meaning or message they get from the data and see if they write down the same meaning from the data as portrayed. Work backwards and forwards with this, take the caption and think about what the data would look like, then take the data portrayal and think about what its meaning is in text.

We also find it valuable to force a management team to do what we call the "data-to-information-to-decision-to-action" exercise. A management team is presented with some data and individually asked to convert that data to information. Then they are individually asked to identify what decisions and actions they would make and take on the basis of the information they have derived. They are encouraged to use their total data and knowledge base in doing this. They don't just utilize the data provided; they must explain other data they employed. Once the members of the management team have completed this, they are requested to share their results with others in the group. Variation is discussed and a group consensus is reached. We find that groups working together struggle with this tremendously. Like practicing the piano, it isn't fun for most, and requires a parent or teacher to "supervise" the practicing to ensure it happens, but when mastered is extremely rewarding. The difference is that we have, ultimately, the choice about whether to learn to play the piano; management teams should not have a choice about whether to learn how to skillfully execute the improvement cycle.

Developmental Guidance for the Change Master

It is clear that use of statistics, exploratory data analysis, and more effective and sophisticated information portrayal methods will be important in the future. The change master will probably need a "minor" (formally or informally) in statistics to be effective. Dr. Deming emphasized statistical thinking as one of the four elements of profound knowledge, and we would agree this is critical for the change master. Specifically, it seems to us that beyond fundamental statistics, the change master will require applied:

- Nonparametric statistics
- Regression analysis (linear and nonlinear)
- Experimental design
- Survey sampling
- Statistical process control/QC/QA.

Learning how to explore data will be invaluable to the change master. This has become known as exploratory data analysis. It is not uncommon for researchers to utilize fairly sophisticated statistical analysis techniques on data sets and never really "play" with or examine the original data set to search for meaning. Some would suggest confirmatory data analysis should always be preceded by exploratory data analysis. Confirmatory data analysis would be exemplified by hypothesis testing, experimental design, and statistically proving signficance and confidence, whereas exploratory data analysis is the search for meaning, playing with data to create better visibility and understanding. In some respects, many of the tools of quality are exploratory tools being taught to those engaged in improvement activities.

In developing knowledge and skill in this area, the change master first must understand the theory and foundations of measurement. This entails the concepts of scales; theory of knowledge (philosophy of science); the theory and concepts of measurement-to-data, data-to-information, information-to-knowledge, knowledge-to-decisions, and decisions-to-actions (Management Systems Model); information systems theory and principles; communication theory (for information portrayal knowledge); and probably fundamentals of accounting and finance. Second, the change master must learn about various tools of measurement. Third, the change master will have to study measurement system design, development, implementation, and enhancement. (See Sink and Tuttle 1989 for the example of a method for doing this.) Fourth, the change master must create opportunities and take them to practice, building or enhancing measurement systems similar to the process explained with planning previously.

PROBLEM SOLVING

Application Issues
We all solve problems, personally and professionally, and we all have somewhat unique problem-solving styles. What is your mental model of problem solving? Do you have a preferred and predictable approach that you follow? Or, do you solve some problems one way and other problems another? What does problem solving include or incorporate, in your mind? Can the quality of the solution to a problem be improved by changing the method used to solve the problem? How do groups and organizations solve problems? How is this different than how individuals solve problems?

A change master must contemplate these questions as he or she begins to think about developing improved knowledge and skill in this area. In many ways, quality and productivity improvement, certainly when approached from a large-scale improvement perspective, is a process of problem solving. The problem is how to improve performance. Managers, leaders, and change masters are confronted with this problem because it is their job; it is in their domain of responsibility.

There are many types of problem solving the change master will be exposed to in efforts to learn more about this area of competency. There is creative problem solving, where the aim is to think outside the box, be creative, withold judgment, suspend assumptions, and believe their are no constraints, only controllables. There is structured problem solving, such as the methodology provided by the Kepner-Tregoe system referred to earlier: It structures the phases of problem solving, frames our inquiry process with questions and forms, and provides learning examples so we can move from theory and method to skill. There is group problem solving, where the issue of agreement and consensus becomes important. There are, of course, big problems and small problems, problems with a high degree of certainty and those with great uncertainty, some that involve significant risk while others involve little. To assume that one problem-solving method will suffice for all these situations is naive.

To assume that one problem-solving method will be equally embraced by those with a variety of styles and preferences is equally naive. Thus, the change master is faced with a dilemma. There is an assumption that the method of solving problems can improve the quality of the solution, but there is also a recognition that acceptance and ownership of both the method and the solution are important to eventual implementation. We need a good method, but we need it accepted, and one method probably won't suffice for all types of situations.

I was first exposed to formal problem solving methodology at Eastman Kodak. Like many organizations, they had adopted the Kepner-Tregoe method to teach employees. I was constantly pressuring my supervisor to let me take the variety of internal courses offered by the company, and one of the courses I took was the Kepner-Tregoe Problem Solving course. As most have discovered, the course, if taught by a reasonably competent instructor, is engaging and logical, and the case applications provide an opportunity for hands on learning and application. The course can also be fun because you are learning in small groups, and you can't fail because you aren't graded.

But, when you get out of the course armed with the book, the workbook, the forms, and you try to apply the method, things start to go awry. Team members you work with haven't all had KT and resent you imposing structure and new language and taking a leadership role. Your bosses patronize you, reinforcing your attempt to apply new knowledge, but you get the sense they don't really believe that problem solving can be improved. The problems you face on the job aren't as neat and clean as the case examples written up in the course. And, perhaps most importantly, you don't have time to go through the fairly elaborate four step, multiform process. When attempting to do the decision-analysis you find it frustrating to have to evaluate alternatives when you really don't have any; you are designing a satisfactory solution, not selecting among a set of already existing solutions.

The change master won't find many managers or technical people who at one time or another in their career haven't been exposed to a structured problem-solving course. However, sitting through a course does not a problem solver make. This truism was reinforced to me in a client setting not long ago.

I was working with a group of division directors, all twenty-plus years into their careers, third level managers in a large organization, all bright, in charge of significant departments, all well educated. We were establishing an affinity group of division directors. The basic task of the affinity group was to identify common problems across the twenty division directors and resolve them.

We struggled for a year with that task. At the end of about six months of struggling, I suggested we do some problem-solving training. To the person, they said they had had all the problem-solving training they needed and weren't interested. When I confronted them with the fact that they couldn't solve problems, they immediately began to externalize the reasons. I concluded it wasn't that they didn't know how to solve problems but that they hadn't developed skill in problem-solving in complex organizations. I also suspected they were avoiding individual responsibility and weren't intellectually honest with themselves.

There was not a consistent method for problem solving being used by the group. In fact, there wasn't a method in some cases. I took a back door approach. After several unsuccessful cycles of problem solving, I asked them to do a cause-and-effect diagram. We isolated some root causes. The most significant were: tackling problems outside their domain of responsibility and authority, no common method, no discipline, no follow-through, inability to make tough decisions and implement them, no support from the next level of management, and no real empowerment to solve problems as an interdependent group.

Each of the problem-solving teams from the unsuccessful attempts documented the process or method they had employed to solve the problem. We brought all those descriptions together and compiled a common method that was in their terms and that they understood. I provided some educational guidance as this was done, but largely it was their methodology. We then applied this methodology in the next round of problem solving.

They improved and made progress. I am convinced that this type of scenario must be followed as post-formal problem-solving training for KT-type approaches to be internalized as a way of doing business. An organization will not be able to increase the rate at which performance is improving if it does not learn how to solve problems more consistently and effectively.

A basic model we employ to depict the steps in the problem-solving process is shown in Figure 43. It is an adaptation from the KT model that has been designed to address some of the application problems mentioned above, and includes the following elements:

- **Situation appraisal** helps to sort out the problems from the issues from the perplexities; it sorts out what is often a mess into pieces, some manageable, some not.
- Situation appraisal leads to **issue and problem identification** and prioritization. An issue, to us, is often emotional, fuzzy, subjective, while a problem is separated from the person, less emotional, more objective.
- Issue and problem identification lead to **issue and problem analysis**. Issue analysis often leads to the identification of additional problems or often the resolution or evaporation of the issue. An example of this is root-cause analysis using a cause-and-effect diagram.
- Problem analysis leads to **design of a satisfactory solution** or the **analysis of alternative solutions** to the problem, called **decision analysis**.
- Decision analysis or design leads to **decision making**.
- Decision making leads to **implementation planning**, the thinking through of how the decision will be implemented. Kepner-Tregoe calls this potential problem analysis.
- Implementation planning leads to **implementation**.
- Implementation leads to **evaluation** (study and act).

The important point is that not all situations call for completion of all the problem-solving stages. It may be the case that one proceeds directly to decision making, implementation, or evaluation, depending on where you happen to be in the problem-solving cycle.

It is important to note several things we have learned about problem solving in the context of quality and productivity improvement over the years. We are almost always confronted with situations. Situations may be problems needing to be solved, projects needing to be managed, perplexities needing to be dealt with, messes needing to be sorted out, processes needing to be developed or improved, programs needing to be started and

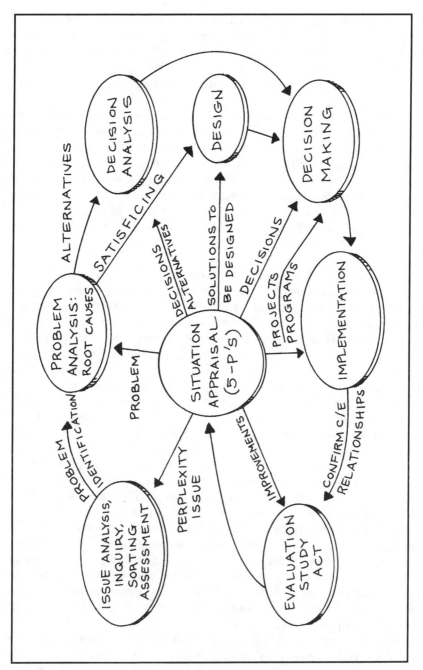

Figure 43. The problem-solving wheel is composed of a set of interrelated components.

managed and maintained, objectives needing to be accomplished, solutions needing to be designed, or opportunities needing to be captured. Pure-form problems that will be resolvable by any methodology, let alone KT, are rare. We must learn to sort out situations and understand "what we have a hold of," so to speak. Different approaches will be required for different situations. This is what KT calls situation appraisal, and that's a good term for it.

We may enter the problem-solving and opportunity-capturing process at different points on the hub of the process. There are submethods and processes for each circle on the hub. They are not necessarily complex or sophisticated. The secret is in practicing problem solving enough so that it becomes second nature. You should be able to teach it or use it in an instant. Our problem-solving methodology is evolving, and in fact has been refined just now as we have written about it for the nth time. Change masters should be at this level of development with respect to problem solving. Moving clients through the phases of change will require effective problem solving; therefore, this must be a tool that you can access and use quickly.

Developmental Guidance for the Change Master

To develop technical competence in problem solving, the change master first must come to grips with his or her current method of problem solving. What is your method? How does it vary in different situations? Do you have a formal method and an informal method, and how are they different? Second, as has been the case in previous core competency areas, the change master should study problem-solving theory and methods, primarily creative, structured, individual, and group problem solving. Select a methodology you like best, feel is most comprehensive and robust, and is most sellable to your clients, and study it carefully. I suggest you become acquainted with Kepner-Tregoe as a foundational methodology. References are provided for this method at the end of the section.

Third, the change master will have to create opportunities to work with individuals and groups in a problem-solving activity. This creates experience that you can then juxtapose against the theory and methods as presented in the literature. The gap between the method as written and as applied with individuals and groups is usually quite large. Application is sloppier, steps get done out of order, and it's more difficult. The change master will find that individuals typically believe they are better at problem solving than they are: There is often a large gap between what they know and have been trained in and what they can do relative to problem solving. Part of the problem is that they simply haven't practiced a problem-solving methodology enough for it to have become habit. So, the change master not only must create his or her own opportunities but also create opportunities for the client.

Systematically document what you are learning as you apply the methodology. Create a short tutorial on the methodology that you share with your clients. Continue to improve this written description of your methodology.

Fourth, the change master will have to develop and internalize a problem-solving methodology (perhaps more than one) that is almost second nature. You must have the problem-solving methodology so well learned that it is indelibly imprinted in your mind, something you can teach, without aid of materials, at the spur of the moment. You must continue to refine your methodology, learning how to apply it and modify it for different situations. You must be able to help groups and individuals apply the method to solve problems, teaching them the method while using it to help them solve the problem.

Concentrate on helping groups learn how to improve their problem-solving skills and use these groups as prototypes from which others can learn.

MOTIVATION

Application Issues

We include motivation, counseling, mentoring, and helping in this area of technical competence because they are all part of the development process. To us they seem to fit together. Motivation addresses understanding why people do or do not do things. In the context of improvement, the change master seeks to understand how to motivate people to engage in "B," often in the midst of being overwhelmed by "A" and "C." How do we motivate people to do their best, to rise to the occasion and to do more than they thought possible when the need arises?

If you agree that most people are willing workers, then motivation may not be an issue. We believe people are, in general, willing workers. They have tremendous potential to excel and to create. But, we also believe that people, although often willing, are not always able. Creating a system that enables each individual's very best to be good enough is the problem we should be solving. Motivating, coaching, mentoring, and counseling people to learn and adopt new methods is what this area of technology is all about, and it is applicable to all levels of the organization.

Another dimension of this area of technical competency deals with helping individuals, groups, and organizations get unstuck. Organizations and groups are like people in some respects. They get ill, and when they do they need help. They often are not motivated to seek help or to get unstuck. They know something is wrong, but they are willing to live with it. Change masters must work to help organizations achieve civility, "consciously motivated organizational behavior that is ethical in submission to a Higher Power" (Peck 1993). They must learn to be civil, to help individuals, groups, and organizations improve performance through development. This will mean they must learn to motivate, manage conflict, and understand human behavior in complex organizations.

This is an important area of technical competence for the change master, and a foundation of theory and method is essential for success. Helping individuals, groups, and organizations get unstuck often requires knowledge of counseling and personal and group development.

As the change master matures in experience and tackles increasingly more complex performance improvement situations, he or she will be called upon to "treat" the effects of stresses and strains on other change masters, leaders, managers, and employees. These stresses and strains are mounting today as we face more rapid change, more complexity, shorter cycle times on improvement, downsizing, restructuring, rapid shifts in technology, and an increasingly global economy. The need for the change master to be part counselor will increase.

Developmental Guidance for the Change Master

First, the change master needs to read and study the four basic theories of motivation introduced in Chapter 8, focusing where possible on methods that are available for operationalizing these theories. Additionally, the change master needs to read and study literature in the area of counseling and group development.

Second, the change master needs to think through the types of behaviors required on the part of management and employees to support improvement efforts. Where are actual behaviors different than desired behaviors and why? It might be useful for the change master to do a force-field analysis, assessing forces in support of improvement and forces against improvement. What can be done to the system to remove or reduce restraining forces? What can be done to reinforce, recognize, and reward improvements? What are the consequences of not cooperating with improvement efforts? What are the consequences for cooperating? What can be done to better manage these consequences?

Third, the change master needs to experiment with motivation theories and techniques. Observe situations where motivation seems to be a problem. Think about which theories seem to explain or perhaps predict the behaviors you observe. On the basis of those theories, what could be done to improve the level of effort, quality of effort, level of commitment, or willingness to cooperate? Think through what "levers" you might be able to influence as a change master to improve motivation. Think about root causes of variation in performance. Is motivation actually a root cause? Currently, the debate over intrinsic versus extrinsic motivation is being waged full-scale. Study this debate (see references at end of section). If quality and productivity improvement efforts work and the organization begins to win, how will you share the results with employees? What happens if you don't? What happens if people are motivated and do cooperate, the organization gets better, needs fewer people or different kinds of people, and those who made improvement possible are let go? How will you manage the interrelationship between the culture front and the motivation front?

Fourth, as with problem solving, the change master should strive to develop a written description of his or her motivation theories and methods. The change master will be called upon frequently to address motivation and development issues in the course of improvement efforts. It will be valuable to have a foundational, personal crystallization of your understanding of this area of technical competence. In this vein, the change master should think through what he or she would recommend as a strategy for moving the motivation front forward in an organization.

On Mentoring

Gaining technical competence in the area of motivation, or in any other area for that matter, will be facilitated by mentorship. Mentoring is a concept not commonly understood. Frankly, I have only recently been exposed to the importance of the mentor/protégé relationship. A mentor, to me, is someone to look up to, someone to learn from, someone you wish to emulate in some respect. Protégés select mentors, and the chemistry is crucial. Often the mentor is "paying forward," doing for a protégé what was done for him or her.

In an informal mentor/protégé relationship, the mentor is not aware that he or she has a protégé. The protégé keeps this quiet, admiring, copying, and learning from the mentor at a distance. In a formal mentor/protégé relationship, the relationship is known and understood by both parties.

Change masters need mentors. Becoming a change master will not come easily or quickly without them; in fact, it may not come at all. Among my mentors have been: Dr. George Smith, my co-author Dr. William Morris, the late Dr. Edwards Deming, Dr. Ed Lawler, Dr. Dominic Monetta, Dr. Harold Kurstedt, Dr. Joe Mize, and Dr. James Tompkins. Most of them probably are not aware that we have a mentor/protégé relationship (Dr. Deming didn't, and Ed Lawler doesn't even know). I've had disagreements with a few of them and don't concur with most of them in every regard. But I've learned a great deal from them.

PROJECT AND PROGRAM MANAGEMENT

Application Issues

We're going to repeat what was said about project management in Chapter 8 because it is short and worth repeating. Then we will share some lessons learned, some application issues, and prescriptions in terms of how the change master can begin to develop in this area.

We have introduced the three-ball problem and the 3^n-ball problem. Clearly, solving the focal problem, allocating resources on improvement projects, and developing and managing implementation strategy represent a project management challenge. In a sense, a change master is a program and project manager. The program is the transformation; the projects are the variety of improvement efforts that will take place over time to make the transformation take place.

It's relatively easy to manage a project in the traditional sense—just focus on the first two balls (solve the problem and allocate resources). Project management gets more complex when we add the third ball (implementation strategy), and when we add multiple improvement projects and end up with the 3^n-ball problem it's a real challenge. This is the task facing a change master attempting to help an organization (or organizations) make the transformation. It's extremely rewarding, but it takes time to acquire the necessary knowledge and skills.

Following are some lessons we have learned on quality and productivity improvement project management for the change master. We have found that ultimately, the project or program manager has to:

1. Envision what has to be done;
2. Sequence what has to be done;
3. Determine who has to do what and when;
4. Determine how to measure to get data and information to support decisions and actions aimed to ensure cost, schedule, and quality;
5. Evaluate performance on an ongoing basis, but, most importantly, at the end of every improvement project so that lessons learned can be incorporated in the future;
6. Make sure the customer(s) and other stakeholders are involved throughout the project;
7. Pay attention to details, stay on top of things (but don't tamper). "The devil is in the details; but so is salvation" (Rickover 1991);
8. Maintain the ability to "zoom-in" and "zoom-out";
9. Utilize a "red team" if and when appropriate; to reiterate, a red team is a group of external honest brokers who are brought in on large, complex, critical projects to provide guidance;
10. Know when to make interventions aimed at keeping up pace—particularly important on large, long, complex projects;
11. Keep all members of the project well informed; involve them in planning, problem

solving and decision making when appropriate; help them understand the big picture;

12. Be able and willing to broker special assistance when appropriate to help the project get unstuck or to spark innovation;

13. Not let ego interfere with objectivity;

14. Know when to "fish or cut bait" on the project or subtasks if things aren't working;

15. Always keep the improvement project in perspective, understand it in the context of the organization's grand strategy;

16. Continually improve skills in organizing, time management, meeting management, delegation, coaching and counseling, team development, professional modes of functioning. Improvement projects are tremendous opportunities to develop change master skills; be willing to experiment and to try new things;

17. Practice patience, persistence, and consistency. It will be important to keep the big picture in mind. There will be critics and doomsayers along the way; if the improvement initiative is worth doing you will have to preach staying the course, share your vision. This is difficult and requires leadership.

Five Key Stages of Project/Program Management

There are five areas associated with project management that are typically more difficult than others to master. The first is envisioning. The change master must be able to envision the end of the project or program, or, if the project or program is large and complex, the change master may have to envision intermediate ends or milestones. The change master must be able to conjure up an image of the desired end state. The change master must be able to articulate this mental picture with clarity and conviction. The "why" question is important in this stage. Why are we doing this? Is it the right thing to do? This is directly related to the effectiveness criterion.

Following envisioning, the change master must think through, in increasing detail, the steps that must be taken to accomplish the desired end state. The what, when, who, and how questions come into play at this stage. Methods are the focus, and quality is the criterion of emphasis. Attention is on ensuring we accomplish what we have envisioned. We want to be creative and nonjudgmental at this point, deferring evaluation and efficiency issues. The aim is to get ideas down, to dream, to develop a living project or program plan. This stage creates a conceptual design, a version 1.0 project or program plan. To strive for perfection is a mistake at this stage.

Third, we seek to expand input on our project or program plan. We begin to involve more inputs from the larger system. We seek to enhance, modify, and improve the detail of our plan. The intent here is to create version 2.0 of the plan.

The fourth stage of project or program planning involves subjecting version 2.0 to critique. Here, we may use a red team or simply allow top management or other experts to review the plan with the intent of finding gaps, omissions, areas of inconsistency, inefficiency, or impracticality. Our intent at this stage is to avoid being defensive. What does the critic see that we didn't? All key stakeholders, targets, sponsors, and champions should be involved in this stage. A "punch list" of changes should be developed and shared with this critic group after the changes have been made. This allows the critics to see what has been incorporated and closes the loop on their input.

By this point we have reached the fifth stage, where we have a version 3.0 or 4.0 project or program plan that is ready to be implemented. Once the project begins, it is highly likely that the plan will become outdated rapidly, perhaps even obsolete. This stresses the need for the change master to consider project and program plans as living plans. The most difficult and yet most important part of project and program management is keeping the plan current. In the implementation phase, it is all too easy to forget about keeping the plan current; we get so busy doing we forget to modify our plan as we study and act. It is the role of the DDT/A&E team and the change master to ensure that this doesn't happen. Regular project or program plan updates should be a required and formal team exercise. Enhancements should be shared with the Steering Committee, highlighting areas where the plan has changed.

Improvement projects and programs are so much easier when we follow the simple advice of "planning the work and then working the plan." If the plan is not current, it is predictable that you will lose sight of the forest for the trees. When this happens, momentum is lost because people are confused as to what happens next. Recall the simple readiness for change model: $C = a \cdot b \cdot d \geq R$. At all times, the vision must be clear, shared, understood, and pain management, dissatisfaction with the status quo, and motivation to keep at the project or program must be maintained. This is difficult, if not impossible, when the project or program plan isn't current.

An Example

With respect to Grand Strategy System Program plans, we have found that the quality of the plan increases significantly with each version. Figure 44 portrays an example of a partial Gantt-chart version of a GSS program plan showing 8 or the 9 fronts. The x-axis represents time. The y-axis represents fronts and specific initiatives within fronts. There needs to be nine major rows, one for each front. Infrastructure, planning, measurement, and education/training/development are clustered together because they are key start-up fronts.

Version 1.0 of the GSS program plan usually is crafted with the Design and Development Team. The GSS model actually prescribes a baseline plan, in that there are certain activities that occur as part of the model. The change master brings a very rough first draft (Version .5) of the GSS plan to the DDT strategy session, and the DDT works from that to further complete the planning matrix.

Early on, it will be a challenge for the DDT to even complete out-month planning for the planning front. They may struggle to enhance the basic elements called for by the planning process or system for twelve or fifteen months. They will, with the help of the change master, be able to add some specific activities in other rows, particularly the start-up fronts. This version 1.0 then can be shared with key stakeholders, targets, and sponsors for enhancement. Again, it is likely that a few enhancements will be made, but the plan will be far from complete. Version 2.0 then can be critiqued by some large-scale organizational change experts or by senior management just prior to startup. This will cull up a number of other additions and enhancements.

We have found that about every three months the DDT, along with the change master, will have to go through another plan update and enhancement session. For these sessions, we use a large white-board and replicate the matrix on the board. We all have copies of the plan as it exists, and we put new activities and milestones on the white-board. We basically just brainstorm. We identify new "whats," think through the "whens,"

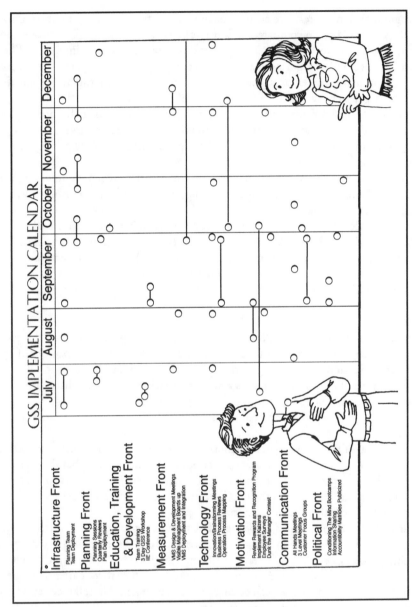

Figure 44. The GSS implementation calendar allows the sequencing of all improvement interventions to be viewed over time.

and tend not to deal with "whos" or "hows" at this stage. Once we are thought out, one person then adds the new items to the old plan, and we distribute that widely for review and critique.

As you continue to do these sessions, your ability to move down the chart and move further out in time will increase. Your depth and breadth of planning will improve as a team. This is part of the large-scale, organizational change learning curve. Learning is occurring with the development of each version of the plan. The chart is a tool to facilitate the ability to think about improvement efforts that are programs rather than just projects. The DDT begins to think more clearly about the 3^n-ball problem. As their collective knowledge of the fronts begins to improve, the quality of their initiatives behind each front improves, and, consequently, the overall performance improvement effort improves.

Developmental Guidance for the Change Master
It is essential that the change master develop project or program management knowledge and skills. First, learn how to be a good project manager. Start with small, relatively simple, low-risk projects. Study tools of project management and try using them to develop discipline. Strive for more attention to detail and to write everything down at first; with experience, tasks will become second nature and you can back off on the detail and explicitness.

Once your knowledge and skills of project management have been developed, you can begin to explore the realm of program management (the 3^n-ball problem). I would not suggest that the inexperienced change master start their career with a GSS, large-scale organizational change program until they had developed good project management skills and a solid foundation in the change matrix and the core areas of technical competence.

Time management, meeting management, stress management, and small-group behavior are knowledge and skill areas that complement project and program management. Getting these skill areas under your belt will be essential to success with project and eventually program management. Understanding the business, and its requirements for success, is also a key. This would suggest that a requirement for an internal change master is some experience with the organization and knowledge of the business. Networking is another key element to success as a project or program manager. Knowing where to go to get information and resources will be crucial. The change master will want to either have or have access to people who are well networked politically, experientially, and technically in the organization.

Again, perfect practice makes perfect. Practicing the tools and acquiring the knowledge of project and program management is necessary to develop solid skills. Discipline will be required; it is often too easy to slack off on rigor and explicitness. Maintaining a high quality, evolving plan for the improvement effort must be the responsibility and accountability of the change master and the DDT.

FINANCIAL DECISION ANALYSIS

Application Issues
As mentioned in Chapter 8, money is the language of management. Improvement efforts will, ultimately, be boiled down to benefits (dollars made or saved) to burdens (dollars

invested, spent) analysis. We can analyze quality improvement, productivity improvement (output/input), innovation, and quality of work life all we want, but managers, owners, and the public are going to want to know about efficiency, about profitability, about more for less.

Perhaps not the bottom line, but certainly an important indicator of improvement, is actual performance in terms of budgetability (what we said we would do compared to what we did in the context of what we said it would cost compared to what it did cost) or profitability (measures of the relationship between revenues and costs). Selling improvement projects and programs will require the change master to be able to speak the language of management. Improvement efforts will have to be sold on the basis of benefits to burdens. Often, detailed financial analysis will be required to justify an investment for a project or within a program. Engineering economic analysis, the ability to forecast or estimate revenue increases and expense increases or decreases over time, and the ability to access accounting and finance data to support decision making, will be required.

Investments of human resources are seemingly less complex than capital investment decisions, as they, on the surface, require only reallocation from one area of effort to another. However, the practical reality of human resource investments is that it is easy to say yes and then later find out that people have been unable to make necessary adjustments in time management. They have overextended themselves and are unwilling or unable to decide what to stop in order to have time to start improvement initiatives. Reallocating resources from one area of endeavor to another is crucial to large-scale organizational change efforts and yet is often the most difficult thing to do. People have a vested interest in keeping things the same. Doing the new is often threatening and therefore resisted. Gaining commitment for the behavior changes necessary for improvement to occur will help to ensure that supporting decisions are made.

What are the theories and models that describe how managers and groups of managers make improvement decisions? What do we know about actual behaviors versus prescribed models of decision making? How can the change master use this understanding to improve the quality of decision making in his or her projects and programs?

Individual, group and organizational decision-making is often complex in the context of improvement projects and programs. Finding resources to support improvement efforts is increasingly difficult today. Justifying improvements that require investments of capital can be technically complex as well as politically challenging. Tools that assist in selling certain investments will be useful and should be used when appropriate. The change master must at least be aware that these tools exist, and although you do not necessarily have to be proficient with respect to these techniques you should be able to access someone who is.

Developmental Guidance for the Change Master
Of course, the first step is for the change master to become acquainted with the language and the literature in the areas of accounting, corporate finance, engineering economic analysis, and decision analysis. The average college graduate would not likely have a background in all four of these areas, so it should become a part of their personal and professional plan of development. One book in each area would serve to at least familiarize the change master with the language, theory, principles, and methods. We list some examples of books that might suffice as a starting point at the end of this section. For additional information and insights, the change master might consult with a cutting-edge

professor at a local university as to the current best reference in each area. We did so, but there will certainly be differences of opinion.

Acquaintance with the field is certainly not sufficient for reduction to practice. This overview serves to let the change master know what they don't know as well as to help them better understand these four related areas. It would be beneficial to be networked to an expert or two in these areas if you are engaged in a program that is of any magnitude and will involve a great deal of decision analysis. Most larger organizations have a staff of financial analysts that can consult with the DDT as they confront complex decisions.

Read and study in these four areas. Develop more detailed knowledge and skills as appropriate. Practice using decision-analysis tools. Work with teams to help them improve their abilities to posture decisions so they are supported. Use specially trained human resources, such as industrial engineers for engineering economic analysis, financial analysts for tax implications and corporate trade-offs, and psychologists, sociologists, or organizational development specialists for group decision-making aid.

Use the appropriate level of decision analysis and support. Balance instinct and intuition with fact and data-based analysis to support improvement decisions. Develop an appropriate amount of structure for teams to utilize as they attempt to make decisions or sell decisions. Most importantly, begin to develop decision rules within the organization in terms of empowerment. We have suggested the three-type rule development—Type I, Type II, and Type III. Build a slate of examples that begin to operationalize these types of decisions within the organization. Teach newcomers these decision rules. In a relatively stable system with adequate education, training, and development, and fairly mature employees, it is a good idea to err on the side of asking for forgiveness rather than permission if, in fact, you are trying to empower and drive rates of improvement and are willing and able to accept a few mistakes along the way. If this is the case, teaching teams and individuals how to think through down-side risk assessment will be useful.

Much has been written recently about the inadequacy of our accounting systems in supporting problem solving and decision making aimed at optimizing the system (see Kaplan as an example). Dr. Deming suggested that the most important figures are "unknown and unknowable." The change master will need to have a firm grasp of the principles of sound measurement to support improvement systems in the context of existing accounting and finance systems. The best measurement and evaluation system is an appropriate blend of the quantitative with the qualitative. The change master must learn to balance these as he or she crafts measurement-to-data-to-information-to-decision and action systems and strategies. Perhaps the challenge is to maintain flexibility, the ability to rely on one approach in one situation while utilizing an opposite approach in another situation.

Decision analysis isn't all tools and techniques and numbers; it's a bit of common sense too.

SYSTEM AND PROCESS IMPROVEMENT

Application Issues
Process improvement has been the foundation or cornerstone of TQM. Many TQM efforts focus, almost exclusively, on training employees how to do process improvement.

Recently, the scope of process improvement has extended to what are called business processes. Business processes are really systems in our language; certainly they are very large, cross-functional processes. In a strict sense, there are just a few (three to seven or so) business processes in any organization. They begin and end with the customer or user. They usually are not "owned," in that no one 'is organizationally responsible for them.

Whether we are improving a small process owned by an individual worker, work team or work cell, or a large process, the method of improvement is fundamentally the same. In industrial engineering we call this methods engineering. It has been around since the earlier part of this century.

Developed originally to simplify work so that unskilled laborers would not introduce excess variation in how a task was performed, methods engineering has evolved, largely due to Japanese innovations, to be a tool used by an increasingly better educated workforce to self-reduce variation in method, thus reducing variation in performance. In the early part of this century, methods improvement was done by industrial engineers to workers; today, industrial engineers are teaching and training employees how to do methods improvement. Again, the methods are essentially the same; the aim is the same; however, the people using methods engineering have changed and expanded.

Figure 45 is an adapted example of a business process re-engineering process flow diagram used by Texas Instruments. Figure 46 depicts an example of a methods engineering process flow diagram as applied to a much smaller process. Note the similarities. The figures portray basically the same method applied to different levels of processes. Applying the methodology to a business process is obviously more complex, just as GSS, large-scale organizational change is more complex than a single improvement project. In fact, business process re-engineering is an example of large-scale organizational change. Texas Instruments and others (Hammer and Champ) reinforce this fact in their descriptions of successful re-engineering projects. It's not the method, as depicted in the figure, that is complex and difficult; it is the peripheral activities that must be managed that create the challenge: learning how to get the organization to optimize the system as opposed to optimizing the subsystems, learning how to create cross-functional trade-offs, learning how to reallocate resources to ensure that the business process is effective and efficient, breaking down barriers, learning how to create bold visions for how the business process should be working—thinking outside the box, if you will.

Developmental Guidance for the Change Master

Increasingly, the change master will be required to understand methods engineering, process improvement, business process engineering or re-engineering. This will be an area of technical competence that must be well developed. In addition, the tools of quality will have to be understood, and the change master must be able to use them and teach them on demand in different situations.

The steps to development of knowledge and skill in this area are similar to those outlined in the other areas. First, read and study. We provide a good list of references to get you started at the end of the section. Practice using the tools. Learn when to take short-cuts and when not to. Don't take short-cuts at first; use the tools as intended even though it seems like over-kill. You want to develop discipline and learn the tools in the right fashion. Practice with simple applications and processes at first and evolve to larger, more complex processes. In working with clients, it is important to know that they will almost

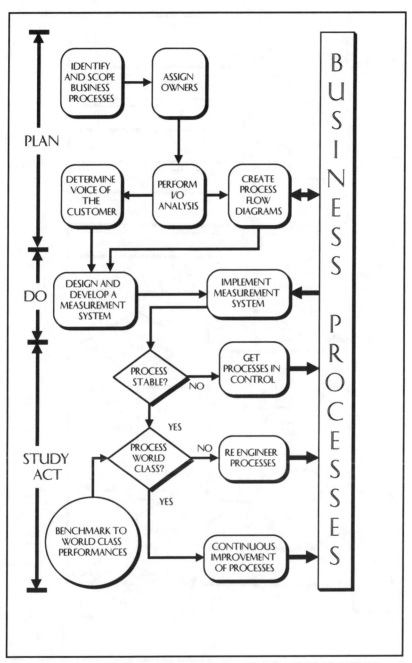

Figure 45. Business process re-engineering in a process flow diagram (adapted from Texas Instruments).

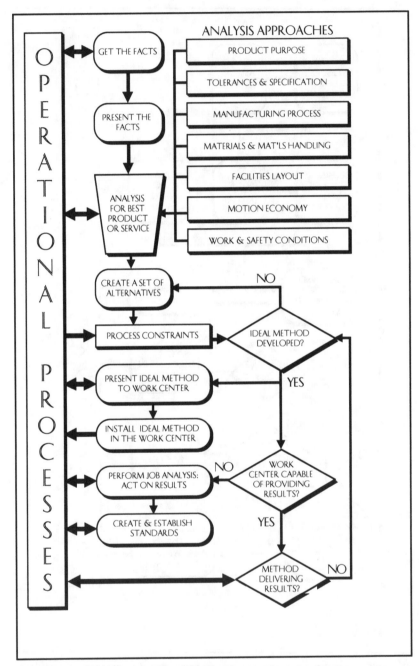

Figure 46. Traditional methods engineering in a process flow diagram (adapted from Niebel).

always defer to short-cuts and sloppy use of the tools. It is a painful exercise, for example, to apply a process flow diagram to a process with which you are very familiar. There are a number of ways to portray any given process, so it is important not to get hung up on perfection while learning to use the technique.

Seek out situations or applications where there is a good fit between the technique and the need. Find situations where process improvement clearly will work and where you can build a successful example inside your particular setting. You then will be able to use this example to sell other attempts within the organization. In general, you want to tackle processes that aren't too small or too large. This sounds obvious, but it is a critical issue. If you tackle a process too small, you may optimize it but not cause any improvement in the larger system; in fact, you might even cause things to get worse; it may be a process that would be eliminated if tackled at the larger system level. On the other hand, if you tackle a process too large, you may have so many uncontrollables that you bog down and eventually fail.

CONCLUSION

It was difficult to know how to approach presenting methods and tools for the change master both in Chapter 8 and in this chapter. Striking the balance between helping you understand the area of technical competence and detail on specific tools was a challenge for us. We opted for ensuring you understand the scope of the area of technical competence and for providing you with more than ample guidance on specific sources of information for professional development in these areas. We understand that there will be "voice of the customer" variation (perhaps wide) in what you expect and require in terms of technical development. We relied on our experience with typical change masters for TQM efforts to guide our presentation of the material.

Clearly, we have presented only sufficient material to introduce you to the area of technical competence; in that respect we have perhaps added only perspective. The development of a growing "tool kit" is a major aim of the change master. You must be learning at a rate more rapid than those around you to succeed. The challenge you face is one of making depth and breadth decisions.

One of my graduate students recently confronted me with a question of whether the change master is a generalist or specialist. I think I surprised the student when I said both. The change master must be a generalist, have a broad but not necessarily deep understanding of all of these areas of technical competence (and probably more), but must at the same time have some Level 3, 4, and even 5 knowledge in certain areas. I consider myself a generalist in all of the areas listed and a specialist in measurement, problem solving, and planning. I have both formally and informally been educated, in some cases trained, in all of the areas. In some cases this means I know enough to be dangerous. Actually, it means I am at least acquainted with Levels 1 and 2 knowledge in these areas, in most cases also Level 3 (methods). It does not mean I could do the methods. I am a student in all of these areas, more active in some than in others. I want to be able to converse intelligently with specialists in all areas. I want to know specialists in all areas, so I can refer clients to them when appropriate. I know what I don't know. This is often as important as the reverse.

The next chapter provides you with a method for managing an individual transformation. We urge you to take a continuous improvement orientation as you develop your personal and professional plan of study and development. Don't evaluate where you are or have been, concentrate on improving your knowledge and skills associated with leading and helping individuals, groups, and organizations improve their performance. This last chapter is the capstone. We can help you with the method for self-designed change, but we can't ensure that you try out new methods and behaviors and reinforce them. You have a lifetime to accomplish your individual transformation. Make the most of it.

CHAPTER 12

A METHOD FOR INDIVIDUAL TRANSFORMATION

This chapter builds on the works of Senge, Covey, Peck, Monetta, Rickover, Baldwin, and others. It assumes that you, the change master, and others in your organization take individual responsibility for personal and professional improvement. It assumes that you can apply the matrix on yourself with the aim of improving. It assumes that you are willing to pay the price to improve personally and professionally. It assumes that you have a "burning platform," that your level of dissatisfaction with the status quo is sufficiently high for you to adopt our proposed next steps.

THE CONCEPTUAL IMAGE DOCUMENT AND PERSONAL/ PROFESSIONAL PLAN OF STUDY AND DEVELOPMENT

The first step is for you to develop what we call a Conceptual Image Document and Personal and Professional Plan of Study and Development. This document is comprised of four parts, and both the personal and professional dimensions of your life should be considered as you address each part.

1. What is your conceptual image of yourself? What are your strengths? What are your weaknesses? What value do you add to your organization? What do you know about your personality, your cognitive style? How do others see you? What are your values, beliefs, principles? Who are you? What do you do?
2. What is your vision for yourself, personally and professionally? If your life were on tape and you could fast forward the tape and see how it plays out, how would it end if you just kept doing what you are doing, kept heading where you are heading? How do you want it to play out? Create two alternative scenarios, how the tape will play out if you just keep doing what you are doing now and how you want the tape to play out.
3. What are your five-year personal and professional goals or objectives? How do these relate to your vision(s)? What do you want to accomplish, personally and professionally, in the next five years?
4. What is your personal and professional plan or program of study and development? What will you read, do, experience, observe, think through, to continue to improve and to move in the direction of your goals and vision? We suggest that you map out your plan of study in three- to six-month intervals and that you have twelve to eighteen months thought through. Have the next three to six months thought through in great detail; the rest of the plan of development can be more vague at this point. We encourage you, as have Peck, Covey and Baldwin, to think through actions you will take to improve spiritually,

physically, mentally, individually and as a couple or family, and as a team within your organization.

What is your initial reaction to these 4 sets of questions and the document they represent?

• Too logical, too rational, too formal;
• I already do this, not quite as formally, but I do it;
• I don't need to do this;
• Sounds interesting, I might try it;
• I'll do it now;
• Sounds hard, would require a lot of thought, would be painful, would force me to address some questions I don't want to think about;
• Thinking of my life on a tape is uncomfortable. Thinking through to the end of my life is depressing; I don't want to do that;
• My life won't end; I've lived previous lives; I'll live future lives; life is just an experience; I go with the flow; I don't need this formal planning;
• This is not my style;
• I'm already improving, don't need this;
• I've had all the learning I need to get through my career and life, the rest is just experiential learning;
• I think this is important. I've read Covey and Senge, and others but I never thought about a method of operationalizing what they have talked about. This sounds like it would be interesting and fun and challenging. I'd like to give it a try, have others in my organization try it, have my spouse try it, and then share our thoughts to spark cooperation and potential synergy.

We have found that these type of reactions are not uncommon. Answering the questions the first time is, for most, very difficult and even painful. There is a tendency to want to get it perfect. We aren't accustomed to answering these types of questions. We often aren't in touch with ourselves as much as we think. We tend not to be very reflective.

As you begin to write your responses to these questions, we suggest you force your "editor" mind out and let your "creative" mind take over. Just put the pencil or pen to paper or fingers to the keyboard and let your thoughts flow. Don't judge what comes out. Just get your thoughts down. Set the product aside for a day. Come back to it and read it carefully, without editing or judging. Jot down notes as you reread the document—your reactions, your questions, your uncertainties. Don't change the words, just take notes on your reactions. Set the result aside and come back to it again in another day or so. Make a separate list of things you would change, at this point, in the original product; don't change the original product, just make the list. Set that list aside and come back to it in another couple of days.

Now, on the basis of what you think and feel at this point, what specific actions are you going to take in the next thirty to 120 days to improve personally and professionally? Answer part 4 again, only this time in much more detail. Now you are ready to manage yourself through the phases of change.

Think about what mode of professional functioning you need to be in with yourself at various phases of change over the next thirty to 120 days. For example, I am constantly setting a goal to exercise more. I am aware of the need to exercise; I know how. I have spent over $3,000 on exercise equipment and yet I continually fail to try out and reinforce new behaviors. I simply am not willing to pay the price. My behaviors suggest I am more willing to accept and live with the consequences than to manage my life differently and change my behaviors. It's not a willingness or ability or skill problem, it's simply a paying the price problem. So, I have to be a challenger with myself. I have to get angry with myself and be tough on myself. I have to enforce more discipline in this area than I have shown in the past. I have to examine forces for and against this area of change and improvement.

So it will be with you. There will be certain areas of change and improvement that will be more painful and difficult than others. The important thing is for you to clearly establish your vision and your next steps; to make your plan and then work your plan. Periodically assess how you are doing. I think it is important not to be too hard on yourself early out. If you are doing any of the things on your personal and professional plan of development, congratulate yourself.

I also find that this somewhat disciplined, formal process "gets on my nerves" after a while, so I give myself a break. I back off for three months and then come back to it when I am re-energized to instill the discipline associated with the process.

At first, I revised the document every six months. I kept the old versions so that I could review the past periodically and reinforce my progress. After a point, the document got to a point where I was pretty satisfied with Parts 1-3, and they became somewhat stable. I spent most of my time, once a year, working on question 4. The document became a living document; I carry it around in my notebook with me and revisit it periodically. I do not manage directly from it. It influences my behavior; it does not constrain my behavior or overly structure what I do. It is a much more informal process of influencing what I do than it might appear on the surface. At the end of the year I look back at progress and performance and am often amazed at how much I have accomplished. Although there are always areas for improvement, areas where I haven't made as much progress as I would have liked, over a period of two or three years I have seen a positive difference.

GUIDANCE ALONG THE WAY

The change master, the leader, the manager, or the target typically want help to improve their knowledge and skills relative to performance improvement. They want to know what they should be reading and studying, what courses they should be taking, what they should be experimenting with, etc. So we have begun to assemble a "cafeteria"-style list that we believe might serve as a baseline from which to work.

We'll reintroduce you to the concept of levels of knowledge and then ask you to audit where you are relative to being a change master. We want you to think about your levels of knowledge relative to phases of change, professional modes of functioning, and the technologies of quality and productivity improvement. This audit will be useful for you as you begin to develop your personal and professional plan of study and development. We also will ask you to think through levels of knowledge for the targets of performance improvement. What knowledge and skills do your sponsors require, and how will you help them along with their own personal and professional plans of development? What knowledge and skills do your clients need, and how will you, as change master, help them improve their abilities to improve performance over time?

LEVELS OF KNOWLEDGE

To reiterate, theories of learning suggest that there are levels of knowledge one can have relative to any given subject. We propose that there are five levels of knowledge relative to quality and productivity improvement:

Level 1   Concepts, Theories, Models, Principles
Level 2   Operational Definitions
Level 3   Methods
Level 4   Skills
Level 5   Profound
       — Can teach, can improve
       — Theory of psychology, appreciation for systems, theory of knowledge, understanding of variation and theory of statistics.

Any subject can be taught at various levels. One can understand the theory of total quality and the transformation but have weak operational definitions. One can have quite a full tool kit and be reasonably skilled at using the tools but not really understand the theory behind them, and thus be restricted in applications and unable to move to Level 5. In general, it is intuitively obvious that one cannot be at Level 5 unless one has passed through Levels 1-4. However, one might not be a master at Level 4 with respect to a given technique yet still may have profound knowledge.

It is not uncommon today for individuals to be trained at Level 3 and fail at Level 4. We believe this is because they are doing something in the absence of understanding why. They know what and how but not why. They end up being a hammer looking for a nail to pound; everything looks like a nail. One could make this observation about SPC zealots; everything can be solved with Statistical Process Control. Or, everything can be solved with strategic planning, or employee involvement, or operations research, or reorganization, or measurement, or better communication, or....

LEVELS OF KNOWLEDGE AS THE BASIS FOR SELF-DESIGNED CHANGE

The change master might begin by auditing his or her level of knowledge relative to the matrix and relative to the tools and technologies of quality and productivity improvement. You will be asked to do this exercise at the end of this chapter. This audit might serve, then, as a foundation for building your professional plan of development. The results would indicate a gap between where you need to be relative to knowledge and skills associated with postive change management and the technologies of improvement. This audit represents a self-awareness phase of change for the change master. The audit serves as an important triggering device. It identifies gaps and helps direct you as you begin to craft your professional plan of development.

Our theory and method (Level 1 and 3) suggest that you would then self-evaluate and develop self-designed change strategies. The key then is to force yourself to move into the last two phases of change. This will require experimentation and the willingness to take some risks. If you are doing this in the context of a larger organizational effort to learn, then you will likely be in a supportive culture. However, if you do not succeed in getting sponsors and targets involved in the professional development exercise, then you may find it is more difficult to experiment with new techniques, methods, and behaviors.

Finding an affinity group of change masters to benchmark to and share experiences with will further support your learning efforts. Professional conferences, divisions or special interest groups in professional societies such as the Institute of Industrial Engineers, Academy of Management, the American Quality and Productivity Managers Association, or the American Society for Quality Control are natural vehicles for such opportunities. Local and regional quality councils are quite common today, and these groups represent geographically focused affinity groups in some respects.

STAGES IN BECOMING A LEARNING ORGANIZATION

Learning organizations are made up of learning individuals. Clearly, the change master must become a learning individual, but how do you translate this process to others and ultimately to the organization? You, as an individual, will go through predictable stages of change as you develop your ability to do the conceptual image process and develop and execute your personal and professional plans of study and development. We have found that, once a critical mass of individuals in the organization embark on this learning and development process, the organization tends to pass through the following five stages relative to learning and to performance improvement.

Stage One: Awareness, enlightenment, "altar calls," sense of urgency, call to arms—all represent one stage of change that you and those in your organization will pass through. Leadership gets its wake-up call. The burning platform is addressed. Leadership understands its obligation. There is a commitment of a critical mass of resources to make the transformation. Thus, Phases 1 and 2 of change are complete, but often Phases 3 and 4 are inadequately addressed or skipped over entirely. Symptoms of jumping to Phase 5 (self-designed change) prematurely include: trying out new behaviors and methods, but not giving them time to work and skipping from one quick fix to the next for awhile. Leadership gets disenchanted and either moves through this as a result of continued learning or abandons the large-scale effort and regresses to the old style and methods. If the organization is doing well enough, this may be an option that appears to be the solution.

Stage Two: This stage is marked by premature enthusiasm and a naive understanding of the scope and magnitude of the change required. In this false learning curve (Figure 47) period, a little knowledge does a lot of damage. Symptoms of this stage include: simple solutions for complex problems, treating symptoms rather than causes, interfaced solutions rather than integrated solutions, compliance rather than commitment, solutions that are not strategically thought through, or aerobic step up, step down approach versus staircase approach. Again, passage to the next stage is a function of the degree of "sticktuitiveness," their strength of vision, and the extent to which leadership continues to learn about the transformation. Benchmarking on the part of leadership is often a key activity in this stage. Recognition that the effort must be staffed and otherwise resourced properly occurs at the tail end of this phase.

Stage Three: Appreciation for a system and large-scale organizational change begins to emerge. Grand Strategy System approaches are "tinkered with." Continuous learning has gotten a critical mass of leadership and managers to this stage. They recognize that quick fixes and interfaced solutions won't work. They are beginning to comprehend the

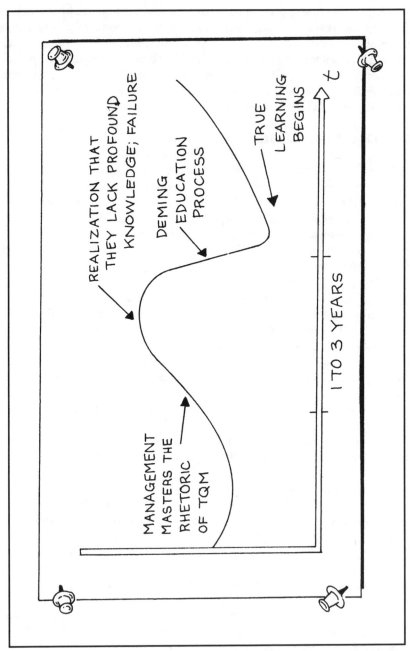

Figure 47. Change masters personally work through the false learning curve in addition to guiding their clients.

"transformation" as described by Dr. Deming and others. They know what they don't know and have plans for systematically acquiring sufficient knowledge and skills for the organization to survive the knowledge revolution described by Drucker. They fully appreciate the importance of proper balance between "B," "A," and "C." They are beginning to understand the interrelationships among the key fronts or subsystems and are systematically driving progress against them via the planning front. The distinction between implementation and system-wide deployment is beginning to sink in. There is still a tremendous amount of inefficiency and ineffectiveness. Communication and coordination are emphasized, although actual improvement is still deficient. Conflict, distrust, fear, and lack of knowledge and skills are still evident within pockets of the organization.

Stage Four: The organization is approaching prime with respect to the transformation. They have done very well in their self-assessments and external assessments with Malcolm Baldrige or U.S. Senate Productivity and Quality Award processes. There are very few pockets of resistance, fear, or distrust. A minimal level of knowledge and skills in terms of improvement exists throughout, and in many areas Levels 1-4 knowledge with respect to basic improvement is pervasive.

The organization is much more proactive; there is a greater degree of alignment and attunement. All fronts are at a stage of development that is at least satisfactory. There is a grand strategy that is clearly thought through for the next three to seven years; it is a living plan, there is widespread visibility for the strategy, and it is deployed within the organization such that it guides all improvement efforts. Most importantly, the measurement systems are beginning to register both quantitative and qualitative results. The organization is exceeding customer requirements, meeting or exceeding expectations, and delighting customers periodically. There is a strong culture supporting various types of improvement. There is a strong sense on the part of all that they are on a winning team. There is a clear understanding of what each and every person can and must do to succeed.

Stage Five: The organization is going beyond being a fast follower and is clearly a leader in the field. They are benchmarked to frequently. "B" is 15-25% of almost everyone's job (in some cases as high as 100%). "C" is uncommon; it exists, but it is almost predictable, in quantity at least, and there are plans for how the organization manages "C." "A" is stable and predictable. Business development is truly strategic.

It is unlikely that the organization will experience financial problems that it cannot survive because the integration of existing products and services is so good that there is a steady stream of new, revenue generating opportunities. Periods of downturn are predicted, and coping mechanisms are so well developed that job security is a non-issue.

The organization is winning with people; it is selecting and retaining the highest caliber professionals. Education, training, and development is 10% of budget on a constant basis, and when people are in areas that suffer downturns their training goes as high as 100%. People are truly seen as the organization's most valuable resource and treated accordingly.

There are ongoing and significant problems that the organization faces, yet they are met as opportunities. The organization is filled with people who accept that succeeding is difficult, who accept that maintaining this stage of success is difficult and are continuously learning how to cope with this difficulty. Rate of learning is so rapid that the organization's leaders are frequently challenged by their followers.

It seems that the change master's most significant task lies in getting the organization from stage one to two, and two to three. Regression is less likely once an organization gets to stage three; however, it is common in stages one and two. The key is to gain enough momentum with the planning front to get key leaders to a point where they are "hooked" enough to press through the first two stages, particularly the false learning curve discussed by Scholtes. As mentioned previously, the education/training/development front (ETD) and the measurement front may be the two most crucial in this regard. ETD ensures they keep learning while measurement ensures they benchmark and that they are provided with feedback and reinforcement.

REQUIREMENTS FOR SUCCESS IN MOVING THE ETD FRONT FORWARD
The secrets to keeping the education/training/development front moving forward at a rate that will support forward progress of other fronts are fivefold:

1. Unrelenting dedication to training as central to survival by the top leadership in the organization;
2. Staffing, restaffing, and retraining or reprogramming properly for leadership in this front and functional area;
3. Protecting appropriate resources for this front;
4. Developing a grand strategy within this front;
5. Ensuring that the Conceptual Image Process and the Personal and Professional Plan of Development Process are pervasive.

Organizational leaders must significantly elevate the functions responsible for education and training in terms of esteem and influence. These functions must be actively, not passively, involved in the organization's grand strategy. One visible leader and champion stands out for us when it comes to the education/training/development front — Bob Galvin of Motorola. The several times I have heard him speak, his dominant theme has always been education and training. His belief in cause-and-effect relations regarding training investment are so strong that he developed his own university within the organization, Motorola U. He is the champion for a program called The University Challenge TQM Partnership (discussed in Case Example 2b) that brings together major private sector organizations and universities in an attempt to promote total quality in higher education. The change master must strive to find a champion within the organization for the education/training/development front and assist that person in becoming visible, vocal, and influential concerning this front.

Training departments and human resource departments, in general, are extremely provider oriented. This has occurred, in our opinion, because they are often poorly staffed and under-resourced. Training and personnel often are not powerful or influential, are not held in high regard, and are seen as being bureaucratic, inefficient, ineffective, and not customer driven. Their model for training seems comprised of two strategies: (a) provide the standard "bill of fare" training at the lowest possible cost to satisfy the common training needs in the organization or (b) when possible and called upon to do so, find the lowest-cost provider of specialized training to meet specific needs of internal customers.

Many training specialists in organizations today do not understand total quality, are striving to optimize the efficiency criterion, and do not evaluate outcomes. However, in their defense, they are usually willing workers who are victims of the system. The system has downgraded the performance of training departments so baldly that re-engineering often is required. We somewhat boldly suggest:

• Completely restaffing the function, the ownership for the education/training/development front, with individuals who are enlightened and will lead this front proactively.

If that is not possible, then:

• Completely retrain or reprogram the training function such that the personnel in that function are proactively driving the grand strategy for that front and the front is an integral component of the organization's overall grand strategy.

I personally don't believe that anything short of these two actions will suffice. I have been working with, through, around, and in spite of training functions for over twenty years. This function is broken and needs fixing. Quality of education and training is extremely poor in most cases, resulting in limited training dollars being thrown away. Educators and instructors are not viewed as partners in the process. Training is not integrated into performance improvement. Education, training, and development ought to be viewed as a crucial means to our end. It should be viewed as a mechanism to help us improve performance; in most cases it is viewed as something that takes us away from our "A" and our "C." Participants most often are prisoners or tourists rather than true participants. Course materials go up on the shelf, course certificates go up on the wall, and nothing changes. We check the boxes and get back to business as usual.

The personnel issue is part of the larger resource issue. As mentioned before, the training budget is the most susceptible to being cut first in periods of downturn. Paradoxically, there seems to be philosophical agreement that it should be the last thing cut during bad times. This is a classic case where we aren't "walking the talk." The emerging benchmark from world-class organizations like Corning and Motorola is that 5-10% of each employee's annual hours, or approximately 100-200 hours, should be spent in education, training, and development. Most organizations average 0.5-1%. Dr. Deming and Mr. Galvin have suggested that the type of training is almost irrelevant, that better people make better organizations. This is why Covey and Baldwin stress the interwoven nature of personal and professional development.

In the organization of the future, individuals will be empowered to take ownership for their personal and professional development. They will coordinate their actions within teams, teams will communicate and coordinate with each other, and the organization will have a front team owner who ensures individuals and groups are making progress on their plans. Building a sufficient budget to achieve and sustain this vision will be a project that the change master, in conjunction with organizational leaders, must address.

To summarize, the deployment of a process by which individuals are expected to create and utilize their own personal and professional plans of development must be an integral part of the overall education, training, and development strategy. I believe that these documents should form the foundation for a completely re-engineered performance assessment process. It may not be possible to throw out performance measurement and evaluation; however, I do think it is possible to re-engineer this process so it supports the aims of continual improvement and the overall aims of the system.

CASE EXAMPLE 4: EDUCATION, TRAINING AND DEVELOPMENT— THE PRESCRIPTION FOR SUCCESS AT OMEGA HOSPITAL

Omega Hospital is a 400 bed, nonprofit health care facility located in Atlanta, Ga. Until the late-1980s, total quality management was a foreign concept to Omega's top management team. Then, largely as a result of visibility created by the National Demonstration Project on Quality Improvement in Health Care (headed by the Juran Institute), Todd, Omega corporate vice president, developed a keen interest in total quality management and its potential benefits.

Todd's interest was well founded. Omega was struggling to control costs and increase productivity in an intensely competitive service environment. A myriad of factors, including the introduction of Diagnostic Related Groups (DRGs) to the Medicare payment system, the rapid growth of Health Maintenance Organizations (HMOs), and heightened government intervention through regulation had culminated in unprecedented operational challenges to health care providers nationwide.

Todd realized that to make total quality management and the notion of Grand Strategy System and large-scale organizational change pervasive would require a strong push on education and training. This would truly be a new way of thinking for his organization.

CAST OF CHARACTERS

Todd — Corporate vice president, Omega Hospital, and the sponsor of Omega's improvement effort.

Cheryl — A research associate at the Georgia Quality and Productivity Center, Cheryl specializes in the education, training, and development front.

Vivian — Director of Omega's School of Leadership.

Karen — A research associate at the Georgia Center, and the Omega Grand Strategy System project manager.

Cheryl stood at the white-board in her office, dry erase marker in hand. She had spent the better part of the day working on the education, training, and development front for Omega Hospital. How could she integrate all the pieces into an approach that would produce results for Omega?

Omega was about nine months into the planning and implementation of a grand strategy system for the hospital. This effort had originated shortly after Todd, the corporate vice president, had heard a presentation by Cheryl's Atlanta-based quality and productivity center and had contacted them for assistance.

At the outset of Omega's effort, a nine-member Design and Development Team had been formed. They had attended one boot camp at the Georgia Quality and Productivity Center and had struggled through the completion of a version 1.0 Grand Strategy System plan. The Design and Development Team was on a steep part of the learning curve, and their frustration had been evident both during and after the boot camp session.

Two months into the project, Cheryl had been brought onto the center's project team to assist with education, training, and development for the DDT. Her function had been to design an intense plan of study and development which would get the team "up to speed" and able to manage the task at hand. However, Todd clearly had additional plans for the education, training, and development front at Omega. He envisioned that in order to sustain rate of improvement for the long term, it would be necessary to create "second generation" change masters, a core group of individuals within the organization who could continue to carry the effort forward well into the future. He tasked Cheryl with establishing this "Change Masters Affinity Group," and with ensuring this group's education and training progressed to meet Omega's emerging needs.

Todd also wanted to improve the quality of Omega's internal training function. Six years earlier, the hospital had created the School of Leadership to ensure a strong focus on the continuing education needs of Omega employees. The School of Leadership currently had four full-time staff members and offered, according to their mission statement, "professional development programs for the purpose of improving efficiency, effectiveness, and the quality of life throughout the organization." The School had come under increasing criticism lately for being too provider-driven and generally ineffective.

Todd had asked Cheryl to conduct a situation appraisal with Vivian, the director of the School of Leadership, and make recommendations for how the School could better align itself to support Omega's improvement efforts. Cheryl had quickly arranged a trip to Omega to facilitate the start-up meeting of the newly formed Change Masters Affinity Group and to initiate a situation appraisal with the School of Leadership.

The Affinity Group meeting had been a breath of fresh air. The twelve group members, hand-picked by Todd, seemed to Cheryl to be bright, eager, and full of potential. The average age of the group members was, Cheryl estimated, approximately 23. Cheryl had concluded that this would be an advantage—no excess "baggage" to contend with, still somewhat of a student mentality, not enough years of experience to have become entrenched within the system.

During the two-hour meeting, Todd had verbally chartered the group, addressed a few questions, then departed, leaving Cheryl to lead the remainder of the meeting. Cheryl facilitated the group through the development of ground rules and meeting procedures, had group members elect individuals to fill the roles of convener, recorder, and reporter, then identifed dates for the next three months' worth of bi-weekly meetings. The meeting adjourned with a great sense of accomplishment and anticipation.

After a hurried lunch in the hospital cafeteria, Cheryl met with Vivian to discuss the School of Leadership. Prior to this meeting, Todd had cautioned Cheryl that Vivian might come across as territorial and protective of "her" function, and Cheryl sensed this was the case, although on the surface Vivian appeared pleased to have Cheryl's assistance. Cheryl was careful to play acceptant listener and avoid the challenger or expert modes. If she were going to work with Vivian and help achieve some significant breakthroughs in the School of Leadership, she would have to tread carefully. Cheryl worked hard in her meeting to get Vivian to articulate key problems and opportunities.

Without being very specific, Vivian talked about her desire to improve the complete training process, from needs assessment to design, development, delivery, and evaluation. She alluded to the fact that the School had lost credibility within the organization. She indicated that staffing and budget constraints had compromised the School's ability to improve existing course offerings and to add new course offerings in a timely and high-quality fashion. Cheryl listened attentively, taking copious notes. Where appropriate, she wove into the conversation benchmarking examples of education and training approaches from other organizations, such as the Saturn plant in Smyrna, Tenn., and Motorola. Vivian expressed a strong interest in learning more about what other organizations were doing in this regard. The meeting concluded with plans for Cheryl to identify which existing courses she could review and enhance and present her recommendations to Vivian.

Back at the Georgia Center, Cheryl had made arrangements for three members of the Omega Design and Development Team to attend an upcoming offering of the Center's Performance Improvement Engineer education and training course. This course had been designed and developed by the Center to help change master teams build their knowledge and skills. Participation in the course was by invitation only and was offered to teams of change masters from selected organizations. Cheryl believed that this course would provide an effective "shot in the arm" for a subset of the Omega DDT and allow for additional work on the organization's Grand Strategy System plan.

The course had gone well, as expected. There were a total of 18 participants representing six diverse organizations. The following topics were presented during the 2.5 day-session:

- Professional modes of functioning and phases of change;
- A Grand Strategy System for performance improvement;
- The Deming philosophy;
- An operational definition of TQM;
- Strategic planning for performance improvement;
- Business process re-engineering;
- Management of change;
- Establishing an infrastructure for continuous improvement;
- Creating a personal and professional education, training, and development plan.

During the training, participants were given two major tasks: one was to create or enhance an eighteen-month grand strategy for their organization, the other was to develop an 18-month personal plan of study. Over the course of the 2.5 days, participants had three opportunities to work on these exercises and present their work, obtaining feedback from both the course instructors and other participants. This small-group work was interspersed with educational interventions. During the repeated presentation of plans, participants gained platform and presentation experience. This also provided them an opportunity to "think (and learn) out loud." Although unplanned, the other participants at times operated in a red team fashion, challenging presenters on perceived gaps, omissions, and faulty logic, which provided valuable input presenters could use to improve their plans.

To assist in the creation of personal development plans, participants had been given an extensive listing of resources — books, conferences, workshops, videotapes, self-assessment instruments, journals — all categorized by front. They were given a template on which to document their past, present, and future with respect to their own personal and professional development. Center associates had a table set up containing some carefully selected books, and during breaks, they watched as small groups of participants gathered around the table and discussed the various resources on display. The opportunity to access resources in this fashion invariably influenced the motivation front for personal and professional development.

The course also was structured for a high degree of participant interaction out of the classroom. Social activities had been planned carefully to give participants an opportunity to benchmark to each other in terms of organizational and personal improvement efforts.

The Omega team had left the course with some definite next steps for their own development, as well a more comprehensive grand strategy for the organization. Cheryl was confident that they had come away with enough new knowledge and skills to mobilize the rest of the DDT for moving forward.

That was six months ago, and this afternoon as Cheryl stood at the white-board in her office, she was both pleased with and worried about events that had unfolded at Omega. The Design and Development Team was performing well. They had continued to refine and expand their Grand Strategy System plan, had established front owners and teams and targeted some specific improvement projects to initiate. Every member of the DDT had completed a conceptual image document and personal and professional development plan, and the DDT members who attended the Performance Improvement Engineer training session had come back to Omega and presented a condensed version of what they had learned to the other team members. Karen, the Georgia Center's project manager and change master for the Omega Grand Strategy System effort, had continued to keep the DDT focused on working through the plan of study Cheryl had laid out, and according to Karen, and to the DDT, it was making a difference.

Cheryl's current role with the DDT was primarily that of a resource adviser — she often received calls or faxes from DDT members who wanted recommendations about what to read or what conference or workshop to attend on a particular topic. Cheryl, too, was proactive in sending packets of articles and reference information to the DDT on a regular basis. She knew the Center had another offering of the Performance Improvement Engineer training session scheduled in two months, and reminded Karen that this would be a good opportunity to get the remaining DDT members through the program. For now, the education, training, and development front for the Omega DDT was "in control."

By contrast, the School of Leadership effort was still somewhat of a perplexity, and the Change Masters Affinity Group seemed to Cheryl to be teetering on the brink of failure. As Cheryl had entered her fourth month as facilitator of the Change Master Affinity Group, to a person members began struggling to understand the purpose of the group. Todd had not provided a written charter and had been fairly inconsistent in the verbal messages he gave the group: during one meeting he stated they were simply there to learn, while at another meeting he said that the group needed to demonstrate some tangible results to the organization; during one meeting he pointed out that members needed to share information about their "A" projects, while at another meeting he said they should discuss "B"-type activities; during one meeting he said that the Change Masters Affinity Group was a top priority for Omega, while at yet another meeting he stressed that all members had jobs to do and could not let their work suffer because of participation in the group.

This last statement highlighted another concern Cheryl had — the amount of time Todd was willing for group members to devote to this effort. They were allowed to meet every other week for two hours, and quarterly for one-day offsite retreats; all other work such as reading, education, and training was to be done entirely on their own time. Cheryl was amazed that Todd would expect this to be sufficient for imparting change master knowledge and skills. She had tried to use an analogy with Todd that she thought he would find relevant — she asked him if it would be reasonable to expect someone to become a surgeon if they had only two hours every two weeks and one day every three months to study and develop their knowledge and skills. Todd had said he understood the point, but the operational realities of the business would not support taking these talented people away from their assigned tasks for more than this short amount of time.

Despite the group's lack of focus, Cheryl was still impressed by the eagerness and willingness she saw among most members. By now there were several prisoners on the team who made little attempt to disguise the fact that their continuing participation was only due to the fact that they didn't want to risk the "wrath of Todd." It was clear to her that they were struggling to understand what this was all about. They wanted direction and clarity in what they were supposed to accomplish and how they were supposed to spend this time. Several group members had mentioned that their department managers were increasingly beginning to question their involvement in the affinity group. What was being accomplished, and what was in it for the department, they wanted to know. Cheryl had begun to ponder these questions herself.

This afternoon, Cheryl wrote on her whiteboard: "Change Masters Affinity Group: Requirements for Success." Underneath this heading she wrote:

1. Written charter from the group's sponsor
2. Management commitment and support
3. Member commitment
4. Clearly documented plan of study.

With these four key requirements identified, she felt she could begin to think through a strategy for getting the group unstuck. She immediately began to draft a plan of study and after two hours' work was pleased with what she had developed. Cheryl decided to adopt a structured approach to learning for the CMAG, with quarterly plans of study and a very specific "curriculum" for each quarter. Affinity Group members would work on small-group assignments, and most importantly would get a chance in group meetings to practice the skills they were acquiring. Figure 48 provides excerpts from the CMAG's first quarter plan of study.

With respect to the School of Leadership, Cheryl had identified a list of existing course offerings she proposed to review and enhance: Process Improvement, Effective Meetings, Facilitation Skills, Managing Change, Teamwork, Advanced Team Management, Creative Thinking, Process Management, Team Problem Solving and Decision Making, Project Management, and Serving Internal Customers as a Team. These courses had only recently been designed and developed, with the intent of supporting Omega's growing focus on total quality management and performance improvement. However, as Cheryl had reviewed the course materials, she got a strong sense that they fell far short of their purpose. She saw little integration of concepts across courses, a piecemeal approach that had no apparent path of progression. As Cheryl flipped through overhead after overhead, she began to suspect that these courses were being conducted for the most part in straight lecture mode, with few opportunities for participation by attendees. Furthermore, for the team-related courses, the School had made no effort to manage enrollment such that the training was attended by actual teams within the organization. Consequently, individual

CHANGE MASTER AFFINITY GROUP (CMAG) 1ST QUARTER PLAN OF STUDY

LEARNING OBJECTIVES:

- TO DEVELOP AN APPLIED UNDERSTANDING OF HOW INDIVIDUALS, GROUPS, AND ORGANIZATIONS MANAGE POSITIVE CHANGE AND IMPROVEMENT;
- TO DEVELOP UNDERSTANDING AND IMPROVED ABILITY TO APPLY PROFESSIONAL MODES OF FUNCTIONING IN SPECIFIC SITUATIONS;
- TO DEVELOP INCREASED KNOWLEDGE OF, VISIBILITY FOR, AND INVOLVEMENT IN IMPROVEMENT EFFORTS UNDERWAY AT OMEGA;
- TO DEVELOP AND IMPLEMENT PERSONAL AND PROFESSIONAL PLANS OF STUDY AND MAINTAIN DISCIPLINED USE OF THOSE PLANS FOR ACQUIRING KNOWLEDGE AND SKILL;
- TO CLARIFY THE ROLE THAT CHANGE MASTERS PLAY IN ORGANIZATIONS TODAY AND IN THE FUTURE;
- TO LEARN DIFFERENT QUALITY TOOLS AND HOW TO APPLY THEM;
- TO IMPROVE PRESENTATION AND COMMUNICATION SKILLS;
- TO HELP EACH OTHER BECOME BETTER TEACHERS AND LEARNERS.

"BY WHAT METHOD" WE WILL LEARN:

MEETING FACILITATION
THROUGHOUT THE QUARTER, TEAMS OF FACILITATORS WILL BE ASSIGNED TO LEAD/FACILITATE ONE CMAG MEETING. FACILITATORS WILL WORK WITH CHERYL AND THE CMAG CONVENER TO ENSURE ADEQUATE PREPARATION FOR "THEIR" MEETING. FACILITATOR TEAMS ARE RESPONSIBLE FOR DEVELOPING NOT ONLY THE METHOD FOR LEADING THE GROUP THROUGH THE TOPICAL DISCUSSION, BUT ALSO FOR THE FEEDBACK AND ASSIGNMENT FOR THAT PARTICULAR MEETING. FACILITATOR TEAMS WILL PRACTICE AND BE EVALUATED ON APPLICATION OF THE PROFESSIONAL MODES OF FUNCTIONING DURING THEIR ASSIGNED MEETING.

BETWEEN MEETING ASSIGNMENTS
READING ASSIGNMENTS, AS OUTLINED IN THE QUARTER PLAN, MUST BE COMPLETED IN A TIMELY FASHION IF CMAG MEMBERS ARE TO PARTICIPATE ACTIVELY IN MEETING DISCUSSIONS AND ACQUIRE KNOWLEDGE AND SKILLS AT AN ACCEPTABLE RATE.

FEEDBACKS
FEEDBACKS WILL BE GIVEN AS SCHEDULED THROUGHOUT THE QUARTER. A FEEDBACK WILL CONSIST OF THREE TO FIVE OPEN ENDED QUESTIONS THAT ENCOURAGE CMAG MEMBERS TO INTEGRATE WHAT THEY ARE LEARNING FROM THEIR GROUP MEETINGS, READINGS, AND PERSONAL EXPERIENCE. FEEDBACKS WILL NOT BE "GRADED;" THEY ARE INTENDED TO PROVIDE CMAG MEMBERS WITH A MECHANISM FOR GUAGING THEIR RETENTION OF MATERIAL AND DEPTH, BREADTH, AND RATE OF LEARNING.

Figure 48. A sample change master plan of study.

employees from different departments were attending these courses with no opportunity to apply what they were learning during the training and little opportunity for post-training application because there was a good chance that their co-workers had not yet been exposed to the training concepts.

Cheryl had pointed out some areas for improvement to Vivian, and Vivian had given her the go ahead to consolidate, integrate, and enhance the courses Cheryl proposed. But Cheryl believed that this effort represented only the tip of the iceberg—there was still much more work to be done to align the School of Leadership with Omega's strategic direction. For example, the School had little to offer to support the needs of the Design and Development Team or the Change Masters Affinity Group. Vivian was vaguely familiar with these two teams, but she had only a superficial knowledge of what they were working on and what their education and training needs were. She had assumed that the School's current course offerings would be sufficient for these groups, but in fact the courses were so generic and basic that they simply were not suitable. Further, Cheryl was waiting for an opportune time to challenge Vivian on the School's purpose statement. Cheryl had kept coming back to the words, "provider of professional development programs." To her this evoked images of educational courses and classroom training types of initiatives. Cheryl believed that the School's purpose should be to facilitate the dissemination of knowledge and information for improving the performance of individuals, groups, and the organization. There were many ways to do this, and classroom instruction was but one mechanism. She had realized that she would have to approach this gradually with Vivian, first successfully completing the course consolidation and enhancement, then coming back with a proposal for re-engineering the School of Leadership.

Having thought through and some definite next steps for the Change Masters Affinity Group, and identified a strategy for the School of Leadership, Cheryl felt optimistic that there would soon be tangible progress on the education, training, and development front for Omega.

CONCLUSION

Becoming a change master requires unrelenting dedication to a career of helping organizational systems improve. There aren't formal curricula or programs of study for becoming a change master. There are some programs that provide a better foundation than others; the option of creating a one-of-a-kind, multidisciplinary program of study and development exists at many universities, and management systems engineering programs within industrial engineering exist in a few universities.

Change masters will come from many backgrounds: human resources, industrial engineering, industrial psychology or sociology, management, organizational development, and statistics to name a few. Augmenting this discipline-specific education is a lifelong process.

In this closing chapter, we have outlined the Conceptual Image Document and Personal and Professional Plan of Development. We encourage you to complete and update this document every six months. We also have expanded our discussion of education and training beyond that of the change master to the organizational system and to the individuals within this system. We have advocated re-engineering the training function within your organization. Further, we have suggested that you, early on, develop an education/training/development front grand strategy that is aligned with and supportive of the overall grand strategy of your organizational system. Finally, we have strongly suggested that you encourage all individuals in the organization to participate in the process of personal and professional planning and development. Learning organizations are made up of learning individuals: We must teach individuals how to establish discipline with respect to their own continuous improvement.

The development work at the end of this section is perhaps the most important of the book. It represents the commitment on your part to put this book to work for you and your organization. It represents Phases 5-7 of the change process for you. It will not be easy to try out these new behaviors.

We would hope that by this point you believe developing a critical mass of change masters within your organization is necessary for success. We are, by training and preference, methodologists. The title "By What Method?" is appropriate for our emphasis. We believe that we have provided at least the following answers to the title question:

• Section 5 provides a method by which a change master can lead and manage quality and productivity improvement—the Change Master Matrix — the integration of phases of change, modes of professional functioning, and technologies of improvement.
• Section 5 provides a method by which to do "large-scale organizational performance improvement"—the Grand Strategy System.
• This last section and chapter provides a method by which you can begin to develop the knowledge and skills of a change master.

We haven't told you enough. It isn't necessarily a failing on our part, it's just that this book must be a living book. It requires participation to make the book useful to you and your organization. You have to do more than read it; you have to study it and you have to engage yourself in the development work. You alone can move from the Levels 1-3 information and knowledge presented here to Level 4 and ultimately level 5. We can challenge you to do this; we have operated in that mode and in the teacher and expert solution provider mode throughout the book. We can't do situation appraisal with you, so we don't know your present phase of change and evolution. We can say this, however: there is no more rewarding a profession than that of a helping profession. There are many needs in our world today — the need for quality and productivity improvement is among the mightiest.

DEVELOPMENT WORK

INQUIRY QUESTIONS
These are questions you have for yourself or for others to help you better understand what was covered in this section.

Inquire First
What didn't you understand, what do you want to know about, what assumptions or beliefs do we posit that you want us to explain, what do you want clarification on?

Advocate Second
What did you disagree with, what do you want to argue about, what didn't you like, what do

you want to challenge, in what areas do we appear to have different assumptions, data bases, beliefs, or attitudes?

LEARNING EXERCISES

LE 6.1 You have, by this point, developed at least one version of your personal and professional plan of study. Take whatever version you have to the next version now that you have completed this book. Use the resources listed at the end of each section as a source of input for your development, but don't be limited to those reading-oriented things. Make sure you have a mix of reading, viewing, experiencing, studying, discussing, teaching, presenting, etc. to ensure that you are developing broadly.

LE 6.2 Update and enhance your matrix and tool kit diagnosis exercise done earlier. At this point you should have the ability to do a good personal diagnosis as to where your strengths and weaknesses (areas for development) are. In doing this exercise, continue to think about the meaning of true intellectual honesty. Are you being honest with yourself when you assess your level of knowledge relative to the change matrix and areas of technical competence?

Level of Knowledge and Skills:
0 Never heard of this, don't have foggiest idea what this is or how to do it;
1 Have heard about them;
2 Know what they are, have read about them;
3 Have studied a method for doing these or have studied the tool itself;
4 Have used the tool at least once, have tried to do this at least once;
5 Have used the tool, done this many times, have experimented with different ways of using/doing in different situations, am quite proficient at the tool or area;
6 Have taught this, written about it, have improved upon the tool, have developed new tools for this area.

Core Technology Areas:
   Planning
   • Nominal Group Technique or Delphi
   • Input/Output Analysis (created appreciation for system)
   • Vision Creation
   • Assumptions Generation and Analysis
   • Guiding Principles Generation
   • Vision to Goals to Objectives to Strategies and Actions to Measures Auditing
   • Hoshin Kanri (policy deployment)
   • Visible Management Systems
   • Planning System (system-wide)
   • Implementation Management
   • Create linkages among I, G, O levels so that plans are better communicated and coordinated

Measurement
   • Total or Multi-Factor Productivity Measurement Model

- Multi-Criteria Performance Measurement Technique (Objectives Matrix)
- Statistics, Statistical Tools, Tools of Quality
  — Control charts
  — Pareto analysis
  — Run charts
  — Histogram
  — Cause-and-effect diagram, root cause analysis
- Information System Design and Development
- Measurement to Data, Data Collection
  — Surveys
  — Logs
  — Observation data collection
  — Time studies
  — Work sampling
  — Archival data collection
- Information portrayal
  — Tables, figures, charts
- Data storage and retrieval, files, filing, architecture
- Exploratory data analysis

Problem-solving
- Kepner-Tregoe or equivalent (structured problem solving)
- Creative problem solving
- Design and development
- Decision analysis and decision making
- Implementation analysis, potential problem solving
- Evaluation

Motivation
- Equity Theory
- Expectancy Theory
- Job Characteristics Theory
  — Job Diagnostic Survey/Job Characteristics Inventory
  — Job Enrichment
- Reinforcement Theory
  — Gainsharing
  — Recognition system

LE 6.3 Work with a group or organization to expose them to the notion of Conceptual Image Document and Personal and Professional Plans of Development. Teach or present the concept and observe carefully the reactions you get.

LE 6.4 Do a cards exercise; start, stop, and continue exercise with yourself first and then with a group, perhaps your own work group or organization. This involves using 3" x 5" index cards to capture the major tasks that are accomplished (take up time) for an individual or group. You can get fancy and use different color cards to represent levels of tasks or types of tasks (e.g., "A", "B", "C"), but it isn't necessary. Once the individual or group has identified most major tasks on cards they can spread them out on a table and begin to process the cards. Which can or should be delegated? Which should be stopped, don't add value, aren't a priority? Which should be continued in same fashion or perhaps in an improved fashion? Which cards aren't on the table that should be? Think about how cards get added, get modified, and get taken off "your plate." How does this exercise relate to time management? Do you always know what is the most important card on your plate at any given point in time? Do you always work the most important card on your plate, or do you work the urgent not necessarily important or the easy or fun or simple? How can you use this exercise to improve your own personal performance?

LE 6.5 It has been observed that you can't build teamwork until the individuals on the teams know themselves and know each other. One approach to doing this is to complete self-diagnosis instruments, perhaps with the aid of experts in those instruments. We have used the Meyers-Briggs Type Indicator, the DISC instrument, and the Thomas-Kilmann Conflict Mode Instrument over the years to assist in doing this. Many organizations use tools like this in one fashion or another. If you haven't been exposed to these type of instruments, take them. The three we mentioned are a place to start. We provide references for these three to assist. Once you or your group have taken them, discuss what insights they provide. What did you confirm about yourself? What did you learn that you didn't know? Were you intellectually honest enough to be willing to share your results (remember these are not tests, there are no wrong or right, good or bad scores or results) with others in your work group? How can these types of data be used individually and in groups to help understand diversity? Note that the MBTI measures preferences for how data are collected, how they are processed, our orientation to the world around us, and our preference for how long we wait to make decisions or take action. DISC is an instrument that gets at personality dimensions. TKCM measures our tendencies to behave in certain ways in conflict-oriented situations.

LE 6.6 Discuss possible ways of handling the following situations:
A. Top management is extremely skeptical of the possibility and value of TQM or any of these "new" approaches to improvement; they are not well read or very enlightened. They want improvement but don't think the method for improvement is critical; they want results now.
B. Early in the change effort, a participant announces that the whole thing is ridiculous and a waste of time.
C. Several participants in pivotal positions of power do not think statistically, do not have an appreciation for system, are not well read and are not learners (not interested in learning about this stuff), want improvement, but think all of this is just common sense and that the organization just needs to work harder.
D. Several key players constantly suggest that the effort is scoped too large, that there are too many constraints and that they should focus on things they can control only, that the appreciation for system concept is interesting but not pragmatic, some degree of suboptimization is inevitable, they argue for downsizing the scope to something manageably.
E. The education, training, and development front for leadership and for the internal

change masters is clearly way behind other fronts. The training department is pre-Neanderthal in thinking and under-resourced. "A" and "C" are so dominant that any suggestions you make for reading and studying are summarily dismissed. There is not a climate of growth and development in the organization. People are stagnating relative to improvement and paradigms are strong.

F. The notion of doing a Conceptual Image Document and a Personal and Professional Plan of Study is summarily rejected as a waste of time or something that is too formal. The leadership is not supportive of education and training being a significant (5-10% of labor hours) portion of the budget. They see education, training and development as an expense rather than an investment, largely because it has been done so poorly in the past and there have not been perceived benefits.

G. Senior leadership thinks succeeding and surviving are simply a matter of meeting requirements, discipline, control, execution, hard work; they think that succeeding only requires "A" and inevitable "C." They are not in favor of a disciplined, structured, comprehensive improvement effort, certainly not one that requires significant resources.

FEEDBACK QUESTIONS

FBQ 6.1 What are the levels of knowledge? How do the levels we presented correspond to your levels of knowledge and skills? Have you ever thought about learning in this fashion?

FBQ 6.2 Explain the difference between inquiry and advocacy. What would your words for these two concepts be? How cognizant or aware are you when you are doing one versus the other?

FBQ 6.3 What term would you use or does your organization use for the type of person for whom this book has been written? Eli Lilly utilizes the term "performance improvement engineer"; we use the term management systems engineer; Kanter utilized the term "change master."

FBQ 6.4 Does the notion of continuing to develop a syllabus and a plan of study after you graduate from formal education appeal to you? Why or why not? Most of us think that our transcript from college or high school is completed when we graduate. What if we considered our transcript a living document; what if we kept a copy and kept adding to it every three to six months? If you follow through with the Conceptual Image Process and the Personal and Professional Plan of Study and Development, do you think that eventually you will become a learning individual?

FBQ 6.5 Why do people stop learning and growing? What can you do to help others, including yourself, keep learning and growing? Does the thought of sharing your Conceptual Image Document and Personal and Professional Plan of Study and Development appeal to you, threaten you, frighten you? How would doing this exercise as a family or as a work group help to transition from learning individuals to learning groups and organizations?

PLAN OF STUDY

What follows is a list of resources that support, in general, the material introduced in this section. Scan the list, indicate which you have read (R), studied (S), attempted to use (U), and which you would like to become acquainted with (TBD).

The bibliography for this section does not duplicate those sources of information and knowledge identified in Section IV. As you complete this book and your personal and professional plan of study and development, we encourage you to return to the extensive bibliography, by area of technical competence, provided in that section.

LITERATURE CITED

Baldwin, B. A. 1985. *It's All In Your Head: Lifestyle Management Strategies for Busy People.* Wilmington, N.C.: Direction Dynamics.

Deming, W. E. 1986. *Out of the Crisis.* Cambridge, Mass.: MIT Center for Advanced Engineering Study.

Deming, W. E. 1993. *The New Economics.* Cambridge, Mass.: MIT Center for Advanced Engineering Study.

Drucker, P. 1968. *The Age of Discontinuity.* New York: HarperCollins.

Drucker, P. 1989. *The New Realities.* New York: HarperCollins.

Drucker, P. F. 1980. *Managing in Turbulent Times.* New York: Harper and Row.

Hammer, M., and J. Champy. 1993. *Reengineering the Corporation: A Manifesto for Business Revolution.* New York: Harper Collins.

Kurstedt, H. A. 1993. *The Industrial Engineer's Systematic Approach to Management.* MSL working draft and articles and responsive systems article. Blacksburg, Va.: Management Systems Laboratories.

Peck, M. S. 1978. *The Road Less Traveled.* New York: Simon and Schuster.

Peck, M. S. 1993. *A World Waiting to be Born: Civility Rediscovered.* New York: Bantam Books.

Scholtes, P. R. 1988. *The Team Handbook.* Madison, Wis.: Joiner Assoc.

Sink, D. S. 1983. Using the nominal group technique effectively. *National Productivity Review.* Spring, pp. 173-184.

Sink, D. S., and T. C. Tuttle. 1989. *Planning and Measurement in Your Organization of the Future.* Norcross, Ga.: Industrial Engineering & Management Press.

Skinner, L., and C. D. Johnson. Business process engineering at Texas Instruments. *Quality and Productivity Management.* 10(3).

BIBLIOGRAPHY

Decision Analysis (Evaluation, Analysis, Decision-Analysis, Financial and Economic Analysis)

Box, G.E.P., W. G. Hunter, and J. S. Hunter. 1978. *Statistics for Experimenters.* New York: John Wiley.

Duncan, A. J. 1986. *Quality Control and Industrial Statistics* (5th edn.). Homewood, Ill.: Irwin.

Feinberg, S. E. 1991. *The Analysis of Cross-Classified Categorical Data.* Cambridge, Mass.: The MIT Press.

Hoaglin, D. C., F. Mosteller, and J. W. Tukey (eds.). 1983. *Understanding Robust and Exploratory Data Analysis.* New York: John Wiley.

Kececioglu, D. 1991. *Reliability Engineering Handbook.* Vols. I and II. Englewood Cliffs, NJ: Prentice-Hall.

Shewhart, W. A. 1980. *Economic Control of Quality of Manufactured Product.* Milwaukee, Wis.: American Society for Quality Control.

Wheeler, D. J. 1993. *Understanding Variation: The Key to Managing Chaos.* Knoxville, Tenn.: SPC Press.

Wheeler, D. J., and D. S. Chambers. 1992. *Understanding Statistical Process Control* (2nd edn.). Knoxville, Tenn.: SPC Press.

Wheeler, D. J., and R. W. Lyday. 1989. *Evaluating the Measurement Process* (2nd edn.). Knoxville, Tenn.: SPC Press.

Wilson, P. F., L. D. Dell, and G. F. Anderson. 1993. *Root Cuase Analysis: A Tool for Total Quality Management.* Milwaukee, Wis.: ASQC Quality Press.

Leadership/Management of Improvement and Change

Bass, B. M. 1985. *Leadership and Performance Beyond Expectations.* New York: The Free Press.

Bass, B. M. 1990. *Bass & Stogdill's Handbook of Leadership: Theory, Research and Managerial Applications* (3rd edn.). New York: McGraw-Hill.

Belasco, J. A. 1990. *Teaching the Elephant to Dance.* New York: Crown Publishers.

Bennis, W. 1989. *On Becoming a Leader.* Reading, Mass.: Addison-Wesley.

Bennis, W., and B. Nanus. 1985. *Leaders: The Strategies for Taking Charge.* New York: Harper and Row.

Bolman, L. G., and T. E. Deal. 1987. *Modern Approaches to Understanding and Managing Organizations.* San Francisco: Jossey-Bass.

Geneen, H. 1984. *Managing.* New York: Doubleday.

Fukuda, R. 1983. *Managerial Engineering: Techniques for Improving Quality and Productivity in the Workplace.* Stamford, Conn.: Productivity Inc..

Goldratt, E. M., and R. E. Fox. 1986. *The Race.* Croton-on-Hudson, N.Y.: North River Press.

Harris, T. G. 1993. The post-capitalist executive: an interview with Peter F. Drucker. *Harvard Business Review.* May-June, pp. 114-122.

Kanter, R. M., B. A. Stein, and T. D. Jick. 1992. *The Challenge of Organizational Change: How Companies Experience It and Leaders Guide It.* New York: The Free Press.

Kelly, M. 1991. *The Adventures of a Self-managing Team.* San Diego: Pfeiffer and Co..

Kotler, P., L. Fahey, and S. Jatusripitak. 1985. *The New Competition.* Englewood Cliffs, N.J.: Prentice-Hall.

Neusch, D. R., and A. F. Siebenaler. 1993. *The High Performance Enterprise: Reinventing the People Side of Your Business.* Essex Junction, Vt.: Oliver Wight Publications.

Mitroff, I. I. 1983. *Stakeholders of the Organizational Mind.* San Francisco: Jossey-Bass.

Peters, T. J., and R. H. Waterman. 1982. *In Search of Excellence: Lessons from America's Best Run Companies.* New York: Warner Books.

Quinn, R. E. 1988. *Beyond Rational Management: Mastering the Paradoxes and Competing Demands of High Performance.* San Francisco: Jossey-Bass.

Reich, R. B. 1987. *Tales of A New America.* New York: Times.

Schein, E. H. 1992. *Organizational Culture and Leadership* (2nd edn.). San Francisco: Jossey-Bass.

Tateisi, K. 1989. *The Eternal Venture Spirit: An Executive's Practical Philosophy.* Cambridge, Mass.: Productivity Press.

Thomas, J. B., S. M. Clark, and D. A. Gioia. 1993. Strategic sensemaking and organizational performance: linkages among scanning, interpretation, action and outcomes. *The Academy of Management Journal.* 36(2): 239-270.

Vroom, V. H., and A. G. Jago. *The New Leadership: Managing Participation in Organizations.* New York: Prentice-Hall.

Wheatley, M. J. 1992. *Leadership and the New Science: Learning about Organization from an Orderly Universe.* San Francisco: Berrett-Koehler.

Management of Participation

Belasco, J. A., and R. C. Stayer. 1993. *Flight of the Buffalo: Soaring to Excellence, Learning to Let Employees Lead.* New York: Warner Books.

Hackman, J. R. 1986. The psychology of self-management in organizations. *Psychology and Work: Productivity, Change and Employment.* Edited by M. S. Pallack and R. O. Perloff. Washington, D.C.: American Psychological Association.

Kanter, R. M. 1983. *The Change Masters.* New York: Simon & Schuster.

Kanter, R. M. 1989. The new managerial work. *Harvard Business Review.* November-December.

Kilman, R., and T. J. Covin. 1989. *Corporate Transformations.* San Francisco: Jossey-Bass.

Klein, J. A. 1984. Why supervisors resist employee involvement. *Harvard Business Review.* September-October.

Lawler, E. E. 1986. *High Involvement Management.* San Francisco: Jossey-Bass.

Lawler, E. E. 1988. Transforming from control to involvement. In *Corporate Transformation.* Edited by R. Kilmann and T. Covin. San Francisco: Jossey-Bass.

Semler, R. 1989. Managing without managers. *Harvard Business Review.* September-October.

Sink, D. S. 1982. The ABC's of theories X, Y, and Z. *IIE Conference Proceedings.* Norcross, Ga.: IEM Press.

Sink, D. S., L. Shetzer, and D. Marion. 1986. Performance action teams: a case study. *National Productivity Review.* Summer.

Sink, D. S., and L. K. Swim. 1983. Participative problem-solving techniques: when are they appropriate? *IIE Conference Proceedings.* Norcross, Ga.: IEM Press.

Waterman, R. H. 1987. *The Renewal Factor.* Toronto: Bantam.

Waterman, R. H. 1990. *AdHocracy: The Power to Change.* Knoxville, Tenn.: Whittle Direct Books.

Measurement

Adam, E. E., J. C. Hershauer, and W. A. Ruch. 1986. *Productivity and Quality: Measurement as a basis of improvement* (2nd edn.). New York: Prentice-Hall.

Anderson, D. R., D. J. Sweeney, and T. A. Williams. 1981. *Introduction to Statistics: An Applications Approach.* St. Paul, Minn.: West Publishing.

Aragon, G. A. 1989. *Financial Management.* Boston, Mass.: Allyn and Bacon.

Balm, G. J. 1992. *Benchmarking: A Practitioner's Guide for Becoming and Staying Best of Best.* Scharumburg, Ill.: QPMA Press.

Bruns, W. J., Jr. 1992. *Performance Measurement, Evaluation, and Incentives.* Boston, Mass.: Havard Business School Press.

Camp, R. C. 1989. *Benchmarking: The Search for Industry Best Practices that Lead to Superior Performance.* Milwaukee, Wis.: Quality Press.

Christopher, W. F., and C. G. Thor (eds.). 1993. *Handbook for Productivity Measurement and Improvement.* Cambridge, Mass.: Productivity Press.

Cosgrove, C. V. 1986. How to report productivity: linking measurements to bottom-line financial results. *National Productivity Review.* Winter.

Churchill, N. C. 1984. Budget choice: planning vs. Control. *Harvard Business Reviews.* July-August, pp. 150-164.

Craig, C. E., and R. C. Harris. Total productivity measurement at the firm level. *Sloan Management Review.* 14(3): 13-29.

Davis, H. S. 1955. *Productivity Accounting.* University of Pennsylvania, The Wharton School Industrial Research Unit. Major Study No. 37. Reprinted in 1978.

Dixon, J. R., A. J. Nanni, and T. E. Vollmann. 1990. *The New Performance Challenge: Measuring Operations for World-Class Competition.* Homewood, Ill.: Business One Irwin.

Gollop, F. M. 1986. Corporate earnings and productivity analysis. *Working Paper.* Boston: Boston College, Department of Economics.

Hayes, R. F., and K. B. Clark. 1986. Why some factories are more productive than others. *Harvard Business Review.* September-October.

Hall, R. W., H. T. Johnson, and P.B.B. Turney. 1991. *Measuring Up: Charting Pathways to Manufacturing Excellence.* Homewood, Ill.: Business One Irwin.

Hollander, M., and D. A. Wolfe. 1973. *Nonparametric Statistical Methods.* New York: John Wiley.

How to Measure Productivity at the Firm Level. 1978. Short course notebook and reference manual. Houston, Tex.: American Productivity Center.

Japan Productivity Center. 1984. *Measuring Productivity: Trends and Comparisons From the First International Productivity Symposium.* New York: Unpublished.

Johnson, H. T. 1992. *Relevance Regained: From Top-down Control to Bottom-up Empowerment.* New York: The Free Press.

Johnson, H. T., and R. S. Kaplan. 1987. *Relevance Lost: The Rise and Fall of Management Accounting.* Boston: Harvard Business School Press.

Kaplan, R. S. 1984. Yesterday's accounting undermines production. *Harvard Business Review.* July-August.

Kaplan, R. S. 1986. Accounting lag: the obsolescence of cost accounting systems. *California Management Review.* 28(2).

Kaplan, R. S. 1993. Measuring manufacturing performance: a new challenge for managerial accounting research. *The Accounting Review.* 58(4).

Kaplan, R. S. (ed.). 1990. *Measures for Manufacturing Excellence.* Boston: Harvard Business School Press.

Kaplan, R. S. and D. P. Norton. 1993. Putting the balanced scorecard to work. *Harvard Business Review.* September-October, pp. 134-147.

Khadem, R., and R. Lorber. 1986. *One Page Management: How to Use Information to Achieve your Goals.* New York: Morrow.

Kinlaw, D. C. 1992. *Continuous Improvement and Measurement for Total Quality.* Homewood, Ill.: Business One Irwin.

Miller, D. 1984. Profitability = productivity + profitability. *Harvard Business Review.* May-June.

Mundel, M. E. 1975. *Measuring and Enhancing the Productivity of Service and Government Organizations.* Tokyo: Asian Productivity Organization.

Nagashima, S. 1973. *100 Management Charts.* Tokyo: Asian Productivity Organization.

Neter, J., and W. Wasserman. 1974. *Applied Statistical Models.* Homewood, Ill.: Irwin.

Ohio State University Productivity Research Group. 1977. Edited by William T. Morris and George L. Smith. *Productivity Measurement Systems for Administrative Computing and Information Services.* Executive summary and user's manual. Columbus, Ohio: NSF-RANN Research Grant.

Olson, V. 1983. *White-Collar Waste.* Englewood Cliffs, N.J.: Prentice-Hall.

Riggs, H. E. 1981. *Accounting Survey.* New York: McGraw-Hill.

Riggs, J. L., and G. H. Felix. 1983. *Productivity by Objectives: Results-Oriented Solutions to the Productivity Puzzle.* Englewood Cliffs, N.J.: Prentice-Hall.

Senju, S., T. Fushimi, and S. Fujita. 1980. *Profitability Analysis: For Managerial and Engineering Decisions.* Tokyo: Asian Productivity Organization.

Sink, D. S. 1985. *Productivity Management: Planning, Measurement and Evaluation, Control and Improvement.* New York: John Wiley.

Sink, D. S., and T. C. Tuttle. 1989. *Planning and Measurement in your Organization of the Future.* Norcross, Ga.: IEM Press.

Sink, D. S., T. C. Tuttle, and S. J. DeVries. 1984. Productivity measurement and evaluation: what is available? *National Productivity Review.* Summer.

Sloma, R. S. 1980. *How to Measure Managerial Performance.* New York: Macmillan.

Sumanth, D. J. 1987. *Productivity Engineering and Management.* New York: McGraw-Hill.

Spendolini, M. J. 1992. *The Benchmarking Book.* New York: amacom Press.

Thor, C. 1986. Capital productivity within the firm. *National Productivity Review.* Autumn.

Tuttle, T. C., R. E. Wilkinson, W. L. Gatewood, and L. Lucke. 1981. *Measuring and Enhancing Organizational Productivity: An Annotated Bibliography.* Air Force Systems Command, AFHRL-81-6, July.

Van Loggerenberg, B. J. 1988. *Productivity Decoding of Financial Signals.* Pretoria, South Africa: Productivity Measurement Associates.

Van Loggerenberg, B. J., and S. J. Cucchiaro. 1981. Productivity measurement and the bottom-line. *National Productivity Review.* Winter.

Motivation

Doyle, R. J. 1983. *Gainsharing and Productivity: A Guide to Planning, Implementation, and Development.* New York: amacom.

Fein, M. 1981. *Improshare: An Alternative to Traditional Managing.* Norcross, Ga.: IEM Press.

Frost, C. F., J. H. Wakely, and R. A. Ruh. 1974. *The Scanlon Plan for Organization Development: identity, participation, and equity.* East Lansing, Mich.: The Michigan State University Press.

Geare, A. J. 1976. Productivity from Scanlon type plans. *Academy of Management Review.* July.

Henderson, R. I. 1985. *Compensation Management: Rewarding Performance* (4th edn.). Reston, Va.: Reston Publishing.

Kanter, R. M. 1987. The attack on pay. *Havard Business Review.* March-April.

Kohn, A. 1993. Why incentive plans cannot work. *Harvard Business Review.* September-October, pp. 54-63.

Lawler, E. E. 1971. *Pay and Organizational Effectiveness: A Psychological View.* New York: McGraw-Hill.

Lawler, E. E. 1973. *Motivation in Work Organizations.* Belmont, Calif.: Wadsworth Publishing.

Lawler, E. E. 1981. *Pay and Organization Development.* Reading, Mass.: Addison Wesley.

Lawler, E. E. 1985. *Gainsharing Research: Findings and Future Directions.* Los Angeles: Center for Effective Organizations, USC.

Lesieur, F. G. (ed.). 1958. *The Scanlon Plan: A Frontier in Labor-Management Cooperation.* Cambridge, Mass.: MIT Press.

Masternak, R. L. 1993. Gainsharing boosts quality and productivity at a BFGoodrich plant. *National Productivity Review.* 12(2): 225-238.

Moore, B. E., and T. L. Ross (eds.). 1983. *Productivity Gainsharing: How Employee Incentive Programs Can Improve Business Performance.* Englewood Cliffs, N.J.: Prentice-Hall.

Patten, T. H., and M. G. Damico. 1993. Survey details profit-sharing plans: is revealing allocation formulas a performance incentive? *National Productivity Review.* 12(3): 383-294.

Rossler, P. E., and C. P. Koelling. 1993. The effect of gainsharing on business performance at a papermill. *National Productivity Review.* 12(3): 365-382.

Organizational Development

Adizes, I. 1979. Organizational passages—diagnosing and treating lifecycle problems of organizations. *Organizational Dynamics.* Summer.

Adizes, I. 1988. *Corporate Lifecycles: How and Why Corporations Grow and Die and What to Do About It.* Englewood Cliffs, N.J.: Prentice-Hall.

Adler, P. S., and R. E. Cole. 1993. Designed for learning: a tale of two auto plants. *Sloan Management Review.* Spring. pp. 85-94.

Argyris, C., and D. Schon. 1978. *Organizational Learning: A Theory of Action Perspective.* Reading, Mass.: Addison-Wesley.

Garvin, D. A. 1993. Building a learning organization. *Harvard Business Review.* July-August. pp. 78-91.

Hatch, M. J. 1993. The dynamics of organizational culture. *The Academy of Management Review.* 18(4): 657-693.

Isaacs, W. N. 1993. Taking flight: dialogue, collective thinking, and organizational learning. *Organizational Dynamics.* Autumn. pp. 24-39.

Kilmann, R. H. 1975. Designing and developing a "real" organization in the classroom. *Academy of Management Journal.* 18(1): 143-148.

Kim, D. H. 1993. The link between individual and organizational learning. *Sloan Management Review.* Fall. pp. 37-50.

Kofman, F., and P. M. Senge. 1993. Communities of commitment: the heart of learning organizations. *Organizational Dynamics.* Autumn. pp. 5-23.

Leonard-Barton, D. 1992. The factory as a learning laboratory. *Sloan Management Review.* Fall. pp. 23-38.

McGill, M. E., J. W. Slocum, and D. Lei. 1992. Management practices in learning organizations. *Organizational Dynamics.* Summer. pp. 5-17.

Plovnick, M. S., R. E. Fry, and W. W. Burke. 1982. *Organization Development: Exercises, Cases, and Readings.* Boston, Mass.: Little, Brown, and Co.

Ryan, K. D., and D. K. Oestreich. *Driving Fear out of the Workplace: How to Overcome the Invisible Barriers to Quality, Productivity and Innovation.* San Francisco: Jossey-Bass.

Schein, E. H. 1993. On dialogue, culture, and organizational learning. *Organizational Dynamics.* Autumn. pp. 40-51.

Personal and Professional Development

Baldwin, B. A. 1985. *It's All In Your Head: Lifestyle Management Strategies for Busy People.* Wilmington, N.C.: Direction Dynamics.

Bennis, W., and B. Nannus. 1985. *Leaders.* New York: Harper and Row.

Benfari, R. 1991. *Understanding Your Management Style.* Lexington, Mass.: Lexington Books.

Block, P. 1981. *Flawless Consulting*. San Diego: University Associates.

Blanchard, K., P. Zigarmi, and D. Zigarmi. 1985. *Leadership and the One Minute Manager*. New York: Morrow.

Covey, S. 1989. *Seven Habits of Highly Effective People*. New York: Simon and Schuster.

Covey, S. 1991. *Principle Centered Leadership*. New York: SummitBooks.

Covey, S. R., A. R. Merrill, and R. R. Merrill. 1994. *First Things First*. New York: Simon and Schuster.

de Bono, E. 1973. *Lateral Thinking: Creativity Step by Step*. New York: Harper and Row.

DePree, M. 1989. *Leadership is an Art*. New York: Doubleday.

Eble, K. E. 1988. *The Craft of Teaching* (2nd edn.). San Francisco: Jossey-Bass.

Fear, R. A., and R. J. Chiron. 1990. *The Evaluation Interview* (4th edn.). New York: McGraw-Hill.

Forsha, H. I. 1992. *The Pursuit of Quality through Personal Change*. Milwaukee, Wis.: ASQC Press.

Gilbert, T. F. 1978. *Human Competence: Engineering Worthy Performance*. New York: McGraw-Hill.

Hamden-Turner, C. 1990. *Charting the Corporate Mind*. New York: Free Press.

Hampden-Turner, C. 1982. *Maps of the Mind*. New York: Collier.

Heider, J. 1985. *Tao of Leadership*. Toronto: Bantam.

Hersey, P. 1984. *The Situational Leader*. New York: Warner Books.

Hunt, D., and P. Hait. 1990. *The Tao of Time: Time Management for the Real-World—A Right-Brain Approach That Gives You the Control You Need and the Freedom You Want*. New York: Simon and Schuster.

Kolb, D. A. 1984. *Experimental Learning: Experience as the Source of Learning and Development*. Englewood Cliffs, N.J.: Prentice-Hall.

Lowman, J. 1985. *Mastering the Techniques of Teaching*. San Francisco: Jossey-Bass.

Minto, B. 1992. *The Pyramid Principle: Logic in Writing and Thinking*. London: Pitman.

Myers, I. B., and P. B. Myers. 1986. *Gifts Differing* (9th edn.). Palo Alto, CA: Consulting Psychologists Press.

Peck, M. S. 1978. *The Road Less Traveled*. New York: Simon and Schuster.

Peck, M. S. 1993. *A World Waiting to be Born: Civility Rediscovered*. New York: Bantam Books.

Peter, L. J. 1975. *The Peter Plan*. New York: Morrow.

Pirsig, R. 1974. *Zen and the Art of Motorcycle Maintenance*. New York: Bantam Books.

Rickover, H. G. 1991. Thoughts on man's purpose in life. *Quality and Productivity Management*. Blacksburg, Va.: VQPC Virginia Tech.

Robey, D., and W. Taggart. Measuring managers' minds: an assessment of style in human information processing. *Academy of Management Review*. 6(3).

Rubin, L. B. 1983. *Intimate Strangers: Men and Women Together*. New York: Harper & Row.

Seligman, M.E.P. 1991. *Learned Optimism*. New York: Alfred Knopf.

Senge, P. 1990. *The Fifth Discipline*. New York: Doubleday.

Tannen, D. 1990. *You Just Don't Understand*. New York: Ballantine Books.

Wonder, J., and P. Donovan. 1984. *Whole Brain Thinking: Working From Both Sides of the Brain to Achieve Peak Job Performance*. New York: Morrow.

Wankat, P. C., and F. S. Oreovicz. 1994. A different way of teaching. *ASEE Prism*. 3(5): 15-19.

Planning

Akao. 1991. *Hoshin Kanri: Policy Deployment for Successful TQM*. Cambridge, Mass.: Productivity Press.

Below, P. J., G. L. Morrisey, and B. L. Acomb. 1987. *The Executive Guide to Strategic Planning*. San Francisco: Jossey-Bass.

DeGeus, A. P. 1988. Planning as learning. *Harvard Business Review*. March-April.

Gray, D. H. 1986. Uses and misuses of strategic planning. *Harvard Business Review*. January-February.

Hayes, R. H. 1985. Strategic planning—forward in reverse? *Harvard Business Review*. November-December.

Juran, J. M. 1988. *Juran on Planning for Quality*. New York: The Free Press.

Kami, M. J. 1988. *Trigger Points*. New York: McGraw-Hill.

McGinnis, M. A. 1984. The key to strategic planning: integrating, analysis, and intuition. *Sloan Management Review*. Fall.

Mintzberg, H. 1990. The design school: reconsidering the basic premises of strategic management. *Strategic Management Journal*. 11(3): 171-195.

Morrisey, G. L, P. J. Below, and B. L. Acomb. 1988. *The Executive Guide to Operational Planning*. San Francisco: Jossey-Bass.

Pfeiffer, W. J. (ed.). 1986. *Strategic Planning: Selected Readings*. San Diego: University Associates.

Pfeiffer, W. J., L. D. Goodstein, and T. M. Nolan. 1986. *Applied Strategic Planning: A How to Do it Guide*. San Diego: University Associates.

Schoemaker, P.J.H. 1992. How to link strategic vision to core capabilities. *Sloan Management Review*. Fall, pp. 67-81.

Quality Management

Aguayo, R. 1990. *Dr. Deming the American who taught the Japanese about Quality*. New York: Carol Publishing.

Albrecht, K. 1988. *At America's Service*. New York: Warner Books.

Albrecht, K. 1990. *Service Within: Solving the Middle Management Leadership Crisis*. Homewood, Ill.: Irwin.

Albrecht, K., and Zemke, R. 1985. *Service America*. Homewood, Ill.: Dow Jones Irwin.

Blackburn, R., and B. Rosen. 1993. Total quality and human resources management: lessons learned from Baldrige Award-winning companies. *The Academy of Management Executive* VII(3): 49-66.

Conway, W. E. 1992. Quality management in an economic downturn. *Quality Progress*. XXV(5): 27-29.

Davis, T. 1993. Effective supply chain management. *Sloan Management Review*. Summer, pp. 35-46.

Dobyns, L., and C. Crawford-Mason, C. 1991. *Quality or Else: The Revolution in World Business* (a companion to the IBM-funded PBS series). Boston: Houghton-Mifflin.

Dyer, J. H., and W. G. Ouchi. 1993. Japanese-style partnerships: giving companies the competitive edge. *Sloan Management Review*. Fall, pp. 51-63.

Easton, G. S. 1993. A Baldrige examiner's view of U.S. total quality management. *California Management Review*. 35(3): 32-54.

Gabor, A. 1990. *The Man Who Discovered Quality: How W. Edwards Deming brought the Quality Revolution to America—the stories of Ford, Xerox and GM*. New York: Penguin Books.

Garvin, D. A. 1988. *Managing Quality*. New York: The Free Press.

Gehani, R. R. 1993. Quality value-chain: a meta-synthesis of frontiers of quality movement. *The Academy of Management Executive*. VII (2): 29-42.

Gitlow, H. S., and S. J. Gitlow. 1987. *The Deming Guide to Quality and Competitive Position.* Englewood Cliffs, N.J.: Prentice-Hall.

Glasser, W. 1990. *The Quality School.* New York: Harper Perennial.

Gluckman, P., and D. R. Roome. 1990. *Everyday Heroes: From Taylor to Deming: the Journey to Higher Productivity.* Knoxville, Tenn.: SPC Press.

Harrington, H. J. 1987. *Poor-Quality Cost.* New York: Marcel Dekker.

Hauser, J. R. 1993. How Puritan-Bennett used the house of quality. *Sloan Management Review.* Spring, pp. 61-70.

Hiam, A. 1992. *Closing the Quality Gap: Lessons from America's Leading Companies.* Englewood Cliffs, N.J.: Prentice-Hall.

Hosotani, K. 1992. *Japanese Quality Concepts: An Overview.* White Plains, N.Y.: Quality Resources.

Hudiburg, J. J. 1991. *Winning with Quality: The FPL Story.* White Plains, N.Y.: Quality Resources.

Hunt, D. V. 1992. *Quality in America: How to Implement a Competitive Quality Program.* Homewood, Ill.: Irwin.

Jacobsen, G., and J. Hillkirk. 1986. *Xerox American Samurai: The behind-the-scenes story of how a corporate giant beat the Japanese at their own game.* New York: Collier.

Juran, J. M. 1989. *Juran on Leadership for Quality: An Executive Handbook.* New York: The Free Press.

Juran, J. M. 1993. Made in U.S.A.: a renaissance in quality" *Harvard Business Review.* July-August, pp. 42-50.

Juran, J. M., and F. M. Gryna. 1993. *Quality Planning and Analysis* (3rd edn.). New York: McGraw-Hill.

Kanatsu, T. 1990. *TQC for Accounting: A New Role in Companywide Improvement.* Cambridge, Mass.: Productivity Press.

Kano, N. 1993. A perspective on quality activities in American firms. *California Management Review.* 35(3): 12-31.

Kilian, C. S. 1992. *The World of W. Edwards Deming* (2nd edn.). Knoxville, Tenn.: SPC Press.

Lawler, E. E., III, S. A. Mohrman, and G. E. Ledford. 1992. *Employee Involvement and Total Quality Management: Practices and Results in Fortune 1000 Companies.* San Francisco: Jossey-Bass.

Luther, D. B. 1992. Advanced TQM: measurements, missteps, and progress through key result indicators at Corning. *National Productivity Review.* 12 (1): 23-36.

Mann, N. R. 1987. *The Keys to Excellence: The Story of the Deming Philosophy.* Los Angeles: Prestwick.

Miller, R. I. (ed.). 1991. *Applying the Deming Method to Higher Education: for more effective human resource management.* Washington, D.C.: College and Personnel Association.

Scherkenbach, W. W. 1988. *The Deming Route to Quality and Productivity: Road Maps and Roadblocks.* Washington, D.C.: Ceep Press.

Scherkenbach, W. W. 1991. *Deming's Road to Continual Improvement.* Knoxville, Tenn.: SPC Press.

Seymour, D. T. 1992. *On Q: Causing Quality in Higher Education.* New York: Macmillan.

Shewhart, W. A. 1986 (original work 1939). *Statistical Method: from the viewpoint of quality control.* New York: Dover Publications.

Shiba, S., A. Graham, and D. Walden. 1993. *A New American TQM: Four Practical Revolutions in Management.* Portland, Ore.: Productivity Press.

Sink, D. S. 1989. TQM: the next frontier or just another bandwagon to jump on? *Quality and Productivity Management.* 7(2).

Sink, D. S. 1990. Total quality management is... *Quality and Productivity Management*. 8(2).

Sink, D. S., and D. D. Acker (eds.). 1988. *Managing Quality and Productivity in Aerospace and Defense*. Fort Belvoir, Va.: Defense Systems Management College.

Steele, J. 1993. Implementing total quality management for long- and short-term bottom-line results. *National Productivity Review*. 12(3): 425-441.

Steeples, M. M. 1992. *The Corporate Guide to the Malcolm Baldrige National Quality Award*. Milwaukee, Wis.: ASQC Press.

Sullivan, L. P. 1986. The seven stages in company-wide quality control. *Quality Progress*. May.

Townsend, P. L., and J. E. Gebhardt. 1992. *Quality in Action*. New York: John Wiley.

Wallace, T. F. 1992. *Customer Driven Strategy: Winning through operational excellence*. Essex Junction, Vt.: Oliver Wight.

Walton, M. 1986. *The Deming Method*. New York: Perigee.

Walton, M. 1990. *Deming Management at Work: six successful companies that use the quality principles of the world-famous W. Edwards Deming*. New York: C.P. Putnam's.

Zeithaml, V. A., A. Parasuraman, and L. L. Berry. 1990. *Delivering Quality Service: Balancing Customer Perceptions and Expectations*. New York: The Free Press.

Quality Principles, Deming's Fourteen Points

Deming's point four: a study. 1988. *Quality Progress*. December.

Meyers, H. N., N. E. Kay, and J.R.P. French. 1965. Split roles in performance appraisal. *Sloan Management Review*. January-February.

Mintzberg, H. 1986. The manager's job: folklore and fact. *Management Classics*. Edited by M. T. Matteson and J. M. Ivancevich (3rd edn.). Plano, Tex.: Business Publications.

Pirsig, R. 1991. *Lila: An Inquiry into Morals*. New York: Bantam Books.

Rosander, A. C. 1991. *Deming's 14 Points Applied to Services*. Milwaukee, Wis.: ASQC Press.

System and Process Improvement

Kaufman, R. S. 1992. Why operations improvement programs fail: four managerial contradictions. *Sloan Management Review*. Fall, pp. 83-93.

Short, J. E., and N. Venkatraman. 1992. Beyond business process redesign: redefining Baxter's business network. *Sloan Management Review*. Fall, pp. 23-38.

Theory of Knowledge/Philosophy of Science

Kuhn, T. S. 1970. *The Structure of Scientific Revolutions*. Chicago: University of Chicago.

Lewis, C. I. 1929. *Mind and The World Order: Outline of a Theory of Knowledge*. New York: Dover Publications.

Tools/Methods of Quality and Productivity Improvement

Akao, Y. (ed.). 1990. *Quality Function Deployment: Customer Requirements into Product Design*. Cambridge, Mass.: Productivity Press.

Akao, Y. (ed.). 1991. *Hoshin Kanri: Policy Deployment Successful TQM*. Cambridge, Mass.: Productivity Press.

Akiyama, K. 1991. *Function Analysis: Systematic Improvement of Quality and Performance*. Cambridge, Mass.: Productivity Press.

Bendell, T., J. Kelly, T. Merry, and F. Sims. 1993. *Quality: Measuring and Monitoring*. London: Century Business.

Bossert, J. L. 1991. *Quality Function Deployment: A Practitioner's Approach.* Milwaukee, Wis.: ASQC Press.

Brassard, M. 1989. *The Memory Jogger Plus.* Methuen, Mass.: Goal/QPC.

Byrne, D. M., and S. Taguchi. 1987. The Taguchi approach to parameter design. In *Quest for Quality* by M. Sepehri. Norcross, Ga.: IIE.

Carr, L. P. 1992. Applying cost of quality to a service business. *Sloan Management Review.* Summer. pp. 72-77.

Competitive Benchmarking: What it is and what it can do for you. 1987. Stamford, Conn.: Xerox Coporate Quality Office, Reference No. 700P90201.

Feigenbaum, A. V. 1983. *Total Quality Control* (3rd edn.). New York: McGraw-Hill.

Gitlow, H., S. Gitlow, A. Oppenheim, and R. Oppenheim. 1989. *Tools Methods for the Improvement of Quality.* Homewood, Ill.: Irwin.

Grant, E. L., and R. S. Leavenworth. 1988. *Statistical Quality Control.* New York: McGraw-Hill.

Harrington, H. J. 1987. *The Improvement Process: How America's Leading Companies Improve Quality.* New York: McGraw-Hill.

Harrington, J. H. 1991. *Business Process Improvement: The Breakthrough Strategy for Total Quality, Productivity, and Competitiveness.* New York: McGraw-Hill.

Hauser, J. R., and D. Clausing. 1988. The house of quality. *Harvard Business Review.* May-June, pp. 66-73.

Imai, M. 1986. *Kaizen: The Key to Japan's Competitive Success.* New York: Random House.

Ishikawa, K. 1982. *Guide to Quality Control.* Tokyo: Asian Productivity Organization.

Ishikawa, K. 1985. *What is Total Quality Control? The Japanese Way.* Englewood Cliffs, N.J.: Prentice-Hall.

Ishikawa, K. 1990. *Introduction to Quality Control.* Tokyo: 3A Corporation.

Japan Quality Control Circles: Quality Control Circle Case Studies. 1972. Tokyo: Asian Productivity Organization.

Juran, J. M. 1992. *Juran on Quality by Design: the New Steps for Planning Quality into Goods and Services.* New York: The Free Press.

Kaizen Teian 1: Developing Systems for Continuous Improvement through Employee Suggestions. 1992. Cambridge, Mass.: Productivity Press.

Kaizen Teian 2: Guiding Continuous Improvement Through Employee Suggestions. 1992. Cambridge, Mass.: Productivity Press.

Krismann, C. 1990. *Quality Control: An Annotated Bibliography (through 1988).* White Plains, N.Y.: Quality Resources.

Mills, C. A. 1989. *The Quality Audit: A Management Tool.* New York: McGraw-Hill.

Mizuno, S. 1990. *Company-wide Total Quality Control.* White Plains, N.Y.: Quality Resources.

Mizuno, S. (ed.). 1988. *Management for Quality Improvement: The 7 New QC Tools.* Cambridge, Mass.: Productivity Press.

Nemoto, M. 1987. *Total Quality Control for Management: Strategies and Techniques from Toyota and Toyoda Gosei.* Englewood Cliffs, N.J.: Prentice-Hall.

Ozeki, K., and T. Asaka. 1990. *Handbook of Quality Tools.* Cambridge, Mass.: Productivity Press.

Quality Control Circles at Work. 1984. Tokyo: Asian Productivity Organization.

Robson, G. D. 1991. *Continuous Process Improvement: Simplifying Work Flow Systems.* New York: The Free Press.

Sullivan, L. P. 1986. Quality function deployment. *Quality Progress.* June.

Taguchi, G., E. A. Elsayed, and T. Hsiang. 1989. *Qualtiy Engineering in Production Systems.* New York: McGraw-Hill.

Talley, D. J. 1991. *Total Quality Management: Performance Cost Measures, the Strategy for Economic Survival.* Milwaukee, Wis.: ASQC Press.

Watson, G. H. 1992. *The Benchmarking Workbook: Adapting Best Practices for Performance Improvement.* Cambridge, Mass.: Productivity Press.

INDEX

About the Authors

D. Scott Sink, Ph.D., P.E., is professor and director of the The Center for Organizational Performance Improvement. Dr. Sink received B.S.I.S.E., M.S.I.S.E., and Ph.D. degrees from The Ohio State University in 1973, 1977, and 1978, respectively. He is a past President of the Institute of Industrial Engineers and the President of the World Academy of Productivity Science. Dr. Sink has authored three books and over fifty papers on the subject of quality and productivity. During the past twenty years, Dr. Sink has been very active as an educator, a researcher, an author, and a consultant. His focus is on reduction to practice of state of the art and science theories, models, and methods in the area of quality and productivity.

William T. Morris' career spanned thirty years in government, education, and industry before he retired in 1981. He received a bachelor of science degree from Massachusetts Institute of Technology in 1950, masters and Ph.D. degrees from The Ohio State University in 1953 and 1956, respectively. Dr. Morris taught and lectured for twenty-eight years, occupying faculty and chair positions at Ohio State. From 1980 to 1981 he was a Fullbright Lecturer at Tribuvan University in Nepal.

Dr. Morris has authored several books on industrial engineering, engineering economy, personal finance, and management. He holds Fellow status with the Institute of Industrial Engineers, the Academy of Management, and the World Academy of Productivity Science,

About The Performance Center
at Virginia Tech

Since 1980, The Performance Center has been helping organizations and individuals worldwide achieve results through quality and productivity management. The Performance Center is a "teaching hospital" type organization housed in the department of Industrial and Systems Engineering at Virginia Tech. The center's purpose is to research, educate, and reduce to practice in the field of quality and productivity improvement. The teaching hospital and professional practice collaborate to provide a wide range of products and services:

Situation Appraisals
One-day situation appraisals are the best way for The Performance Center to get to know your organization and for you to get to know ours. We assess your quality and productivity improvement requirements and expectations, meet with senior leadership and management, and provide an executive summary of our findings and recommendations.

Grand Strategy System (GSS)/Large-scale organizational change
Documented and described extensively in this book, Grand Strategy System represents a major area of research and reduction to practice for the Performance Center. GSS has proven to be an effective method for helping organizations integrate and manage total system change and improvement. We serve as "chief architects and engineers" for GSS efforts.

Strategic Performance Improvement Process
We help organizations integrate Strategic Planning with TQM. Our Strategic Performance Improvement Planning Process is extensively used in a wide range of organizations and is the basic model chosen in the Department of the Navy. This service ranges from facilitation of your planning offsites (3-5 days) to an eighteen month planning system start-up.

Visible Management Systems
We help organizations design, develop, implement and deploy enhanced performance measurement systems. These efforts normally are integrated with planning efforts so as to ensure that strategies, actions and measures are integrated.

Bootcamps
Five days in duration, our bootcamps focus on both individual and organizational

transformation by blending opportunities for personal growth with applied education and training about methods for leading organizational improvement.

By What Method Public Offering Short Course
The Performance Center offers a three-day short course on *By What Method?* annually in conjunction with the Institute of Industrial Engineers Conference. Additional public offers short courses are scheduled periodically throughout the year. Contact The Performance Center for most current schedule.

Performance Improvement Engineer (PIE) Education and Training Program
We committed to the education, training and development of a new breed of managers and leaders — those who are equipped to lead the transformation to the organizations of the future. Our PIE education and training/research program is an integral component of the change master curriculum.

ISE at Virginia Tech also offers a formal Masters and Ph.D. option in **Management Systems Engineering**.

The Performance Center Internship Program
Designed to provide a rigorous educational opportunity for change masters, the internship program is 9–12 months in length and combines classroom instruction with experiential learning. Interns are required to relocate to Blacksburg, Virginia while participating in the program.

Customized Education and Training
We offer a wide range of education and training programs in the area of quality and productivity improvement, all customized to meet organizational needs. Example topics are: motivation, measurement, culture, performance, planning basics; Benchmarking; Re-engineering; and management of change.

QPM Sourcebook
The *QPM Sourcebook* is an education and development tool for practicing change agents, TQM coordinators, and others who are expected to manage organizational improvement efforts. The sourcebook consists of a three-ring binder, partitioned into the major fronts or topical areas affecting performance improvement efforts. Subscribers are sent developmental readings and learning exercises on a regular basis. Edited by D. Scott Sink.

Other Publications
We have an extensive library of publications available, position papers, theses, dissertations, and case studies. The Performance Center also offers a number of books, including: *Planning and Measurement in Your Organization of the Future* by D. Scott Sink and Tom Tuttle (1989), *Productivity Management: Planning, Measurement and Evaluation, Control and Improvement* (1985), and *Managing Quality and Productivity in Aerospace and Defense* (1988).

Implementing a Total Safety Culture
We help organizations implement safety improvement processes based on principles of

psychology. Principles of behavior-based psychology guide the development of strategies for motivating increased safe work practices, while principles of person-based psychology are employed to foster an "actively caring" environment and to encourage employee involvement in and ownership of the change efforts.

If you or your organization would like to engage in a learning partnership with the Performance Center, please call (703) 231-3501 or fax (703) 231-3538.